America's Battle for Media Democracy

How did the American media system become what it is today? Why do American media have so few public interest regulations compared with other democratic nations? How did the system become dominated by a few corporations, and why are structural problems like market failures routinely avoided in media policy discourse? By tracing the answers to many of these questions back to media policy battles in the 1940s, this book explains how this happened and why it matters today. Drawing from extensive archival research, the analysis uncovers the American media system's historical roots and normative foundations. It charts the rise and fall of a forgotten media reform movement to recover alternatives and paths not taken. As much about the present and future as it is about the past, the book proposes policies for remaking media founded on democratic values for the digital age.

Victor Pickard is an assistant professor in the Annenberg School for Communication at the University of Pennsylvania. His research explores the history and political economy of media institutions, media activism, and the politics and normative foundations of media policy. Previously he taught media studies at New York University and the University of Virginia and worked on media policy in Washington, DC. He served as a Policy Fellow for Congresswoman Diane Watson and as a Senior Research Fellow at the media reform organization Free Press and the think tank the New America Foundation. His work has been published in numerous scholarly journals and anthologies, and with Robert McChesney he coedited the book *Will the Last Reporter Please Turn out the Lights?* He frequently speaks to the press about media-related issues and his op-eds have appeared in venues like the *Guardian*, the *Seattle Times*, the *Philadelphia Inquirer*, and the *Huffington Post*.

D0907808

Communication, Society and Politics

Editors

W. Lance Bennett, *University of Washington*
Robert M. Entman, *The George Washington University*

Politics and relations among individuals in societies across the world are being transformed by new technologies for targeting individuals and sophisticated methods for shaping personalized messages. The new technologies challenge boundaries of many kinds – between news, information, entertainment, and advertising; between media, with the arrival of the World Wide Web; and even between nations. Communication, Society and Politics probes the political and social impacts of these new communication systems in national, comparative, and global perspective.

Other Books in the Series

(Continued after index)

America's Battle for Media Democracy

The Triumph of Corporate Libertarianism and the Future of Media Reform

VICTOR PICKARD
University of Pennsylvania

CAMBRIDGE
UNIVERSITY PRESS

CAMBRIDGE
UNIVERSITY PRESS

32 Avenue of the Americas, New York, NY 10013-2473, USA

Cambridge University Press is part of the University of Cambridge.

It furthers the University's mission by disseminating knowledge in the pursuit of education, learning, and research at the highest international levels of excellence.

www.cambridge.org
Information on this title: www.cambridge.org/9781107694750

© Victor Pickard 2015

First published 2015

Printed in the United States of America

A catalog record for this publication is available from the British Library.

Library of Congress Cataloging in Publication data
Pickard, Victor W.
America's battle for media democracy : the triumph of corporate Libertarianism and the future of media reform / Victor Pickard, University of Pennsylvania.
    pages   cm. – (Communication, society and politics)
Includes bibliographical references and index.
ISBN 978-1-107-03833-2 (hardback) – ISBN 978-1-107-69475-0 (pbk.)
1. Mass media policy – United States – History.   2. Broadcasting policy –
United States – History.   I. Title.
P92.U5P44   2014
302.23–dc23   2014015034

ISBN 978-1-107-03833-2 Hardback
ISBN 978-1-107-69475-0 Paperback

Contents

Acknowledgments

America's Battle for Media Democracy was made possible with the help of innumerable friends, family members, mentors, and colleagues. This nearly decade-long project began during my doctoral studies at the Institute of Communications Research at the University of Illinois, where I had the good fortune to work with top-notch faculty, staff, and graduate students who created a rich intellectual environment. Special recognition goes to my mentor and friend, Robert McChesney, whose exemplary work first led me to the field of communication. Bob gave me excellent guidance as my dissertation advisor, and he also graciously shared some of his hard-earned archival materials, which helped me understand the depth of 1940s radio criticism. Also joining my dissertation committee of all-star scholars were John Nerone, Dan Schiller, and Bruce Williams. Their collective wisdom on the historical relationships involving media, democracy, and policy helped set my focus on 1940s media reform efforts. Another valued mentor and friend (and co-editor of this book series), Lance Bennett, inspired me to look at normative questions about the role of media in a democratic society. Lance encouraged me to publish with Cambridge, and through him I met Robert Entman, the other co-editor of this series. I was very fortunate to work with Bob, a fantastic editor who challenged me to sharpen my critical analysis.

In addition to these core advisors was a solid intellectual community of friends and colleagues who encouraged me along the way and offered constructive criticism. It is impossible for me to thank all of them, but those whose conversations and advice informed various aspects of this project include: John Anderson, Jack Bratich, Kevin Coe, Jeff Cohen, Matt Crain, James Curran, Brian Dolber, David Domke, Susan Douglas, John Downing, Matt Ehrlich, Mark Fackler, Liz Fones-Wolf, Des Freedman, Lew Friedland, Kelly Gates, Jay Hamilton, James Hay, Deepa Kumar, Mark Leff, Marie Leger, Steve Livingston, Mark Lloyd, Steve Macek, Rick Maxwell, Sascha Meinrath, Tony

Nadler, Phil Napoli, Russ Newman, John Nichols, Molly Niesen, Janice Peck, Jeff Pooley, Matt Powers, Andrea Press, Craig Robertson, Amit Schejter, Andy Schwartzman, Ben Scott, Josh Silver, Pete Simonson, Michael Socolow, Laura Stein, Inger Stole, Sharon Strover, and Siva Vaidhyanathan. Conversations with my good friends Christina Dunbar-Hester and Todd Wolfson, whose books are coming out at the same time as mine, were particularly therapeutic. Ed Baker, one of my intellectual heroes, who was quickly becoming a close mentor before he passed away, gave me key advice about my book's Conclusion. The late Norman Corwin and Everett Parker generously allowed me to interview them at length about their experiences with 1940s media reform efforts.

A number of individuals deserve special thanks for reading and commenting on specific chapters and early drafts of articles, including Mark Cooper, Mike Kittross, Ben Lennett, John Nerone, Allison Perlman, Manuel Puppis, Michael Schudson, Michael Stamm, Josh Stearns, and Chris Sterling. Michael Copps, Richard John, and Chris Ali generously read the entire book and offered valuable feedback. My dear friend Joseph McCombs carefully copyedited the entire book. Joe is one of the top copy editors in the nation, and this manuscript greatly benefited from his expert attention. My "best man" Jonathan Evans read an early draft of the book and offered spirited encouragement.

All of my colleagues at the University of Pennsylvania have been very supportive and offered helpful suggestions on all manner of book-related issues, especially Michael Delli Carpini, Peter Decherney, Marwan Kraidy, Carolyn Marvin, Monroe Price, Joe Turow, and Barbie Zelizer. I would also like to thank my former NYU colleagues, particularly Rod Benson, Brett Gary, Eric Klinenberg, and Mark Miller, for their camaraderie and for their feedback on my work. Marita Sturken was a wonderful departmental chair during my time at NYU. This book also benefited from the attention of a number of superb research assistants, including Doug Allen, Chris Cimaglio, Tim Libert, Beza Merid, Samantha Oliver, Luke Stark, Doron Taussig, and Alex Williams. I often tasked these young scholars with tracking down and researching obscure historical literature, and they always exceeded my expectations. Chris deserves special recognition for proofreading the entire book, editing all of my footnotes, and offering sharp feedback. Doug and Tim's feedback on my Conclusion chapter helped strengthen a number of key points. Annenberg is incredibly fortunate to have an amazing staff, and I especially thank Joe Diorio, our communications director, and Sharon Black, our librarian, for crucial book-related assistance. And I am deeply indebted to Lew Bateman and Shaun Vigil at Cambridge, who always kept things on track, handled my first-time-author anxieties with great aplomb, and made sure that the book was published. Of course, any errors are entirely on me.

Archival work is expensive, labor-intensive, and time-consuming. These factors make financial support from academic institutions and professional aid from archivists absolutely essential. Along these lines, I thank my past and present academic homes: the University of Illinois, New York University, and the

Annenberg School for Communication at the University of Pennsylvania. I also thank the archivists at libraries and collections who offered me tremendous professional assistance, including those based at the Alabama Department of Archives and History, Dallas Smythe Collection at Simon Fraser University, the Library of American Broadcasting at the University of Maryland, the Library of Congress, the National Archives in College Park, the Rare Book & Manuscript Library at Columbia University, the Special Collections Division at the University of Washington, and the University of Chicago's Regenstein Library. Sections of this book appeared in earlier form in various journal articles, which I reference at the beginning of specific chapters. The media reform organization Free Press and the public policy think tank New America offered intellectual and institutional support as I was finishing my dissertation and during the early stages of book writing. I would also like to thank the media activists and progressive policy makers, past and present, whose struggle I hope to honor with this project.

I want to thank my family for their unconditional love and help over the years. My sister Lara Bury and her family – Steve, Willow, and Ryan – were crucial in providing me the strength to complete this project. I would also like to thank my wife's family members, especially Julilly Kohler, Chuck and Jean Hausmann, and Issa Kohler-Hausmann and her partner, Marty LaFalce, who have always been incredibly supportive during these often challenging years.

I thank my two vivacious children, Zaden and Lilia, for reminding me every day that I am first and foremost "Daddy" and that there are more important things in this world beyond writing books. Beginning an academic career at the same moment as creating a new family is not the most ideal in terms of timing or sanity. But I could not ask for a better-suited companion with whom to share this crazy adventure than my amazing wife, Julilly Kohler-Hausmann. In addition to being an incredible mother and loving partner, Julilly is a world-class historian, and her spot-on comments on each chapter of my book were invaluable. Julilly was with me during every stage of this book process and I am forever deeply in her debt. I am so blessed to have her in my life.

Finally, this book – and, indeed, my existence – would not be possible without the love and support from my parents. Victor Willoughby Pickard, Jr., who passed away during my first year of grad school, taught me to not back down from my convictions and was always very encouraging of my writing (even when he disagreed with its arguments). Kay Pickard, who for many years worked long, difficult hours, often away from home, to put me through college, taught me to work hard, read deeply, and enjoy the many wonders of life. It is to this amazing woman, my mother and my hero, that this book is dedicated.

Introduction

The Policy Origins and Normative Foundations of American Media

To live in modern society today is to be immersed in media. We spend much of our waking lives reading, viewing, listening to, and interacting with the products and processes that we refer to generally as "media" or a "media system." Yet most of us know little about the policies that structure the media surrounding us. Particularly in the United States vast sectors of communications are heavily commercialized, dominated by corporate duopolies and oligopolies, with relatively little public input or oversight. How did Americans come to inherit this particular media system? More specifically, when and how did the U.S. polity determine media's normative role in a democratic society – its social responsibilities and commitments to the public interest? Everyone learns in school that an independent press is necessary for democratic self-governance, but American citizens rarely pause to reflect on what this means. How did American society decide upon media's public service obligations? Commercial media institutions receive many benefits, from indirect subsidies and tax breaks to monopolistic use of the public airwaves; what do they owe society in return?

This book shows that many of these answers lie in the 1940s, when core constituencies fought over questions about the American media system's governance and design. The following historical analysis retraces policy trajectories, ideas, and discourses to a moment before received assumptions about media's role in society took on an air of inevitability. By uncovering a key chapter of this history, this project is as much about the present and future as it is about the past. Once we realize that the status quo was contingent, that there were other options, other roads not taken, we can begin to imagine that a very different media system was – and still is – possible.

Contested and constantly renegotiated, policy arrangements are always in flux to varying degrees. At any given point of development, resistance to a commercial media system is usually detectable.[1] However, not all kinds of resistance are equivalent, whether in terms of degree or impact. During specific moments – what previous scholars have termed "critical junctures" and "constitutive moments" – inordinate disruptions occur, usually caused by sociopolitical and technological turmoil, as status quo relationships are jolted before settling into new, path-dependent trajectories.[2] Therefore, policy decisions during these periods can carry tremendous weight, often determining a media system's contours for generations to come.[3] The Marxist thinker Antonio Gramsci referred to these recurring patterns as "conjunctural moments," marked by shifting historical blocs and fleeting political opportunities.[4] Describing hegemonic processes by which an elite consensus comes to dominate commonsensical notions about how society should operate, a Gramscian framework also allows for constant conflict and challenges from below. Often characterized by crisis, these conjunctural moments create openings into which radical ideas and experimental models – banished to the far reaches of acceptable discourse during less tumultuous times – are suddenly treated with serious consideration.

This book focuses on one of these pivotal moments. It shows how specific arrangements shaping many of American media's core foundations, particularly its dominance by commercial interests and unusually weak (compared to other advanced democracies) public service obligations and regulation,[5] trace back to policy decisions made in the 1940s. During this period, political elites, social movement groups, and communication industries grappled over defining media's role in a democratic society. In the 1940s, alternate media trajectories differing from today's market-driven system were still in play. Recovering these forgotten antecedents and lost alternatives denaturalizes the commercial status quo by underscoring its contingency. Furthermore, though drawing parallels is an inherently fraught and risky enterprise, this historical work yields fresh insights and potential lessons applicable to contemporary policy challenges.

---

[1] The term "commercial media" used throughout this book generally refers to for-profit media; in many cases it is synonymous with "capitalist" or "corporate media."

[2] Robert McChesney, *Communication Revolution: Critical Junctures and the Future of Media* (New York: New Press, 2007); Paul Starr, *Creation of the Media* (New York: Basic Books, 2004). Some scholars understand this process as a "punctuated equilibrium," although this framing suggests more harmony than is typically present in contentious policy processes.

[3] For more on critical junctures and path dependencies, see Ruth Berins Collier and David Collier, *Shaping the Political Arena: Critical Junctures, the Labor Movement, and Regime Dynamics in Latin America* (Princeton, NJ: Princeton University Press, 1991); Kathleen Thelen, "Historical Institutionalism in Comparative Politics," *Annual Review of Political Science* 2 (1999): 369–404.

[4] Antonio Gramsci, *Selections from the Prison Notebooks* (New York: International, 1971). I elaborate on this critical historical approach in "'Whether the Giants Should Be Slain or Persuaded to Be Good': Revisiting the Hutchins Commission and the Role of Media in a Democratic Society," *Critical Studies in Media Communication* 27, no. 4 (2010): 391–411; see especially 395–6.

[5] Daniel Hallin and Paolo Mancini, *Comparing Media Systems: Three Models of Media and Politics* (Cambridge: Cambridge University Press, 2004).

Then, as now, vexing policy questions faced a still-new medium – commercial radio broadcasting was at approximately the same stage of development as the Internet today – as well as a newspaper industry in structural crisis. This book, based on extensive archival research, historicizes media policies and reform efforts by contextualizing them within ongoing struggles for a more public-oriented media system.

The 1940s was a decade of transition and reform. As American society converted to a peacetime economy, national and geopolitical power relations were in flux. Although New Deal liberalism had begun to falter, a window of opportunity arose in the early to mid-1940s, when structural reform of the American media system still seemed viable. Elements of the 1930s Popular Front – uniting radical leftists, Progressives, and New Deal liberals – persisted, and American power centers like Washington, DC were not yet dominated by anti-communist hysteria. Until the late 1940s, many social movements, especially those supporting labor and civil rights, continued to advance a reformist agenda. During and immediately after World War II, a three-pronged assault against commercial media arose from above and below, led by grassroots activist groups, progressive policy makers, and everyday American listeners and readers who were upset with specific aspects of their media system, especially its excessive commercialism. This disenchantment gave rise to various forms of media criticism and activism as coalitions composed of labor unions, civil rights organizers, civil libertarians, disaffected intellectuals, progressive groups, educators, and religious organizations sought to reform their media system. Media reform activists helped advance policy interventions and experimental models, ranging from nonprofit ventures to strong public interest mandates for commercial news organizations.

Within this political and intellectual landscape, a number of policy debates rose to the fore in ways rarely seen, calling into question the implicit laissez-faire relationships among U.S. media institutions, the public, and the state. A nascent media reform movement set the stage for a cluster of progressive court decisions and policy interventions, including the Federal Communications Commission's (FCC) 1943 anti-monopoly measures against chain broadcasters, which forced NBC to divest itself of a major network; the Supreme Court's 1945 antitrust ruling against the Associated Press, which affirmed the government's duty to encourage in the press "diverse and antagonistic voices"; the 1946 "Blue Book," which mandated broadcasters' public service responsibilities; the 1947 Hutchins Commission on Freedom of the Press, which established journalism's democratic benchmarks; and, finally, the 1949 Fairness Doctrine, which outlined key public interest obligations for broadcasters.

Not all of these initiatives were successful, but they all sought to ensure that profit was not the sole imperative of the American news media. They also all shared an expansive view of the First Amendment, one that protected the audience's "positive" right *to* information as much as broadcasters' and publishers' "negative" rights protecting their speech and property *from* government intervention.[6] In other words, these initiatives prioritized the collective rights of the public's "freedom to read, see, and hear" over the individual rights of media producers and owners.[7] And, as important, they all assumed a proactive role for government to guarantee these rights affirmatively. Had this trajectory not been averted, much of the American media system might look very different today.

Taken together, these policy interventions composed a broader impulse, one defined by a "social democratic" view of media, what I refer to as "media democracy" in the title of this book. More established in other advanced democracies, "social democracy," like the term "liberal" in many nations, refers to both a type of political party and an ideological project. Drawing from the normative foundations of the latter, a specific policy framework comes into focus, one that emphasizes media's public service mission instead of treating it as only a business commodity. Privileging social benefits over property rights, this perspective assesses a media system's value by how it benefits all of society rather than how it serves individual freedoms, private property rights, and profits for a relative few. As Thomas Meyer wrote in *The Theory of Social Democracy*, two normative premises unite all versions of social democracy: "First, 'libertarian particularism' ... is rejected in favor of a universal conception of liberty that ranks negative and positive liberty on par. Second, the identification of freedom and property is jettisoned in favor of a universal conception of liberty that balances the liberties of all parties."[8] That is, social democracy elevates a positive liberty in which universal and collective rights – pertaining to publics, audiences, and communities – are at least as important as the individual freedoms most cherished within libertarianism and classical liberalism.

Reaching its greatest expression in the United States during the New Deal era, social democracy legitimates an activist state that allocates resources in an egalitarian fashion. Skeptical of unregulated capitalism and wary of "market failure,"[9] this ideological project values a mixed economy and structural diversity. It sees crucial services like education as public goods that warrant special protections and subsidies. Instead of leaving the public sector entirely dependent on the market's mercy, social democracy seeks to reinforce civil society's foundations by promoting public investments in critical infrastructures and institutions like strong labor unions, universal health care, public media, libraries, and schools. The historian Tony Judt observed that a social democratic society's normative foundation begins with determining whether a policy is good or just, not whether it is profitable or efficient.[10]

[6] Isaiah Berlin, "Two Concepts of Liberty," in *Four Essays on Liberty* (London: Oxford University Press, 1969).
[7] See Morris Ernst, "Freedom to Read, See, and Hear," *Harper's Magazine*, July 1945, 51–3; see also Lee Bollinger, *Images of a Free Press* (Chicago: University of Chicago Press, 1991).
[8] Thomas Meyer, *The Theory of Social Democracy* (Cambridge: Polity Press, 2007), 16.
[9] I expand on media market failure in the Conclusion.
[10] Tony Judt, *Ill Fares the Land* (New York: Penguin Press, 2010).

This book uncovers a paradigmatic challenge in the 1940s. when a social democratic vision that major news media should not be organized primarily by market relationships was buoyed by social movements and a New Deal ethos. By focusing particularly on case studies of policy formations around the Blue Book, the Fairness Doctrine, and the Hutchins Commission, the book charts the rise and fall of a reform movement that envisioned a different media system. It shows how these reform efforts were largely coopted and quelled, resulting in a "postwar settlement" for American media. This settlement was defined by several overlapping assumptions: that media should remain self-regulated, adhere to a negative conception of the First Amendment – a freedom of the press privileging media producers' and owners' individual rights over the collective rights of listeners, readers, and the broader public – and, in return, practice a mostly industry-defined version of social responsibility. Within this framework, press freedoms were understood as primarily protecting commercial media institutions, a logic perhaps best described as "corporate libertarianism." This ideological framework attaches individual freedoms to corporate entities and assumes that an unregulated market is the most efficient and therefore the most socially desirable means for allocating important resources.[11] An apotheosis of market fundamentalism that combines the exaltation of absolute individual liberty with the delegitimation of redistributive policies, the logic of corporate libertarianism encourages media self-regulation and weak public interest standards.

The resultant changes from these policy debates in the 1940s were subtle but significant. Under the guise of "social responsibility," media were now nominally accountable to the public interest, but government would play only a minor role in defining and mandating these obligations. The implicit social contract that emerged among the state, the polity, and commercial media institutions consolidated an industry-friendly arrangement that contained reform movements, foreclosed on alternative models, and discouraged structural critiques of the U.S. media system. The failure of a social democratic challenge to an increasingly corporate libertarian policy orientation left a lasting imprint on much of the media Americans interact with today.

Legacies from these debates, particularly the delegitimation of public policy interventions in media, continue to straitjacket discussions about the future of news media. For example, the retreat or absence of the regulatory state – a turn usually pegged to 1980s "deregulation," but that had already begun by the late 1940s – is a key assumption in contemporary discourse about how we as

---

[11] For a more in-depth discussion of corporate libertarianism, see Victor Pickard, "Social Democracy or Corporate Libertarianism? Conflicting Media Policy Narratives in the Wake of Market Failure," *Communication Theory*, 23, no. 4 (2013): 336–55. David Korten used this term, especially in characterizing global neoliberal instruments like the World Trade Organization and the International Monetary Fund. See *When Corporations Rule the World* (West Hartford, CT: Kumarian Press, 1995).

a society can sustain journalistic media that are no longer market supported. This book shows how this deference to the market was not natural, inevitable, nor necessarily ideal; it was first and foremost the result of policy decisions and political struggles. Therefore, such market centrism should be subjected to rigorous interrogation and debate. Indeed, given the frequent and ongoing failures of America's crisis-prone news media system, the history of these foundational normative debates is central to questions about the future of journalism and news media more generally.[12] This history helps explain how American society came to have a particular media system largely defined by commercialism and self-regulation, and it can clarify policy options moving forward.

Thus far, little research has focused on 1940s media reform efforts, although several leading scholars have signaled the period's importance and suggested that it warrants scholarly attention.[13] Dan Schiller, for example, noted a significant confluence of progressive media policy initiatives in the mid-1940s, observing that they had "yet to find their historian."[14] Similarly, Robert Horwitz situated these years as the second of three key media reform periods, occurring after questions of broadcast media ownership and control were decided in the 1930s and before public broadcasting was established in the 1960s.[15] A number of more recent books have focused on specific postwar radio reform issues, including Elizabeth Fones-Wolf's *Waves of Opposition*, Kathy Newman's *Radio Active,* Michael Stamm's *Sound Business*, Matt Ehrlich's *Radio Utopia,* and Inger Stole's *Advertising at War*.[16] For a revisionist history of print media, David Davies offered a very useful analysis in *The Postwar Decline of American Newspapers*.[17] However, these and other important studies notwithstanding, few existing works examine the period's broader political and ideological contexts in relation to media policy, and none offers a detailed discussion of the

---

[12] W. Lance Bennett, Regina Lawrence, and Steven Livingston, *When the Press Fails: Political Power and the News Media from Iraq to Katrina* (Chicago: University of Chicago Press, 2007).

[13] Exceptions are Margaret Blanchard, "Press Criticism and National Reform Movements: The Progressive Era and the New Deal," *Journalism History* 5, no. 2 (1978): 33–7, 54–5; Marion Marzolf, *Civilizing Voices: American Press Criticism, 1880–1950* (New York: Longman, 1991).

[14] Dan Schiller, *Theorizing Communication: A History* (New York: Oxford University Press, 1996), 53.

[15] Robert Horwitz, "Broadcast Reform Revisited: Reverend Everett C. Parker and the 'Standing' Case," *Communication Review* 2, no. 3 (1997): 311–48.

[16] Elizabeth Fones-Wolf, *Waves of Opposition: Labor, Business, and the Struggle for Democratic Radio* (Urbana: University of Illinois Press, 2006); Kathy Newman, *Radio Active: Advertising and Consumer Activism, 1935–1947* (Berkeley: University of California Press, 2004); Michael Stamm, *Sound Business: Newspapers, Radio, and the Politics of New Media* (Philadelphia: University of Pennsylvania Press, 2011); Matt Ehrlich, *Radio Utopia: Postwar Audio Documentary in the Public Interest* (Urbana: University of Illinois Press, 2011); Inger Stole, *Advertising at War: Business, Consumers, and Government in the 1940s* (Urbana: University of Illinois Press, 2012).

[17] David Davies, *The Postwar Decline of American Newspapers, 1945–1965* (Westport, CT: Praeger, 2006).

1940s policy battles that gave birth to many of the intellectual foundations and normative assumptions that continue to structure the American media system. In particular, a dearth of scholarship has attempted to historically contextualize contemporary issues like the journalism crisis and questions around digital media governance. On a more theoretical level, relatively little work has explored the American media system's normative foundations, especially the politics that historically shaped them.[18] The media system that has developed in the United States – one that is lightly regulated and whose public service components receive minimal subsidies – stands in stark contrast to systems that developed in other advanced democracies. The historical decisions and events that led to this kind of "American exceptionalism" deserve closer analysis. This book focuses attention on a neglected but formative period in the American media system's development – a period that holds profound implications for the present moment.

The following chapters trace the rise and fall of a social democratic vision of the press. The book is divided into a broadcast media section and a print media section. The former receives a longer treatment largely because the technology was newer and thus subjected to more developments and reform proposals. Chapter 1 begins with an overview of 1940s radio criticism that served as the political and intellectual landscape for the policy initiatives discussed in the following three chapters. The book then proceeds chronologically through Chapters 2–4, covering case studies of key policy battles. By discussing early-1940s media ownership debates and anti-monopoly initiatives, Chapter 2 sets up the antecedents and political conditions that led to the Blue Book episode. Close attention is given to debates and policy battles around the FCC's Blue Book in Chapter 3. Chapter 4 focuses on the deliberations leading to what later became known as the Fairness Doctrine. Chapter 5 presents the political economic context, especially the abundant press criticism that drove regulatory threats against the 1940s newspaper industry, and discusses the Hutchins Commission's genesis. Chapter 6 traces the Hutchins Commission's debates, resolutions, and implications. Chapter 7 provides an analytical overview of the preceding chapters' case studies. I conclude with an epilogue that discusses why this history matters especially now, and its implications for American media policy's future trajectory.

Before proceeding, several caveats are in order. In the name of self-reflexivity, I should state up front that I am sympathetic with many of the 1940s media policy reform efforts. In my view, reformers were attempting to create a media system more aligned with the liberal democratic ideals upon which the United States was purportedly founded. Nonetheless, I am critical of how these reformers strategically advanced their goals – which often were thwarted

---

[18] An exception is Clifford Christians, Theodore Glasser, Denis McQuail, Kaarle Nordenstreng, and Robert White, *Normative Theories of the Media: Journalism in Democratic Societies* (Urbana: University of Illinois Press, 2009).

as much by liberals' nervousness as conservatives' obstruction – and I try to be generous toward commercial media owners' and operators' objectives. I do not see them as nefarious; rather, they were acting rationally within the parameters of a commercial media system. I also grant that perhaps many pro-industry spokespeople believed that their arguments were not merely in service to profit motives; they may have genuinely felt that democratic principles were at stake, that an unregulated commercial media system was an ideal model, and that any move toward closer governmental oversight was a slide toward statism or even totalitarianism.

I should be clear, though, that my analysis leads me to believe that the corporate libertarian position – which, save for a few significant exceptions, became the dominant policy paradigm – has set the American media system on a dangerous trajectory, a point to which I return in the final chapters of the book. There is much to learn, and perhaps recover, from the social democratic vision of media that briefly flowered in the United States in the 1940s. I do not wish to exaggerate the impact of the period's reform efforts. That many of them came to naught, however, does not negate their significance for subsequent policy developments. Nor do I mean to suggest an overly deterministic narrative; resistance to commercial media has never fully abated, and organized reform efforts have flared up again periodically in the ensuing decades. Moreover, a historical debate about exact periodization is not the intervention I hope to make with this book; rather I am drawing attention to an ideological formation that is historically situated. Finally, I should note that although this book's focus is clearly on American policy, it offers many important parallels and disjunctures with the histories of other countries' media systems. Furthermore, it holds significant implications for international media policy debates – especially since contemporary media crises are increasingly global in scope.

The following chapters call attention to this long-neglected history and its relevance for many contemporary regulatory challenges, from Internet policies like net neutrality to debates about the future of news and public media. Given the ongoing dissolution of journalism, the decline of broadcast media, and the failed promises of digital communication, this history suggests that now is an opportune moment for renegotiating the resolutions of the 1940s – a second chance to forge a new social contract, one that rescues media from endemic market failures to create a more democratic system.

I

The Revolt against Radio

In 1940s America, radio was the preeminent communications medium, fully integrated into millions of households. Although its programs were much loved, grievances were also commonplace, particularly concerning overcommercialization. Access to a variety of high-quality programs was not guaranteed, especially in rural areas. Growing concerns around excessive advertising and the medium's failure to reach its full democratic promise prompted grassroots activism and proposals for government intervention. In 1947, near the fortieth anniversary of his invention of the Audion tube, Lee de Forest, often considered "the father of radio," wrote a widely distributed letter to the National Association of Broadcasters (NAB):

What have you gentlemen done with my child? He was conceived as a potent instrumentality for culture, fine music, the uplifting of America's mass intelligence. You have debased the child … made him a laughing stock…. The occasional fine program is periodically smeared with impudent insistence to buy or try…. Soap opera without end or sense floods each household daily. Murder mysteries rule the waves by night, and children are rendered psychopathic by your bedtime stories. This child of mine has been resolutely kept to the average intelligence of 13 years … as though you and your sponsors believe the majority of listeners have only moron minds. Nay, the curse of your commercials has grown consistently more cursed, year by year.[1]

De Forest's anguish over how commercialization undermined radio's potential as an enlightening and democratizing instrument – degrading it with excessive advertising and low-quality programming – echoed across much of the media criticism that was proliferating in the 1940s. The analysis that follows shows how these central critiques shaped media reformers' intellectual arsenal and helped them move from criticism to activism. Following in a rich tradition that

---

[1] "Radio: Debased Child," *Time*, February 10, 1947. Also printed in, for example, *Chicago Tribune*, October 28, 1946.

anticipates contemporary media-related crises and opportunities, this criticism reminds us that the modern American media system faced significant dissent. It resulted from a profound struggle to define media's social responsibilities – and government's ability to mandate them – in a democratic society.

The Political Economy of 1940s American Radio

American radio in the 1940s was an increasingly concentrated and powerful industry. The commercial broadcasting system had roots going back to the 1920s, but it was officially codified by the 1934 Communications Act. Through this legislation, Congress largely sanctioned commercial broadcasting at the expense of alternatives pushed by educators and other reformers. Thus a strong public broadcasting system did not take root during American radio's early days as it did in many other democratic nations. Instead, American radio was dominated by an oligopoly of large networks and the same commercial interests were monopolizing FM radio.

Although these pre-television years are often celebrated as radio's golden age, public service responsibilities were ill defined. Most broadcasters viewed their primary role as that of selling airtime to individual advertisers who would then use their rented time slot to develop programs and promote their product. Advertisers – usually referred to as "sponsors" – would buy entire time segments ("dayparts") of programming from a commercial broadcaster, usually an affiliate of one of the major networks. Shows like "soap operas," the term given to 1940s radio serials because of frequent soap company sponsorship, gave sponsors free rein to air numerous commercials and even sometimes to influence actual programming.

Radio's expansion was accompanied by media conglomeration and concentration. By the mid-1940s, the broadcast industry was dominated by four networks: the National Broadcasting Company (NBC), the Columbia Broadcasting System (CBS), the Mutual Broadcasting System (MBS), and the American Broadcasting Company (ABC – formerly NBC's Blue Network, until 1943). By the end of 1946, MBS had 384 affiliates; ABC, 238; NBC, 162; and CBS, 162.[2] Local stations were largely dependent on the networks, with approximately two-thirds of the nine hundred AM stations affiliated with, and thus taking syndicated nonlocal content from, one or more of the big four. The major networks commanded about 95 percent of the entire country's nighttime programming, with independent commercial broadcasters and about twenty-eight noncommercial stations producing the remaining 5 percent.[3] Such intensive concentration and commercialization had an impact on radio content. Describing the American broadcast media system as one in which nominally

---

[2] White, *American Radio*, 35.
[3] Eugene Konecky, *The American Communications Conspiracy* (New York: People's Radio Foundation, 1948).

public channels are surrendered to "the hands of the four national networks and then ... [to] the major advertising agencies," the *New Republic* declared in 1944 that in terms of programming diversity, "No regular radio listener needs to be told that our national policy of ensuring a free radio ... is a failure."[4]

Nonetheless, radio was deployed to mobilize publics for various national-istic and commercial agendas, from FDR's fireside chats to advertising cam-paigns aimed at promoting consumer culture. During World War II, radio's role in the rise of European fascism yielded a new appreciation and concern regarding its capacity to sway publics.[5] Radio also played a key role on the home front. The Federal Communications Commission (FCC) War Problems Division was responsible for monitoring U.S. foreign-language stations for subversive broadcasts,[6] while commercial stations ran patriotic advertisements and provided firsthand reportage from the front lines. Despite broadcasters' good corporate citizenship and patriotism during the war, public criticism of radio's overcommercialism began to simmer in the late 1930s and early 1940s, and only intensified as the decade wore on.

A contentious issue also emerged around "sustaining programs," which were usually public affairs programs not sponsored by commercial interests. Many critics argued that, as a condition for receiving or renewing their licenses, all broadcasters should devote regular segments to sustaining programs that cov-ered "education, information, or enlightenment – specifically ... controversial issues and problems, national and local."[7] While pro-industry groups coun-tered that the burgeoning FM broadcast band and television would render such regulations moot, others voiced concerns about path dependencies – patterns established with AM radio – that would prefigure new media. One prominent literary critic, Bernard Smith, argued that "sound programmatic public service standards" established for AM radio "will be carried over into FM and tele-vision." If regulated by a "watchful FCC to observe the proposed minimum [public service] standards," he concluded, broadcasters' profits and the sta-tions' sale prices "would not get out of hand."[8]

Another important political economic concern – similar to concerns about broadband Internet access today – was the bleak rate of radio penetration in rural communities. An article in the periodical *Forum* observed that some areas had "only two or three stations available," whose broadcasts were filled with "sponsored network programs consisting of soap operas, thrillers, and comic

4 "Radio's New Chance," *New Republic* 110, no. 26 (1944): 841–2. For breakdowns of advertis-ing revenue, see White, 59–60.
5 This impression was further concretized in the post–World War II treason trials of "Axis Sally" and "Tokyo Rose," who propagandized via radio to undermine Allied war efforts.
6 Mickie Edwardson, "The FCC's War Problems Division: Partner in a Forgotten Blacklist," *Journal of Radio Studies* 6, no. 2 (1999): 270–86.
7 Bernard Smith, "The Radio Boom and the Public Interest," *Harper's Magazine* 190, no. 1138 (March 1945): 315–20.
8 Ibid., 320.

programs."[9] One analysis of commercial radio's rural service inadequacies suggested that a significant chunk of the United States had less radio penetration than Britain; even war-torn Finland fared better by some measures.[10]

At first, optimists saw a fresh start with FM radio. Broadcasting had become immensely profitable in a relatively brief time, effectively pricing most potential buyers out of the AM market. Presumably, the new FM channels could provide a wider variety of stations and services. However, incumbents quickly established prime positions in the new media landscape; the FCC authorized FM frequencies for commercial licensing and the major networks quickly acquired new FM stations.[11] Those most invested in developing alternative radio programming, like educators and progressive activists, feared that television would follow suit.

The FCC did set aside five nonprofit FM channels for educational stations[12] – a victory of sorts, but it paled in comparison to the far more significant allocations that were fought for and lost in the 1930s.[13] Despite these disappointments, early 1940s programming suggests glimmers of an alternative vision for radio. Paul Robeson, Norman Corwin, Richard Durham, and other left-leaning artists and intellectuals were able to produce occasional radio programming with strong progressive themes of racial solidarity, class egalitarianism, and internationalism.[14] Public affairs programs like *America's Town Meeting of the Air*, which ran on the Blue Network from 1935 to 1956, exemplified radio's democratic potential by airing a wide array of viewpoints on pressing political issues, conducted in front of engaged audiences.[15] Its debut

[9] Max Knepper, "Why Broadcasting Has Failed." *Forum* CIX, no. 1 (January 1948): 8.
[10] Eleanor Timberg, "The Mythology of Broadcasting," *Antioch Review* (1946): 354–5.
[11] Although FM was heralded as an improvement over AM – it was more immune from electrical interference and offered greater fidelity for music broadcasts – early political and technical developments hindered its democratic potential. The FCC had authorized its frequency allotment at 42–50 MHz, but after lobbying by AM station owners and newspaper publishers who feared competition for advertising, the FCC moved the FM band to the 88–108 MHz range. This sudden switch rendered all existing FM radios obsolete and retarded FM growth until the 1950s. See Lawrence Longley, "The FM Shift in 1945," *Journal of Broadcasting* 12 (Fall 1968): 353–65. For more details on this and other technological developments in the 1940s, see the thoroughly researched book, Hugh Slotten, *Radio and Television Regulation: Broadcast Technology in the United States, 1920–1960* (Baltimore: Johns Hopkins University Press, 2000).
[12] Edwardson, "James Lawrence Fly's Fight for a Free Marketplace of Ideas," 28.
[13] For the authoritative history on this period, see Robert McChesney, *Telecommunications, Mass Media and Democracy: The Battle for the Control of U.S. Broadcasting, 1928–1935* (New York: The Oxford University Press, 1993).
[14] See Judith Smith, "Radio's Cultural Front, 1938–1948," in *Radio Reader: Essays in the Cultural History of Radio*, ed. Michele Hilmes and Jason Loviglio (New York: Routledge, 2002): 209–30. See also Matthew Ehrlich, "A Pathfinding Radio Documentary Series: Norman Corwin's One World Flight," *American Journalism* 23 (Fall 2006): 35–59.
[15] For an account of radio coverage of racial issues, see Barbara Savage, "Radio and the Political Discourse of Racial Equality," in *Radio Reader: Essays in the Cultural History of Radio*, ed. Michele Hilmes and Jason Loviglio (New York: Routledge, 2002): 231–55.

program was titled "Which Way America – Communism, Fascism, Socialism or Democracy?" and the show's moderator invited representatives from each ideological position.[16] Yet these, as well as a "vox pop" movement that put some diverse voices on the air, were exceptions for typical programming that was otherwise often relatively homogeneous.

Dissatisfaction was felt perhaps most acutely on the creative side of radio programming. The well-known radio writer Norman Corwin and the play-wright Arch Boler complained publicly about commercial network policies and advertising agencies' stifling creativity. Similarly, the radio writer Norman Rosten observed, "The sponsor and the advertising agency have taken over radio quietly in this matter of writing." He wondered, "Shall the singing commercial and the Lone Ranger inherit the earth?"[17] The *New York Times* radio critic, Jack Gould, distilled this criticism when he described radio writing as "simply an adjunct to advertising" because the "word is fitted to the Product" and "The Product is God." By this calculus, "The word is the interval between the announcements of God."[18] Ultimately, for radio workers and the public at large to wrest control over programming from advertising agencies would require radical reform at a deeply structural level.

Radio's Reckoning

The vehemence with which segments of the American public criticized 1940s radio is difficult to overstate. A tradition of radio criticism emerged in the 1930s, particularly from intellectuals like James Rorty and Ring Lardner,[19] but critical voices became more prominent in the 1940s. Although precise numbers are difficult to obtain, proclamations in the press and elsewhere suggest a shift in the quantity and tone of 1940s radio criticism. In its 1946 year-end review, the *New York Times* found "radio subjected to more obverse and insistent criticism than the industry had experienced in the whole of its previous twenty-five years, the main burden of the complaint against the ethereal art being excessive commercialism."[20] Another article claimed, "Criticism of radio is not new, but in 1946, as the industry enters its third decade richer, more powerful and

---

[16] Discussed in Jason Loviglio, *Radio's Intimate Public: Network Broadcasting and Mass-mediated Democracy* (Minneapolis: University of Minnesota Press, 2005), 38–69. See also Michele Hilmes, *Radio Voices: American Broadcasting, 1922–1952* (Minneapolis: University of Minnesota Press, 1997).

[17] All quoted in Eleanor Timberg, "The Mythology of Broadcasting," *Antioch Review* (1946): 354.

[18] *New York Times*, July 15, 1945.

[19] Bruce Lenthall, "Critical Reception: Public Intellectuals Decry Depression-era Radio, Mass Culture, and Modern America," in *Radio Reader: Essays in the Cultural History of Radio*, ed. Michele Hilmes and Jason Loviglio (New York: Routledge, 2002), 343–66.

[20] Jack Gould, "Backward Glance: Radio in 1946 Suffered Strong Criticism," *New York Times*, December, 29, 1946.

more excruciatingly vulgar and meaningless than ever before, impatience has reached a higher peak of articulate disgust."[21] Capturing what was becoming a consensus notion among intellectuals, a 1945 Harvard report on American media noted, "One need be no soft paternalist to believe that never in the history of the world have vulgarity and debilitation beat so insistently on the mind as they do now from screen, radio, and newsstand."[22] While there was significant agitation toward media in general, most of it was focused on the airwaves, leading *Fortune* magazine in 1947 to dub the uptick in criticism the "revolt against radio."[23]

The archival record suggests that the depth and breadth of public disquiet extended beyond malcontent intellectuals and activists. FCC files stuffed with listeners' complaints indicated a pronounced anger toward radio. Community radio "listening councils" sprang up across the country to monitor local programming for its quality of public service. Major newspapers and opinion journals railed against the overcommercialization of American broadcasting – not only left-leaning magazines like *Harpers*, the *New Republic*, the *Nation*, and the *Atlantic*, but also mainstream popular magazines like *Reader's Digest*, *Time*, and *Life*, and even business journals like *Fortune* and *Business Week*. Media criticism also appeared in less likely places: general interest journals and specialized publications as diverse as the *Antioch Review*, the *Saturday Review of Literature*, the *American Mercury*, *Tide*, and *Variety*.

The *New York Times Magazine* echoed the theme in a long article by the *Public Opinion Quarterly* editor Lloyd Free, who lambasted broadcasters' "binge of commercialism." Encouraging listeners "to make their pressure felt" through collective action, the article concluded that the "program which advertisers believe will sell goods has become the god of the industry," ignoring the desires of "minority groups" like "farmers, labor union people, women; lovers not only of fine music but of serious drama and literature, listeners interested in science, in problems of health and social betterment, in international affairs, in the great issues before Congress." The article described 1940s' radio as a "handmaiden to the advertisers … increasingly permeated by their commercial philosophy," one that dictates that "only broadcasts which attract mass audiences are considered important and 'successful.'"[24] A Scripps Howard columnist argued that commercialism rendered all radio "corny, strident, boresome, florid, inane, repetitive, irritating, offensive, moronic, adolescent, or nauseating."[25] A columnist in the adless newspaper *PM* declared: "Nobody can be

[21] Vernon Young, "The Big Noise of the Hucksters," *Arizona Quarterly*, 1946, 5–12.
[22] Harvard University, "Committee on the Objectives of a General Education in a Free Society," *General Education in a Free Society* (Cambridge, MA: Harvard University Press, 1945).
[23] "The Revolt against Radio," *Fortune* 35, no. 102 (March 1947).
[24] Lloyd Free, "What Can Be Done to Improve Radio?" *New York Times Magazine*, August 25, 1946, 9, 50, 52.
[25] Quoted in Fones-Wolf, *Waves of Opposition*, 126–7.

found today who will deny that the radio commercial in its present form is the most offensive breach of good taste the Nation has ever seen."[26]

Media Reform Rises

Historical narratives describing the 1940s often overlook what in retrospect was a fleeting window of opportunity for sociopolitical change.[27] Media policy debates during these years unfolded before Cold War imperatives and red-scare hysteria firmly took hold, and many reformers still believed that New Deal aspirations could be further realized. During this transitional moment, a variety of progressive social movements were ascendant. Even as New Deal liberalism began to falter in the 1940s with the rise of anti-communism and a conservative resurgence,[28] labor and civil rights activists continued to agitate for structural reform. Unions launched massive strike waves.[29] African American veterans returned from the war with demands for equal opportunity.[30] These groups increasingly saw media as an essential battleground for advancing social justice and racial equality. While seeking fairer representation within radio programming, activists also attempted interventions at the policy level to make the medium less hostile toward their political messages. As verities about the commercial media system's inviolability came under fire – especially its laissez-faire relationship with government and various publics – reformers hoped that American mass communications could be restructured along more democratic lines.

---

[26] Quoted in Konecky, *The American Communications Conspiracy*, 19.
[27] The 1940s are gradually receiving more attention, especially from revisionist historians who complicate the commonly held notion that the decade is defined by the emergence of a "liberal consensus." See, for example, Gary Gerstle, "The Crucial Decade: The 1940s and Beyond," *Journal of American History* 92, no. 4 (March 2006): 1292–9. Gerstle notes that more revisionist accounts recognize that "the significance of the 1940s lies as much in what failed to occur as in what did occur." Moreover, he observes that "the liberalism that did emerge from the 1940s was tamer and less confrontational than many reformers and radicals of the 1940s had wanted." Much of the political history literature on public policy changes and state building in the 1940s places emphasis on WWII and/or fears of totalitarianism. See, for example, James Sparrow, *Warfare State: World War II Americans and the Age of Big Government* (New York: Oxford University Press, 2011) and David Ciepley, *Liberalism in the Shadow of Totalitarianism* (Boston: Harvard University Press, 2007).
[28] Alan Brinkley, *The End of Reform: New Deal Liberalism in Recession and War* (New York: Vintage Books, 1995). Brinkley sees the New Deal impulse expiring by the late 1930s and early 1940s. Ira Katznelson sees the New Deal's influence extending through the Truman administration in *Fear Itself: The New Deal and the Origins of Our Time* (New York: W. W. Norton, 2013).
[29] George Lipsitz, *Rainbow at Midnight: Labor and Culture in the 1940s* (Urbana: University of Illinois Press, 1994).
[30] William Barlow, *Voice Over: The Making of Black Radio* (Philadelphia: Temple University Press, 1999).

This was particularly true for radio, which saw a wide array of constituencies organize against its corporate consolidation to advocate for a more democratic system. Although some of this activism clearly had roots in the 1930s, historians have noted that the New Deal arrived later and stayed longer at the FCC than at other government agencies.[31] This shift helps explain the sudden flurry of policy initiatives in the 1940s aimed at limiting radio's commercialism and advertiser-influenced programming while mandating social responsibility and accountability to local communities. Emboldening these DC-based policy efforts was a nascent broadcast reform movement coalescing at the grass roots.

By recovering significant dissent toward commercial media, this history shows how the American media system's development was the direct result of political struggle that involved suppressing those who agitated for creating less market-dominated media institutions. This little-known history of resistance against the dominant commercial media model and its attendant self-regulatory regime holds much contemporary relevance. Many of the tensions negotiated then are still challenging us today: concerns about media concentration, excessive commercialism, misrepresentation of minority groups and viewpoints, lack of independent journalism, and loss of local media. Furthermore, competing logics of self-regulation and regulatory oversight of commercial media are still central to current policy debates. Understanding the sudden rise and fall of a social democratic challenge to the American commercial system in the 1940s is crucial to assessing many of the problems facing U.S. media today – problems that are at least indirectly linked to various policy failures and industry self-regulation. A contextual overview of the vibrant criticism and activism assailing 1940s commercial broadcast media brings into focus these broader paradigmatic challenges.

The Anatomy of 1940s Radio Criticism

The wave of radio criticism in articles, books, and activist pamphlets that emerged at this time fell generally into four categories: structural, ideological, racial, and commercial. While there was significant overlap, teasing out these major themes with representative examples is instructive, for they provided the necessary milieu for progressive policy initiatives. Repeated across a broad canvas of journal articles and books, the structural critique saw commercial broadcasting as excessively profit driven, monopolistic, and advertiser controlled. Specifically, this critique charged that advertisers had too much power in shaping radio programming and that increasingly concentrated private ownership of news outlets led to overly commercialized fare.

[31] Erik Barnouw, *The Golden Web: A History of Broadcasting in the United States* (New York: Oxford University Press, 1968), 169; Brinkley, *The End of Reform*, 153.

In the *Atlantic Monthly*, for example, Gilbert Seldes lamented the type of mass appeal programming that a commercial system was likely to produce. Since profit imperatives necessitated large audiences, broadcasters' "first principle" was to serve a "monolithic mass" with an "established zone of interest" instead of offering creative and experimental programming. With cultural and public affairs programming disappearing, Seldes urged broadcasters to consider America's diverse composite of "many large groups, many small ones, and individuals belonging to several major and several minor groups at the same time." Instead, radio opted to make "people listen to the commercial," and after "entertainment has reduced the listener to a passive, noncritical state, the announcer moves in with his clubs or machine guns or soothing syrup and finishes the job." Our entertainment industries, he warned, were creating a "cultural proletariat: the intellectually disinherited, the emotional homeless, whose function is only to answer the telephone and say what program they are listening to." According to this debased model, "the commercial is sacred" for it is the "sponsor's private property."[32]

Much of this criticism suggested that without immediate structural reform, American broadcasting's democratic potential would be squandered. A piece in the *Antioch Review* phrased it dramatically: "These next few years of physical development are crucial for the salvation of broadcasting's soul." By "contemplating our vanishing freedoms," the article declared, we must be "armed for the impending battle of the air."[33] Similarly, a two-part series published in *Forum* addressing the question "Why Broadcasting Has Failed" came up with four major causes: low quality of entertainment, excessive commercialism and advertising, lack of local talent, and lack of public service programs. Unbeknownst to many listeners, the article suggested, commercial radio was amenable to reform, because the airwaves upon which stations broadcast were public property and "not the private preserve of those lucky few who got there first."[34]

Broadcasters' lack of public service was another recurring structural media critique. One representative article noted that national advertisers who "consume very nearly all the precious evening time of the principal networks" shirked public interest provisions because their primary concern was selling "breakfast foods, drugs, soaps and cigarettes they manufacture by extolling the virtues of their products ... [during] broadcasts designed to attract mass audiences."[35] Without "criteria of public service," the article cautioned, commercialism was "bound to increase rapidly in the postwar period" to become "light entertainment" like "the comic strip and motion picture," preventing the

---

[32] Gilbert Seldes, "How Dense Is the Mass?" *Atlantic Monthly* 182, no. 5 (November 1948): 23–7.
[33] Eleanor Timberg, "The Mythology of Broadcasting," *Antioch Review* 1946, 354–5.
[34] Max Knepper, "Why Broadcasting Has Failed," *Forum* CIX, no. 1, January 1948, 7–8.
[35] Ibid.

public from becoming "an informed and thinking citizenry, without which a truly democratic government cannot survive."[36]

Whereas the structural critique saw the primary problem as how the broadcast system was organized – especially that it was market driven – the ideological critique saw commercial broadcasting as an inherently conservative medium and derived much grist for its charges from radio's apparent rightward shift in the mid-1940s. Radio arguably had reached a kind of ideological equilibrium during the war, as progressive views gained more access to the airwaves. The *New Republic* went so far as to run an article in early 1945 titled "Is Radio Going Liberal?"[37] President Roosevelt saw radio as hospitable terrain, and Democrats' frequent representation on the air prompted one prominent radio analyst to call for an "equal time" provision between Democrats and Republicans – though not for Communists or Socialists, he clarified, because "ours is a two-party system."[38] As the decade progressed, however, ideological imbalance became a frequent lament among liberals.

As early as November 1943, an *Atlantic Monthly* news analyst wrote that an emphasis on audience appeal "puts a premium on sensationalism," creating a de facto conservative slant in broadcasting. "The serious news broadcaster … finds himself under pressure from two quarters," the author asserted. The broadcaster must attract "the widest possible audience" and "slant his interpretation" according to his sponsor's worldview. Recent months had seen "sponsors snap up the news programs with a conservative slant as they never snapped up the programs with a liberal slant," he observed. When sponsoring a news program, "nine times out of ten" an advertiser preferred an "analyst who at least does no violence to the National Association of Manufacturers." With the political landscape shifting from New Deal liberalism to the "big wartime profits of American industry," he suggested, corporate interests were "exerting more indirect pressure" and liberal commentators increasingly "get into trouble with their sponsors."[39]

This and similar critiques responded to a clear pattern of left-leaning and labor-friendly voices rapidly disappearing from radio. What had been a relative balance between liberal and conservative commentators quickly gave way to a right-wing skew. By one count, the four major radio networks eliminated two dozen left-leaning commentators in less than a two-year span.[40] The casualty list included liberal luminaries like Don Hollenbeck, Raymond Gram Swing, John Vandercook, Don Goddard, Frank Kingdon, Robert St. John, and the

[36] Bernard Smith, "The People's Stake in Radio," *New Republic*, July 13, 1944.
[37] Emil Corwin and Alan Reitman, "Is Radio Going Liberal?" *New Republic*, February 12, 1945, 220.
[38] Rolf Kaltenborn, "Is Radio Politically Impartial?" *American Mercury* LXII, no. 270 (June 1946): 665–9.
[39] Quincy Howe, "Policing the Commentator: A News Analysis," *Atlantic Monthly*, November 1943.
[40] Barnouw, *The Golden Web*, 241.

former New York City mayor Fiorello LaGuardia. By the late 1940s, as one historian observed, the networks took on "a decidedly conservative cast," and even respected analysts like Edward R. Murrow and Eric Sevareid were barred by CBS from interpreting the news. Other than ABC's Elmer Davis, only conservative commentators were heard more than once a week on network prime time, including H. V. Kaltenborn, Earl Godwin, Fulton Lewis Jr., Henry J. Taylor, and Gabriel Heatter.[41] One representative letter of hundreds sent to the FCC decried broadcasting companies' "very obvious trend" of "systematically suppress[ing]" information "that does not fit the strait-jacket" on advertisers' thinking. "The latest – and probably not the last – victim of this crusade to kill free information," the writer claimed, was "William Shirer, a commentator who believed that news is a public trust, not an advertiser's puff." Tying together commercial radio's ideological and structural biases, the letter concluded: "We the people own the [airwaves]. They are not the private preserve of huge corporations currently abusing their leased property."[42]

A *New Republic* article titled "Thought Control – American Style" struck an alarmist note: "To protect our minds and their pocketbooks, networks are dropping liberal commentators from coast to coast." Noting increasing pressures to "tone down news which is sympathetic to organized labor and to Russia," the article captured what many progressives were feeling by the mid- to late 1940s – namely, a sense that American radio was increasingly hostile to not only liberal ideas but intelligent discourse in general as broadcasters replaced informative programming with cheaply produced entertainment. While some thought the networks themselves, not advertisers, were behind "a concerted reactionary drive" to "purge liberals from the air," others perceived a return to "old-time commercialism of the most blatant sort." Whatever the main cause, the article observed, "the result adds up to ... the increasing refusal of the networks to give adequate room to anything but stand-pat interpretation of the news."[43] This purge did not go unnoticed by the public, media, and Congress, but the tide against all things left-of-center nonetheless proved devastating for radio's liberals.

As Cold War imperatives provided cover for right-wing forces to drive progressives from the air, few issues or groups suffered as much as labor, even if unions maintained a small radio presence by acquiring several stations. The *CIO News* called out commercial broadcasters as "moneyed masters" who let loose "their mechanized hounds of the press and radio" to attack "the American working people and their unions."[44] One radical pamphleteer argued that "Big

[41] Fones-Wolf, *Waves of Opposition*, 133.
[42] R. Davis to the FCC, April 22, 1947, Box 53, FCC papers. Office of Executive Director, General Correspondence 1947–56.
[43] Bryce Oliver, "Thought Control – American Style," *New Republic*, January 13, 1947, 13.
[44] Quoted in Elizabeth Fones-Wolf, "Defending Listeners' Rights: Labour and Media Reform in Postwar America," *Canadian Journal of Communication* 31, no. 3 (2006): 499–518.

Business interests – the monopoly corporations, the old-system standard (AM) broadcasting giants, and the big-money publishers and newspaper owners ... have taken FM from labor and the people."[45] Similarly, piles of letters to the FCC decried radio's anti-labor slant. Pleading that "labor and capital both be heard equally," one representative letter stated, "It is regrettable that a means of disseminating knowledge such as the radio should be utilized so exclusively for sheer advertising and propaganda purposes."[46]

The racial critique of 1940s radio shifted the focus from structure to content, particularly toward popular radio programs and films that regularly trafficked in racist stereotypes of African Americans. The most emblematic of these was *Amos 'n' Andy*, a comedy show that featured a pair of white actors speaking in caricatured black dialect (and later, on television, performing in blackface). Although it was enormously popular and boasted large audiences, many African Americans found the show deeply offensive. The boxer-turned-actor Canada Lee told a crowd in 1949 that in media, "with rare exceptions, it is the lazy gambler, the shiftless, thieving, razor-wielding Negro that has come to represent the totality of Negro life." These portrayals did violence to African Americans on multiple levels. For radio listeners, "we do not exist," Lee observed. "Our problems need no solution.... Our people need not be respected, need not be given equal rights ... for we are not a people according to radio." These omissions, Lee suggested, were as detrimental as the gross misrepresentations. "Negro life, its richness, its humor, its warmth and humanity, and its fighting spirit, is not felt to be a fit subject for depiction on the air." Instead, radio "is that of a white world." "Almost never," he charged, "will a Negro enter into these stories except as a menial, or a loyal maid, who lives through and suffers the agonies of her white mistress." Even on quiz shows, "white people stop the music, white people guess the answers, white people hit the jackpot." To create more balance, Lee saw a need for policies enabling African Americans to operate their own radio stations.[47]

Many of the charges leveled against commercial radio made the crucial link between station ownership and programming. In 1947, there were only 16 African-American disc jockeys regularly working in the entire United States, only approximately 200 of 30,000 white-collar jobs in the entire industry were held by African Americans, and there were no black station owners.[48] Also at this time only four radio stations nationwide used formats appealing directly

---

[45] Eugene Konecky, *Monopoly Steals FM from the People* (Provisional Committee for Democracy in Radio), 2.

[46] C. Nations to the FCC, January 6, 1946, Office of Executive Director, General Correspondence 1927–46, Box 60, Federal Communications Commission Archives, National Archives and Records Administration, College Park, MD (hereafter cited as FCC Archives).

[47] Quoted in Martha Biondi, *To Stand and Fight: The Struggle for Civil Rights in Postwar New York City* (Cambridge, MA: Harvard University Press, 2003), 94–5.

[48] Ward, *Radio and the Struggle for Civil Rights*, 25. This changed slightly in 1949 when two African-American entrepreneurs purchased radio stations. Barlow, *Voice Over*, 247.

to African-American audiences.[49] A letter to the FCC from a prominent member of the National Negro Congress defined radio discrimination for African Americans as twofold: "First, the widespread discrimination in the employment of Negroes in almost every job category; and second, the stereotyping of Negro characters over the air."[50] The Committee for the Negro in the Arts documented African Americans' exclusion from the radio industry – especially as stakeholders like producers, directors, commentators, technicians, and executives – and the perpetuation of abhorrent stereotypes in radio programming. "The truth about the American Negro is not held a fit subject for radio," it concluded. The report posed the question "Is the greatness and humanity of Negro America, of Crispus Attucks, Frederick Douglass, Marian Anderson, Paul Robeson and Jackie Robinson, to be presented over the radio channels forever in terms of Amos 'n' Andy and Beulah?"[51]

During a "Social Responsibility of Radio" discussion at the Institute for Education by Radio, Lester Granger, a National Urban League representative, noted that his organization's "first concern" was the "equality of economic opportunities for Negro citizens."[52] But radio perpetuated "stock characterizations and caricatures of the printed word, the stage, and the screen, thus advancing stereotypes and continuing racial misconception." His greatest indictment against radio was the lack of job opportunities for African Americans: For instance, black bands were routinely passed over for contracts given to white bands. Beyond entertainers like musicians, singers, actors, and comedians,

there are scarcely two dozen colored men and women employed in the radio industry, behind the scenes where the wheels of radio are turning. And there are thousands of jobs in an industry that provides 130 million people with almost continuous radio listening. And there are hundreds of job classifications – pages and pagettes, file clerks, messengers, stenographers, typists, cashiers, bookkeepers, teletypists, research assistants, librarians, sound effects technicians, electricians; studio, maintenance, and recording engineers; artists, telephone operators, news analysts, announcers, scriptwriters, carpenters, firemen, private police – but almost no faces of my hue appear until ... the janitors, the porters, the maids![53]

Similarly, African Americans were hired temporarily as freelance voice coaches or programming consultants but rarely hired as permanent staff.[54] Discrimination even pervaded radio advertising. According to a listener from Gainesville, Florida, despite the community's "substantial proportion" of

[49] Hilmes, *Radio Voices,* 273.
[50] Vivian Cadden to Clifford Durr, February 20, 1947, Box 31, Folder 2, Clifford J. Durr Papers, Alabama Department of Archives and History, Montgomery (hereafter cited as CJDP).
[51] Quoted in Barlow, *Voice Over,* 77–8.
[52] I. Keith Tyler and Nancy Mason Dasher, "Education on the Air," *Sixteenth Yearbook of the Institute for Education by Radio,* 1946.
[53] Ibid., 162–6.
[54] Eric Rothenbuhler and Tom McCourt, "Radio Redefines Itself, 1947–1962," in *Radio Reader,* 373.

African-American listeners and businesses, "all radio stations in the community refuse to accept advertising by Negro businesses at any time, on more or less spurious grounds."[55] Civil rights organizations drew from these criticisms to organize for radio reform.[56]

Overlapping with the other types of criticism, a commercial critique held that American broadcasting's profit-driven system typically provided low-quality, homogenized, unintelligent programming. Many critics discerned an underlying pattern: programming was cheaply produced, crafted barely to pass the lowest quality threshold and still be acceptable to large audiences. Broadcasters typically employed established names instead of developing new creative talent, especially with widely syndicated programs like soap operas, resulting in a loss of local programming and a lack of diversity. The most passionate indictment by far was aimed at excessive commercialism in the form of invasive on-air advertising, particularly the widely reviled jingles referred to as "singing commercials" and the disruptive ads known as "plug-uglies."

A 1942 *Reader's Digest* article titled "Radio's Plug-Uglies" presented its 7 million readers with embarrassing transcripts from typical radio advertisements about bodily functions and hygiene products. The article tapped into a wellspring of anger, eliciting thousands of letters from listeners disgusted with radio advertising. Responding to the growing offensiveness of these "plug-uglies" (a phrase referring to a political gang or group of thugs), fed-up NYC listeners formed the Plug Shrinkers Club to campaign against them.[57] Describing those "terrible commercials" that "continue to be a favorite American gripe," Marjorie Kelly wrote in the *Washington Post* in 1943 that "despite the anguished howls of thousands of listeners ... a vast number of plug-uglies remain on the air." "Infuriating the public and undermining respect for American radio," the commercials were condemned by listeners for being too long, repetitious, silly, and "an insult to our intelligence."[58] Also annoying were "cowcatchers" (plugs that preceded a radio program, intended to advertise a sponsor's less important products) and "hitchhikers" (plugs for a second product after promotion of the sponsor's featured product). The media reformer and scholar Charles Siepmann noted that such "new language has had to be invented to keep apace with [advertisers'] enterprising innovations."[59]

55 Letter to the Southern Conference for Human Welfare copied in James Dombrowski's letter to Clifford Durr, April 23, 1947, Box 31, Folder 3, CJDP.
56 Biondi, *To Stand and Fight*, 94–5; Barbara Savage, *Broadcasting Freedom: Radio, War, and the Politics of Race, 1938–1948* (Chapel Hill: University of North Carolina Press, 1999), 230–45; Brian Ward, *Radio and the Struggle for Civil Rights in the South* (Gainesville: University of Florida Press, 2004).
57 Robert Littell, "Radio's Plug-Uglies," *Reader's Digest*, August 1942; "Report on Plug Shrinkers," *Reader's Digest*, October, 1942, 58–61. See also Gerd Horten, *Radio Goes to War: The Cultural Politics of Propaganda during World War* (Berkeley: University of California Press, 2002), 100–1.
58 Marjorie Kelly, "'Terrible Commercials' Still Terrible: No One Is Proud of Them – There's One Slight Hope in Sight," *Washington Post*, October 31, 1943.
59 Charles Siepmann, *Radio's Second Chance* (Boston: Little, Brown, 1946), 135–6.

Beginning in January 1945, the *St. Louis Post-Dispatch* led a months-long national campaign to end offensive radio commercials like plug-uglies via a series of editorials and articles. Tracing its lineage to "earlier crusades to keep the public domain from being cluttered by the excesses of American publicity," one article likened the anti-plug-ugly campaign to a controversy in 1860 in which an oil advertisement was painted on the rocks at Niagara Falls, prompting the first outdoor advertising restrictions.[60] Under the title "Radio Chains Don't Want Reform," the *Post-Dispatch* informed readers about the major networks' advertising policies in a report that spanned several columns. It advised the networks to eliminate "interrupting plugs and objectionable sponsorship," including "remedies for kidney trouble, body odors, hangovers and the like." Also singled out were "middle commercials" that interrupted the "news in dead center to permit an effusive description of the sponsor's product." "A related nuisance," the *Post-Dispatch* continued, "is the 'self-announcer' newscaster who springs from a news report to commercial blurb, frequently tricking the listener's attention ... [by] using the same voice for news and commercial."[61]

Eighteen days after launching the campaign, the *Post-Dispatch* reported widespread support from leading radio newscasters who detested the "hideous" practice of interrupting newscasts, especially during reporting on important issues such as the war. The article claimed support from the FCC – and even some leading advertisers; du Pont's advertising director was quoted as saying, "I am sure something must be done by the industry or will be done for it." Reminding broadcasters of the looming threat of governmental intervention, the article noted that a recent bill forbidding all advertising in newscasts "is dormant but not dead."[62] The radio critic Jack Gould also joined the growing *Post-Dispatch* editorial campaign. He saw it contesting "two of the most prevalent evils in connection with the presentation of news on the radio ... the interruption of news broadcasts with a commercial spiel and the sponsorship of such programs by 'objectionable advertisers.'" "The public is entitled to hear ... war news which may vitally involve loved ones," Gould wrote, "without being forced to listen to a plug for a product." Although "listeners, commentators and a few of the more thoughtful advertisers have voiced their full support [of the *Post-Dispatch's* campaign]," he groused, industry had done little beyond "profess[ing] to be uneasy" about overcommercialization.[63] Radio's drift toward advertiser control, he argued, degrades everyone involved – from the producers to the audience. Although broadcasters might disclaim obligation

[60] Dixon Wecter, "The Public Domain of the Air," *Saturday Review of Literature* IXIX, no. 20 (May 18, 1946): 5.
[61] "Radio Chains Don't Want Reform," *St. Louis Post-Dispatch*, February 17, 1945.
[62] "The Revolt against Radio Plug Uglies," *St. Louis Post-Dispatch*, February, 1945, 2B. The article was referring to the White-Wheeler bill, discussed in Chapter 3.
[63] Jack Gould, "Plug-Uglies," *New York Times*, 1945, 7.

to "reform the public taste," Gould noted, "it certainly is the broadcaster's responsibility not to lower it."[64]

The *Post-Dispatch* campaign gained wide national attention and reportedly led to some improvement, with a few individual stations voluntarily complying with its suggestions. But despite further endorsements from print media like the *New York Times,* the *New Republic,* and even the pro-industry *Broadcasting,* the networks largely ignored the campaigns. Urging them "to put aside the indiscretions of youth," the *Post-Dispatch* opined that the networks "ought long ago to have reached maturity. Their income now is higher than ever, and they can well afford to reject ... commercials which annoy the public."[65]

Harlow Shapley, a famous astronomer, channeled this widespread disgust toward plug-uglies and singing commercials in a high-profile address. He excoriated broadcasters for their "propaganda against government regulation" and for employing the "totally false use of a trite slogan – freedom of speech ... to ask the government not to try to protect us." Instead of worrying about government control, he argued, broadcasters should resist "the much more dangerous control by ... a few advertising agencies." Shapley exhorted his fellow intellectuals and scientists to oppose advertisers and their allied industries' vast resources with "a budget of good will towards American culture in the post war world." He suggested they "may even help to preserve higher standards for FM," especially from "that current vulgar inanity – the singing commercial."[66]

Shapley's critique resonated widely and was picked up by a *Times* editorial: "Life in America does threaten to become pretty sad if something is not done soon about those commercial jingles which drive Professor Shapley crazy with millions of others." Responding to the firestorm, the NBC president, Niles Trammell, offered Shapley an opportunity to express, as he artfully termed it, "reactions to certain phases of the broadcasting enterprise." Shapley happily complied. He described a recent experience of "immense appreciation" while listening to the symphony on NBC. It was, he said, as if listeners were "communicants in a majestic ethereal cathedral."

Then suddenly ... a revolting, leering vulgarian defecated in the altar before us all, desecrating the cathedral, destroying the ecstasy of the communicants, defaming the symphony and the artists.... Before we could defend ourselves, a squalling, dissonant, hasty singing commercial burst in on the mood. The impostor used the same medium of music used by the high priest Toscanini. The vast audience would have been quite willing at that time to hear General Motors tell of further concert plans, or even tell with dignity suitable to the occasion about the products of General Motors. But what we got was a hideous jingle about soap; and we could not protect ourselves. The great art had been prostituted in the interests of immediate cash return to the broadcasting industry and its commercial patron.[67]

[64] Ibid.
[65] "Networks Trail the Parade," *St. Louis Post-Dispatch,* February 20, 1945.
[66] Harlow Shapley, National Wartime Conference Address, New York, June 2, 1944.
[67] Harlow Shapley to Niles Trammell, August 29, 1944, Box 30, Folder 1, CJDP.

Shapley widely distributed copies of his letter, including to NBC advisory board members and the FCC, which he saw as "the fight of the timid public against the bold advertising monopolies."[68] That same week, *Business Week* reported, "Radio listeners may take hope that the epidemic of singing commercials which began with the Pepsi-Cola's 'Nickel, nickel, nickel, nickel' ... is finally running its course."[69]

Radio commercials did not end, but neither did public pressure to reform them. Most American listeners were not familiar with other countries' broadcast systems, but those who traveled were often the most cutting in their critique. The *New Republic* noted that, with noncommercial programming nonexistent or relegated to times when few listened, America was unique among democracies in permitting "the homes of its citizens to be invaded by vulgar and often false claims of private individuals and corporations seeking to make money."[70] Likewise, after listening to the "sedate programs of the BBC" during the war, the *New York Herald Tribune's* book critic, Lewis Gannett, wrote that his "ears were horrified" upon his return to hear "enough laxative advertising to convince a visitor to this country ... that the chief wartime occupation of the USA was performed in its [toilets]." Gannett gathered that "we were a nation of sufferers from acid stomach, chronic headaches, inadequate elimination, and general physical incompetence." He wondered whether "perhaps the public ... would revolt," especially after returning military members became "plumb disgusted with radio commercials." "When the boys come home," Gannett hoped, "they'll be aware of [radio's] perversion as never before." The BBC gave them "their radio pure," and now they might join "a revolt of the civilians."[71] After receiving many supportive letters, Gannett allowed that "radio commercials didn't express the basic metabolism of America after all." He ventured that "If more of us stood up and shouted what we feel as we hear, night after night, the shoddy nastinesses of everyday radio commercials, the industry would listen."[72]

Many critics insisted that radio did not reflect public demand. The *Evening Bulletin* in Providence, Rhode Island, editorialized that it was inexcusable for radio to pretend "such unmitigated tripe" was "what the people want." It asked, "Are they really reflecting the mores of this great nation?"[73] A torrent of angry letters sent to the FCC and radio networks suggests otherwise. After calculating a typical broadcast's allocated time to commercials and vapid commentary, a listener wrote, "Do not delude yourself ... the American listening public is not getting what it wants on the radio – it is, on the contrary, taking

[68] Harlow Shapley to Clifford Durr, September 9 and November 24, 1944, Box 30, Folder 2, CJDP.
[69] *Business Week*, December 2, 1944.
[70] "Radio Revisited," *New Republic*, February 26, 1945, 296–8.
[71] Lewis Gannett, "Feeling Tired?" *Atlantic*, August 1945, 115–17.
[72] Lewis Gannett, *This Week Magazine*, February 28, 1945.
[73] *Evening Bulletin*, June 27, 1944.

unbelievable amounts of mental punishment."[74] Many commentators singled out daytime programming as the nadir of this commercial logic when, as the broadcast critic John Crosby argued, radio "presents its sorriest spectacle."[75]

Reinforcing this critique were complaints to the FCC about its disservice to women. A female listener wrote that she was keenly aware that the "saccharine tripe of Helen's tears and Paul's love affairs" was aimed to sell soap to women. Suggesting that the "quality and quantity" of soap operas "constitute an insult to American intelligence," this listener, a nursing magazine editor, described her recent exposure to radio while recovering from an illness: "Pretty shocked" by the low-quality programming, she felt that "the radio industry and its patrons have an obligation ... to promote something more than emotional binges." Noting the lack of children's programming, she asked, "Why isn't there anything available for the two to five year olds, especially in the morning hours?" Describing how "awful" she and other women found daytime radio, she remarked how grateful mothers would be "if some of the soap opera time would go into programs for our youngsters!" "Not only is the great bulk of women capable of absorbing better stuff than they're getting," she continued, "they would welcome programs that would enable them to grasp world affairs better – and thus hold their own in the family dinner discussions."[76] A self-described housewife wrote to the FCC that after illness left her bedridden and subjected to daytime programs whose quality was "abysmally low," she was compelled to write letters and "take up the cudgels" for reform, especially for "the aged, the sick in homes and hospitals, the house-wives" who had few options in daytime radio. She urged the FCC, "Please keep up the fight. If it means government control better that than sponsor control."[77]

A much-discussed exposé appeared in the March 1946 issue of *Fortune* criticizing soap operas. With the caption "Manufactured at low cost, it pleases advertisers and flatters women," the article noted that about 20 million women listened daily to more than forty soap operas on the air. While apologists referred to them as "daytime serials or serial dramas" and claimed they offered good storytelling, others called them "soapers, washboard weepers and cliffhangers" and summarized their content as "at best ... tedious bilge and at worst ... stark, revolting morbidity." These naysayers denied that "it is what the housewife wants"; she listened "only because she has been conditioned by years of trash."[78] While at times this critique smacked of paternalism and even sexism, it zeroed in on soap operas' underlying economic rationale: They

[74] A. Ruff to Congressman B. Carroll Reece, May 18, 1946, Box 30, Folder 6, CJDP.
[75] John Crosby, "Radio and Who Makes It," *Atlantic,* January, 1948, 28.
[76] Janet Geister to Clifford Durr, June 30, 1946, Box 30, Folder 6, CJDP. See also Jennifer Wang, "The Case of the Radio-active Housewife: Relocating Radio in the Age of Television," in *Radio Reader: Essays in the Cultural History of Radio,"* 343–66.
[77] Belle Ragsdale to Clifford Durr, June 27, 1946, box 30, folder 6, CJDP.
[78] "Soap Opera," *Fortune,* 33, no. 1 (March 1946): 119–29.

could be produced at "a fraction of the cost of a musical program having comparable appeal." The article described how advertisers essentially coproduced soap operas, typically purchasing a serial as a package deal and hiring the writers, actors, organist, director, and announcer, while supervising the whole affair. Thus, a network's role was reduced to approving scripts and keeping one person in the control room, because the "serial story itself is mere bait to persuade the housewife to listen to the commercial announcement." Commercials typically ran more than 3 minutes within 15-minute daytime programs, often given more attention than the programs themselves, and "delivered by well-paid announcers, men at once chatty and orotund, confidential and pontifical, sweet and portentous." Some commercials, the article suggested, were "purposely irritating because of an advertising theory that certain kinds of exacerbation have sales value."[79]

Although soap operas claimed to give audiences what they wanted, their formulaic plot constructions and stereotypical characters left glaring omissions and distortions. The *Fortune* article noted that "working people almost never appear," and when politicians are introduced, "their political views are foggy, if stated at all." Women were typically presented as being virtuous but subservient, commanding a "homely wisdom" to comfort men. Insisting that women "only listen [to soap operas] because they can find nothing better," the article cited Department of Agriculture findings that half of all rural women listened to serials, but only a quarter liked them and another quarter disliked them intensely. Similarly, the article noted, ABC found that 36 percent of women surveyed thought there were too many serials, and even among frequent listeners, 28 percent thought there were too many. Based on content analyses of daytime programming across all networks, daytime radio quality was "abysmally low, primarily because advertisers aim at the lowest common denominator." "Something ought to be done about this excessively shabby art," the article concluded, but little would change "unless the people insist – or the networks belatedly recall – that the air belongs to the people and ought to be used for their benefit."[80]

Extant analyses (of varying degrees of reliability) suggest popular disgust toward advertising. For example, the Committee on Consumer Relations in Advertising reported that nearly 75 percent of people polled felt that radio advertising was worse than any other type,[81] and several contemporaneous polls from newspapers and other organizations found that most listeners detested commercials and wanted better programming.[82] While progressive

[79] Ibid.
[80] Ibid.
[81] Max Knepper, "Why Broadcasting Has Failed," *Forum* CIX, no. 1 (January 1948): 9.
[82] For a more detailed description of these surveys, see Victor Pickard, "Media Democracy Deferred: The Postwar Settlement for U.S. Communications, 1945–1949" (Doctoral dissertation, University of Illinois, Urbana, 2008), 66–8.

FCC commissioners would happily trot out whatever polls emerged that supported their positions, reliable survey data from this period about people's views toward radio are scarce. The most scientific public opinion study from this period on attitudes toward radio was a 150-page report commissioned by the National Association of Broadcasters (NAB) and co-authored by the leading social scientist Paul Lazarsfeld.[83] While the researchers did find that between 20 to 40 percent of those surveyed held "grievances on a variety of items,"[84] commercial radio's defenders were quick to highlight some surprising numbers: Only 7 percent thought advertising should be banned; 26 percent did not like it but would put up with it; 41 percent did not particularly mind advertising; and 23 percent said they were in favor of advertising.

Llewellyn White, whose radio research for the Hutchins Commission is discussed later, noted that for listeners to "not particularly mind advertising" was not a ringing endorsement. Among broadcasters' "many curious and untenable positions during their quarter century in business," White countered, "none is more insecure (and insincere) than the bland contention ... that the listener does not want anything he is not now getting." The assertion that if listeners wish for something different they need "only to ask for it" is absurd, White observed, because the "public cannot ask for something it does not know exists or could exist."[85] Lazarsfeld himself stressed a similar weakness inherent in this kind of study:

It must be admitted, however, that a direct inquiry into people's dissatisfactions may not yield the most valid results. It is widely recognized in many fields of social research that, psychologically speaking, supply creates demand.... Within certain limits, it is a recognized fact that people like what they get. It is also a fact that nobody knows whether or not a different program fare would be equally, or even more, acceptable to average listeners than the present program structure. And few would gainsay that the man in the street lacks the ability to envisage what he would like to hear that is different from what he can listen to now.... A survey like the present one cannot tell what people would like if they had the opportunity to listen to different radio fare.[86]

Despite Lazarsfeld's significant – but usually overlooked – caveat, leading media historians would conclude from this study that people were generally pleased with their radio fare and uncritical of its oligopolistic foundations,[87]

[83] Paul Lazarsfeld and Harry Field, *The People Look at Radio* (Chapel Hill: University of North Carolina Press, 1946). With Patricia Kendall, he conducted a similar NAB-sponsored study a year later, *Radio Listening in America* (New York: Prentice-Hall, 1948). Again, those surveyed generally liked radio. Lazarsfeld coedited another book on 1940s radio with CBS's Frank Stanton, *Radio Research 1942–43* (New York: Hawthorn Books, 1944).
[84] Ibid., 10.
[85] Llewelyn White, *The American Radio* (Chicago: University of Chicago Press, 1947), 221.
[86] Lazarsfeld & Field, *The People Look at Radio*, 10–12.
[87] James Baughman, *The Republic of Mass Culture: Journalism, Filmmaking, and Broadcasting in America since 1941*, 3rd ed. (Baltimore: Johns Hopkins University Press, 2006), 16–21.

and that significant media reform efforts had ended by the mid-1940s.[88] A substantial written record does not support such conclusions.

Critical Books and Novels

Despite high-profile articles and editorials, radio criticism was not a regular beat for most news organizations. A 1946 survey by *Variety* found that of the 1,700 daily U.S. newspapers, only 324 employed full-time radio editors, and of these, few provided careful analysis.[89] Books of satirical and polemical media criticism were arguably more effective in reaching large audiences with reformist ideas. These works tended to be authored by liberal intellectuals, progressive journalists, and former New Deal policy makers who became radicalized in their opposition to commercial media. Their publications both echoed and helped shape popular frustrations while proposing structural reforms. In the mid- to late 1940s these included a notable trio of books: Llewellyn White's *American Radio*, Morris Ernst's *The First Freedom*, and Charles Siepmann's *Radio's Second Chance*. Also noteworthy were two pamphlets: Jerome Spingarn's *Radio Is Yours* and Eugene Konecky's *The American Communications Conspiracy*. Calling for radical systemic change and encouraging Americans to mobilize listeners' groups and radio councils, this literature was readily embraced by media reform activists.

In *Radio Is Yours*, Spingarn, a lawyer and former Senate staffer, explained how "the listener pays" when public airwaves are surrendered to corporate interests.[90] "Radio is no gift horse," he advised; "you definitely pay for your entertainment, and radio owes good broadcast service." A radio listener is not "a small boy sneaking a free peek at a ball game through a hole in the fence," Spingarn argued, but rather "a King in a royal box, witnessing a command performance." With cartoons detailing how broadcasters bilked listeners, the pamphlet emphasized that insipid programming, shot through with annoying commercials, reflected not popular taste but cheap production costs and profit motives.

Konecky's more radical pamphlet stated that a "gigantic conspiracy of monopoly interests has seized hold of American communications," including radio, television, and newspapers. As a result, Americans are "robbed of billions of dollars" and do not benefit from a "superior radio system – FM – which the monopolists have strangled."[91] Konecky urged reformers to make their "main line of struggle" radical structural change of the entire media system, requiring "the people's forces to shatter the corporation conspiracy to control the mass communications' monopoly."[92] Ernst likewise advocated

[88] See also McChesney, *Telecommunications, Mass Media, and Democracy*, 251.

[89] *Variety*, January, 1946.

[90] Jerome Spingarn, *Radio Is Yours* (New York: Public Affairs Committee, 1946), 3.

[91] Konecky, *The American Communications Conspiracy*, 4.

[92] Ibid., 166.

structural interventions, dedicating his anti-monopoly book *The First Freedom* to Congress, who must "restore free enterprise in movies, radio and press." While calling for "reversing the monopoly trend and upsetting the present cartelization of press, radio and movies," Ernst was also deeply concerned about governmental censorship. But he concluded that "far more is kept from our minds by lack of diversity of ownership of the means of communication than by government interference."[93]

White's *American Radio*, a book-length study by the Hutchins Commission (discussed later), also insisted that commercial radio had failed in its "special responsibilities toward society."[94] The lack of "enlightened businessmen operating within the framework of profit-motive free enterprise," he pointed out, stemmed from the "tendency to confuse public service with public relations." With "advertiser domination of radio," he noted, broadcasters' "raison d'être" was to "sell goods and services" to large audiences, and thus favor uncontroversial programming that would not make listeners "think or tax their consciences" in ways that might discourage them from consuming advertised products. Indeed, "the advertising man" would prefer to "copy a successful formula than try a new one" and would rather "resist change and experimentation" and avoid "strictly local programs."[95] White concluded: "What we have here is a continuing contest between two diametrically opposed approaches to the problem of public service in radio – one based on long-range citizen need as the criterion, the other based on Hooper ratings and sales charts."[96]

Siepmann's *Radio's Second Chance* saw FM providing a potential alternative to AM's radio monopolies, unchecked commercialism, and dependence on advertisers. Echoing Spingarn's critique, in a section titled "Who Pays for Radio?" Siepmann observed that "big business has attempted to propagate a convenient but misleading idea" that we owe our "fine" programming to their "annual investment of millions of dollars in radio." Similarly absurd, Siepmann averred, was the claim that "we, the public, are therefore somehow beholden to the advertiser and to the networks and stations, as though a benefit had been conferred for which we should be grateful." With people feeling like "fortunate beneficiaries of a generous patron," such a "dangerously sentimental state of mind" leads to public "subservience." Rather, radio is "a system of exchange" whereby the public leases its airwaves, listens to advertisements and often subpar programming, and substantially subsidizes radio equipment, while broadcasters reap enormous profits. "If gratitude enters in at all," wrote Siepmann, "it is owed by the radio industry and by big business to the listener."[97] Ultimately,

93 Morris Ernst, *The First Freedom* (New York: Macmillan, 1946), xiv.
94 White, *The American Radio*, 2–3. This book is one of the Hutchins Commission's six major reports.
95 Ibid., 88, 91–4.
96 Ibid., 94–6, 210–27.
97 Ibid., 157–8.

only long-term struggle would change the system – "always by protest, by costly and prolonged petitions."[98]

Media criticism also took root within popular culture, especially novels. The mid-1940s saw a quick succession of fictional works satirizing and negatively portraying American radio. One review described them as reflecting "popular criticisms of the imbecility and corruption of one of our largest 'public services,' radio broadcasting," which instead of airing "the best and liveliest, most honest, profound, or critical in our culture" was dedicated "to a few mammoth soap-and-cigarette interests, to a few thousand third-rate merchants the country over, and to many thousands of their satellites, the advertising charlatans." In these novels, the "assembled hucksters have no higher objective" than to flood the market with products through "cajolery, downright lies, and the most abysmally trashy substitutes for entertainment." The novels drew attention to the industry's "over-commercialization, extirpation of critical ideas, regency of mediocre taste in all departments" and content that was "conditioned, vulgarized, circumscribed, or controlled" according to sponsors' "strictly mercantile aims."[99]

This view was epitomized in Frederic Wakeman's 1946 best-selling satirical novel *The Hucksters*, named after a common epithet for radio advertisers. The author, a former employee of a prominent advertising firm, provided a fictionalized account of his experiences of the backstage world of radio production that linked mediocre programming to greedy radio station owners and advertising agents. Other popular books with similar themes coincided – such as *Aurora Down* by the well-known novelist Herman Wouk and two novels by the *Fortune* magazine publisher[100] – but *The Hucksters* was by far the most prominent, peaking at number 4 and remaining on the *New York Times* Best Seller list for fifty-eight weeks, selling well more than 700,000 copies.[101] Attracting significant audiences and press attention, the popular book was made into a film of the same title starring Clark Gable. Becoming a common reference point for media reformers, the novel, according to one critic, "brought into public focus one of the most acute evils of radio, the vicious invasion of advertising in the form of swarms of spot announcements, singing commercials, middle commercials and other verbal selling devices."[102] "The

[98] Siepmann, *Radio's Second Chance*, 115.
[99] Young, "The Big Noise of the Hucksters," 5–12.
[100] Frederic Wakeman, *The Hucksters* (New York: Rinehart, 1946); Herman Wouk, *Aurora Down* (New York: Simon & Schuster, 1947); Eric Hodgins, *Mr. Blandings Builds His Dream House* (New York: Simon & Schuster, 1946) and *Blanding's Way* (New York: Simon & Schuster, 1950). See also: Arkady Leokum, *Please Send Me Absolutely Free* (New York: Harper, 1946); Fielden Farrington, *The Big Noise* (New York: Crown, 1946); and S. J. Perelman, "Garnish Your Face with Parsley, and Serve" in *Keep It Crisp* (New York: Random House, 1946).
[101] Susan Smulyan, *Popular Ideologies, Mass Culture at Mid-Century* (Philadelphia: University of Pennsylvania Press, 2007), 186.
[102] Konecky, *The American Communications Conspiracy*, 19.

sad truth is," Wakeman said on *Town Meeting of the Air*, the "people who should be the creators of radio, responsible to the public, are today nothing but salesmen responsible to their sponsors." Wakeman urged broadcasters to "take back your networks. Take back your stations and do your own programming" regardless of "what any sponsor thinks any program should be."[103] The criticism resonated far and wide: One in four Americans read the book or watched the movie. The researchers Lazarsfeld and Kendall found that those exposed to Wakeman's satire were "considerably more critical of commercials" and that for those who were already critical, their "criticism is strengthened and reinforced by [their] exposure."[104]

Internal documents from the NBC archives suggest that commercial broadcasters felt threatened by the film, especially depictions of public disgust toward advertising's role in radio. One particular exchange shows the extreme measures NBC was considering (although ultimately electing to go with a more moderate tone) to discredit the film and Hollywood in general.[105] After describing "the most dangerous part of the entire film," in which Clark Gable claims that commercial radio did not reflect public desires but rather the sponsor's, NBC's advertising director urged NBC president Niles Trammell to "get MGM to pull this out of the film." An NBC publicist provided a list of other suggested amendments to scenes deemed too critical of commercial broadcasting, and even suggested that NBC provide a "public service to its many listeners" with a new program series called "Spotlight on Hollywood" that drew attention to "suits now pending against the leading movie companies." He proposed pursuing the question of "whether Hollywood ... is making a real contribution to the American way of life, or is engaged solely in the exposition of sex," and launching an investigation of the "movie industry's attitude towards Communistic writers and producers."[106] Picking up on this latter theme, one of the proposed statements about the film resorted to red baiting by denouncing the "vicious and untruthful attack on our American system of advertising which is generally recognized by all except left wingers as the bulwark of the American system of free enterprise." The statement concluded that the "vast audience of radio listeners, the people who turn the dials and flip the switches, know that they and they alone dictate what they shall hear on the air."[107] Although ultimately not leading to the kind of public uprising that broadcasters feared, *The Hucksters*

[103] *Education*, May 1947.
[104] Paul Lazarsfeld and Patricia Kendall, *Radio Listening in America* (New York: Prentice-Hall, 1948), 77–9.
[105] Charles Hammond to Niles Trammell, June 26, 1947, Folder 17, Box 115, National Broadcasting Company Records, State Historical Society of Wisconsin Archive, Madison, WI (hereafter NBC papers).
[106] Syd Eiges to Niles Trammell, June 27, 1947, Folder 17, Box 115, NBC papers.
[107] Syd Eiges to Niles Trammell, "Proposed Statement by Niles Trammell on 'The Hucksters,'" July 1, 1947, Folder 17, Box 115, NBC papers.

effectively focused American society's attention on advertisers' often-hidden control over American broadcasting and steered discourse about radio in a more critical direction.[108]

From Criticism to Activism

The 1940s provided the driving narratives for a vibrant media reform movement.[109] This criticism took shape in grassroots organizations, in commentary in newspapers and opinion journals, and thousands of letters from average listeners to broadcasters and the FCC.[110] Dissident intellectuals provided further coherence by extending this critique into trenchant polemics embraced by social movement groups. However, intellectual critique alone does not make a social movement. Organized activist groups must connect this critique with action by channeling the discontent felt among the wider populace toward a targeted set of actions and social change. In particular, much media reform activism necessitates engaging the FCC, which, as one critic warned, "will not exert the [regulatory] power unless the people so demand."[111]

In the 1940s, media critics dialectically combined with grassroots organizations to launch a vibrant, if nascent and inchoate, reform movement, fostering the intellectual heft and moral imperative to spur what the historian Elizabeth Fones-Wolf describes as a "loose media reform coalition," consisting of disaffected intellectuals, progressive FCC commissioners, and remnants of the Popular Front.[112] These reformers contested "unchecked commercialism, promoted public service, and sought to make radio more representative and democratic and to increase community control."[113] Joining this coalition were religious groups, educators, political progressives, and civil rights activists who pressured broadcasters via petitions, call-ins, and letter-writing campaigns to

[108] Alan Havig, "Frederic Wakeman's The Hucksters and the Postwar Debate over Commercial Radio," *Journal of Broadcasting* 29, no. 2 (1984), 197.
[109] I expand on this period's media reform activism and criticism in the following: "The Revolt against Radio: Postwar Media Criticism and the Struggle for Broadcast Reform," in *A Moment of Danger: Critical Studies in the History of U.S. Communication since 1945*, ed. Janice Peck and Inger Stole (Milwaukee: New Marquette University Press, 2011), 35–56; "The Air Belongs to the People": The Rise and Fall of a Postwar Radio Reform Movement, *Critical Studies in Media Communication*, 2012; "The Postwar Media Insurgency: Radio Activism from Above and Below," in *Media Interventions*, ed. Kevin Howley (New York: Peter Lang, 2013), 247–66.
[110] White suggests a rough estimate of "fifty thousand unsolicited letters a year to the FCC," though presumably some of them were simply advocating different kinds of programming. See White, *American Radio*, 232.
[111] Oliver, "Thought Control – American Style," 13.
[112] Fones-Wolf, *Waves of Opposition*, 4.
[113] Ibid., 126.

radio stations and the FCC, urging them to democratize the public airwaves and to improve programming.[114]

A signature model of 1940s radio activism was the neighborhood listener council.[115] Created by local communities – oftentimes by parents, educators, and minority groups – listener councils monitored programming and lobbied radio stations and the FCC to privilege localism and curb excessive commercialism. By the mid-1940s, listener councils were established in Cleveland, Columbus, and New York City, and in more rural areas like central Wisconsin and northern California.[116] As these councils emerged across the country, reformers advocated their broader deployment to countervail against commercial broadcasters' political juggernaut. Some reformers hoped that the councils could extend to the state level and coordinate nationally, thereby harmonizing their standards and survey techniques with the FCC and perhaps an overarching public national council. They proposed that councils receive local government support or be volunteer based to provide institutional backing for groups collecting research on the state of broadcasting. Armed with these data, listener councils could pressure radio stations with the threat of presenting critical evaluations to the FCC during broadcasters' renewal procedures.[117] Listener councils' potential generated much enthusiasm, even if they never became a major force within policy debates. Siepmann, for example, saw listener councils as the "community's best safeguard against the exploitation of the people's wavelengths and the surest guarantee [that radio stations consider] ... its needs."[118] By devising blueprints for high-quality local programming, Siepmann opined, the councils serve as "watchdogs for the listener, ready and able to protest the abuse of airtime and to promote its better use."[119]

Many activist groups participating in the 1940s media reform coalition also created their own alternative media, contested negative imagery, and exploited opportunities within commercial media to disseminate their political messages. Labor unions succeeded in buying a number of stations

[114] Other groups involved in 1940s media reform campaigns include the ACLU, Jewish organizations, and women's groups. For an interesting case study of the latter, one that was often pro-industry and anti–media regulation, see Jennifer Proffitt, "War, Peace, and Free Radio: The Women's National Radio Committee's Efforts to Promote Democracy, 1939–1946," *Journal of Radio & Audio Media*, 17, no. 1, (2010): 2–17.

[115] Not to be confused with "listener clubs," or discussion groups that were sometimes formed around specific programs, especially those that had educational value such as "America's Town Meeting of the Air."

[116] For an overview of different models of "radio councils," see Judith Waller, *Radio: The Fifth Estate* (Boston: Houghton Mifflin, 1946), 311–31. See also Christopher Sterling and John M. Kittross, *Stay Tuned: A Concise History of American Broadcasting*, 2001 ed. (Belmont, CA: Wadsworth,), 336–7.

[117] See White, *American Radio*, 231–34.

[118] Siepmann, *Radio's Second Chance*, 51–2.

[119] Ibid., 50–2.

and instructed their members how to produce their own shows or insert labor-friendly scripts into commercial radio programming. The Congress of Industrial Organizations (CIO) galvanized reformers with its *Radio Handbook*, a pamphlet that contained instructions for getting on the air and promoting "freedom to listen" and "freedom of the air." It insisted that workers have not exercised "their *right* to use radio broadcasting." "Labor has a voice," the pamphlet stated, and "the people have a right to hear it." Although broadcasters own radio stations' equipment, "the air over which the broadcasts are made does not belong to companies or corporations. *The air belongs to the people.*"[120] The handbook instructed activists on how to gain radio time for a labor perspective via different techniques and formats, including the Straight Talk, the Round Table Discussion, the Spot Announcement, and the Dramatic Radio Play. It encouraged activists to generate good publicity and to coordinate with consumer groups, cooperatives, women's organizations, and religious organizations.[121] The CIO handbook provided advice about choosing optimal airtime, tips on making high-quality programs, and sample scripts for announcements and dramatizations, including "Full Employment for Workers after the War," "Child Care and School Lunch Programs," "G. I. Joe and CIO," "Why We Are for FDR," "The Need for Farm-Labor Unity," "The Negro in 1944," and "Women War Workers."[122] These instructions demonstrated a savvy approach to influencing commercial radio in ways that legitimated labor unions, even as the political landscape turned rightward.

The NAACP attempted to advance the coalition's politics and strategic vision by creating a permanent radio reform organization in partnership with labor and religious groups. Inspired by the CIO's radio activism handbook, the NAACP convened in 1946 a media reform conference as part of a larger effort to "call in every existing agency working in the field of race relations, religious and nationality minorities" to create a "coordinating agency" that impressed upon broadcasters that these media reform groups "represent the entire ... minority field." Representing "millions of listeners," their goal was to "request, not beg for air time," to counteract discriminatory programming, and ultimately reform commercial radio.[123] The groups constituting this media reform coalition shared grievances, critiques, tactics, and strategies to engage in media policy debates in Washington, DC Media reformers continuously pressured the FCC and commercial broadcasters to include diverse perspectives in radio programming. Their objectives converged around specific policy interventions, often backed by progressive allies at the FCC.

---

[120] Congress of Industrial Organizations (CIO), *Radio Handbook* (their emphases), 1944, 6.
[121] Ibid., 25.
[122] Ibid., 23.
[123] Quoted in Toro, 53.

Ferment for Media Reform

The 1940s witnessed pronounced dissatisfaction – what some sources even described as a "revolt" – among various interest groups as well as everyday American listeners who were upset with their typical radio fare. One irate listener captured this multifaceted challenge against commercial broadcasters in a letter to MBS: "The Hucksters, the FCC's so-called Blue Book, The N.Y. *PM*'s campaign, Crosby, Gould et al. critics, discussion on ABC's Town Meeting ... the adverse editorials and your own listeners' letters, has put your industry-spokesmen ... on the defensive, apologetically insisting that radio does operate in the public interest."[124] Condemnation of radio's excessive commercialism galvanized a broad array of media criticism and activism. Exhortations to change the media system in the 1940s were not merely routine calls for a public conversation on a pressing issue. They carried an urgency that recognized the gravity of the moment and demanded systemic change, leading to a wide array of media critiques in book-length reports and polemics, popular culture, and organized opposition. Popular media representations in novels and films like *The Hucksters* dovetailed with the structural critique that advertisers had too much power in shaping programming; that radio's increasingly concentrated ownership led to privileging profits at the expense of local programming, high-quality fare, and information-rich newscasts; and that these systemic flaws prevented broadcasting from realizing its democratic potential. This criticism combined with disruptive new media technologies like FM radio, and soon television – as well as the support of sympathetic policy elites – to create the necessary historical conditions for a critical juncture in American media policy.

This juncture was characterized by two contrasting policy visions: One, corporate libertarianism, saw commercial media institutions as the primary beneficiaries of First Amendment protections and assumed that media corporations should be regulated primarily by market relationships.[125] The other, social democracy, saw the need for an activist state that ensured media accountability based on local communities' communication needs and other democratic criteria. Although there were degrees of difference in between, these competing positions crystallized within 1940s media policy debates. Many believed the progressive changes sweeping American society at this time could extend to structural media reform. Reformers hoped to establish a social democratic vision of media – a paradigm shift in the relationship among media, government, and the public – that would challenge the self-regulatory regime.

This social democratic vision of media gained its fullest expression with policy initiatives in the 1940s. At this time, a New Deal interventionist approach

[124] Fred Miller to MBS, January 20, 1947, Box 31, Folder 2, CJDP.
[125] A glaring contradiction occurs when media companies benefit from government largesse, including radio spectrum giveaways to broadcasters.

to corporate monopolies was leaving an imprint on media policy. This impulse came to fruition under an activist FCC chairman, James Lawrence Fly, who would leave the commission before many of the progressive initiatives he helped set in motion were debated. The following three chapters chronicle these media reform efforts. They trace the rise and fall of a progressive regulatory project that attempted to restructure radio broadcasting along social democratic lines, culminating with the policy battles over the FCC Blue Book and the Fairness Doctrine. The outcomes of these policy struggles would help shape the American media landscape for generations to come.

2

A Progressive Turn at the FCC

Despite its New Deal origins, the Federal Communications Commission (FCC) did not begin with a reformist agenda. The commission's early years saw few policy challenges to American radio's increasing commercialization. The inveterate media reformer Everett Parker, recalling how the FCC's genesis was characterized by close ties to media corporations, quipped that prior to its formation, "four commissioners were vetted by AT&T and three by broadcasters."[1] Given such proclivities, the FCC would not seem to be a natural progressive ally. Although the 1934 Communications Act – the FCC's founding charter and the blueprint for its regulatory power – gave it a mandate to serve the always-contested "public interest, convenience and necessity," the commission was largely nonconfrontational in its interactions with commercial broadcasters.[2] Indeed, what is known as "regulatory capture" – when federal agencies seemingly act in concert with the industries they purportedly regulate – gives a fairly accurate picture of how the FCC typically operates, then and now. However, under new leadership in the early 1940s, the FCC changed its behavior markedly. It confronted media corporations and aggressively defended public interest principles while facing considerable political opposition.

Few would have predicted such a turn. The FCC was preceded by the Federal Radio Commission (FRC), a temporary agency founded in 1927 to provide regulatory stability, particularly around technical issues, for the increasingly contested airwaves. Congress soon deemed the FRC inadequate to keep up with expanding communication technologies, and regulation of all interstate communications was consolidated under the new agency of the FCC, giving it authority over telephony and broadcast media. While its purview did not include potentially contentious duties like overseeing industry profits or rate

[1] Interview with author, December 23, 2008.
[2] Their behavior toward the telecom industry was at times more confrontational.

38

structures, the FCC nonetheless faced several regulatory quandaries. As with the FRC, the FCC was tasked with granting licenses, inspecting equipment, and ensuring that broadcasting stations served a public interest mission. However, programming regulation was a thorny terrain because the FCC was forbidden by law to practice censorship as described in the Communications Act.[3] Moreover, the standards by which licensees were judged remained ill defined, thereby inviting charges of arbitrariness. Thus any FCC attempt to establish public interest standards invited conflict with the commercial broadcast industry, including accusations of paternalism and infringement of free speech. These power struggles often hinged on the question of government's role in media regulation and disagreements over First Amendment interpretations.

Given these tensions, the FCC would seem an obvious target for liberal reform, but it was initially spared serious scrutiny. The agency lacked the zeal that characterized other New Deal regulatory bodies, and FDR largely ignored it during its early years. Many of the first FCC appointments were uninspiring, described years later in *Newsweek* as "political hacks and has-beens who were content to draw their paychecks."[4] FDR's cozy relationship with broadcasters may have encouraged complacency toward the increasingly concentrated industry and commercialized medium. This conciliatory disposition, however, began to change by the late 1930s when newspapers rapidly bought up radio stations and, in some cases, exerted editorial authority over radio programming. FDR saw in this consolidation a threat to democracy – and perhaps more alarmingly, a political challenge to his New Deal agenda. He needed a proxy to make an intervention.

Chairman Fly: Anti-monopolist Crusader

James Lawrence (Larry) Fly's appointment to the FCC chairmanship in July 1939 marked a decidedly different turn for the commission, initiating a nearly decade-long progressive regulatory orientation for American media policy. A strong-willed New Dealer from Texas, Fly had studied with Supreme Court Justice Felix Frankfurter at Harvard Law School and inherited from his mentor a deep-seated suspicion of monopoly power, believing that capitalism foundered without competition. Having cut his teeth on progressive policy battles during the mid- to late 1930s heading the Tennessee Valley Authority's legal department, Fly developed a reputation as a tough liberal who relished a good fight and did not fear provoking powerful industries. *Broadcasting* magazine

---

[3] Bollinger, 63. See generally William Ray, *FCC: The Ups and Downs of Radio-TV Regulation*, 1st ed. (Ames: Iowa State University Press, 1990).

[4] *Newsweek*, September 1961, 63, cited in Joon-Mann Kang, "Franklin D. Roosevelt and James L. Fly: The Politics of Broadcast Regulation, 1941–1944," *Journal of American Culture* 10, no. 2 (Summer 1987): 24. See also Lawrence Lichty, "The Impact of FRC and FCC Commissioners' Backgrounds on the Regulation of Broadcasting," *Journal of Broadcasting* 6 (1962): 102.

described him as a "mailed-fist regulator ... who brooked no opposition."[5] The corporate attorney and Republican presidential candidate Wendell Willkie called Fly "the most dangerous man in America – to have on the other side."[6]

For many, Fly represented the New Deal's last hope, and, in many ways, the FCC became the last stand for the American social democratic project. Harry Plotkin, the FCC's assistant general counsel under Fly, remembered, "When the New Deal was dying everywhere else, it came to the FCC, when Larry came to the FCC." Young liberals were drawn to Fly, whom Plotkin described as "a real strong towering man" committed to carrying out a progressive agenda. "The whole concept of public responsibility of broadcast licensees got a strong impetus from Fly," Plotkin recalled. "Everything that the Commission ultimately did [for the public interest] stems from the fact that he put his shoulder behind the wheel."[7] Specifically, Plotkin credited Fly with transforming the FCC from being a mere "traffic cop" concerned only with "technical requirements" into an institution that disciplined broadcasters according to a "strong public service responsibility," so that program quality became "as important as the technical quality of the transmission."[8] Fly believed that such programming objectives required government-driven structural interventions. One historian noted that Fly was "steadfast in his desire to use the federal government as a countervailing force to private power," taking with him to the FCC a "deep commitment to promoting diversity of ownership among the corporations shaping the public sphere."[9]

Fly's many writings and public speeches clearly reflected this New Deal policy orientation, in which three broad themes stand out. First, Fly saw open access to the airwaves for a wide range of voices as a prerequisite for liberty and democracy. Considering the public's "freedom to listen" as paramount,[10] he firmly believed this freedom was predicated on the positive liberty that guaranteed public access to a diversity of media content. Fly described his personal regulatory philosophy as one that assumed self-governance depended on people's access "to the information necessary to the exercise of an intelligent judgment." Therefore, "freedom of speech is not so much a right of the individual to express himself as it is a right of the people to hear – a right to information untarnished and fairly presented."[11] Fly did not go so far as to suggest that government "propaganda stations" – what some referred to as a "TVA of the

[5] "Fly Leaves FCC Nov. 15" *Broadcasting* November 6, 1944, 18.
[6] "Battler's Exit," *Time*, November 13, 1944.
[7] Sally Fly Connell, interview with Harry Plotkin, December 27, 1967, 3, James Lawrence Fly Project, Oral History Research Office, Sally Fly Connell Papers, Special Collections, Columbia University, New York (hereafter cited as Fly Connell Papers).
[8] Ibid., 25–6.
[9] Stamm, *Sound Business*, 112.
[10] Fones-Wolf, *Waves of Opposition*, 111.
[11] James Lawrence Fly, "Regulation of Radio in the Public Interest," *Annals of the American Academy of Political and Social Science* 213 (January 1941): 105.

air" – were needed, but he believed in strict democratic criteria for commercial radio. It was broadcasters' mandate to fulfill the cherished liberal ideal of the "marketplace of ideas" by presenting "all the facts and all the points of view." After all, Fly asserted, the radio spectrum "belongs to the people; it may be used only in the public interest."[12] In his first significant speech as FCC chairman – which happened to be at a National Association of Broadcasters (NAB) convention – Fly emphasized that providing the public with diverse programming was a "responsibility ... [that] rests with the licensee." "The broadcaster," he asserted,

owes to the public whose facility he occupies – and to the democracy he is bound to preserve – the inescapable duty of full and fair reporting, balanced treatment, and honest and impartial comment on all facts and information of public concern; and adequate coverage on all public issues by two-sided discussions and equality of facility and representation.[13]

Fly did not seek diverse programming through content regulation but rather through structural regulation, namely, through mandating a diversity of media ownership. This leads to his second core principle: breaking up media concentration.

Fly's tenure at the FCC was marked by a decidedly anti-monopoly approach. Drawing upon a New Deal orientation of general hostility toward concentrated capital, Fly believed that monopolies were a corruption of the free enterprise system, dangerous for competition and, more important, for the survival of democratic governance. Therefore, he believed, government must intervene on the public's behalf against media monopolies to encourage diverse voices and viewpoints. He saw Americans living in an age of "monopolies and near monopolies" with a "present-day threat" of "increasing domination of the media of communication by a few economic entities, and the resultant lessening of opportunities for the full, free spread of all kinds and shades of opinion." This threat, he believed, was "the begotten child of technology and big business."[14] To diversify the airwaves, Fly aimed to promote competition by applying the weight of the FCC's still ill-defined regulatory powers.

A third underpinning to Fly's regulatory orientation was an unremitting defense of civil liberties. Later in life, Fly confided to his grandchildren that his

[12] Ibid., 107. The "marketplace of ideas" was not the exact phrase uttered by Justice Holmes and is not used in the article, but rather "competition of the market."

[13] James Lawrence Fly, "Radio Faces the Future," address to National Association of Broadcasters convention, San Francisco, August 5, 1940, James Lawrence Fly Papers, Rare Book & Manuscript Library, Columbia University, New York (hereafter cited as Fly Papers). Quoted in Mickie Edwardson, "James Lawrence Fly's Fight for a Free Marketplace of Ideas," *American Journalism* 14, no. 1 (Winter 1997): 22.

[14] Larry Fly, "Freedom of Speech and the Press," in *Safeguarding Civil Liberty Today*, 66 (Edward Bernays lectures of 1944 given at Cornell University). Ithaca, NY: Cornell University Press, 1945. Also quoted in Edwardson, "James Lawrence Fly's Fight for a Free Marketplace of Ideas," 24.

sole regret was his "failure in teaching John Edgar Hoover the Bill of Rights."[15] In particular, he was an ardent foe of governmental wiretapping of phones. According to FDR's deputy attorney general James Rowe, Fly was "against it no matter what," while "FDR was on the fence."[16] However, Fly saw threats of surveillance, censorship, and propaganda originating in private commercial interests as much as, if not more than, in an overreaching government. In a talk about international communications during a civil liberties union luncheon, he suggested that "the main restraints on our speech and press are not those of a governmental character." He invoked John Milton and Justice Oliver Wendell Holmes to embrace "the free exchange of ideas in the greatest of all marketplaces – the marketplace of thought" instead of solely relying on the commercial marketplace.[17] Fly's civil libertarianism continued during his post-FCC years as the ACLU director, when he defended people like the labor leader Harry Bridges against deportation from the United States for alleged Communist Party membership.[18]

Fly's fight against concentrated power, reflected in his attitudes regarding media monopolies, listeners' rights, and civil liberties, helped define a new progressive era at the FCC. His chairmanship sets up a rise-and-fall narrative arc for structural media reform in the 1940s, because in many ways, Fly's tenure was a high point for imagining alternative trajectories for commercial radio, and it was followed by a gradual discursive narrowing of possibilities. However, the following story amounts to more than a simple tale of declension; it sets the context for a number of subsequent policy battles and holds many parallels with and lessons for contemporary debates over media ownership, monopoly power, and the public's positive liberties in a democratic society.

Clifford Durr Bolsters FCC Progressivism

Fly's regulatory agenda was not his alone. A cadre of liberal commissioners formed a progressive majority on the FCC around him. In the fall of 1941, with several key reforms already advancing, the equally progressive Clifford Durr joined Fly to challenge broadcasting monopolies, triumph over right-wing congressional opponents, and formulate progressive policy positions on a number of media issues.[19] Charles Siepmann later recalled that Durr was "the only

[15] Quoted in Mickie Edwardson, "James Lawrence Fly, the FBI, and Wiretapping," *Historian* 61 (1999).

[16] Interview with James Rowe, August 1, 1967, Box 55, Fly Papers.

[17] Larry Fly talk at Civil Liberties Union luncheon, World Freedom of Speech and Press Town Hall Club, May 16, 1945, Box 49, Fly Papers.

[18] Siepmann recalled how much he admired Fly and how they were both deeply committed to the ACLU. Charles Siepmann to Sally Fly Connell, May 17, 1967, Box 55, Fly Papers.

[19] John Salmond, *The Conscience of a Lawyer* (Tuscaloosa: University of Alabama Press, 1990), 72–97.

other commissioner who ... matched [Fly's] courage and integrity."[20] While Fly faced some opposition on the commission – particularly from the pro-industry democrat T. A. M. Craven – other commissioners composed a fairly reliable liberal bloc, including the progressive California Republican Ray Wakefield and the populist Oklahoma Democrat Paul Walker.

Durr in particular would become a progressive stalwart on the FCC and the go-to person for a wide array of activist groups on issues like educational broadcasting, public service programming, and civil liberty protections. He ventured to DC in the early 1930s as a young Oxford-trained attorney to work for the Reconstruction Finance Corporation as part of FDR's New Deal – an opportunity facilitated by his influential brother-in-law, the former Alabama senator and Supreme Court justice Hugo Black, whose liberal politics would deeply influence both Clifford and his increasingly activist wife, Virginia. Also influential was DC's tight-knit community of New Deal policy advocates; frequent social gatherings included luminaries ranging from political figures like Lyndon Johnson to artists like Pete Seeger. Durr's biographer noted, "The New Deal community was full of vitality, shared ideals, and the sense of being part of something bigger than oneself. Even at the parties the talk would most often turn to politics, their jobs ... and their hopes for the future."[21] New Deal agencies attracted hundreds of idealistic attorneys like Durr who sought meaningful employment in public service.[22] These young progressives came to identify "with the aims of federal policy and ... its reformist directions."[23] The well-known activist and friend of the Durrs Jessica Mitford noted that, unlike Virginia, who more easily assumed leftist politics, Clifford was "not one of nature's radicals" but rather was "flung by history into a radical role."[24] The New Deal gave rise to legions of such unlikely radicals who went to DC to embrace the social democratic view that government could tame market savageries, nurture a strong public sector, and actualize democratic ideals.

Durr carried these values to the FCC, an appointment facilitated by Alabama political connections and FDR's approval.[25] He took his advocacy for progressive media policy to diverse constituencies beyond DC circles via talks, letters, and articles. In his widely discussed article "Freedom of Speech for Whom?" he drew connections between media ownership structures and First Amendment protections, arguing that "the only barriers to the complete occupation of the air by advertisers, and the consequent total elimination of public service programs" were broadcasters' "self-restraint" – fortified by listeners' complaints – and the

---

[20] Siepmann to Connell, May 17, 1965, Box 55, Fly Papers.
[21] Salmond, 57–8. For a biography describing Hugo Black's legal philosophy, see Howard Bell, *The Vision and the Dream of Justice Hugo L. Black: An Examination of a Judicial Philosophy* (University: University of Alabama Press, 1975).
[22] Salmond, *The Conscience of a Lawyer*, 50.
[23] Ibid., 52.
[24] Ibid., 59.
[25] Salmond, *The Conscience of a Lawyer*, 73–4.

"public interest provisions of the Communications Act."[26] He emphasized that economic inequities were as significant as political constraints on freedom of speech and access to a diverse range of information. Durr feared that "the average listener [perceives radio] ... as a matter of course" and thus does not adequately fear the "economic control of information and ideas."[27]

In an article titled "How Free Is Radio?" Durr warned that radio was becoming "predominantly an advertising medium" that "moved from diversification to concentration," placing acute commercial pressures on stations and squeezing out public service programs. Radio also was becoming an "active battlefront" for the First Amendment, he observed. "Propaganda against government regulation" tempted people to ask that government not protect them, but Durr dismissed the "many solemn warnings during the past year or so that despotic government bureaucrats are plotting to snatch away ... freedom of speech." Corporate power was the true enemy, for "concentration of economic power" would subject Americans "to dangers far more serious and immediate than any threat from the government." Durr felt this was especially true given that 144 advertisers controlled 97 percent of the national networks' advertising and 74 percent of four national networks' total billings were from four industry groups: food, beverages, and confections; drugs; soaps and cleaners; and tobacco.[28] Because advertising dominance of commercial radio impoverished the medium's democratic potential, in Durr's view, government needed to intervene.

Another important member of the new progressive faction was the FCC's first chief economist, Dallas Smythe, a Canadian who was later red-baited as a "premature anti-fascist."[29] Smythe, a self-described "New Dealer left-wing economist," explained in his autobiography why he left his economist position at the Interstate Commerce Commission (ICC) for the promise of continuing progressive work. "By 1942 I realized that the ICC was a tool of the railroads and hopelessly sterile. The FCC, under New Deal leadership, however, was a place where the public interest might be served." Smythe was especially interested to see what he could do "to influence policy toward communication monopolies."[30] Fly's decision to hire Smythe – both for his

---

[26] Clifford Durr, "Freedom of Speech for Whom?" *Public Opinion Quarterly* 8 (Fall 1944): 391–406.

[27] Durr to Peter Odegard, November 17, 1944, Box 30, Folder 2, CJDP.

[28] Clifford Durr, "How Free Is Radio?" *Journal of the National Education Association* 33, no. 7 (1944): 167.

[29] In addition to Smythe's personal Papers, three books provide background on his FCC years: Dallas Smythe and Thomas Guback, *Counterclockwise: Perspectives on Communication* (Boulder, CO: Westview Press, 1994), especially pages 26–37; John Lent, *A Different Road Taken: Profiles in Critical Communication* (Boulder, CO: Westview Press, 1995), especially page 30; and Janet Wasko, Vincent Mosco, and Manju Pendakur, *Illuminating the Blindspots: Essays Honoring Dallas W. Smythe* (Norwood, NJ: Ablex, 1993), especially pages 222–3.

[30] Wasko et al., *Illuminating the Blindspots*, 2; Smythe, *Counterclockwise*, 26–7.

progressivism and for his highly desirable economic skills – signifies what the FCC was gearing up to do: go after broadcasters' monopolistic power at a structural level.[31]

Investigating Newspaper-Owned Radio

The incoming chairman Larry Fly hit the ground running when he arrived at the FCC. Along with having a number of fellow New Deal progressives on the committee, Fly's direct access to the president was a significant asset. Much archival evidence suggests that he coordinated with the Roosevelt administration to challenge media concentration. It was a fairly open secret that FDR tasked Fly with tackling what he saw as a major threat to both democracy and his administration's agenda: newspapers owning radio stations.[32] Memos were sent back and forth, and at key moments the two would meet at the White House.[33] While FDR made it clear that he could not publicly endorse an aggressive regulatory agenda against broadcasters and newspapers, he supported it from behind the scenes.

Up until this point, newspapers had been on a mad dash toward acquiring radio stations. Press control of radio grew from 11 percent of all stations on the air in 1931 to nearly 31 percent in 1940.[34] During this time, in ninety-eight localities, the only radio station was owned by the only newspaper.[35] In 1941 there were 241 newspaper-associated AM stations, and many of the initial applicants for newly available FM licenses were newspapers, leading to increased fears about local news monopolies.[36] Throughout the 1940s, newspapers would control from one-fourth to one-third of all AM radio licenses, a trend that continued with FM.[37] By 1941, the FCC had given nearly 25 percent of FM authorizations to newspapers.[38] According to one source, by the summer of 1941 newspapers had filed 43 of 99 FM applications.[39]

---

[31] Smythe notes that he was introduced to Fly through his union friends, perhaps in the American Communications Association. Lent, *A Different Road Taken*, 30.

[32] FDR's concern was well known, discussed in Barnouw, *The Golden Web*, 169–70; Salmond, *The Conscience of a Lawyer*, 73. See also the Sally Fly Connell interviews with Ed Brecher, 17; Harry Plotkin, 30; and Paul Porter, 18, Fly Connell Papers.

[33] Kang, "Franklin D. Roosevelt and James L. Fly," 26–7.

[34] Christopher Sterling, "Newspaper Ownership of Broadcast Stations, 1920–68," *Journalism Quarterly* (Summer 1969): 229. These numbers have differed slightly according to several historians.

[35] Kang, "Franklin D. Roosevelt and James L. Fly," 24. See also Barnouw, *The Golden Web*, 169–70.

[36] Earl Minderman, Memorandum to Clifford Durr in preparation for his Nieman address, March 3, 1944, Box 34, Folder 2, CJDP.

[37] Sterling, "Newspaper Ownership," 232, 234.

[38] Sterling, "Newspaper Ownership," 231; "FCC vs Press," *Business Week*, July 26, 1941, 32.

[39] Daniel Toohey, "Newspaper Ownership of Broadcast Facilities," *Federal Communications Bar Journal* 20, no. 1 (1966): 47. Cited in Sterling, "Newspaper Ownership," 231.

Given the increased attention from regulators, broadcasters saw strategic value in joining forces with newspapers for both political and economic
reasons. As early as the mid-1930s, Louis Caldwell, a leading advocate for
commercial broadcasters, had noted in the *Annals of the American Academy
of Politics and Social Science* that newspapers and radio shared a "common
cause." He cautioned that "a defeat by either will eventually expose the other
to flank attack."[40] Calls for a united front – even if just for joint economic
benefits – continued into the 1940s. *Editor & Publisher* wrote in 1944 that
given radio's "comparatively low cost" and "tremendous future," newspaper
publishers "are missing a bet if they do not immediately obtain an option" to
set up an FM station "on the highest building in town" or atop "the highest
hill or mountain in their vicinity."[41] Two years later, in response to the FCC's
decision to consider newspapers' editorial policy among other criteria when
evaluating their application for a radio license, *Editor & Publisher* noted
that "leaders in the radio industry have been calling for a joint press-radio
front."[42]

Many commentators took note of this growing juggernaut. Radical critics like Eugene Konecky, who viewed media corporations' privileged position
in society as a threat to democratic culture, declared the emergence of the
"American Communications Monopoly." Alarmed by their growing political
power, especially their later collective opposition to Henry Wallace's presidential campaign, he asserted that "if and when monopoly radio and monopoly newspapers are confronted by an anti-monopoly movement organized by
the American people – the radio and press monopolists will make common
cause against the people."[43] Beyond left-wing radicals, concerns about newspapers owning radio stations registered at the highest reaches of the political
establishment.

Shortly after winning his third term, FDR sent Fly a single sentence: "Will
you let me know when you propose to have a hearing on newspaper ownership of radio stations."[44] Fly responded that he was "in wholehearted agreement that the problem of newspaper ownership of radio stations should be
given a thorough airing so that the desirability of having as many *independent*
channels of information and communication as possible may be brought home
to the public."[45] Fly set out to investigate newspaper-radio conglomerates to
uncover how they were anti-competitive and not serving democracy. But he did
so with some reservations. The archival record makes clear that this impetus

---

[40] Quoted in Konecky, "The American Communications Conspiracy," 111.
[41] *Editor & Publisher*, February 26, 1944.
[42] *Editor & Publisher*, December 28, 1946.
[43] Konecky, *The American Communications Conspiracy*, 112.
[44] Fly papers, Box 55, also quoted in multiple places, including Barnouw, *The Golden Web*, 170.
[45] Fly, "Memorandum to the president," December 23, 1940, Fly Papers (emphasis in original).
Also quoted in Edwardson, "James Lawrence Fly's Fight for a Free Marketplace of Ideas," 30.

for an investigation of cross-ownership was orchestrated by FDR himself. In a "Memorandum to the President," Fly wrote in late 1940,

I have sounded out members of the Commission informally on the question of an early investigation of newspaper ownership of radio stations. Although I believe a majority of the Commission would be prepared to authorize the investigation, particularly in view of your own interest, I find considerable reluctance to move at this particular moment.

Fly warned, "All too frequently in the past the Commission has been a public whipping boy. Right now the chains are prepared to seek the destruction of the Commission if any substantial network regulation is attempted." Before the commission could go after newspapers, he felt, this "problem must be dealt with promptly and the resulting criticism absorbed." Otherwise, "the Commission's position," Fly feared, "might be impaired if the press were provoked to join the attack."[46] Before loosening their hold on newspapers, he wanted to weaken broadcasters' political power by breaking up the chains, lest the commission face a united front of radio and newspaper owners.

These trepidations notwithstanding, Fly's FCC proceeded forthwith. After the commissioners narrowly supported the decision by one vote, Order No. 79 was issued on March 21, 1941, officially launching the FCC investigation. The order called for "an immediate investigation to determine what statement of policy or rules, if any, should be issued concerning applications for high frequency (FM) with which are associated persons also associated with the publication of one or more newspapers."[47] In addition to calling for public hearings, the order froze pending FM applications and halted the unfinished construction of new stations.[48] Focusing on whether newspapers should be barred from owning more stations, the FCC immediately began subpoenaing expert witnesses for hearings to be held that summer.

Broadcasters' reactions were swift and vicious. *Broadcasting* condemned Fly and the FCC for discriminating against newspapers and warned that "a battle of goodly magnitude was brewing."[49] Many observers saw this initiative as a barely hidden partisan ploy to clip newspaper publishers' growing political and economic power. In response, more than 150 newspaper and radio executives assembled to form a new alliance whose primary function was to contest the investigation: the Newspaper-Radio Committee. It was chaired by the *Louisville Courier-Journal* publisher and former NAB president Mark Ethridge. Despite incessant attacks from industry spokesmen and a promised

[46] See also James Rowe Jr. Papers, Administrative Asst to President 1938–41, Container 13 File FCC-1, FDR Presidential Library, Hyde Park, New York. See especially "Memorandum to the President," From Larry Fly, December 23, 1940. I thank Dan Schiller for bringing these materials to my attention.

[47] Federal Communications Commission, "Order No. 79," *Federal Register* 6, March 22, 1941, 1580.

[48] The delay in construction lasted for only several months.

[49] Quoted in Stamm, *Sound Business*, 113.

investigation from Congress, Fly was not cowed. In one historian's words, broadcasters' protests "only emboldened Fly to make the FCC's investigation more aggressive."[50]

Several months after the initial order, the FCC issued Order No. 79-A, which contained ten specific questions to be considered during the upcoming hearings, indicating an even wider investigation that scrutinized the commercial broadcast industry's fundamental ownership structures.[51] The report announced that these questions would consider whether "free and fair presentation of public issues and information" contained "prejudice" and whether news had been restricted or distorted so as to "limit the sources of news to the public."[52] The FCC also sent 14-page questionnaires to radio-station-owning newspapers probing the financial relationships among their various media holdings, including program listings and advertising practices. These aggressive inquiries further enflamed critics, who saw the FCC investigation as a strong-arm tactic. The FCC's real agenda, they believed, was to indirectly regulate newspaper publishing.

Two weeks later, at the National Archives Building in Washington, DC, Fly commenced the FCC's hearings in front of an audience that included a large number of editors and publishers. The newspaper industry went into full battle mode. It pursued a legal strategy to stop the hearings immediately by filing a petition that challenged the FCC's jurisdiction to launch a general inquiry into the newspaper publishing business. Their charges of unconstitutionality were to no avail: The FCC denied the petition, explaining that it was precisely for the purpose of holding such general hearings that administrative agencies were established. The melee saw two opposing stables of academics and intellectuals voicing their respective critiques, as the FCC requested expert witnesses to give testimony and the American Newspaper Publishers Association countered with its own industry-friendly witnesses. The FCC called up eminent intellectuals like the aforementioned Morris Ernst, the NYU sociologist and newspaper historian Alfred McClung Lee, and Elmo Roper, a Columbia University journalism professor and director of a prominent public opinion survey. The newspaper industry recruited Arthur Garfield Hays, a senior counsel for the ACLU; Paul Lazarsfeld, a founding figure of communication research and the director of the Office of Radio Research; Frank Luther Mott, a journalism historian; and the law professor Roscoe Pound. In many ways, the range of these expert testimonies would set the parameters for possible policy resolutions.[53]

[50] Ibid., 114.
[51] Federal Communications Commission, "Order No. 79-A," *Federal Register* 6, July 8, 1941, 3302.
[52] Ibid.
[53] Much of the following synopsis draws from the detailed analysis in Stamm, *Sound Business*, 113–45.

The ensuing intellectual debates revolved around core normative questions about the relationship of media and democracy – and the legitimacy of government to monitor and regulate that relationship. Sparring between the pro-industry experts and their libertarian positions and the reformists and their social democratic positions often hinged on dueling historical narratives. According to the former group, American society enjoyed unparalleled press freedom that resulted from a triumphalist story of American can-do and rugged entrepreneurialism. The newspaper-radio combines were merely the latest evolutionary stage in this frictionless progression that promised untold benefits for society writ large. The pro-regulation camp, on the other hand, emphasized the deleterious transformations in the newspaper industry's economic structures. For them, diminished diversity, as exemplified by the decreasing number of newspapers combined with the ascendance of media conglomerates, was deeply troubling. For example, Alfred McClung Lee noted in his testimony that outside big cities, most readers had access to only one newspaper and editorial pluralism was nonexistent. Also noted was the sheer financial impossibility for most people to start up a newspaper. For the pro-industry side, the specter of an overreaching state warranted the most fear.

Both sides appealed to democratic theory for their arguments. For industry supporters, the FCC did not have administrative authority to conduct such interventions into the marketplace, and, more alarmingly, empowering the state with such authority would amount to creeping totalitarianism. For the pro-regulation camp, this regulatory power was required for government to create the structures necessary for a marketplace of ideas – an ideal that necessitated diverse voices and viewpoints within the nation's news media system. In a role similar to the one he would later play on the Hutchins Commission (discussed in Chapter 6), Morris Ernst articulated the most critical perspective, one resembling FDR's and Fly's. Ernst was alarmed by commercial media giants' potential gatekeeping, and he believed that an activist state should serve as a countervailing force against concentrated corporate power. In terms of a marketplace-of-ideas approach, he argued that no newspaper publisher should also own radio stations.

In response, industry representatives sought to weaken the argument that assumed a link between media ownership diversity and information quality. Paul Lazarsfeld's quantitative comparisons assisted this polemic by finding little difference between the programming of fifty newspaper-owned and fifty non-newspaper-owned stations.[54] Pro-industry academics like Frank Luther Mott celebrated the press's contributions to American culture and argued that media consolidation had often improved news media quality. Finally Arthur

[54] Privately, Lazarsfeld expressed sympathy for reform efforts to improve radio programming, but he also expressed skepticism that a strong relationship existed between media ownership structures and media content. Nonetheless, broadcasters were quick to hold up his findings as scientific truth.

Garfield Hays refuted his civil libertarian colleague Morris Ernst by presenting an absolutist First Amendment argument that any abridgment of any form of speech – commercial or not – created a slippery slope to state-sanctioned censorship and therefore was a priori unacceptable. Ultimately, it was Zechariah Chafee who struck what became the middle road. Chafee, who played a central role in the Hutchins Commission as well as other major debates about media regulation, tended toward a First Amendment libertarianism.[55] He allowed that government could help protect a healthy marketplace of ideas against the threats of monopoly and excessive commercialism, but he did not think that preventing media conglomeration justified aggressive state intervention. Thus he recommended that the FCC approach the cross-ownership issue on an individual basis, and that is largely what the commission decided to do.

Hearings continued at various intervals until January 1943, when the investigation came to a gradual stop. By that point, $250,000 had been spent to gather thirty-five hundred pages of conflicting testimony that offered little clarity on the issue.[56] Fly had not been deterred by industry critics, but congressional investigations (described later) and opposition within his own FCC created numerous challenges. After the investigation officially closed in early 1944, the FCC reported to Congress that no official rule would be set; instead a case-by-case approach would be exercised. Meanwhile, even though cross-ownership declined somewhat in AM radio, in FM and TV it continued to rise. Clifford Durr observed this trend in a late-1944 memo to Jonathan Daniels, the president's administrative assistant, saying that he was "clearly convinced that the arithmetic of broadcasting shows too much concentrated control over the realm of ideas." Durr noted that "the chain newspapers are in radio in a big way":

For example, the Cowles group owns six standard broadcasting stations, has already applied for four FM stations, and has plans under way for television as well. The Hearst group has five standard broadcasting stations and there is at least one more controlled by its top officials. Applications are on file for six FM stations and three television stations, in addition to an experimental television station already operating in New York. Gannett owns seven standard stations and one FM station and has applied for two more FMs. Scripps Howard owns or controls four standard stations and has applied for two FM stations and a television station.[57]

Although media concentration would continue to alarm reformers, specific reforms preventing cross-ownership were never implemented. The media historian Michael Stamm noted that this lack of reform was not a "willing reconciliation" but instead the result of aggressive opposition from newspaper

---

55 This libertarianism probably stems in part from his early experiences arguing against the Justice Department's prosecutions under the Espionage and Sedition Acts. Thus he had reason to be highly skeptical of the government's involvement in media.
56 Sterling, "Newspaper Ownership," 232.
57 Clifford Durr to Jonathan Daniels, November 39, 1944, Box 30, Folder 2, CJDP.

publishers and their allies, lukewarm support from the ACLU against media concentration, and constant attacks from congressional conservatives against the FCC.[58]

Nonetheless, cross-ownership would continue to face significant resistance from the FCC. Although the FCC did not prevent newspapers from purchasing stations, it did adopt a general principle that media ownership diversity was "desirable"; thus, when faced with competing applicants, the FCC would sometimes invoke diversity as a public interest consideration in choosing the non-newspaper applicant.[59] These efforts notwithstanding, by the early 1940s, newspapers owned almost a third of all broadcast stations, and as the decade progressed, they also acquired newly licensed FM stations and, increasingly, television stations.[60] By 1950, of the 97 television stations in operation, newspapers owned at least 40.[61] It would be several decades before the FCC placed restrictions on media cross-ownership, a policy that remains fiercely contentious to the present day.

The Report on Chain Broadcasting

An even more significant political battle than taking on newspaper-radio combines was the fight against radio monopolies. One of Chairman Fly's first acts, with President Roosevelt's blessing, was to reinvigorate an ineffectual FCC study (begun in 1938) of chain broadcasting's increasing market power. This study would serve as the vehicle by which Fly enacted an aggressive agenda to rein in chain broadcasters' domination of local radio stations via their network affiliations. Ultimately, these efforts led to the 1941 *Report on Chain Broadcasting*, often referred to as the "Monopoly Report," and then to perhaps the FCC's most significant regulatory action against media conglomeration.[62] Unlike the radio and newspaper cross-ownership investigation, this study would lead to substantive reform. The report outlined the FCC's "Chain Broadcasting Regulations," eight rules that would dramatically restructure commercial broadcasting, including the divestiture of NBC's Blue Network.[63] Fly characterized the new rules as "based ultimately upon the premise that

---

[58] Stamm, *Sound Business*, 144.
[59] Federal Communications Commission, "Newspaper Ownership of Radio Stations, Notice of Dismissal of Proceeding," *Federal Register* 9, January 18, 1944, 702–3. Stamm notes how the FCC's approach was incoherent and inconsistent.
[60] Stamm, *Sound Business*, 4.
[61] James Baughman, "'Wounded but Not Slain': The Orderly Retreat of the American Newspaper, 1945–2000," in *The History of the Book in America*, vol. 5, ed. David Paul Nord, Joan Shelley Rubin, and Michael Schudson (Chapel Hill: University of North Carolina Press, 2009), 122.
[62] For a general description, see James Baughman, *Television's Guardians: The FCC and the Politics of Programming, 1958–1967* (Knoxville: University of Tennessee Press, 1985), 9; Barnouw, *The Golden Web*, 180; Salmond, *The Conscience of a Lawyer*, 73.
[63] Commentary, "The Impact of the FCC's Chain Broadcasting Rules," *Yale Law Journal* 60, no. 1 (January 1951): 78–111.

responsibility for broadcasting must remain in the hands of the more than nine hundred station licensees all over the country, rather than gravitating into the hands of the three or four nationwide network organizations."[64]

This investigation was an early priority of Fly's – even more so than FDR's. There were times when the president seemed to lack enthusiasm, perhaps in part because he and his press secretary, Steve Early, were good friends with many broadcasters and therefore reluctant to upset them.[65] The Roosevelt administration tried to delay publishing the report, but Fly essentially defied its orders.[66] At one critical point, Fly even lied to the administration, claiming that the report was already published and therefore a fait accompli.[67] Harry Plotkin would later recollect how Fly "really fought to get through the chain broadcasting report."[68]

Indeed, Fly's unremitting activism against media monopolies at times seemed obsessive, but his efforts produced a rigorous political economic study of the commercial broadcast industry.[69] The report framed the problem in stark terms, finding that competition in the commercial broadcast industry would "necessarily remain a thing of shadow rather than of substance as long as conditions now prevailing are permitted to continue." Demonstrating that stations' "profitable operation" made them overly reliant on the national networks' broadcasts, the report noted that NBC and CBS were able to dominate the field because "their ownership and operation of important radio stations and their restrictive long-term contracts with other stations enable them to maintain indefinitely their present monopolistic position." "These conditions," the report argued, "prevent their one existing competitor [Mutual Broadcasting] from seriously encroaching on their domain and practically foreclose the possibility of new competition; affiliated stations are treated as, and constitute, mere adjuncts of NBC and CBS."[70] The report concluded that the FCC's chain-broadcasting regulations would "decentralize the tremendous power over what the public may hear which is now lodged in the major network organizations, and will remove existing constraints upon competition without interfering unduly with the operations of the network organizations."[71]

[64] James Lawrence Fly, "Review of Thomas Porter Robinson's *Radio Networks and the Federal Government*," *Annals of the American Academy of Political and Social Science* 230 (1943): 231–2.

[65] "Interview with James Rowe," August 1, 1967, Box 55, Fly Papers.

[66] "Reminder for Steve Early," Memo to Fly, January 26, 1940, Box 55, Fly Papers.

[67] Michael Socolow, "To Network a Nation: NBC, CBS and the Development of National Network Radio in the United States, 1925–1950" (Ph.D. dissertation, Georgetown University, 2001), 175.

[68] Sally Fly Connell, interview with Harry Plotkin, December 27, 1967, 3, Fly Connell papers.

[69] For a thorough overview of the ensuing battles over the report, see Mickie Edwardson, "James Lawrence Fly's Report on Chain Broadcasting (1941) and the Regulation of Monopoly in America," *Historical Journal of Film, Radio and Television* 22, no. 4 (2002).

[70] Federal Communications Commission, *Report on Chain Broadcasting*, 48.

[71] FCC Supplemental Report on Chain Broadcasting, quoted in *Federal Communications Bar Journal*, 6 (1941–2): 41.

The FCC's new rules stated that networks could no longer demand options on large amounts of station time; an affiliate could reject network programs that it believed failed to uphold the public interest; networks could not control a station's advertising rates outside the network programs; and network affiliation contracts would be limited to one year. Another area of concern was "artist bureaus," which essentially allowed broadcasters to negotiate terms that benefited them instead of the artists themselves. Even though the report said this conflict of interest would require regulators' ongoing attention, no actual rule was pushed. Nonetheless, the mere threat of regulation prompted broadcasters to divest themselves of these agencies.[72]

The report was unequivocal about the dangers of media concentration. "To the extent that the ownership and control of radio-broadcast stations falls into fewer and fewer hands," the FCC concluded, "the free dissemination of ideas and information, upon which our democracy depends, is threatened."[73] Following the critique presented in its monopoly report, the FCC made the dramatic rule changes of barring one company from owning more than one station per metropolitan area and by breaking up the largest broadcast company by forcing NBC to divest its Blue Network, which became ABC in 1945. The divorcement actually came about indirectly because the FCC had licensing power over individual stations and not entire networks.[74] It negotiated this problem strategically: "No license shall be issued to a standard broadcast station affiliated with a network organization which maintains more than one network."[75]

Broadcasters were livid. The CBS president, William Paley, referred to the report as a "torpedoing operation" that threatened radio's freedom, and he retorted via a widely circulated 33-page report that roundly condemned the FCC.[76] The NAB president, Neville Miller, and NBC president, Niles Trammell, issued similar statements. The historian Eric Barnouw noted that "free enterprise itself was declared at stake" and that the NAB "resolved to fight the FCC to the finish," including efforts "to negate the FCC moves through congressional and other action."[77] The most dramatic exchange occurred during what historians would refer to as the "Battle of St. Louis." The altercation took place on May 14, 1941, at the NAB's annual convention. Invited to explain the FCC's Monopoly Report, Fly conceded to a reporter upon his arrival that broadcasters were "a little vexed." But he shrugged it off by saying, "What the hell – there's nothing I like better than a good fight."[78] He probably did not anticipate the ambush awaiting him.

[72] Discussed in Barnouw, *The Golden Web*, 171–2.
[73] *Report on Chain Broadcasting*, 99.
[74] Barnouw, *The Golden Web*, 171.
[75] Report on Chain Broadcasting, 92. For a detailed overview see Charles Siepmann, *Radio, Television, and Society* (New York: Oxford University Press, 1950), 27–33.
[76] Edwardson, "James Lawrence Fly's Report on Chain Broadcasting," 402.
[77] Barnouw, *The Golden Web*, 169.
[78] Sally Fly Connell, "The Red and the Blue," 1, Box 55, Fly Papers.

In his speech at the conference, Fly described the Monopoly Report as the "Magna Carta of American broadcasting stations" and clarified that the FCC was "opposed to concentration of power in the hands of Government as we are opposed to concentration in the hands of a few networks." He asserted, "The way to avoid abuse of the power is to decentralize it – to return it ... [to] the individual licensees." These words were provocative enough, but Fly also included in his remarks a rather impolitic statement, added via a handwritten note late in the revision process. This sentence, which became the most quoted part of his speech, did not put broadcasting industry leaders in the kindest light: "These men, to divert attention from the fact of monopolistic control in their hands, conjure up insistently the bogeyman of government operation."[79]

The next day, Mark Ethridge responded to the report by attacking the FCC and Fly (who was sitting on the panel with him), dismissing their efforts as the product of "bad temper, impatience and vindictiveness [that was] intended to be punitive, not constructive." Ethridge declared allegiance to the New Deal but maintained that the FCC "under cover of an alleged fear that some group would gain control of mass communication ... seeks to remake radically the system which it has set up itself." Ethridge saw this as "transferring a latent power" to the FCC, "where it may be abused." He felt legitimacy rested with Congress instead of the commission, and he called on broadcasters to support congressional efforts to investigate the FCC's abuse of power.[80] The speech, later published as a stand-alone report titled "A Fair Deal for Radio," was received with wild applause from an audience of twelve hundred broadcasters. The panel was then quickly adjourned before Fly, who had been taking notes during Ethridge's diatribe, was allowed his promised opportunity to respond.[81] This snub infuriated Fly. Afterward he accused industry leaders of "mental and moral flexibility"[82] and made his infamous statement to reporters that commercial radio management reminded him of "a dead mackerel in the moonlight – it both shines and stinks."[83]

As this back and forth continued, Fly was called upon eight times over a span of several months to testify in front of Congress about the FCC's regulatory activism. Spurred on by Fly's nemesis Representative Eugene Cox, Congress launched an investigation of the FCC, focusing criticism on Fly's leadership.[84] The Roosevelt administration confused nearly all parties as to where its loyalties

---

[79] Quoted and discussed in Edwardson, "James Lawrence Fly's Report on Chain Broadcasting," 406.
[80] Mark Ethridge, "A Fair Deal for Radio," St. Louis Missouri, May 14, 1941, published by the National Association of Broadcasters, Washington, DC, 6–7.
[81] This dramatic exchange is described in detail in Edwardson, "James Lawrence Fly's Report on Chain Broadcasting," 405–8. See also Barnouw, *The Golden Web*, 173.
[82] Edwardson, "James Lawrence Fly's Report on Chain Broadcasting," 407.
[83] This infamous quote has appeared in many places, including "Battler's Exit," *Time*, November 13, 1944.
[84] Socolow, "To Network a Nation," 188–9.

lay as industry tried to contest the regulatory implications of the new rules outlined in the report. NBC's lawsuit against the FCC rules eventually made it to the Supreme Court. In a 5-2 decision, the court determined in *NBC et al. v. U.S. Department of Justice* that the new chain regulations were permissible and that the FCC did indeed have a mandate to regulate stations' programming.[85] Justice Frankfurter, Fly's Harvard Law School professor, wrote for the majority that the Communications Act makes clear that "the Commission's powers are not limited to the engineering and technical aspects of regulation of radio communication," and it "does not restrict the Commission merely to supervision of the traffic." Rather, the mandate establishes that the commission holds "the burden of determining the composition of that traffic."[86]

Citing duopoly concerns and the fact that broadcast frequencies were necessarily finite and thus unavailable to everyone (what would later be known as the "scarcity principle"), the court maintained that this regulation did not interfere with broadcasters' First Amendment protections. The Supreme Court's decision was arguably the most important legacy of these policy battles. However, Justice Frankfurter's decision placed the FCC in a regulatory quandary in coming up with criteria for evaluating program content, which would set the stage for the next round of policy battles (discussed in the next chapter) between progressive policy reformers and commercial broadcasters.[87]

In terms of outcomes and lasting effects of this aggressive structural intervention, the forced divestiture was far from a crippling blow against NBC. In retrospect, broadcasters' concerns that actions like the Blue Network divestment would cause great suffering were largely unfounded. The networks and their affiliates' gross revenues almost doubled from 1940 to 1945. For independent stations, revenues more than doubled.[88] However, just as it did little actual harm to commercial broadcasters, the intervention did little to help noncommercial broadcasters. Nonetheless, the decision etched a regulatory high-water mark, and it would be the FCC's last successful effort to promote fundamental structural change in the radio industry for the foreseeable future. Meanwhile, a discussion in Congress entertaining an even bolder intervention arose, albeit briefly.

Nationalize the Airwaves?

Most serious discussion about establishing government-supported, noncommercial broadcasting ceased after the early 1930s when commercial

---

[85] For a through treatment of this case, see Socolow, "To Network a Nation," 187–90.

[86] *NBC v U.S.*, 319 U.S. 190 at 216 (1943).

[87] See Herbert Rosenberg, "Program Content: A Criterion of Public Interest in FCC Licensing," *Western Political Quarterly* 2, no. 3 (1949): 375–401.

[88] Christopher Sterling and John M. Kittross, *Stay Tuned: A Concise History of American Broadcasting* (Belmont, CA: Wadsworth, 1978), 233.

broadcasters successfully disabled radio reform efforts like the 1934 Wagner-Hatfield Act, which would have reserved 25 percent of all radio frequencies for nonprofit broadcasting.[89] Occasionally, however, the subject would reemerge within policy discourse, particularly with the government-supported BBC model existing in such stark contrast to the American advertising-dominated model. One influential politician who seemed sympathetic to the argument was Senator Burton Wheeler, a longtime critic of the commercial broadcast industry. In 1944, Wheeler published ten indictments that summed up many of the systemic problems with commercial broadcasting, including how the industry insists "on regarding itself as a private enterprise to the detriment of all other considerations; sees its license as a monopoly right to private property instead of a public good; and is dominated and controlled by absentee owners."[90] In March 1945, at a Senate Interstate Commerce subcommittee hearing, Wheeler remarked that broadcasting "probably should be a common carrier," subject to special rules and strict regulations – such as nondiscrimination safeguards – that apply to other systems such as telecommunications. In an article titled "Wheeler Hints at Government Control," *Broadcasting* quoted him as saying that "a company ought to serve the public generally and take the less profitable business, too." In his view, Congress should mandate that radio broadcasters serve smaller towns. "They claim they're not common carriers," Wheeler observed, conceding, "Congress has agreed to that, temporarily."[91]

Several months later, the House Appropriations Committee chairman, Congressman Clarence Cannon, caused controversy by criticizing the American broadcasting system. Under the headline "Cannon Demands Government Ownership," *Broadcasting* reported that during an Appropriations subcommittee hearing conversation turned toward juxtaposing broadcasters' 200 percent profits with their woeful public service records and unfavorably comparing American radio to the British broadcast system. Congressman Cannon reportedly argued that "Under the English system the government owns the radio channels, and there is no advertising at all. That is a happy situation." Cannon contended that under the American system, private industry received free frequency – a "great natural resource" that he likened to "oil in the ground, or coal or uranium." Noting that little was given in return, Cannon wondered, "Why isn't our government treated by the radio industry as the British government?" After Paul Porter, who had replaced Fly as FCC chair, suggested that the American and British systems were different because their populations' listening habits differed, Cannon responded:

Their system is that the government gets the money and our system is that the private firms come in and are given a monopoly as a free and gracious gift and get the money.

[89] For 1930s radio reform efforts, see McChesney, *Telecommunications, Mass Media & Democracy*.
[90] Burton Wheeler, "The Shocking Truth about Radio," *Progressive*, November 6, 1944.
[91] Bill Bailey, "Wheeler Hints at Government Control," *Broadcasting*, March 26, 1945, 16, 42.

Furthermore, these private systems come in and litter the air with continual advertising, commercials, plug-uglies.... You cannot turn on your radio at any time but what they are telling you about somebody's beer or bills.[92]

"Why take taxes when we can take it all?" Cannon asked those at the hearing. "Why not ... relieve the American people of this constant din in our ears, people who are selling something over the air? Many parents do not want their children continually importuned to patronize many of the vendors who cry their wares over the radio." With the BBC, Cannon noted, "you get a program without interference from somebody trying to sell you something."[93]

Industry defenders like Congressman Clifton Woodrum argued that the American system and its advertisers made possible the "wonderful talent we get on our radio here." Conceding some systemic shortcomings with the commercial model, Porter added his own defense of the American system, claiming that the BBC did not have "the ingenuity, the brilliant technique, and the type of program talent that characterized the private enterprise system of American broadcasting at its best." When Porter asked Cannon directly whether government should be in charge of radio, the congressman answered, "Handle it as other nations handle it. There is a great complaint everywhere."[94] Yet despite what many liberals still felt – that compared with profit-obsessed commercial owners, government ownership was the lesser of two evils – rarely was government ownership of radio seriously advocated.

Commissioner Durr expressed some ambivalence to a listener who wondered "how the public can be served" by a monopolistic commercial system that allowed offensive broadcasts exemplified by the anti-Semitic Father Charles Coughlin in the 1930s. The listener saw little hope for radio unless it was "placed strictly under government ownership and supported by taxation" to encourage "broadcasts of perhaps educational value." Durr agreed that all evidence suggested that "broadcasting is becoming primarily an advertising medium rather than a medium of public service supported by advertising." But Durr saw this trend as "inevitable" given broadcasters' commercial logic since no one can "expect people who are in the business for profit not to do the very thing they are in business to do." Durr did not outright advocate government control but found other scenarios even more objectionable: "government monopoly has its dangers as well as a private monopoly, although if we were faced with only these two alternatives, I would have no hesitation in taking the first." Like Fly, Durr still felt that "our best hope is in diversification of control, with a maximum of competition." Making clear that such competition should be for listeners and not advertising business, he clung to the hope

---

[92] Appropriations Subcommittee Hearing, October 22, 1945. Quoted in "Cannon Demands Government Ownership: Congress Men Show Great Interest in Radio Profit," *Broadcasting*, November 26, 1945, 20, 85.

[93] Ibid.

[94] Ibid.

that by inserting a noncommercial pocket within the American broadcast system, the commercial model could someday be overtaken or at least forced to reform. Durr saw "considerable promise in this direction," exemplified by the commission's setting aside specific FM frequencies for nonprofit educational institutions' exclusive use. Durr felt that "educators are, at last, fully awake to the possibilities of broadcasting and are not going to let their second chance [after losing AM in the 1930s] go by."[95]

Yet most political elites considered the topic of government ownership of broadcast media to be unworthy of serious consideration, and Congress did little to challenge the commercial radio industry's dominance. As progressive initiatives faltered in Congress, radio reform efforts gained momentum at the FCC – especially as Durr took on a more pronounced role at the commission – but even these initiatives were constantly undercut by red-baiting and other reactionary politics unleashed by pro-industry interests and their conservative allies, especially in Congress.

Combating Right-Wing Attacks

Throughout the 1940s, the FCC had repeated run-ins with conservative politicos, and Larry Fly's progressive agenda was frequently undercut by right-wing attacks. The agency had the dubious distinction of being at the center of one of the earliest communist witch hunts – what the FCC staffer Ed Brecher later jokingly referred to as "premature McCarthyism."[96] Several weeks before the Pearl Harbor attack, Durr and Fly were implicated in a right-wing imbroglio involving two FCC employees, William Dodd and Goodwin Watson, who were targeted by the Dies Committee. An early version of the infamous House Un-American Activities Committee (HUAC), the Dies Committee (named after its chairman, Congressman Martin Dies) was founded in 1938 to investigate Nazi sympathizers, but during the years 1939–41 it retooled to focus increasingly on left-wing organizations like consumer advocacy and theater groups. The committee falsely charged Dodd and Watson with being communists and led investigations that dragged on for two years. Dies's attempts to freeze the accused employees' salaries proved to be particularly scandalous.[97] Despite endless hearings and the House Appropriations Committee's voting to cut the FCC budget by 25 percent, Fly and Durr successfully repelled the attacks, and the employees prevailed in the Supreme Court, which forbade Dies's actions.[98] This victory was tempered, however, by ominous signs that Congress lacked

[95] Clifford Durr to Cecil Sarver, January 4, 1945, Box 30, Folder 3, CJDP.
[96] Brecher, 6, Fly Connell Papers.
[97] See Susan Brinson, *The Red Scare, Politics, and the Federal Communications Commission, 1941–1960* (Westport, CT: Praeger/Greenwood Publishing Group, 2004). See also Salmond, *The Conscience of a Lawyer*, 98–104.
[98] *United States v. Lovett*, 328 U.S. 303 (1946).

the resolve to defend constitutionally protected liberties. The confrontation also earned Durr his first of many run-ins with the FBI's J. Edgar Hoover.[99]

The Dies attack was followed by the even more dramatic Cox episode. The powerful Congressman Eugene Cox was a Dies ally, but his FCC attacks were perhaps motivated less by ideology than by an illegal business deal involving a broadcast license. The Herald Publishing Company had been broadcasting on the wrong frequency, but Cox helped it override FCC engineers. In return, it was later revealed, he received stock in the radio station. The FCC prepared a case against the station but was thwarted by Cox – who then sought revenge, as described by Durr's biographer, by launching "a campaign of systematic abuse and calumny against Fly and the FCC," culminating with a congressional resolution calling for investigating the commission. With a colorful metaphorical flair, the resolution alleged that the "FCC had set up a Gestapo the equal of which had never been seen under a free government" that was also a "nest of reds" and the "nastiest nest of rats to be found in this entire country."[100]

Cox chaired the investigating committee, and for weeks it resorted to underhanded tactics like illegal seizure of FCC records, character smears, and outrageous charges. A turning point was a "smoking gun" discovery that revealed Cox's corruption: a $2,500 check for services rendered to the Herald Publishing Company. In a clever publicity stunt, Durr made a hundred photocopies of the $2,500 check for display on the FCC's press table and for members of Congress. Durr also made sure that duplicates were sent to key representatives of the press, including the conservative editor and publisher of the *Washington Post*, Eugene Meyer, who reprinted a copy of the check in the newspaper. The unlikely alliance with Durr led Meyer to publish an editorial that defended the FCC while condemning Cox.[101] This editorial was echoed by papers across the country and was joined by hundreds of letters from the public. Cox was forced to resign, and the liberal newspaper *PM* proclaimed a "personal triumph for FCC Commissioner Clifford Durr, who risked his official position to force the issue against the powerful [Congressman Cox]."[102]

In another fight with Congress, as Brecher later recounted, Fly singlehandedly defeated Congressman Jared Sanders from Louisiana, who attempted to pass a bill curtailing FCC powers. According to Brecher, Sanders's loss in the following election stemmed from his role in the FCC battle, his embarrassing defeat at the hands of a government agency, and his unabashed lobbying for the broadcast industry.[103] Despite winning many of these power struggles, historians have noted, "Fly paid a price for his activism"[104] and was "harassed as

[99] See generally Salmond, *The Conscience of a Lawyer*, 98–104.
[100] Quoted in Salmond, *The Conscience of a Lawyer*, 106.
[101] Ibid., 106–9. See also Fly Connell Papers, especially Brecher, 18–20.
[102] *PM*, October 1, 1943.
[103] See Brecher, 24–6, Fly Connell Papers.
[104] Mickie Edwardson, "James Lawrence Fly's Fight for a Free Marketplace of Ideas," *American Journalism* 14, no. 1 (Winter 1997): 12.

few public servants have been," as "Dies, Cox, interstate commerce and other committee hearings battered away at him."[105] Even while standing his ground, Fly became dispirited, with many of his reformist plans stymied by drawn-out investigations. As he prepared to depart the FCC, however, the seeds of an even larger policy battle were being planted by Commissioner Durr.

Gearing Up for the Battle Royale

Fly left the FCC in 1944, but he continued advocating media reform issues, especially after he became the ACLU director in 1949. He would later express ambivalence about his FCC tenure, conceding that his aggressive efforts yielded few substantive systemic changes.[106] Nonetheless, he helped set in motion a number of reforms. In addition to the two major investigations of media industries, Fly pressured the NAB to change its code, making it easier for labor issues to be covered on radio, and he established the Mayflower Rule, which constrained broadcasters' political editorializing (discussed in Chapter 4). Taken together, these interventions in media markets marked a turn toward a more muscular regulatory approach. Durr would carry on this progressive project for several years after Fly left the FCC. Fly and Durr were often seen as having similar democratic principles and a willingness to fight for them, but they derived slightly different lessons from these early policy battles with broadcasters. Whereas Fly sought to diversify media ownership and then allow media entities to have nearly absolute freedom of speech (with some significant exceptions), Durr felt that this tactic had failed, and he began to see programming regulation as a potential site for policy intervention. These differing styles and tactics came into view with the next big target: broadcast license renewals.

Controversies around license renewal processes were not unprecedented. As early as 1930, the FRC resolved the Brinkley case (an infamous "goat gland doctor" who was seen as threatening public health) and the Shuler case (an inflammatory preacher whose sermons accused public officials of corruption) by revoking the offenders' licenses because of their broadcasts' content. However, this occurred while the FRC was trying to formalize a renewal process consistent with a public interest mandate, and similar actions would almost never be replicated after 1934, when denying licenses became exceedingly rare.[107] Furthermore, to revoke a license or deny a renewal usually required a rationale based on programming regulations. Thus, policing broadcast licenses was inextricably bound up with content regulation because it forced the FCC to evaluate

---

[105] Barnouw, *The Golden Web*, 174.

[106] Document 16, p. 1–15, Meetings, June 19–20, 1944, Folder 2–18, Box 2, Commission on Freedom of the Press Records, Accession No. 0078-011, Special Collections Division, University of Washington Libraries, Seattle, Washington (hereafter cited as Commission on Freedom of the Press).

[107] The FRC's renewal criteria are discussed in Lucas Powe Jr., *American Broadcasting and the First Amendment* (Berkeley: University of California Press, 1987).

programming according to some set of public interest criteria. Predictably, this kind of intervention incurred charges of censorship from broadcasters.

Broadcasters often argued that *any* new regulation proffered was unconstitutional or illegitimate, not just programming-related policies. They knew that the threat of continued government regulation had not yet been deterred. According to some reports, broadcasters saw the likelihood of government intervention increasing with Fly leaving the FCC.[108] Though not as activist as Fly, Paul Porter, who became the new FCC chairman in late 1944, encouraged public engagement in the regulatory process. Despite his having worked for CBS for a few years, many observers assumed that Porter, an ardent New Dealer, would carry on Fly's aggressive campaigns. There were, however, some indications of a more conciliatory approach toward industry and its congressional supporters.[109] For example, during hearings on broadcast policy, Senator Wallace White took note of Porter's deferring several times to Congress's authority instead of taking a position on some contentious issue. White quipped, "I'm quite overcome by this new deference shown to Congressional wishes."[110]

Yet Porter demonstrated that he also could deliver scathing critiques, even when deep in broadcasters' territory. In front of a high-powered audience of congressmen and business leaders at a NAB meeting commemorating the industry's 25th year, he scolded broadcasters for "excessive commercialism" and declared that there was "no back door to his office." He also quoted President Hoover's prophecies that "the quickest way to kill radio would be to use it for direct advertising" and that "advertising in the intrusive sense will dull the interest of the listener and will thus defeat the industry." Porter concluded that "there must be a determination" as to whether broadcasting would be in the public interest.[111] He warned broadcasters that the FCC would pay closer attention to their programming decisions, and for the short time he was on the commission, he remained true to his word. Along with the remaining liberal commissioners, Porter advocated more consumer representation and public input to legitimate the commission's regulatory authority.

Most progressive activism, however, would be carried on by Clifford Durr. Durr had lost his closest ally with Fly's departure, but a liberal bloc continued to set much of the agency's agenda, even as right-wing pressures intensified. Increasingly Durr found himself at the heart of grueling political battles. He had developed a thick skin, but nothing could have prepared him for the battle of the Blue Book.

---

[108] *Time*, November 13, 1944, 73.

[109] Ironically, Porter would become a media reform nemesis years later when he represented broadcasters during the famous WLBT case.

[110] Bill Bailey, "Wheeler Hints at Government Control," *Broadcasting*, March 26, 1945, 16.

[111] "Radio Editor," *Advertiser* 46, no. 3 (March 1945).

3

The Battle of the Blue Book

In March 1946, FCC Commissioner Clifford Durr received a three-page letter from William Tymous, an African American World War II veteran who was outraged by the radio programming greeting him upon his return home:

On the battlefields of France, on Okinawa, on Iwo Jima ... we fought the devils of fascism, discrimination, hate, prejudice, and Jim Crow. We won that fight. We have come home to find that these same enemies are very much alive here.... It is too often the practice of vehicles of American propaganda such as the movie industry and the radio to depict the American Negro as a buffoon, lazy, shiftless, superstitious, ignorant, loose and servile.... This is not the democratic way of life for which so many of our fallen comrades paid so dearly with their lives. This is the Hitler pattern. This is American fascism.

Racist caricatures in radio programs abounded, Tymous observed: "Rochester in the Jack Benny program, Bill and Beulah in Beulah, the maid in Crime Doctor, the maid in The Great Gildersleeve, the maid in the Judy Canova program and the Amos and Andy troupe." Tymous worried that these sketches were "nailing down in the minds of millions of listeners derogatory and false judgments of fellow-citizens." He feared that listeners were "conditioned" by these stereotypes to see "nothing wrong in such disguised fostering of race hatred." He indicted the "sponsors, producers and executives of networks who permit such bigotry and anti-racial pieces on the air."[1]

Durr responded that he was sympathetic with Tymous's views, enclosing with his letter a recently issued report that presented "a pretty fair idea of where the commission stands on the over-all responsibility of station licensees

---

[1] William Tymous to Clifford Durr, March 12, 1946, Box 16–8, Folder 2–14, Dallas Smythe Collection, Simon Fraser University, British Columbia (hereafter cited as Smythe Papers). Tymous was a secretary for a group called Washington Veterans' Congress. A discussion of this letter, the Blue Book, and other sections in this chapter appears in Victor Pickard, "The Battle over the FCC Blue Book: Determining the Role of Broadcast Media in a Democratic Society, 1945–1948," *Media, Culture & Society* 33, no. 2, (2011): 171–91.

for programming" and offered listeners ideas for contesting "the seamier aspects of broadcasting."[2] The report arrived in a blue cover, its title in bold black lettering: "Public Service Responsibility of Broadcast Licensees."

The Forgotten History of the Blue Book

The "Blue Book," as it soon came to be known, remains one of the FCC's most progressive initiatives ever attempted. It made the privilege of holding a broadcast license contingent upon meeting substantive public interest requirements for its programming, and it established standards by which these responsibilities could be judged. A station's failure to adhere to the guidelines would result in public hearings and possibly the loss of its broadcast license, thus ending its operations – a regulatory action unthinkable today. Since its rapid rise and fall, however, the Blue Book has been largely forgotten, receiving little attention in scholarly literature or elsewhere. Given its historical significance and relevance for current media policy debates, this gap in policy research is troubling. Most accounts thus far have focused primarily on the colorful trade-press reactions to the Blue Book.[3] General accounts often characterize it as an interesting historical anomaly. For example, Tom Streeter noted the Blue Book's heresy of suggesting that unlimited profits for broadcasters might conflict with public interest standards, and Erik Barnouw referred to the Blue Book as "one of the most enlightening of FCC documents."[4]

A deeper archival investigation of the Blue Book and its major actors illuminates the normative debates, political strategies, and historical context absent from existing accounts of this critical policy battle. By engaging the perspectives of multiple players and institutions, a thick historical analysis of this key policy debate uncovers the formation of the social contract among government, media industries, and various publics. Like other central policy battles in the 1940s, the Blue Book controversy is a defining confrontation between social democratic and corporate libertarian visions of media. This chapter traces how these paradigms clashed during a power struggle over radio regulations

---

[2] Durr to Tymous, March 16, 1946, Box 16–8, Folder 2–14, Smythe Papers.

[3] See Dave Berkman, "The 'Blue Book' and Charles Siepmann – as Reported in Broadcasting Magazine," *American Journalism* 2, no. 1 (1985): 37–48. See also Dave Berkman, "Charles Arthur Siepmann 1899–1985: A Biographical Tribute and Personal Reminiscence," *Television Quarterly* 22, no. 1 (1986): 77–84. Another authoritative article on trade press coverage is Richard Meyer, "Reaction to the 'Blue Book,'" *Journal of Broadcasting* 7 (1962): 295–312. See also Chad Dell's unpublished paper, "Red-baiting, Regulation and the Broadcast Industry: A Revisionist History of the 'Blue Book,'" presented at the Association for Education in Journalism and Mass Communication (New Orleans, Louisiana, August 3–8, 1999). Socolow's article discusses advertisers' influence on radio programming and the public's reaction: Michael Socolow, "Questioning Advertising's Influence over American Radio: The Blue Book Controversy of 1945–1947," *Journal of Radio Studies* 9 (2002): 292–302.

[4] Tom Streeter, *Selling the Air: A Critique of the Policy of Commercial Broadcasting in the United States* (Chicago: University of Chicago Press, 1996), 147; Barnouw, *The Golden Web*, 229.

outlined in the Blue Book, considers the failure of the report's implementation, and discusses the implications of this outcome for the trajectory of postwar American media policy.

The 1940s progressive shift in FCC regulatory politics that ushered in the Blue Book can be attributed in part to the historical happenstance of individual appointments, particularly that of Clifford Durr. But more significantly, as demonstrated in the previous two chapters, it reflected growing public concerns about commercial excesses in mainstream mass news media, especially radio. Listeners' grievances also included the absence of local accountability, the loss of liberal commentators, and anti-labor programming. From the grass roots to rarefied intellectual circles, many social movement groups began to see media as an essential battleground and began mobilizing media reform groups. Progressive political elites like Durr advanced reformist media policies inside Washington, while activists within social movements strove to exploit these political opportunities.

Public discontent began to manifest at the policy level in significant ways. Dallas Smythe recalled that the Blue Book was a direct response to "the substantial public criticism of the vulgarity of radio commercials."[5] According to Smythe, public affairs programs that typically received no advertiser support "were vanishing from network feeds." Making appearances even worse, Smythe noted, "broadcast profits had soared during wartime" yet there was no noticeable improvement in programming – in fact, many critics believed programming quality was worsening. Feeling that they had public opinion on their side, the commissioners tried to leverage their regulatory power over a recalcitrant broadcasting industry by shifting from a strategy of fostering competition to one that involved directly regulating content.

Promise versus Performance

One of the FCC's major functions is to allocate scarce radio spectrum by leasing licenses to broadcasters. These licenses periodically were due for renewal – in the 1940s, the cycle was every three years; today, every eight. From the FCC's inception, this process had been largely a mere formality. Even under Larry Fly, the FCC shied away from intervening directly in programming, instead finding more structural means to steer programming in certain directions. In cases when the FCC did consider content – for example, its ban on broadcasters' political editorializing – it rarely specified explicit public interest guidelines for programming. With previous reform efforts largely failing to diversify the commercialized airwaves, Durr considered a new approach. While studying license renewal criteria as prescribed in the 1934 Communications Act, he found the following statement: "All renewals shall be governed by the same considerations

---

[5] Dallas Smythe to Jelena Grcic Polic and Oscar Gandy, June 26, 1991, Box 16–6, Folder 16-1-4-7, Smythe Papers.

as original grants." In other words, the FCC's official policy dictated that for broadcasters to renew their monopoly control over scarce public spectrum, they should be held to their original promises, including providing public affairs programming to their local communities. In practice, however, renewal criteria had been based mostly on technical issues such as questions of interference. Smythe recalled how "the FCC was routinely renewing broadcast licenses unless the licensees had been derelict about their engineering standards or had concealed the identity of one of their owners."[6]

The Communications Act made clear that a broadcast license did not equal a property right. The act stated that the federal government reserved ultimate control over all radio channels and provides "for the use of such channels, *but not the ownership thereof*, by persons for limited periods of time, under licenses granted by Federal authority" (emphasis added). The act clarified that "no such license shall be construed to create any right, beyond the terms, conditions, and periods of the license."[7] Nonetheless, then as now, licenses for exclusive use of this public resource were often treated not as leases but as deeds to private property, and renewal applications were generally rubber-stamped for approval. When Durr looked into broadcasters' composite program logs and checked them against original obligations, he found little relationship between their initial promises to the local community when the license was granted and their actual performance during the term of the license. This led him to conclude that the FCC was granting renewals to "not the best applicant, but the biggest liar."[8] The evidence was so startling that all twenty-two stations up for renewal at that time were given only temporary licenses.[9] Arguing that the compiled data illustrated how the process shortchanged both the public and competing applicants, Durr convinced the new FCC chair, Paul Porter, that an in-depth study was necessary to evaluate broadcasters' performance.

At the March 12, 1945, National Association of Broadcasters (NAB) meeting, Porter announced that a study had launched "whereby promises will be compared with performance."[10] Specifically, the study was meant to evaluate broadcasters' pledges to the local community that "time will be made available for civic, educational, agricultural and other public service programs." This project, he suggested, was "designed to strengthen renewal procedures and give the Commission a more definite picture of the station's overall operation when licenses come up for renewal."[11] Officially initiated on April 10, 1945,

[6] Ibid.
[7] Communications Act of 1934, SEC, 301.
[8] A. Tullos and C. Waid, "Clifford Durr: The FCC Years," *Southern Exposure* 2 (1975): 18.
[9] Barnouw, *The Golden Web*, 228.
[10] FCC (Federal Communications Commission), Public Service Responsibility of Broadcast Licensees [hereafter cited as "Blue Book"], Washington, DC, March 7, 1946, 3.
[11] Ibid.

the study would take a year to publish though the bulk of it was assembled quickly. Durr described it years later:

I was appointed to head up the study and given a little money to hire two or three people from the outside, including Charles Siepmann, who was quite knowledgeable about broadcasting. I put Dallas Smythe and Ed Brecher from our staff on it too with the result that instead of this study dragging on for a couple of years, in a month it was complete.[12]

Approved unanimously by the commission, the Blue Book relied heavily on Smythe's data analysis and Siepmann's policy vision. Siepmann was a British-born, recently naturalized American citizen, and a former programming director for the BBC. Though he avowed respect for the American system, Siepmann conferred on the Blue Book BBC-inspired notions that radio's public service mission should be defined by programs devoted to local culture, education, and community affairs. Despite the broadcast industry's preemptive attacks on the report's authors, especially Siepmann, the Blue Book was put on an expedited schedule and assembled for release on March 7, 1946.

The Blue Book's Requirements

The Blue Book was the first comprehensive report that defined the FCC's regulatory authority over programming policy. Although a 1943 Supreme Court decision had affirmed that the FCC had authority to establish programming guidelines, the commission had yet to issue a protocol. The Blue Book was also the first major effort to clarify the commission's position on radio's public interest standard, addressing concerns about localism and commercialism by setting programming guidelines for judging licensees' performance at renewal time. Because applicants oftentimes competed for frequencies within a finite electromagnetic spectrum, practical imperatives prompted the FCC to define its selection process. More an attempt at codifying a synopsis of FCC thinking than at implementing new rules for licensees, the guidelines assumed a general compact: Commercial entities that used the publicly owned airwaves were obligated to perform public services in return.

In this spirit, the 59-page Blue Book was divided into five parts. The first part stressed the importance of local broadcasting and demonstrated that at least some stations had broken their initial promises to the communities they served. The second part asserted the FCC's jurisdiction in evaluating broadcasters' public service performance:

The contention has at times been made that Section 326 of the Communications Act, which prohibits censorship or interference with free speech by the Commission, precludes any concern on the part of the Commission with the program service of licensees. This contention overlooks the legislative history of the Radio Act of 1927 ... [and]

---

[12] Tullos and Waid, "Clifford Durr: The FCC Years," 18.

the re-enactment of identical provisions in the Communications Act of 1934 with full knowledge by the Congress that the language covered a Commission concern with program service, the relevant court decisions, and this Commission's concern with program service since 1934.[13]

The section concluded that these precedents clarified "not only that the Commission has the authority to concern itself with program service, but that it is under an affirmative duty, in its public interest determinations, to give full consideration to program service."[14]

The third part of the Blue Book dealt with the FCC's consideration of local ownership and programming when two or more applicants were vying for the same frequency. It also discussed the kinds of programming that would satisfy public service obligations. In particular, it defined "sustaining programs" – as opposed to commercial, advertising-supported programs – as having "five distinctive and outstanding functions": that they provide "balanced interpretation of public needs," that they "by their very nature may not be sponsored" and that they include "programs for significant minority tastes and interests," "programs devoted to the needs and purposes of non-profit organizations," and experimental programs liberated from the "restrictions" characteristic of "programs in which the advertiser's interest in selling goods predominates."[15]

A general suspicion of profit-driven programming coursed through the report. It referred to sustaining programs as the "balance-wheel" that redresses "the imbalance of a station's or network's program structure" resulting from "commercial decisions."[16] After explicating the functions of a well-balanced program schedule serving "significant minority tastes and interests" that fall outside "dominant needs and tastes," it presented graphs showing stations' ratios of sustaining and commercial programming, with the latter far more often represented, especially among larger stations. These graphs also illustrated that stations typically aired public affairs programs when few people were listening, reserving prime hours for advertising-supported programming. Last, the third part of the report devoted significant space to detailing public criticism of "advertising excesses."

The Blue Book's fourth section presented tables of economic statistics indicating that broadcasters' profits increased dramatically during the war years, undercutting arguments that industry could not afford public service programming or improve the quality of their entertainment fare.[17] In the fifth part, the Blue Book laid out four requirements for broadcast licensees: They must

---

[13] Blue Book, 9.
[14] Ibid., 12.
[15] Ibid.
[16] Ibid.
[17] Chris Sterling has noted that these years may have been atypical since they occurred during the war.

sustain experimental programs unlikely to attract advertisers, promote local live programs, devote programs to the discussion of local public issues, and eliminate "excessive advertising."[18] Failing to meet these social responsibility criteria would subject broadcast licensees to public hearings and possible termination of their licenses.

Though clearly meant to encourage broadcasters to be more accountable to local communities, the Blue Book did not provide great detail about how these criteria would be defined or enforced. Nonetheless, the FCC saw the Blue Book as a direct intervention against the industry-friendly status quo, despite later disavowals aimed at diminishing broadcasters' fury. By a unanimous vote on the report's release, the FCC substantiated its regulatory oversight and sent a clear message to commercial broadcasters: If they failed to reform, they would lose their claim to the public airwaves. When the finished draft was submitted to FCC Chairman Porter, he left a note for a staffer: "I know now how Truman felt when they told him he had an atom bomb."[19] The report would indeed have the immediate impact of a bombshell, though not as the FCC commissioners had imagined.

Reactions to the Blue Book

Initially, the Blue Book's positive reviews overshadowed the negative, particularly given its immense grassroots appeal among diverse constituencies. While policy experts and intellectuals saw much to celebrate in the Blue Book – the Hutchins Commission hailed it as "the most significant milestone in the entire history of radio regulation"[20] – many of Durr's activist allies could barely contain their enthusiasm. Using another atomic bomb metaphor, H. B. McCarty, a prominent educational broadcaster, gushed to him, "You must feel something like the fellow who opened the bomb bays and released the atomic bomb on Hiroshima. Such a reaction to the FCC report! Such violence – and such utter nonsense – from certain quarters." He assured Durr that educational broadcasters were "profoundly grateful" for the Blue Book and that listeners were becoming "more aroused" and "more organized" toward actualizing its ideals.[21] Durr recalled later that once the Blue Book circulated, people in local communities, "whether it was the Girl Scouts or the Boy Scouts or the PTA," went to their local radio stations "armed with the Blue Book."[22]

Public interest advocates embraced the Blue Book as a needed corrective, and its principles were eagerly discussed on special conference panels

[18] Blue Book, 55.
[19] Barnouw, *The Golden Web*, 229.
[20] Llewellyn White, *The American Radio* (Chicago: University of Chicago Press, 1947), 184.
[21] H. B. McCarty to Clifford Durr, April 22, 1946, Box 30, Folder 5, CJDP.
[22] Amy Toro, "Standing Up for Listener's Rights: A History of Public Participation at the Federal Communications Commission" (Ph.D. dissertation, University of California, Berkeley, 2000), 23.

and radio shows. Keith Tyler, a leading radio reform activist, invited Durr to speak at the Institute for Education by Radio Conference about the social and economic implications of the "extremely important" Blue Book.[23] McCarty invited Siepmann and Durr to discuss their policy approach, which he believed was "the soundest assurance of anything constructive in American radio," at a new Public Service Radio Institute conference in Madison, Wisconsin.[24] Inspired by Blue Book principles, the institute's panels included "Programming the Public Service Station" and "Public Service Responsibility of the Local Station."[25] At yet another radio conference, Durr appeared on a Blue Book–themed panel with Siepmann and William Hocking (a member of the Hutchins Commission) titled "Radio's Postwar Responsibilities." Panelists discussed whether radio's public service would "justify itself as free enterprise" and whether radio had assumed its "postwar obligations." The executive secretary of a leading radio council later reported to Durr that his "tolerant, easygoing disposition" had led to the conference's "complete acceptance of the Blue Book." Speaking for "those of us interested in public service radio," she said, "our point of view could not have been represented more adequately."[26] Durr became publicly recognized as the Blue Book's driving force, though he tried to downplay this perception. In a correction to a *Time* article, he stated that the Blue Book "represents unanimous action of the Commission and not the views of any one member." Durr explained that although Chairman Porter left the FCC before the report was formally issued, "he publicly added his hearty 'amen.'"[27] Nonetheless, Durr was in constant demand to give talks, write articles, and participate in public debates on Blue Book–related issues.

Meanwhile, copies of the report were running out at a surprising pace, resulting from requests from nervous broadcasters, gleeful activists, and even average listeners. After Durr generated publicity by debating broadcasters about the Blue Book at a conference in Columbus, Ohio, FCC staffers were forced to rush-order more copies to be printed. Upon hearing the debate, one woman from the Federation of Protestant Welfare Agencies wrote to Durr that she might sound "over-enthusiastic" if she "actually tried to commit to paper the comments" that she and many others made about his arguments. To "reach as many people ... as possible," she asked for 125 Blue Book copies.[28] The media reform advocate Everett Parker made the Blue Book "required reading" at the University of Chicago Religious Radio workshop.[29] Celebrating its "good use"

[23] See, for example, Keith Tyler to Clifford Durr, April 6, 1946, Box 30, Folder 5, CJDP.
[24] Ibid.
[25] Public Service Radio Institute Conference Program, Box 30, Folder 5, CJDP.
[26] Mrs. Bruce Williams to Clifford Durr, July 12, 1946, Box 30, Folder 7, CJDP.
[27] Clifford Durr to "The Editor," June 21, 1946, Box 30, Folder 6, CJDP.
[28] Charlotte Demorest to Clifford Durr, May 8, 1946, Box 30, Folder 6, CJDP.
[29] Everett Parker to Clifford Durr, May 21, 1946; Durr to Parker, May 24, 1946, Box 30, Folder 6, CJDP.

of 75 copies, Parker wrote to Durr, "You will note the influence of the 'Blue Book,'" and attached the workshop's official policy statement.[30] Although such requests left the FCC short on copies, Durr sent as many as could be spared, often enclosing a Blue Book in his mailed responses to listeners' complaints about radio programming.

Durr's Blue Book publicity inspired some broadcasters as well. An NBC representative invited Durr to give a talk on educational radio at NBC's Summer Radio Institute, explaining that it was "surely educational and democratic" for people working in radio, especially "youngsters coming up in the profession," to hear "leaders [like Durr] discuss all sides of disputed questions."[31] After congratulating Durr on his "grand job," Keith Tyler wrote that "a number of station representatives felt that this face-to-face contact with you had won them completely – not to your views, but to you as a person … [in light of] your honesty and sincerity and … courage." Tyler hoped Durr would persuade other commissioners to become more engaged, to help "humanize the whole business of regulation by a governmental body."[32] CBS's Frank Stanton, an industry leader, also congratulated Durr but noted that these discussions were held "six months to a year too late," suggesting that an earlier conversation could have obviated any need for the Blue Book.[33] Months later, a Durr ally working at a major station credited the Blue Book for encouraging "new [programming] in the very near future." The informant noted, "grumble as [broadcasters] will, there's little doubt in my mind that they have been favorably affected."[34]

Despite blowback from predictable quarters – the conservative *Chicago Tribune* described the Blue Book as "censorship through blackmail"[35] – mainstream media offered some measured support. The Blue Book received early plaudits from such media outlets as *Variety, Life,* and *Time* magazine.[36] The latter described it as correcting "radio's most common and obvious faults: soap operas, too many commercials, allowing the sponsor to have free rein." *Time* noted that the FCC found "commercials have been getting longer, more frequent, and more offensive," as one station in 1945 hit an all-time high: In "one 133-hour period of broadcasting, it carried 2,215 plug-uglies, an average of 16.7 an hour." The article confirmed what many broadcasters feared and reformers fantasized: that "If these faults continue," the FCC would "consider suspending some licenses."[37] Writing that the FCC recommendations could "stand as a primer for the operation of a good radio station," *Variety* held no

[30] Parker to Durr, July 1, 1946, Box 30, Folder 7; Parker to Durr, Sept. 5, 1946, Box 30, Folder 8, CJDP.
[31] Judith Waller to Clifford Durr, May 14, 1946, Box 30, Folder 6, CJDP.
[32] Keith Tyler to Clifford Durr, May 31, 1946, Box 30, Folder 6, CJDP.
[33] Frank Stanton to Clifford Durr, May 10, 1946, Box 30 Folder 6, CJDP.
[34] H. B. McCarty to Clifford Durr, Jan. 20, 1947, Box 31, Folder 2, CJDP.
[35] "Blue Book Is Grist for Editorial Mills," *Broadcasting*, May 6, 1946, 67.
[36] "Life Can Be Beautiful," *Broadcasting*, May 20, 1946, 15.
[37] "Worst," *Time*, March 18, 1946.

sympathy for commercial broadcasters: "Obviously, the industry has brought upon itself the FCC proposals by its abuses," which it tried to obscure "by resorting to frantic flag-waving."[38] The *St. Louis Post-Dispatch* found the recommendations praiseworthy in the eyes of "millions of radio listeners," as did the *Hartford Courant*, which editorialized, "Hats off to the FCC" and "FCC to the rescue."[39]

The *New York Times Magazine* saw the FCC as simply – and belatedly – carrying out its official duty. Given advertisers' "commanding position ... in dictating the contents of the day's radio programs, especially during good listening hours," which leads to "excessive commercialism" and "advertising chatter," the story advocated that "it is up to the FCC, backed by the listening public, to enforce strictly the recommendations of the 'Blue Book.'" Dismissing industry's charges that "the FCC has even a remote intention of censoring what the broadcasters say over the air," the article argued that the only means of "counter-balancing excessive commercialism in a radio industry which is privately owned and operated is through a governmental agency acting as guardian of the public interest – which means the FCC." The Blue Book was the "first step in this direction."[40]

Durr often shared and commented on specific articles, noting to one correspondent that many journals had taken up reformist themes since the Blue Book's publication.[41] He and his allies saw the proliferation of broadcast criticism in the nation's leading print news outlets as evidence that the people had awakened. With this positive outpouring, a short-lived enthusiasm arose that history was on the reformers' side. The Blue Book seemingly resonated with public support for radio reform. Commercial broadcasters' reactions were another matter altogether.

Broadcasters' Counterattack

Although the Blue Book's specific proposals were relatively cautious – one historian characterized them as "eminently reasonable and non-revolutionary"[42] – commercial broadcasters responded as if their very existence were in question. The NAB president, Justin Miller, considered the situation, as Eric Barnouw put it, "a life-or-death matter" that required "the industry to discredit and defeat the Blue Book."[43] Broadcasters had reason to make the Blue Book's demise an absolute imperative; at stake was nothing less than the contract

[38] "Let's Face it," *Variety*, March 13, 1946, 35.
[39] Richard Meyer, "Reaction to the 'Blue Book,'" *Journal of Broadcasting* 7 (1962): 305–6; and Barnouw, *The Golden Web*, 231.
[40] Lloyd Free, "What Can Be Done to Improve Radio?" *New York Times Magazine*, August 25, 1946, 9, 50, 52.
[41] Clifford Durr to Edward Heffron, July 14, 1947, Box 31, Folder 4, CJDP.
[42] Berkman, "The 'Blue Book' and Charles Siepmann," 38.
[43] Barnouw, *The Golden Web*, 231.

defining commercial broadcasters' power in society. If they were to lose here, the very logic of their control over the industry could unravel. What if government, backed by a burgeoning media reform movement, determined that the people's airwaves should be entirely decommercialized? If regulators could revoke licenses, could they also prohibit certain types, or all types, of advertising? How would commercial radio retain legitimacy as an enterprise? Indeed, how would it survive? In its relatively short existence, the commercial broadcast industry was already accustomed to vast privilege and profit. It was not about to relinquish such power without a fight.

Broadcasters' counterattack was quick and no-holds-barred. The hostility and ideological zeal with which they assailed the FCC and the Blue Book authors – pouncing on them with a viciousness rarely seen even in political realms known for their contentious nature – are difficult to capture. A *New York Times* article described the rancor as "immediate and clamorous,"[44] while historians have termed it as a "torrent of vitriol" and "apoplectic."[45] Their attacks took many forms and were most pronounced in the trade press, in industry literature, and in Miller's public statements. Also abetting broadcasters were the American Legion and the National Association of Manufacturers (NAM). In a 1947 address to the NAB, the NAM chairman, Robert Wason, urged broadcasters to expunge from government and from the airwaves all of the "remaining communists and fellow travelers," promising them that "industry and commerce will join you to restore freedom to the radio industry."[46]

After hearing of the Blue Book study, commercial broadcasters, particularly the NAB, preemptively attacked the FCC, and the industry backlash only intensified after the report's publication in March 1946. The NAB's Miller spearheaded the anti–Blue Book campaign, claiming the FCC's agenda was to censor and control radio programming. Miller called the Blue Book authors "stooges for Communists," "obfuscators," "professional appeasers," and "astigmatic perverts."[47] In public speeches during the months prior to and following the Blue Book's publication, Miller called on potential allies in print media to join forces against a common enemy in the "strong government boys" found among the usual suspects: "sophomoric professors, selfish special interests, religious fanatics, power-crazed bureaucrats, and irascible legislators." These sinister conspirators had made common cause "to emasculate the media of free communication." While commercial media's "enemies chortle with glee," Miller warned, the government's machinations toward radio "can be done

[44] Free, "What Can Be Done to Improve Radio?" 9, 50.
[45] Barnouw, *The Golden Web*, 231. Michael Socolow, "To Network a Nation: CBS, NBC, and the Development of National Network Radio in the United States, 1925–1950" (Ph.D. dissertation, Georgetown University, 2001), 289.
[46] "NAM Chief Urges Anti-Truman Stand," *Broadcasting*, September 22, 1947, 38.
[47] Meyer, "Reactions to the 'Blue Book,'" 301. See also Charles Siepmann, "Radio," in *The Communication of Ideas*, ed. Lyman Bryson (New York: Institute for Religious and Social Studies, 1948), 181.

to the press, newspapers, magazines, books and all varied forms of printed publications."[48] Fending off a regulatory assault against all media required a united front. Miller called for a "program of militant resistance to further encroachments of Government ... upon radio's freedom."[49] He characterized "talk about 'the people owning the air' as a 'lot of hooey and nonsense.'"[50]

While most of the mainstream press treated the FCC more fairly, editorials printed in *Broadcasting*, the industry's leading trade magazine, were bent on the Blue Book's destruction. Beginning eleven days after its publication, and continuing on a weekly basis for fifteen weeks until June 17, 1946, *Broadcasting* issued screeds against the Blue Book and its authors. The first such salvo dubbed the FCC the "Federal Censorship Commission" and depicted broadcasters as the defenders of constitutional freedoms against a fascist tyranny similar to that of the "Pied Pipers of destruction who led the German and Italian people down a dismal road by the sweet sound of their treacherous voices on a radio which they programmed." It likened the Blue Book to the Nazi "Hermann's planes" because it called for "a wider public criticism of *commercial* broadcasting" (their emphasis). The editorial declared that the Blue Book attacked "free radio" because "its authors are disconcerted that there has been no organized revolution against the medium."[51] Many of these editorials were later compiled by the NBC president, Niles Trammell – who, after Miller, was the most visible spokesman for the broadcast industry – in a red-covered booklet imaginatively titled "The Red Book Looks at the Blue Book."[52]

Broadcasters' counterattack centered on linking the Blue Book's authors to socialism. When broadcasters heard of the British-born Siepmann's involvement, they "welcomed like manna from Heaven" his BBC past, which made him a convenient red-baiting target.[53] They charged that Siepmann's appointment signaled the FCC's agenda to "BBC-ize American broadcasting," by making radio less commercial and advertising supported and more public.[54] Referring to the Blue Book as "The Pink Book,"[55] broadcasters alleged that Siepmann was in league with communist infiltrators – a claim that intensified after he published *Radio's Second Chance*, which expanded on many of the

[48] Justin Miller, Purpose of Meeting, Opening Remarks to the All-media Conference of Freedom of Expression, Washington DC June 26, 1947; "Attacks on Freedom of Communication," address to American Society of Newspaper Editors Convention, Statler Hotel, Washington, DC, 1949. These are quoted in Stamm, *Sound Business*, 148–9.
[49] "Miller Calls for Halt to FCC, AFM Inroads," *Broadcasting*, January 14, 1946, 17.
[50] This comment, made in the spring of 1946, was reprinted in multiple sources, including the following year in "Radio Listeners Be Damned" *Kiplinger's Personal Finance*, February 1947, 8.
[51] *Broadcasting* (1946) F(ederal) C(ensorship) C(ommission), 30, March 18, 1946, 58.
[52] *The Red Book Looks at the Blue Book* (NBC Publications, 1946).
[53] Barnouw, *The Golden Web*, 232.
[54] R. K. Richards, "BBC Expert Probes Procedure for FCC," *Broadcasting* 29, July 30, 1945, 16f., quoted in Meyer, "Reaction to the 'Blue Book.'"
[55] Sally Fly, interview with Paul Porter, 24, Fly Connell Papers.

Blue Book's proposals. Indeed, broadcasters were nothing if not creative in their red-baiting. A piece in *Broadcasting* observed that Durr "lists to portside in his social philosophies" because he "believes there is too much commercialism in American radio."[56] Another *Broadcasting* column characterized Durr as "the FCC's knight errant," the "be-tasseled champion of the Pennsylvania Avenue Cardinals" who "enters the joust in righteous splendor, garbed in an academic grey suit and gripping tightly in one hand – the Blue Book" and in his other "the banner he bears high – is it the white of purity, or is there a hint of pink?"[57]

Broadcasting's editorials alternately attacked Siepmann, Durr, or both at once. One editorial questioned "the manner in which the book emerged from the cloistered chambers which gave its birth. Inevitably it must be asked – is Charles Siepmann its father or is he a midwife who stood in patient attendance at the bower of Clifford J. Durr?"[58] Durr thought it was particularly cowardly and dishonest when his nemesis Sol Taishoff wrote: "Is Commissioner C. J. Durr, chronic dissenter of the FCC, actually a proponent of Government ownership of American radio? He has never said so flatly."[59] These attacks continued intermittently for months. One friend of Durr's, congratulating him for fighting radio's commercialism, saw broadcasters' attacks as a badge of honor. "I certainly resent the sarcasm so often used in the magazine *Broadcasting* concerning you," he said. However, it "singles you out as people's champion, and operates as a boost."[60] Judging by many of his letters from this time, however, the assaults took their toll on Durr and his allies.

Broadcasters' retaliation took the FCC by surprise. One historian observed that the commission was "dazed" and slow to recover from its "bafflement" from the post–Blue Book onslaught.[61] Whereas Durr seemingly grasped the systemic critique of commercial broadcasting that recognized the inherent limitations of a market-driven media system, most liberal policy makers, to their great disadvantage, never fully understood the logical conclusions following from their own arguments. Despite their sometimes-aggressive tactics, they never perceived their critique and regulatory approach as striking at the heart of the commercial model of media. Nor did they clearly grasp that a profit-driven broadcast system could not rationalize sacrificing financial gain for the benefit of public service, and therefore they never fully appreciated the systemic threat that initiatives like the Blue Book posed to commercial broadcasters.

The Blue Book, after all, was not a communism-inspired tract but merely an attempt to define public service responsibilities and the FCC's role as their

[56] Richards, "BBC Expert Probes Procedure."
[57] Quoted in Meyer, "Reaction to the 'Blue Book,'" 303.
[58] R. K. Richards, "Radio's Second Chance: Free to Broadcasters, $2.50 to Listeners," *Broadcasting*, April 8, 1946, 20, 27.
[59] Sol Taishoff, *Broadcasting*, July 8, 1946.
[60] Henry Johnson to Clifford Durr, October 2, 1946, Box 30, Folder 8, CJDP.
[61] Barnouw, *The Golden Web*, 233.

enforcer. The outgoing FCC chairman Porter argued as much in an article, "Radio Must Grow Up," suggesting that the commission was trying to help broadcasters help themselves – using a carrot-and-stick approach – before it was too late. As he put it, "There is a saying about 'putting your house in order, before the law does it for you with a rough hand.' It is an old, trite saying, but still true, as many a proud industry ... knows to its sorrow."[62] Similarly, the new chairman, Charles Denny, described the Blue Book as a "rationalization of renewal policy" and stressed that "we are not interested in program content ... but we are concerned that licensees make good on their representations."[63] Nonetheless, broadcasters acted rationally given the true extent of the regulatory threat, and liberals were unprepared to withstand their reactions.

The constant smears were devastating to the cause of progressive radio reform and mirrored the gathering storm of reactionary politics across the nation. With the Blue Book and its supporters as primary targets, the broadcasting industry mobilized a broad front and ultimately overwhelmed the media reform movement, exploiting early Cold War rhetoric to delegitimate it. As with other postwar social movements, the presence of some actual socialists within the reformers' ranks rendered all of them vulnerable to red-baiting. One historian observed that industry advocates tarred "even the most politically moderate radio reformers as Communists out to destroy the American broadcasting system."[64] Beyond the central tactic of red-baiting, other rhetorical strategies and ideological assumptions underpinning their arguments merit a closer examination.

Broadcasters' Arguments

In the weeks following the Blue Book's publication, broadcasters won the war of words. In their rapid mobilization to contest the Blue Book and remain unencumbered by government regulation, the broadcasters employed lines of argument that were remarkably uniform. Drawing from a libertarian discourse that treated listeners as primarily consumers to whom broadcasters owed little beyond entertainment, their arguments centered on three themes. First, they argued that public interest regulations like those outlined in the Blue Book were an attempt to censor free speech and thus an infringement of their First Amendment rights. A second standard line of reasoning was that structural interventions that established educational and nonprofit set-asides of spectrum

---

[62] "Porter Reaffirms Belief in U.S. Broadcasting and Lists Abuses," *Broadcasting*, September 10, 1945, 16, 74.

[63] "Denny Promises Swift Handling of Cases," *Broadcasting*, March 4, 1946, 15. The previous two quotes are found in Dell, "Red-baiting, Regulation, and the Broadcast Industry." Dell attributes much of the Blue Book's mismanagement to Denny's incompetence, noting also that within a 13-month span the FCC was led by three different chairmen, contributing to institutional confusion.

[64] Fones-Wolf, *Waves of Opposition*, 152–3.

were unnecessary since the commercial system already provided optimal programming. The third argument asserted that any kind of regulation of radio
smacked of socialism, was anti-business, and was therefore inherently nefarious
and un-American. Assuming that radio had been invented and driven purely by
private enterprise, they argued that any deviation from the free market was a
betrayal of radio's first principles.

This last point presented an obvious mischaracterization; broadcasters' state-
guaranteed monopoly rights to the public airwaves were antithetical to free-mar-
ket relationships. Nonetheless, former NAB president, J. Harold Ryan, neglected
to consider this reliance on the state when he informed a group of Kiwanians,
"American radio today is the product of business!"[65] Anticipating the Reagan
era FCC chairman Mark Fowler's infamous statement that television was nothing more than "a toaster with pictures,"[66] Ryan insisted radio should be treated
as a commodity: "It is just as much the kind of product as the vacuum cleaner,
the washing machine, the automobile and the airplane." Pegging 1935 as the
time when "radio and its advertisers really began to get together and progress
began," he asserted that "many a station operator who might have had a personal preference for poetry and the opera learned some sound lessons in selling
and merchandising under tutelage of America's good, hard-headed businessmen,
and it was the best thing that could have happened to him."[67]

The most common trope in broadcasters' rhetoric was the notion of "free
radio," a liberty that mostly translated to "freedom from governmental regulation." Variations of the theme recurred in *Broadcasting* magazine and in
many editorials and books. For example, the NBC president, Niles Trammell's,
congressional testimony, published as a pamphlet titled "Radio Must Remain
Free," urged the senators in attendance to give radio a "new freedom from
fear, the fear of the blight of government control."[68] Likewise, the NAB issued
a thick book titled *Broadcasting and the Bill of Rights* based on statements
made during another set of congressional hearings, particularly the NAB president Miller's anti-regulation arguments.[69] The "free radio" motif was usually
expressed by industry representatives but occasionally appeared elsewhere. For
example, one FCC letter-writer mocked, "The BBC? What have THEY got that
we haven't GOT – and no doubt with all our faults ours is better than theirs.
The important thing is to keep radio FREE!"[70]

---

[65] Quoted in Dixon Wecter, "The Public Domain of the Air," *Saturday Review of Literature* IXIX,
no. 20 (May 18, 1946): 5–6, 36–8. Also contained in Box 33, Folder 7, CJDP.
[66] Peter Boyer, "Under Fowler, FCC Treated TV as Commerce," *New York Times*, January
19, 1987.
[67] Quoted in Wecter, "The Public Domain of the Air."
[68] Niles Trammell, "Radio Must Remain Free," statement given before the Senate Interstate
Commerce Committee, December 7–8, 1943, 6.
[69] NAB, *Broadcasting and the Bill of Rights*, statements presented by representatives of the broadcasting industry during hearings in the White Bill (s. 1333) to amend the Communications Act
of 1934, before a subcommittee on Interstate and Foreign Commerce, June 17–27, 1947.
[70] H. Tarkington to Clifford Durr et al. Dec. 12, 1946, Box 31, Folder 1, CJDP.

However, like that of all normative claims, "free radio's" precise meaning was contested. Progressives posited their own definition in venues like the *Journal of the National Education Association,* which framed free radio as a positive liberty that privileged the audience over individual broadcasters, encouraging "the widest possible range of information, entertainment, and ideas."[71] But in the 1940s, corporate libertarians captured the term along with many normative frameworks for regulating media. The Republican presidential candidate Thomas Dewey demonstrated its centrality in conservative ideology by declaring in 1944: "I believe that the FCC should have no right of censorship, that it should not control the content of radio programs. It should stay in the field of regulating technical facilities. And when the FCC starts to control program content, free radio goes out the window."[72]

Newspaper publishers, particularly those eager to acquire radio stations, also kept the libertarian free-radio motif in circulation. The *Chicago Tribune* publisher Colonel McCormick – who owned a radio station and was interested in acquiring more – argued that the FCC's regulatory power to review license renewals should be discontinued so that "wave lengths will become property and be protected in the courts like any other property."[73] The free-radio frame was also prominent in Hearst-owned newspapers' editorials, especially since the license of the Hearst-owned WBAL station was being challenged by local radio reformers (discussed later). A representative piece was titled "The American Radio Must Be Free."[74] It declared:

[The U.S. Constitution] should be amended to give the American radio the same recognition it gives the American press, and to assure it the same FREEDOM.... There is already a great deal of legislation respecting control of radio ... but none of it has served to keep the radio FREE. The inherent weakness of such legislation ... is that it depends for interpretation and enforcement upon bureaucratic agencies ... which distort the law and assume and usurp powers under it in defiance of the authority of Congress and in contempt of the vital rights of the American people.[75]

Accusing the FCC of censorship and of parroting the Democratic Party, the editorial quoted the Republican National Committee chair, Congressman Carroll Reece, that radio "'has fallen under the rule of seven bureaucrats setting themselves up as judges of what seventy million American radio listeners should be allowed to listen to,'" an action "typical of the bureaucratic state where the private citizen is pushed around with arrogant contempt and allowed to listen only to those things which document the dogma of his masters."[76]

[71] *Journal of the National Education Association,* 33, 1944.
[72] Wecter, "The Public Domain of the Air."
[73] Ibid.
[74] Ivon Newman to Clifford Durr, May 28, 1946, Box 30, Folder 6, CJDP.
[75] "The American Radio Must Be Free," *Boston Daily Record,* May 24, 1946.
[76] Ibid.

Much of this rhetoric originated with political and industry elites, but occasionally it also registered at the grass roots. In the many letters of complaint to the FCC about broadcasters' commercial excesses and the need for radio reform were also some libertarian sentiments. For example, after reading in the *New York Times* about proposed radio regulations, one concerned citizen wrote to Chairman Denny that he should be "classed as a meddler and if not an actual Socialist, then something closely akin to it." Arguing that Congress had given the FCC the power to censor radio programs, he wrote, "Perhaps the radio programs and the advertising plugs are moronic, but if that is what the people of the country want, why punish the radio stations and networks? Just remember that you were not selected to public office. You are there by sufferance."[77] After hearing Durr debate policy on the radio, another listener wrote: "It is appropriate that I find time on Independence Day to tell you how contemptible your [position] was. Would that there were a freedom bath into which men of your alien mind could be immersed to come out clean and American."[78]

One listener saw the FCC's regulatory position as resting on five presuppositions: "The law setting up the FCC was wise and good"; "the interpretation of the law by the FCC is wise and good and necessary"; "the public is not wise and 'Papa' [or] a bureau knows best"; "the public is not vocal, hence [it] must have a voice [expressed by] that of a bureau"; and "private enterprise cannot be trusted." The listener continued, "This attitude, low and bitter to free American citizens, stirs me to an indignation and sadness I cannot express." He asked, "How do you know the public needs uplifting by radio? How do you know what percentage of time should be devoted to this or that, or at what time of day certain types of programs should be put on?" Suggesting that initiatives like the Blue Book were a waste of taxpayers' money, the listener concluded: "This attitude is paternalism, it is not trust in the 'common man.'"[79]

The charge of paternalism carried some legitimacy. After all, much 1940s radio criticism shaded into elitist presumptions about mass society's tastes and sensibilities and radio's ability to dumb down the public. Thus the question, Why should a group of unelected, highly educated bureaucrats – that they were all white men was noteworthy though rarely mentioned – determine the programming and public service needs for all of society? However, this argument was a bit of a red herring. As the Blue Book's content analyses made abundantly clear, public affairs shows, cultural programming appealing to "minority tastes," non-advertising-supported fare, local coverage – all were disappearing from the public airwaves.[80] The FCC argued that instead of dictating specific

---

[77] Leah McClelland to Charles Denny, March 8, 1946, Box 30, Folder 5, CJDP.
[78] Elmer Luehr to Clifford Durr, July 4, 1946, Box 30, Folder 7, CJDP.
[79] Jane McGinnis to Clifford Durr, July 21, 1946, Box 30, Folder 7, CJDP.
[80] Christopher Sterling points out that this may have partly resulted from the decline of wartime taxation – the "10-cent dollars" advertisers had used during World War II.

programming it proposed general parameters for ensuring a degree of diverse, local, decommercialized, and information-rich programming. Running counter to the elitism charge, the FCC sought measures giving local communities more control over programming instead of having their radio fare decided for them by commercial broadcasters and advertisers.

Nonetheless, many of the pro-advertising and anti-regulation arguments rested on a kind of anti-elitism – what might be called "commercial populism." Ralph Smith, general manager of the ad agency Duane Jones (which reportedly was airing more than two thousand weekly commercials at the time), defended radio advertising by explaining, without a trace of irony, the class politics behind commercials: "Persons who complain about commercials are as a rule disgustingly healthy or so strongly fortified financially that grocery bills are no problem."[81] According to Smith, "commercials are not written for such as these. Commercials are written as a form of service to persons who hope to cut budgets or find new methods and products of personal value." Smith claimed that except for the "critical minority who are either professional or amateur objectors," people enjoy commercials and benefit immensely from the information contained within them. "People listen to radio commercials by choice, regardless of where they are placed in the program," he averred. Implying that a handful of killjoys were trying to prevent average listeners who "love to look at the ads in the papers and hear the ads on the radio" from enjoying their simple pleasures, Smith ended with an appeal to American principles: "Freedom of speech is one of the Four Freedoms Americans are fighting for!"

The debate's framing as one over free radio and free speech placed reformers on the defensive from the beginning. Perhaps in part because of their decisive defeats in the 1930s on core issues of media ownership and control, many reformers made a point of denying that they were, for example, advocating a British-style government-supported broadcast system.[82] In public debates with commercial media representatives, progressive policy elites often were prevented from addressing substantive issues and instead corralled into contesting inflammatory yet vacuous topics such as whether they were opposed to free enterprise. Despite their focus on core normative issues, reformers rarely were given – nor did they seize – the opportunity to argue that significant regulation was necessary for a commercial media system to operate at a level required for democratic society.

Media reformers like Durr were the rare holdouts who could level strong counterarguments to commercial populism. "They say we must have 'free radio,'" Durr said in 1945. "I agree. Let us have a radio that is truly free – as free from economic domination and overweening greed as from government

---

[81] *Time*, 1945.
[82] Similar "free radio" tactics were used against 1930s legislative efforts to reserve education channels.

censorship."[83] These social democratic arguments were founded on positive liberties and called for a public-interest-oriented state. However, by the mid- to late 1940s, many liberals had already conceded that arguing for a proactive regulatory state was not unlike tilting at windmills. Indicative of this regulatory retreat, one leading reformer noted that since "democratic thought" seemed to be "swinging away from governmental checks," radio's deficiencies might "have to be worked out between the industry and the listening public."[84]

Industry arguments casting radio regulation as antithetical to cherished American freedoms made matters even more challenging for reformers. Equating deregulated radio with freedom was more than just convenient sloganeering. Staking out "freedom" in American political discourse is the ultimate prize in rhetorical warfare. Broadcasters' framing their arguments in terms of "free radio" allowed them to lay claim to "American freedom" and all its favorable associations. Once commercial broadcasters and their allies commanded that esteemed position, they could dismiss any counterargument as un-American. Indeed, although its definition is inherently unstable and contestable – meaning different things to different people at different times – anything not in line with "freedom" in American political discourse is a priori alien, cast outside the bounds of acceptable practice. Such discursive wrangling suggests that the struggle centered on the role of the state as much as media. It also suggests that the struggle was for much more than just control of radio or media in general; it was a struggle for political economic power – one that extended across many sectors of society and struck at the core of American corporate privilege. Claiming individual freedoms such as First Amendment protections for commercial media entities became a core component of the corporate libertarianism that triumphed in the 1940s.

An Embattled Durr

Feeling besieged, Durr found his spirits bolstered somewhat by allies' supportive letters. After hearing about his possible FCC departure, the famous radio writer Norman Corwin sent Durr an "urgent and earnest plea to stick with it." Corwin, who served as the Progressive Citizens of America's radio division chairman, immediately called on the radio committees of major citizens groups to launch a campaign to keep Durr at the FCC and "make it a commission worthy of [Durr's] ideals and performance." Corwin suggested to Durr that he should be promoted to FCC chair, hoping that "maybe we can arouse enough citizens to make it worth your while."[85] Durr replied that his recent "low moments" had been "due to general developments in Washington rather than to the activities of the FCC itself." But Durr pledged to "plug along,"

[83] "Durr Airs Radio Views," *NAB Reports*, June 29, 1945, 264. Cited in Socolow, 194.
[84] White, *American Radio*, 10.
[85] Norman Corwin to Clifford Durr, March 8, 1946, Box 30, Folder 5, CJDP.

hoping that he could at least "focus some attention upon a few basic problems." Durr added, "As government agencies go these days, I think the FCC is a pretty good organization, but unfortunately the heavy pressures all come from the wrong direction."[86]

Other friends lent moral support. Robert Stephan, the *Cleveland Plain Dealer*'s radio editor, reported that the "FCC program report still gets rumbles," inviting "the NAB's red herrings of 'control' and 'free speech.'" However, Stephan believed neutral observers would discern the Blue Book's "value and intent," distinguishing "instantly between an honest attempt to curb over-commercialization" and false charges of "interference with free speech."[87] Durr also took heart from public letters of support. Many such letters encouraged Durr in his ongoing debate with the RNC Chairman Reece, who declared that contesting the FCC's regulatory authority was a central plank of the Republican platform and electoral strategy.[88] After Reece's on-air defense of commercial broadcasting, a Wichita, Kansas, listener despaired:

To whom can we appeal? I have seen numbers of letters written to editorial columns of radio magazines and newspapers, all of the same tenor as this letter, but no improvement is ever noted. Commercials get longer, more frequent, more idiotic and intellectually insulting each season. What has become of the hours of symphony music, to which, believe it or not, thousands of us would listen to if we could?[89]

Describing himself as "not a long-haired musician" but a "strictly run-of-the-mill average citizen with only a high school education," the listener insisted he could perceive when he was "decently entertained" and when his "intelligence or [his] sanity is being questioned." After talking to "too many people," who "feel more or less as I do," he asserted, "Some sort of regulation is imperative to prevent the despoiling of another of the great gifts granted mankind, from which so pitifully few of the once glowing possibilities have been realized."[90] Durr responded that such "intelligent and well-expressed listener protests" could effect change "in the long run if they come with sufficient frequency and in reasonable numbers." He noted that "thousands of radio listeners share your views" but that few "have the gift of making their own feelings articulate."[91] Durr felt that his actions on the FCC represented this silent multitude, even as his struggles became more solitary and seemingly futile.

Intellectual reinforcement arrived during the thick of the Blue Book controversy in the form of Charles Siepmann's provocative book *Radio's Second Chance*, which presented the argument that the new FM frequencies offered public service opportunities that had been squandered on AM radio.

---

[86] Durr to Corwin, March 14, 1946, Box 30, Folder 5, CJDP.
[87] Robert Stephan to Clifford Durr, March 29, 1946, Box 30, Folder 5, CJDP.
[88] Barnouw, *The Golden Web*, 232.
[89] A. Ruff to Congressman B. Carroll Reece, May 18, 1946, Box 30, Folder 6, CJDP.
[90] Ibid.
[91] Durr to Ruff, June 12, 1946, Box 30, Folder 6, CJDP.

The polemic quickly became a proxy for the Blue Book's criticisms and recommendations. Seeing the two works as complementary, Durr hailed *Radio's
Second Chance* as "the most readable and valuable book on broadcasting so far
produced."[92] Durr felt each could boost the other's prominence. He wrote to a
friend that the Blue Book had "really stirred things up" and that "if the NAB
continues the furor, it will make Charles Siepmann's book a best seller."[93]

Siepmann welcomed the attention but felt "far away and out of touch"
from the fight. Busy directing a new communications department at NYU –
one of the nation's first – Siepmann was nonetheless eager to reenter the fray.
Although his academic workload kept him "remote from developments," he
asked Durr to keep him informed of policy battles he was "anxious to follow."[94] After participating in a policy debate on CBS radio that elicited "fan
mail running into hundreds of letters," Siepmann hoped that "maybe after all,
we may get the listener aroused," making it even more important "that the
Commission should carry its message to the people vigorously." He felt that
Durr should not shoulder "the whole burden of public relations" and wondered whether Chairman Denny could be recruited to become more active in
Blue Book battles.[95] Unfortunately for Durr, Denny was unevenly supportive,
and staffers who had worked on the Blue Book – Siepmann and Ed Brecher,
most notably – had departed. Dallas Smythe remained, but was not directly
involved in defending the Blue Book. Durr, "the Dissenter," increasingly waged
a one-person struggle at the FCC.

Siepmann tried to provide support from afar, repeatedly requesting data
for oppositional research. In one letter, he asked for the number of FM and
AM licenses granted to newspaper owners, the number of FM frequencies
applied for and reserved for educational radio, and "any information on decisions by the FCC or pending problems of which you think I ought to know."[96]
Three days later he sent more research questions: "How many cities in the
United States enjoy adequate reception of the four networks' stations? How
many cities and towns have a choice of less than four programs?" Siepmann
also urged that Blue Books be sent to Luella Lawdin, who, as the chair of
the National Council of Women, the National Federation of Women's Clubs,
and the National Council of Church Women, wielded considerable influence.[97] He was later "appalled" when Durr sent only five copies instead of
the requested fifty. "If in my own small way I have succeeded in promoting
interest," he wondered, "what must be the potential demand from similar

[92] Clifford Durr to Anne Ford, March 28, 1946, Box 30, Folder 5, CJDP.
[93] Clifford Durr to Bontecou, April 16, 1946, Box 30, Folder 5, CJDP.
[94] See, for example, Charles Siepmann to Clifford Durr, received July 17, 1946, Box 30, Folder
     7, CJDP.
[95] Siepmann to Durr, May 15, 1946, Box 30, Folder 6, CJDP.
[96] Siepmann to Durr, June 4, 1946, Box 30, Folder 6, CJDP.
[97] Siepmann to Durr, June 7, 1946, Box 30, Folder 6, CJDP.

backers of the FCC throughout the country?" Fearing they were squandering a fleeting opportunity, he asked Durr what undercut "your labors and your policy so fatally."[98]

Durr hoped that increased circulation of *Radio's Second Chance* would pick up the slack, though he agreed that more Blue Books were needed. He asked Siepmann to collect economic data and explore "the extent and degree of advertiser control over broadcasting and the effect on programming." Hoping that NYU's imprimatur "might add to the impressiveness of the result," Durr thought such a study could provide "an authoritative account of where our radio programs come from, how the script is written, and who makes the real decisions as to what the listener shall hear."[99] That particular study never fully materialized, but Siepmann nonetheless became a publishing powerhouse for the cause, writing strongly worded polemics in a variety of popular venues,[100] including a Blue Book–related piece for the *American Mercury* titled "Storm in the Radio World." "Nervous of [momentum] lapsing," Siepmann told Durr that he wanted "to keep the heat on" and "keep the controversy alive." However, he expressed concern that his colleague Ed Brecher – whose advocacy piece for the *Atlantic Monthly* titled "Whose Radio?" was timed to coincide with Siepmann's – was "in trouble" and indicated that broadcasters' recent attack against him "sounds like dirty business."[101]

Siepmann's and Brecher's articles attempted to rally supporters as well as the FCC. Brecher described the Blue Book's mission and declared that the "real danger" was the FCC's failure to implement "with competence and with vigor" its own policies. He emphasized that the "Blue Book is not a self-enforcing document; its full effect will not be felt by listeners until its general principles are applied in specific cases." Whether the FCC would enforce the Blue Book, he admitted, "is still in doubt."[102] In his article, Siepmann lamented that "while the trade publications have been seething with the controversy," very little "has been heard directly from the listening public, the long-suffering group which has the most at stake." He noted that many Americans would "allow commercial enterprise free scope where the manufacture and distribution of commodities is concerned" but may be much less "tolerant" with radio when the "dissemination of ideas and ideals" is at stake. He called for a confrontation between the FCC and broadcasters because the Blue Book could be tested only

---

[98] Siepmann to Durr, received July 25, 1946, Box 30, Folder 7, CJDP.

[99] Durr to Siepmann, July 26, 1946, Box 30, Folder 7, CJDP.

[100] Throughout the mid- to late 1940s, Siepmann would often publish in opinion magazines, especially the *Nation*, trying to galvanize popular support for broadcast reform. See, for example, Siepmann, "Radio: Tool of the Reactionaries," *Nation*, July 5, 1947, 15–16; Siepmann, "New Wine in Old Bottles," *Nation*, September 27, 1947, 312–13; and Siepmann, "Shall Radio Take Sides," *Nation*, February 21, 1948, 210–11.

[101] Siepmann to Durr, received July 17, 1946, Box 30, Folder 7, CJDP.

[102] Ed Brecher, "Whose Radio?" *Atlantic Monthly*, August 1946, 47–51.

by the radio industry's challenging "some future action of the FCC that stems from the revised procedures outlined in the report."[103] Blue Book proponents would soon get their challenge.

The Blue Book's First Test

The first real test for the Blue Book arrived in the autumn of 1946, involving the Hearst-owned Baltimore radio station WBAL. WBAL had been one of five stations singled out in the Blue Book report for a close study of its public service infractions, making it an apt test case. A group calling itself the Public Service Radio Corporation (PSRC), headed by the well-known newspaper columnists and radio newsmen Robert Allen and Drew Pearson, was trying to claim WBAL's license because it failed to provide public services to the local community and was part of an unaccountable media conglomerate. Allen and Pearson believed that as a relatively new medium, radio had democratic potential and a capacity for journalism that was increasingly scarce in profit-driven newspapers. In taking on an incumbent licensee with a proven poor track record, the PSRC drew inspiration – including its very name – from the Blue Book to make its case. It charged that extreme media concentration and "absentee ownership" – in this case, a national newspaper chain owning a radio station, a newspaper, and a recently acquired television station in one city market – were contrary to the FCC's stated principles.

The WBAL case occurred at a critical moment and its outcome, according to Siepmann, was of "climactic importance" because it would test the FCC's "adherence to the principles of the Blue Book." Siepmann asked Durr immediately to send him evidence of WBAL's recent programming to ascertain whether its directors had fulfilled their promise "to mend their ways."[104] However, Durr was out of the country, his absence prompting another letter from Siepmann emphasizing that the commission's WBAL decision would be "decisive in relation to the Blue Book and the implementation of [its] standards." Anxious to "carry this issue to the public," Siepmann wrote an exposé on the WBAL case for the *Nation*.[105] Citing public indifference as radio reform's biggest obstacle, he pleaded with readers to pay attention to this crucial test case, offer testimony, and seize on radio's democratic potential. Siepmann described the FCC's authority as only a "reserve of power" within the American tradition of checks and balances; public pressure was essential.[106]

---

[103] Charles Siepmann, "Storm in the Radio World," *American Mercury* 63 (August 1946): 201–7.
[104] Siepmann to Durr, September 25, 1946, Box 30, Folder 8, CJDP. Barnouw, *The Golden Web*, 233. The FCC had already recently allowed WBAL to purchase a television station without a hearing. For a more detailed account, see Stamm, *Sound Business*, 171–80.
[105] Siepmann to Charles Cliff, October 3, 1946, Box 30, Folder 8, CJDP.
[106] Siepmann, "Radio's Operation Crossroads," *Nation*, December 7, 1946, 644.

Considering that the FCC had thus far denied fewer than twenty renewals of thousands requested since 1934, the challenge was an uphill struggle. But local activists and Blue Book advocates hoped that a reformist spirit had fundamentally changed this calculus and that incumbent media institutions were no longer immune to community opposition. The commercial broadcast community saw this struggle for the WBAL license as a clearly Blue Book–inspired campaign and was quick to defend the embattled station. During hearings and in the trade press, the Blue Book was regularly derided, and Hearst radio made an unsuccessful attempt at pressing a lawsuit against the FCC for slander. For their part, Allen and Pearson coordinated efforts with local media reform groups and influential Baltimore residents to campaign aggressively for changing WBAL ownership. Canvassing the local community, they found that many people were "constantly talking about the over-commercialization" of their local radio, and few wanted to keep the station in Hearst's hands.[107] If activists could win there, it would show the nation that engaged communities had the power to banish broadcasters who had shirked their public service duties.

Ultimately, the reformers' efforts would not prevail in the WBAL decision. Lively hearings were held over twenty-eight days between November 1947 and February 1948, but the FCC stalled on reaching a final conclusion. The PSRC even tried to force the aging William Randolph Hearst himself to give testimony – believing that having the media mogul on the stand would galvanize public opposition – but to no avail.[108] After long delays, with WBAL kept on the air with a temporary license, whatever public engagement had been stirred up dissipated. The final decision, which was not made until several years after Durr had left the FCC, amounted to the opinion of a lone commissioner. After listening to the case behind closed doors (a common procedure at the time), Commissioner Rosel Hyde concluded that despite imperfections, WBAL had a record of "demonstrated competence." Long deadlocked in a 3-3 split,[109] the decision was officially voted on in 1951 by the entire FCC and was upheld by a 3-2 decision with two commissioners abstaining.[110] In his dissent, Commissioner Wayne Coy articulated a progressive counternarrative that diverse media ownership better serves local communities and that the FCC should not treat a broadcast license as a de facto property right. Ultimately, this view did not hold sway, and the Blue Book's first, and only, decisive test case ended in failure.

---

[107] Quoted in Stamm, *Sound Business*, 176.
[108] Ibid., 179.
[109] *Broadcasting*, "Closed Circuit," 1950, March 6, 4.
[110] Quoted in Barnouw, *The Golden Web*, 233. See *FCC Reports*, 1950–1, Hearst Radio, Inc. (WBAL), 15 F.C.C. 1149–1189 (1951) and Rosel H. Hyde, "FCC Policy and Procedures Relating to Hearings on Broadcast Applications in Which a New Applicant Seeks to Displace a Licensee Seeking Renewal," *Duke Law Journal* no. 2 (May 1975): 253–78.

The Battle for the Public

Even as the Blue Book struggled at the policy level, it still inspired a spirited debate among some sectors of the public. Despite some colorful negative reactions like those noted previously, the great bulk of public responses to the FCC's actions consisted of positive letters like the following: "Three cheers and a slap on the back for a man after my own heart." Speaking "for many millions of my equally annoyed but less articulate fellow citizens," this listener added, "Although one man against Procter and Gamble is pretty poor odds, make it a good fight for a higher intellectual level of radio broadcasting, and we're with you one hundred percent."[111] Another writer expressed skepticism that radio could be liberated from advertisers: "Here we have a three-hundred million dollar industry with its high pressure lobbyists in every form in constant descent upon members of Congress as well as your commission on one side, and the public like myself on the other side." Given these circumstances, the listener wondered, "What can we do to halt" commercial control of radio, a medium that rightfully "should have belonged to the people?"[112]

Durr responded that he would be "the last to contend that commercial radio can be entirely free from the domination of its advertisers" – he was "fully conscious of the pressures" of financially sustaining a station – but felt that that "constant vigilance" could improve it. Articulating a version of regulatory capture theory, Durr conceded that "those with large financial interests are organized and articulate," while the public, except during those rare occasions when it is "really aroused," is "unorganized and inarticulate." Thus, Durr noted that "administrative agencies or regulatory bodies can, on occasion, stand up against these pressures, but in the long run the pressures have their effect."

Despite dealing with a corrupted political process, Durr had not given up hope on noncommercial alternatives. Citing a recent and rare victory of setting aside twenty educational channels, Durr firmly believed that once these educational FM stations were established throughout the country, "the whole level of programming will be raised." He did not believe "that commercial broadcasting is today giving people ... what they want." Once people "get a taste of good radio programs," he asserted, "they will demand more of them." Durr invoked a common belief among reformers: They cannot "know what they want until they have been offered some samples."[113]

On December 12, 1946, Durr appeared on ABC radio's *America's Town Meeting of the Air* with the *Hucksters* author, Frederic Wakeman, to debate two radio industry representatives, the ABC president, Mark Woods, and the general counsel for Broadcast Music Inc (BMI), Sidney Kaye. After asking

---

[111] Alex Bingel to Clifford Durr, July 22, 1946, Box 30, Folder 7, CJDP. He also thanked Durr for reserving FM channels for ex-servicemen.
[112] Frederick Nelson to Clifford Durr, August 12, 1946, Box 30, Folder 7, CJDP.
[113] Clifford Durr to Frederick Nelson, August 14, 1946, Box 30, Folder 7, CJDP.

listeners to mail in their opinions, the show producers selected from stacks of letters numbering in the hundreds a sample of about 330 letters. Lopsidedly sympathetic to Durr, the letters also included detractors. One suggested that the market already sufficiently regulates radio; poor programmers would "kill themselves by their own folly" if people simply turned off the radio or turned to another channel. Another wrote, "After the past 12 years of being told how to eat, sleep and breathe by a lot of Do-Gooders I was interested to know that we still have someone who still thinks he is capable of telling more than 140 million what they should hear. If you don't like a program why don't you turn it off?"[114] Some simply wrote to complain: "A word about radio advertising: The broadcasters are slowly killing the goose that is laying the golden eggs. A man's home is his castle – until he turns on his radio and finds his castle filled with aggressive voices selling laxatives and haranguing about patent medicines."[115] A more representative letter stated, "Bravo! Your honest comments without fear or favor were really a healthy breath of air in this fouled atmosphere of patent medicine, soap and tobacco smoke." Adding that he was "sure someone must have called you a Commie by now," he warned that if right-wing political players like Hearst were listening, "You may be out of a job."[116]

Durr's responses were telling. He agreed with one letter writer that new broadcasting models should be considered and suggested a town hall program focused on the question "Is the American System of Broadcasting the Best in the World?" with "good CBC and BBC representatives on the negative." Durr speculated that such programming might impress upon the public "interesting and worthwhile things going on in broadcasting outside of our own borders."[117] Durr replied to an ABC representative who had sent him a copy of a show about radio's future that "I hope by the time my children's children would be ready to listen to such a program ... [these concerns] will be moot."[118] But even if Durr and his allies were winning debates and persuading people about the Blue Book's merits, radio's systemic problems would persist.

The Final Confrontations of 1947

The last official FCC action in support of the Blue Book occurred a little more than six months after its publication, when the FCC remanded six license renewals for a public hearing on the basis of poor public service. Yet this intervention contained even softer language than that of the Blue Book itself.[119] All of these license renewals, which initially had been deemed problematic for

[114] Jon Dewson to Clifford Durr, Dec. 12, 1946, Box 31, Folder 1, CJDP.
[115] Herbert Lyser to Clifford Durr, Dec. 15, 1946, Box 31, Folder 1, CJDP.
[116] Johniah Meets to Clifford Durr, Dec. 12, 1946, Box 31, Folder 1, CJDP.
[117] Clifford Durr to E. Brown, Jan. 27, 1947, Box 31, Folder 2, CJDP.
[118] Clifford Durr to Robert Kinter, December 27, 1946, Box 31, Folder 1, CJDP.
[119] R. Crater, "FCC Cites 6 for Programs on Renewals," *Broadcasting*, September 23, 1946, 15.

various infractions, were granted despite Durr's dissents. The FCC's resolve was clearly weakening, and broadcasters all but declared victory after the first of these renewals, calling it the Blue Book's "first outright abdication."[120]

Nothing in Durr's letters from late 1946 and 1947 indicates that he thought the FCC was on the verge of turning the tide against broadcasters. However, he clearly saw himself fighting the good fight, even as he grew despondent over the reactionary shift in DC politics, especially after the congressional Republican rout in the 1946 midterm elections. He commiserated with his friend Thomas Emerson, the Yale Law School dean: "Washington *is* rather depressing these days, but I am expecting a slight turn for the better when the Republicans really take over. There is nothing more conservative than a Democrat who clings to the hope that he may be able to get in with the Republicans. I am afraid we have a lot of them in Washington."[121]

With the 1946 elections, politics took a decided turn for the worse for the few scattered New Dealers remaining in government. The Republicans' "Had Enough?" campaign slogan proved remarkably effective, and a raft of conservative politicians were swept into power. *Broadcasting*'s editorials could barely contain their delight, relishing the FCC investigations that were sure to come. One headline read: "Hell Is Located on a Washington Hill – At Least That's the Way It Looks Now for the FCC." The story predicted that "the FCC will be given one of the most thorough-going investigations ever attempted."[122] *Broadcasting*'s Sol Taishoff speculated that "Clifford Durr would be singled out for special attention by Congress." Indeed, Taishoff suggested that "Commissioner Durr, arch liberal Wallace-school New Dealer, is certain to figure in any Republican onslaught involving the FCC." The magazine reported elsewhere that a Harry Truman–backed commission was being organized to "to ferret out disloyal elements in Government" that "can be expected to forage in FCC pasture."[123] Any remaining prospects for progressive FCC activism were increasingly remote.

Nonetheless, Durr and his handful of allies soldiered on, as evidenced by a March 1947 strategy memo titled "Notes for an Outline of a Progressive Radio Program" that was circulated among FCC staffers, including Smythe.[124] It is unclear who authored the memo, but considering its content and that it was authored a full year after the Blue Book's publication, it appears the FCC was continuing to push for reform despite growing resistance. Stating that "at present, Blue Book policy remains on paper due to industry and political opposition," the memo called for a united front requiring "attention from

[120] "Blue Book Deserted in KGFJ Renewal," *Broadcasting*, December 2, 1946, 81.
[121] Clifford Durr to Thomas Emerson, December 9, 1946, Box 31, Folder 1, CJDP.
[122] Bill Bailey, "Hell Is Located on a Washington Hill," *Broadcasting*, November 1, 1946, 115, 72–3.
[123] Quoted in Dell, "Red-baiting, Regulation, and the Broadcast Industry," 23.
[124] "Notes for an Outline of a Progressive Radio Program," March 1947, Box 16–5, Folder 1–9, Smythe Papers.

progressives at least proportionate to that which has stalled it." As a remedy, the memo suggested introducing a congressional resolution announcing the Blue Book as a national policy applied to every individual station's three-year license renewal. Going beyond even Blue Book rules, the memo stated, "Effective democracy needs free or almost free access to the air for political candidates." Other proposals included a "network for labor and other progressive stations," an "anti-monopoly program" aimed at newspaper-owned radio stations, and, given what many thought would be a popular new technology, a "progressive facsimile service."[125] During this time, Chairman Denny, who headed the commission after Truman appointed Porter to chair another agency, still gave speeches declaring that "the Blue Book will not be bleached" and wrote letters endorsing its precepts.[126] He announced at the 25th annual NAB convention, on September 17, 1947: "The Blue Book stands as fundamental FCC policy."[127]

In early 1947, a dramatic showdown in an unlikely location transpired between the nation's two leading Blue Book advocates and two of its leading adversaries. Durr and Siepmann were invited to a radio forum organized by Yale law students to debate the Blue Book and related issues with Robert Richards, *Broadcasting*'s editorial director, and Louis Caldwell, a veteran attorney for commercial broadcasters, MBS counsel, and scourge of the 1930s broadcast reform movement.[128] A candid and aggressive confrontation would ensue before a private audience.

Siepmann and Durr had prepared for the fight. Pegging their opponents as a "tough lawyer and an unscrupulous journalist," they arranged to "conspire and compare notes" and make "complementing statements" to "divide the field."[129] According to the plan, Durr would dispute industry's charge that the FCC infringed upon broadcasters' rights, arguing that freedom of speech would remain as long as "the courts are still sitting" and the people "have safeguards against government encroachments, under the express language of the Communications Act, as well as of the First Amendment." They acknowledged "subtle but nevertheless very real problems" in combating their opponents' rhetoric, which they referred to as the "deliberate creation of emotional blockages against the penetration of facts." Durr anticipated their oft-repeated red herrings: "the cry of 'Americanism' and 'free enterprise' which have by now become somewhat threadbare and less effective than the cry 'communistic,'

---

[125] Ibid.
[126] Tullos and Waid, "Clifford Durr: The FCC Years," 8.
[127] Speech delivered at the 25th annual NAB convention in Atlantic City, NJ, September 17, 1947.
[128] For an in-depth chronicle of these battles, see Robert McChesney, "Louis G. Caldwell, the American Bar Association and the Debate over the Free Speech Implications of Broadcast Regulation, 1928–1938," *American Journal of Legal History* 35, no. 4 (October 1991): 351–92. See also McChesney, *Telecommunications, Mass Media and Democracy*, 130–9.
[129] Siepmann to Durr, December 27, 1946, Box 31, Folder 1, CJDP.

which should be worn out by now but is still used to pretty dangerous ends. 'Siepmann is a foreigner' is another."[130]

The debate was lively.[131] The Blue Book partisans seemed to come out ahead, but their opponents accused the organizers of setting them up because the students in the audience were Blue Book sympathizers. Although he admitted to being thankful that their opponents "drew most of the fire from the audience,"[132] Durr felt compelled to debunk systematically what he called the "we wuz framed" argument. Richards had accused the FCC of "usurping power Congress had never given it" and thus practicing "the well-known technique of 'cessation and gradualism,'" and "driving in the entering wedge for communism." Siepmann responded in "dignified" but "somewhat sharp terms," Durr recounted, adding that the audience was "more impressed by Mr. Siepmann's reply than by Mr. Richards' oratory." But he insisted this was not evidence of a setup, especially since Durr and Siepmann, unlike their opponents, were never alone with the students prior to the panel. Rather, it resulted from having a sophisticated, well-informed audience unsusceptible to red-baiting. The crowd reportedly emitted "what used to be referred to as a 'Bronx cheer'" in response to Caldwell's claim that regulatory oversight was unnecessary because the first applicant "invariably proved to be the better broadcaster." "I am sure," Durr allowed, "their remarks would have been well received at any gathering of the NAB. Unfortunately, the training to which Law School students are submitted makes them unappreciative of Mr. Caldwell's and Mr. Richards' particular type of offerings, excellent as they may have been for other occasions and other audiences."[133]

Beyond these isolated victories, moments of hope punctuated what otherwise was a gradual retreat from structural radio reform. Durr's ally Robert Stephan reported back from a broadcasters' gathering that Durr's name had come up repeatedly during arguments "concerning what is commonly known in radio circles as 'public service,'" causing "hurry and the scurry about the offices."[134] Durr and his allies also saw some hopeful signs in educational and religious radio, which even the NAB president, Miller, purported to accept.[135] Impressed with Everett Parker's fellow religious radio reformers, Durr speculated that

---

[130] Durr to Siepmann, January 3, 1947, Box 31, Folder 2, CJDP.
[131] John Lindsay to Clifford Durr, January 11, 1947, Box 31, Folder 2, CJDP.
[132] Durr to Lindsay, January 14, 1947, Box 31, Folder 2, CJDP.
[133] Inter-Office Memorandum, January 22, 1947, Box 31, Folder 2, CJDP. Durr also corrected Richards that the Blue Book's policy statements "were not new ones, as practically every principle laid down in the Blue Book had been expressed previously by the Commission or the Radio Commission in decisions made in individual cases, or else had been taken from statements made before Congressional Committees by members of the industry themselves or by members of the Commission."
[134] Robert Stephan to Clifford Durr, undated, Box 31, Folder 2, CJDP.
[135] Justin Miller to Clifford Durr, September 24, 1947; Durr to Miller, September 25, 1947, Box 31, Folder 5, CJDP. The two adversaries agreed for Miller to publish the exchange in the NAB's weekly reports.

"maybe a few years from now they will be able to accomplish some of the things you and I have been working for."[136] A progressive broadcaster enthused about a recently established New York City–based religious station: "In all of the defeats which the progressives of this country are now suffering, your victory with the Methodist Church is one that sings out like Gabriel's Horn. How you managed to do this sounds like a miracle from where I sit."[137] Despite "plenty of thunder clouds and storms lately," an educational broadcaster wrote, "the sun shines through occasionally, and here in Wisconsin we're feeling very hopeful and downright optimistic about the future of educational broadcasting."[138] Another positive development was the launch of the Madison-based educational station WHA-FM, the first such FM station in Wisconsin. Around three thousand people attended its opening festivities, and Durr wired a statement that WHA's historic public service mission set "an example which I hope will soon be followed by educational institutions throughout the nation."[139]

In March 1947, Durr received a prestigious award from *Variety*, described in the congressional record as the "most influential publication in the entertainment industry."[140] The tribute praised Durr for being "one of the few Commissioners" in FCC history who, unlike "lawyers and engineers," insisted that the "decisive criterion of radio service is not primarily the coverage pattern, the balance sheet … but what comes out of the loudspeaker: the program." Refusing "to corrode the foundations of a truly free and unmonopolized radio," *Variety* continued, the "Great Dissenter" stated his position "publicly and in lucid terms, stumping the country from end to end to preach the gospel of democracy in radio" as the "guardian of the American people's stake in the air they nominally own."[141] Many friends and allies congratulated Durr, including Harold Engel, the president of the National Association of Educational Broadcasters. Encouraged by the recent high-profile media criticism in the likes of the *Fortune* article "Revolt against Radio," Engel wrote, "The light is beginning to shine through."[142]

The Battle in Congress and the Courts

These encouraging signs notwithstanding, the FCC never received the congressional and judicial support necessary to enact its progressive agenda. In the months following the Blue Book's release, congressional intervention on the

---

[136] Clifford Durr to Everett Parker, April 30, 1947, Box 31, Folder 3, CJDP.

[137] Ira Hirschmann to Clifford Durr, November 7, 1947, Box 31, Folder 6, CJDP.

[138] H. B. McCarty to Clifford Durr, July 26, 1947, Box 31, Folder 4, CJDP. Durr later noted to McCarty, "About all I have done is take back to the Commission a little of what you old-timers in educational radio have poured into me from time to time." Durr to McCarty, November 5, 1947, Box 31, Folder 6, CJDP.

[139] McCarty to Durr, April 5, 1947; Durr to Harold Engel, March 28, 1947, Box 31, Folder 3, CJDP.

[140] Congressional Record, Tribute to Commissioner Durr, March 21, 1947.

[141] *Variety*, March 12, 1947.

[142] Harold Engel to Clifford Durr, March 14, 1947, Box 31, Folder 3, CJDP.

FCC's behalf seemed increasingly unlikely. The rightward shift in the political landscape had cleared out or silenced many potential liberal allies, and the FCC was under increased scrutiny from a hostile Congress and other quarters. Nonetheless, in a letter to an ally, Durr seemed unfazed that "*Broadcasting* magazine is making some dire threats about Congressional investigations of the FCC." If such public exposure were to happen, he noted with sarcasm, "broadcasters will be very enthusiastic about Congressional hearings on the subject of the Blue Book."[143] In truth, they probably preferred to let the Blue Book die quietly rather than risk more public debate on its merits.

While most congressional activity at this time did not defy broadcasters' interests, noteworthy exceptions arose, such as the criticism leveled by the powerful Interstate Commerce Committee chairman, the Republican senator Wallace White. White, a veteran of radio policy battles, had made previous attempts to rein in the broadcast industry and did not fear its ire. He said of the Blue Book, "Generally, I approve it."[144] On the verge of retirement, he drafted what became known – because of the Republican representative Charles Wolverton's companion bill in the House – as the White-Wolverton Bill, which sought clearer regulatory guidelines for the FCC and more constraints on broadcasters. An ideological hybrid, the White-Wolverton Bill called for limiting the FCC's discretionary authority by preventing "discrimination" in granting licenses, but it also adopted specific Blue Book provisions by granting the FCC ultimate authority in examining any station's overall public service performance. The bill also proscribed the FCC from preventing newspapers from owning radio stations, a stipulation unpalatable to most anti-monopoly liberals. White campaigned aggressively, declaring on the Senate floor that the bill was "the result of more than seven years of congressional investigations, studies, and hearings by committees in both houses of Congress."[145]

Broadcasters' hostility toward any affirmative standard for radio programming was on full display during the bill's hearings. The NAB, CBS, and MBS were represented, respectively, by Judge Justin Miller, Frank Stanton, and Edward Kobak. A composite picture of the broadcast industry's positions was reflected in their comments regarding regulatory attempts to establish programming guidelines.[146] Predictably, Miller claimed that granting the FCC any regulatory authority over programming amounted to a gross abridgment of the First Amendment.[147] Arguing that the FCC should be limited to maintaining

[143] Clifford Durr to H. B. McCarty, Jan 28, 1947, Box 31, Folder 2, CJDP.
[144] R. K. Richards, "Freedom of Air at Stake, Solons Declare," *Broadcasting*, March 18, 1946, 15, 101–2.
[145] Congressional Record, vol. 93, 80th Congress, 1st Session, 5707.
[146] See Herbert Rosenberg, "Program Content: A Criterion of Public Interest in FCC Licensing," *The Western Political Quarterly* 2, no. 3 (1949): 375–401.
[147] U.S. Congress, Senate, A Bill to Amend the Communications Act of 1934, Hearings before a Sub-committee of the Committee on Interstate and Foreign Commerce, U.S. Senate, 80th Congress, 1st session on S. Bill 1333, June 17–20, 23–5, 27, 194 (Washington, DC, Government Printing Office, 1947).

technical standards, the industry representatives maintained that the agency should hold no authority whatsoever over content.[148]

Ultimately, the bill dissatisfied both media reformers and the broadcast industry. Left-wing groups such as the Voice of Freedom Committee contested the bill, but broadcasters had more to lose from its passing.[149] Industry benefited from keeping FCC powers ambiguous; vague rules and public interest standards helped maintain a weak FCC, vulnerable to automatic contestation whenever it intervened on the public's behalf. If even the curtailed powers suggested in the White-Wolverton Bill were clearly defined, broadcasters could face a serious regulatory mandate, albeit a minimal one. With costs outweighing benefits, broadcasters fought aggressively to maintain the status quo. In typical fashion, industry representatives employed overblown rhetoric – the NBC president, Trammell, likened the bill to Nazi censorship – and intense opposition helped kill the bill. Although the powerful Committee on Interstate and Foreign Commerce recommended its passage in June 1948, it never received a vote in either the full House or Senate and was soon forgotten.[150]

The Blue Book fared little better in the government's judicial branch. Although it passed muster in the courts, it never went to trial as a high-profile case as did the earlier NBC decision. In *Bay State Beacon, Inc. v. FCC,* the Court of Appeals found that the Blue Book did not violate the Communications Act's prohibition against censorship.[151] Another court case that tested the Blue Book's viability dealt with the FCC's refusal to license a broadcaster who openly refused to provide local programming. In denying the broadcaster, the FCC stated: "Such a program policy which makes no effort whatsoever to tailor the programs offered by the national network organization to the particular needs of the community served does not meet the public service responsibilities of a radio broadcast licensee." The FCC's decision was appealed to the DC Court of Appeals, where it was upheld largely on the basis of Justice Felix Frankfurter's earlier decision in the NBC case that set a precedent for the FCC to use affirmative programming criteria in its decisions.[152] But these court decisions came down too late to have a major impact on Blue Book–related debates. Without significant congressional or judicial assistance, the Blue Book and its progressive promise – a national broadcast policy that would put radio

[148] Rosenberg, "Program Content," 395.

[149] Konecky, *The American Communications Conspiracy,* 110; Robert Sears McMahon, "Federal Regulation and Television Broadcast Industry in the United States, 1927–1959" (Ph.D. dissertation, Ohio State University, 1959), 146–50.

[150] Socolow, "To Network a Nation," 298–300; Horwitz, *The Irony of Regulatory Reform,* 164–5; Rosenberg, "Program Content," 394–6.

[151] 171 F. 2nd 826, DC Cir. 1948.

[152] *Simmons v. FCC,* 169 F. 2d 670 (1948). This case is discussed in Rosenberg, "Program Content," 393. See also, "FCC Decision on Lack of Local Programming Tacitly Upheld," *Broadcasting,* October 25, 1948; and "U.S. Supreme Court Backs FCC 'Program Contest' Power vs. WADC," *Variety,* October 20, 1948.

under some local control and unhook its programming from the sole imperative of profit – were doomed.

The Blue Book's Defeat

As the months ticked by, the Blue Book became increasingly invalidated. Plans
to hold hearings on broadcasters who failed Blue Book criteria were dropped.
The broadcast industry's assaults forced the inexperienced chairman Denny to
stall and then backtrack on the Blue Book's principles. By applying constant
political pressure, commercial broadcasters calculated that they could weather
the storm, which largely subsided by the end of 1947.[153] Whereas Durr and Fly
fended off conservative attacks in the early 1940s, the FCC's position by the
late 1940s had considerably weakened. J. Edgar Hoover frequently harassed
the FCC,[154] and Durr was often isolated in his unyielding defense of civil liberties, unsupported by even the remaining progressive members.[155] In April
1947, Durr gave a series of speeches lambasting his colleagues for shirking
their duty to uphold the public interest.[156] Later that year Denny left the FCC
to become a vice president and general counsel of NBC – a move indicative of
the oft-lamented "revolving door" between industry and the agencies charged
with regulating it.

Perhaps irrationally, the original Blue Book authors clung to some hope.
Although he felt the Blue Book had "aroused the industry to fury but largely
escaped the attention of the listening public," Siepmann still envisioned its
reincarnation in other forms. In 1948, he authored a pamphlet for the Jewish
Anti-Defamation League describing the Blue Book as "a first, partial draft of
a listener's Bill of Rights." He suggested that listeners shared responsibility
with the FCC in protecting the Blue Book's principles. Since the FCC's purpose
exceeds mere "wavelength allocation" also to "hold radio to its contract, to prevent extreme abuses and to fight a rearguard action for the listener," Siepmann
saw the FCC as "a court of appeal" for listeners' complaints, there to "support
the unorganized listening public in its uneven struggle with an organized and
powerful industry."[157] By 1950, however, Siepmann conceded that "neither the
letter nor the spirit of its regulatory decisions has been honored by action on
the FCC's part in its license-renewal policy," allowing industry to consider it
a dead letter.[158] Such disappointments seemed to answer a prescient question

---

[153] Socolow, "To Network a Nation," 300.
[154] See Erik Barnouw, "Blacklisted: How FCC Commissioner Clifford Durr Earned His Place on
the Cold War's Roll of Honor," *Television Quarterly* 28 (1996): 60–6.
[155] Susan Brinson, *The Red Scare, Politics, and the FCC, 1941–1960* (Westport, CT: Praeger,
2004).
[156] R. Crater, "Durr Charges Colleagues with Laxity," *Broadcasting*, April 21, 1947, 13, 90.
[157] Siepmann, *Listeners' Bill of Rights*, 10–11.
[158] Siepmann, *Radio, Television and Society* (New York: Oxford University Press, 1950), 37, 336.
Quoted in Meyer, "Reaction to the Blue Book," 309–10.

posed several years earlier by a prominent media reformer: "Will the Blue Book become the basis upon which future station grants will be made? Or will it merely become another praise-worthy addition to the National Archives?"[159]

The Blue Book's Legacy

The Blue Book campaign was not entirely stillborn. It inspired other reports, including the Hutchins Commission's critical analysis of American radio, for which the commission interviewed Clifford Durr and Larry Fly and closely studied the Blue Book to draw its own conclusions. But the Blue Book had relatively little impact on those it was supposed to influence the most: commercial broadcasters. Anecdotally, the broadcast industry responded to the Blue Book by making more of an effort to comply with the public's and the FCC's expectations.[160] The CBS research director conceded that the Blue Book was resented by the radio industry but added, "Any fair-minded person in the industry must also admit, however, that it had a very marked effect on broadcasting practices, and has stimulated certain reforms which are still in the process of maturing."[161]

Even if the Blue Book's reforms were never given a chance to mature and only briefly prompted broadcasters to become more socially responsible, they did have some ripple effects on media policy. The media historians Robert Hilliard and Michael Keith have suggested that the Blue Book and other progressive policy initiatives such as the earlier chain broadcasting rules led, at least indirectly, to an increase in small stations.[162] Another leading broadcast historian has argued that the Blue Book had a significant impact on subsequent policy debates – just not in the United States. According to Michele Hilmes, it influenced the high-profile Beveridge report on British broadcasting, which helped solidify the BBC's social mission.[163] Similarly, a CBC report comparing Canadian broadcasting's strengths and weaknesses to those of the BBC and American models credited the Blue Book report as the "reason for the American networks' increasing awareness of their public service obligations."[164]

Evidence supporting such causal connections is suggested in letters to Durr from incumbent broadcasters and new applicants professing their adherence to

[159] Jerome Spingarn, *Radio Is Yours* (New York: Public Affairs Committee, 1946), 31.

[160] Horwitz, *The Irony of Regulatory Reform*; Sterling and Kittross, *Stay Tuned*, 305.

[161] E. Wilson to Coleman Griffith, 1948, Box 16-1, Folder 1-1, Smythe Papers.

[162] Robert Hilliard and Michael Keith, *The Quieted Voice: The Rise and Demise of Localism in American Radio* (Carbondale: Southern Illinois University Press, 2005), 53; see also Susan Douglas, *Listening In: Radio and the American Imagination, from Amos 'n' Andy and Edward R. Murrow to Wolfman Jack and Howard Stern* (New York: Times Books, 1999), 124–5.

[163] Michele Hilmes, *Network Nations: A Transnational History of British and American Broadcasting* (New York: Routledge, 2011), 181–6.

[164] "CBC 10th Anniversary Radio Talks," 1946, 2, Box 30, Folder 8, CJDP.

the Blue Book.[165] Matthew Ehrlich has argued that the Blue Book also helped usher in a golden era of radio documentary.[166] Even Siepmann suggested in an analysis of network coverage of the documentary "To Secure These Rights" that a proliferation of such programming in the late 1940s was a "partial answer" to FCC's insistence that "radio devote more and better time to programs in the public interest."[167] Supporting this view are the words of the late radio icon Norman Corwin, who made the surprising claim in a phone interview that he "owes his career to the Blue Book" because it encouraged CBS "to include more culture in its programming." Corwin maintained that the "Blue Book had an immense effect on broadcasting," lamenting that such public interest protections have been increasingly "lessened over the years by an impoverished FCC" that is anything but a "model of liberalism." Observing that many of the same problems of postwar broadcasting persist today, in 2008 he advocated an even "broader edition of the Blue Book."[168] On a similar note, Everett Parker suggested during a phone interview that activism around the Blue Book helped establish a postwar media reform tradition, especially as an educational tool for diverse communities, that provided the foundation for policy victories in later decades.[169]

While the Blue Book was not a radical tract, its implications were bold. It staged nothing less than a full frontal attack on what has since come to be seen as inevitable, natural, and benign: a largely self-regulated commercial media system. A *Broadcasting* editorial titled "Self-Regulation Means Self-Preservation" reflected these fears, stating that "We contend it is none of the Commission's business whether radio is commercial, too commercial, quasi-commercial or pseudo-commercial. We contend the Blue Book is a travesty."[170] Ultimately, however, the commercial broadcasters' fears were not borne out. Both the Blue Book's immediate and long-term impacts were relatively minor, largely because it never reached the level of enforceable policy. And unlike contemporaneous policy initiatives like the Hutchins Commission and the Fairness Doctrine, the Blue Book did not ignite an enduring conversation that continues to reverberate through contemporary policy discourse. Although license renewal forms were recalibrated to comply with the Blue Book, the FCC neither formally adopted its prescriptions nor repudiated them. Most tellingly, not a single station was ever closed for violating the Blue Book. In short, the ethic of industry self-regulation prevailed over governmental intervention.

[165] See, for example, W. Partlow to Clifford Durr, September 16, 1946. Box 30, Folder 8, CJDP.
[166] Matthew Ehrlich, "Radio Utopia: Promoting Public Interest in a 1940s Radio Documentary," *Journalism Studies* 9, no. 6 (2008): 859–73.
[167] Charles Siepmann and Sidney Reisberg, "'To Secure These Rights': Coverage of a Radio Documentary," *Public Opinion Quarterly* (Winter 1948–9): 650.
[168] Norman Corwin interview with the author, December 11, 2008.
[169] Everett Parker interview with the author, December 23, 2008.
[170] "Self-Regulation Means Self-Preservation," *Broadcasting*, September 22, 1947, 14.

These policy decisions for radio were transferred to early television, defining it as a lightly regulated medium with even fewer public interest safeguards.[171] Had the Blue Book been implemented, much of the U.S. media system might look very different today. But from the moment the Blue Book was issued, broadcast industry leaders and their political allies viciously attacked it and successfully red-baited its authors for undermining "free radio." By 1948, with the Blue Book all but dead, broadcasters already were gearing up for their next target: defeating the FCC's ban on broadcasters' political editorializing, a rule established by Chairman Fly earlier in the decade. As this next conflict took shape, progressive policy reformers like Durr and engaged members of the public would play an instrumental role in ongoing debates over broadcasters' public service responsibilities – debates that would culminate by the decade's end with the controversial Fairness Doctrine, which we turn to in the next chapter.

[171] Stamm, *Sound Business*, 188.

4

The Origins of the Fairness Doctrine

Barely a year had passed since the Blue Book controversy when similar conflicts over public interest regulation reemerged. This round of contentious debates centered on whether to repeal the Mayflower Doctrine,[1] which prohibited broadcasters' political editorializing. Broadcasters' growing political power emboldened them to challenge the Larry Fly era FCC decision, which would spark the last major radio reform battle in the 1940s. Fearing a further commercialized, conservative-biased, and corporate-dominated medium should broadcasters gain the right to editorialize, many progressives saw at stake, as one news article put it, "the future of radio as an instrument of service to the people."[2] Reformers marshaled considerable support from the still-intact coalitions from the Blue Book debates to rally for the Mayflower Decision's preservation. Similar to those debates, broadcasters attacked the reformers' position with First Amendment arguments that aimed to delegitimate the FCC's regulatory authority over programming.

This episode involved a number of ironies. Most notably, the controversial rule that later became known as the Fairness Doctrine – which to this day is often invoked by progressives as the high-water mark for enlightened media policy – actually came about as a kind of consolation prize for postwar liberals who were advocating stricter regulation. The following chapter recovers this forgotten history. In doing so, it lays bare a number of early tensions and contradictions that closed out a decade of contentious policy debates around normative understandings of media's democratic role. This history throws into sharp relief several significant parallels and connections to twenty-first-century

---

[1] Depending somewhat on the context, it was variously referred to in the policy literature as the Mayflower Doctrine, Mayflower Rule, and Mayflower Decision.

[2] "Hold Hearings on Radio Question," *The Cooperative Consumer*, March 16, 1948, Docket no. 8516, Box 3383, Federal Communications Commission Docket Section, FCC Archives.

media challenges, particularly around the question of whether government has any affirmative regulatory authority over media.

A Gathering Storm

Toward the end of the 1940s, progressive forces were in disarray. The remains of the Popular Front, including many New Deal liberals, were largely disintegrated, especially after the Progressive Party's disastrous loss in the 1948 election. What had been a rising social democratic challenge was now widely seen as dangerously socialistic, even in its diminished state. With a communist witch hunt in full swing, the broadcast industry exploited Cold War politics to discredit reformers by claiming that their real agenda was to destroy free radio. J. Edgar Hoover harassed the FCC on a regular basis with letters and unsolicited reports on "subversive" broadcasters, and the FCC's actions were aggressively scrutinized as Congress and the FBI put the commission on notice for a number of unofficial investigations. Writing to Larry Fly about the endless red-baiting, Clifford Durr confided, "When I read of the present plans to protect the country against the dangerous thinking of us bureaucrats, I am inclined to look back with nostalgia to the days when the Commission stood more or less firmly against our friend J. Edgar."[3] By the late 1940s, the FCC's more progressive wing aside from Durr became more passive on issues related to regulatory oversight of broadcast programming. The tide clearly had turned in commercial broadcasters' favor.

Rendering the landscape even less hospitable for media reform, the industry attacks against the FCC coincided with an increasingly right-wing tilt in DC politics. Even before the 1948 presidential election, liberals were in various stages of retreat: FDR had died, the New Deal agenda lay in tatters, and Republicans were coming off a congressional sweep in the 1946 midterm elections. The Democrats would regain some ground electorally by taking back Congress in 1948, but the ideological shift was more permanent. During his campaign, President Truman characterized 1948 as a decisive "Year of Challenge," with the primary choice "between a parcel labeled progressive liberalism and a parcel labeled reactionary conservatism."[4] However, Truman's liberalism often proved to be largely rhetorical. After he eked out a victory in a four-way race, his administration quickly shied away from the previous administration's aggressive liberalism, ever mindful of southern conservative Democrats and Republicans nipping at his right flank.

Truman's market-friendly orientation led him to espouse commercial broadcasters' policy positions. Invoking his support for the "American system" of

---

[3] Clifford Durr to Larry Fly, August 15, 1947, Box 31, Folder 5, CJDP.
[4] Harry Truman, "A Year of Challenge: Liberalism or Conservatism," Delivered at Jefferson-Jackson Day dinner, Washington, DC, February 19, 1948. Printed in *Vital Speeches of the Day* XIV, no. 10 (March 1, 1948).

broadcasting, he insisted in an open letter to *Broadcasting*'s Sol Taishoff that "America, as the birthplace of radio, should have a free, competitive system, unfettered by artificial barriers and regulated only as to the laws of nature and the limitation of facilities." Deferring to the laws of the market, he argued, is "preferred over rigid Government regulation of a medium that by its very nature must be maintained as free as the press." The same issue of *Broadcasting* contained an editorial amplifying Truman's message to the FCC that regulation was off the table.[5] A similar statement followed ten months later, with *Broadcasting* triumphantly announcing that Truman "emphatically reaffirmed his belief in a completely free radio," which, according to the editors, translated to a "declaration on behalf of a broadcasting system unshackled by un-American controls."[6]

At the same time, the FCC was losing most of its progressives, including Commissioner Ray Wakefield, who was not reappointed when his term expired. Initially, President Truman had nominated him for another six-year term, but after a Senate subcommittee began investigating Wakefield's political affiliations, Truman suddenly withdrew the nomination without any explanation.[7] For many reformers, the withdrawal of Wakefield's reappointment came as a dispiriting shock. His departure from the FCC would particularly hurt the cause of educational broadcasting, prompting one reformer to write that he was "stirred up and fighting mad."[8] Durr expressed his dismay to a trusted ally: "[Wakefield] has been a good honest public servant and not particularly controversial. It would make more sense if it had happened to me."[9] Wakefield, who committed suicide two years later, had been treated "outrageously," only strengthening Durr's inclination to leave the FCC the following year when his term was up for renewal.[10] Durr could not bear seven more years of constant tension, describing to a fellow reformer "a sense of complete frustration," and he predicted even darker times ahead. "I have a suspicion that before my present term is up, I shall have got myself in even more trouble," Durr confided, because much is "going on around here that I don't like, and I am afraid I shall find myself unable to resist the temptation to say so."[11]

---

[5] Harry Truman, "In Support of Broadcasting," *Broadcasting*, July 9, 1945, 15 and "Truman's Radio Credo," *Broadcasting*, July 9, 1945, 46.

[6] J. F. Beatty, "Truman Reaffirms Stand on Free Radio," *Broadcasting*, May 13, 1946, 15–16.

[7] Gerald Flannery, *Commissioners of the FCC* (Lanham, MD: University Press of America, 1995), 64. According to *Billboard*, the hastily withdrawn nomination resulted from a GOP-led backlash because Wakefield was not a "genuine Republican." The article predicted Durr would also "face a hostile barrage from GOP senators" should he be renominated. "Durr Next on GOP Hatchet List? Jones Sure of OK," *Billboard*, June 28, 1947, p. 5.

[8] Harold Engel to Clifford Durr, July 1, 1947, Box 31, Folder 4, CJDP.

[9] Clifford Durr to Harold McCarty, July 1, 1947, Box 31, Folder 4, CJDP.

[10] Clifford Durr to Harold Engel, June 25, 1947, Box 31, Folder 4, CJDP.

[11] Clifford Durr to Harold B. McCarty, August 29, 1947, Box 31, Folder 5, CJDP.

Amid ominous signs, Durr took some solace in the fact that Commissioner Paul Walker was appointed as acting chairman and another vacancy on the commission was filled by Wayne Coy, a Democrat who leaned progressive on some policy issues and would soon become the FCC chair.[12] Despite these small consolations, Durr was increasingly isolated on the commission, particularly in his fight against the loyalty order.

The Final Days of Durr the Dissenter

In the final months of his FCC tenure, Durr fought two major battles. The extensive Mayflower hearings on broadcast editorializing conducted throughout 1948 would take up much of his and other media reformers' energies for the rest of the decade. Durr's other major battle focused on a more overarching question of civil liberties, one that would color much of the American political landscape. An immediate sea change occurred in DC after President Truman responded to growing fears of communist infiltration by signing the 1947 executive order institutionalizing a loyalty program. This program encouraged background checks – and, in turn, blacklists – of individuals suspected of associating with political parties that advocated violent revolution. Within a broader "Red Scare," it helped create a guilty-until-proven-innocent atmosphere, and harmed the careers and livelihoods of innocent people, especially liberal-leaning public employees and progressive activists. Consequently, Durr found himself drawn into yet another fight over democratic freedoms – one that would continue into his post-FCC activism.

In 1947 Durr gave two high-profile speeches on civil liberties. The first was presented in New York to the Associated Church Press on the executive order's dangerous impact,[13] which the *Chicago Sun* described as "a member of President Truman's administration [raising] a grave and serious challenge to the White House executive order directing a sweeping purge of disloyal employees in the federal government."[14] In a second speech, Durr warned that after the Hollywood House Un-American Activities Committee (HUAC) trials, which many viewed as part of a larger witch hunt to root out progressives, "radio would be the next victim, perhaps followed by the schools and universities." Shortly thereafter he explained in a letter to the leading civil liberties scholar Thomas Emerson that "the Un-American Committee proceedings were the less dangerous part of the program." Rather, the "secret reports of the military security agencies and the FBI were far more dangerous," Durr argued,

[12] Durr to McCarty, November 10, 1947, Box 31, Folder 6, CJDP. Durr observed that Commissioner Coy was "taking hold of things in a very intelligent way." Under his chairmanship, Durr believed, "we shall make progress in the right direction." Clifford Durr to Ray Wakefield, March 29, 1948, Box 31, Folder 7, CJDP.
[13] William Ming to Clifford Durr, April 23, 1947, Box 31, Folder 3, CJDP.
[14] Clipping from "Inside Washington," April 1947, Box 31, Folder 3, CJDP.

"because the victims never knew what they were charged with and had no opportunity to answer."[15] In response to his charge that the FBI was furnishing the FCC with "unsolicited reports on private individuals connected with radio," the talk was greeted with, in Durr's words, "fireworks." The FBI would not fully let up on its reprisals against Durr until the mid-1960s.[16]

Despite mostly silence from the few remaining liberals in places of power, civil libertarians rallied to Durr's cause, telling the story of an often-silent constituency. One letter representative of dozens stated: "I admire your stand ... and only wish there were more people around wise enough to resist Gestapo tactics in all forms and at all levels of our society."[17] Another letter writer thanking Durr for his "courageous and forceful stand against [FBI] snooping" remarked how it was "horrible to realize" that so soon after FDR's passing America would suffer from "forces of neo-Fascism."[18] After reading Durr's speech, Supreme Court Justice Frankfurter wrote him a long letter, capturing this dark moment in American history:

Doubtless you know many people who in their heart of hearts echo your concern over the way which loyalty to our country is sought to be vindicated. Not the least undesirable aspect of the temper of our time is that they fail to express their sentiments ... [for] fear of being smeared by current discrediting slogans. Even one who has the deep convictions that I have about the duty of members of this Court to observe the austerest standards of abstention from political affairs, both in public and in private, would feel self-enslaved not to send you a word of appreciation for your courage and wisdom – your wisdom in appealing to the traditional articles of the American faith and your courage avowing them.[19]

Not all letters were so kind. One listener chided Durr's displeasure with radio stations for their failure to follow the "infamous Blue Book." "So who are you to tell what should be broadcast and what should not?" the listener asked. "I presume you would like all stations to devote their time to CIO-PAC broadcasts." The letter concluded, "I suspect that you are a communist and therefore should resign from the Commission."[20] Despite the increasingly toxic atmosphere within and outside DC, Durr continued his activism, believing that constitutional freedoms were at stake.

Meanwhile, in the view of many progressives, radio continued to become more reactionary. An article by George Seldes, which opened with the line "The big American radio networks are selling their freedom for a pot of advertising gold," provided some statistics on radio's increasing conservatism. Seldes commissioned a survey that found that only three liberal

[15] Clifford Durr to Thomas Emerson, December 8, 1947, Box 31, Folder 6, CJDP.
[16] Ibid.; Salmond, *The Conscience of a Lawyer*, 113–21.
[17] Elizabeth Patton to Clifford Durr, December 10, 1947, Box 31, Folder 6, CJDP.
[18] Elliott Dexter to Clifford Durr, December 29, 1947, Box 31, Folder 6, CJDP.
[19] Felix Frankfurter to Clifford Durr, December 31, 1947, Box 31 Folder 6, CJDP.
[20] Leah McClelland to Clifford Durr, 1947, Box 31, Folder 3, CJDP.

national radio commentators remained after a dozen had been removed from the airwaves, while seven "arch reactionaries" commanded a combined audience of 31 million listeners, with millions more listening to self-described conservative commentators. According to FCC data, more than half of all radio stations were newspaper owned and advertising was dominated by four firms. Seldes described this as a "quiet coup d'état which enabled the most reactionary big business circles to capture control of this important public opinion molding media."

Seldes noted that broadcasters were aiming to expand their power on two fronts. One was renewing pressure on the FCC to permit "perpetual licenses," and the other was to overturn the Mayflower Doctrine's ban on political editorializing. Seldes captured what many media reformers felt when he described the anti–Mayflower Doctrine campaign as "so much nonsense" because "through their hand-picked commentators" the businessmen who own and control radio already "editorialize to their heart's desire." "What the proposal actually means," according to Seldes, "is that owners will be able to dictate what goes on the air and what goes off without having to account to the FCC for bias, falsehood, distortions and smears."[21] In other words, more than a specific policy dispute, this confrontation was a fundamental power struggle over regulatory authority.

The Battle over the Mayflower Doctrine

The Mayflower Doctrine had since 1941 constrained broadcasters' political power to some degree by forbidding station owners to editorialize.[22] In the wake of the Blue Book's defeat, however, the no-editorializing rule fell under broadcasters' sights. Although this rule had been unassailable earlier in the decade when suspicion of corporate influence over media carried the day and the FCC could pass rules curtailing broadcasters' political power, the industry felt emboldened by its win over the Blue Book and saw the regulatory authority represented in the Mayflower Doctrine as ripe for what many would refer to today as "deregulation." Unsurprisingly, broadcasters framed the doctrine as an infringement on their First Amendment rights, best described as an appeal for a negative liberty (freedom *from* government intrusion). In contrast, many progressives sought to preserve the rule on the basis of a structural analysis of media power that entailed a First Amendment defined by a positive liberty (freedom *for* diverse media access). Despite some concessions to the latter, the former vision of the First Amendment would ultimately prevail.

---

[21] George Seldes, "Radio Nets Sell Out to Hucksters; Survey Lists 7 Reactionaries on 1724 Outlets, 31 Million Victims," *In Fact* XVI, no. 2 (October 13, 1947).

[22] For contemporary scholarly treatment of the Mayflower Doctrine, see the *Yale Law Journal* 2 (December 1947): 287–9.

The battle over the Mayflower Doctrine gave progressive media reformers both hope and pause: hope because of the intense public engagement around the issue of whether to allow broadcasters to editorialize, but also pause, since defeat was a distinct possibility and many reformers feared the consequences of commercial broadcasters' gaining yet more political power. With the recent and ongoing purge of liberal commentators from the airwaves, progressives had good reason to assume that any new freedom to editorialize would probably skew sharply to the right. For this and other reasons, most progressive groups campaigned against any relaxation of the ban on broadcasters' editorializing – including what would become the Fairness Doctrine.

A Move toward Fairness

A fairness criterion can be traced to earlier legislative doctrine such as the 1927 Federal Radio Commission's public interest standard. However, throughout much of the 1930s, a de facto libertarian ethos governed radio speech as radio programming largely accorded with broadcasters' commercial imperatives. Although disenfranchised groups had often decried bias, concerns about fairness and balance became more pronounced as fears of fascism spiked in the early years of World War II. Even the 1939 NAB code encouraged broadcasters to avoid overt politicking, and many stations adopted no-editorializing policies.[23]

In its 1941 Mayflower decision the FCC mandated that broadcasters must "provide full and equal opportunity for the presentation to the public of all sides of public issues" because "as one licensed to operate in a public domain, the licensee has assumed the obligation of presenting all sides of important public questions, fairly, objectively and without bias." The decision occurred during the renewal process for station WAAB, whose record indicated that several years earlier it had broadcasted the station owners' editorial views. In response, the FCC clarified its no-editorializing position: "Under the American system of broadcasting ... the limitations in frequencies inherent in the nature of radio, the public interest can never be served by a dedication of any broadcast facility to the support of his own partisan ends." While this "scarcity rationale" lay at the center of the FCC's policy position, the commission also worried that broadcasters could attack any person or idea at will without allowing the offended parties to reply. The FCC's Mayflower decision signaled to broadcasters that such practices were forbidden. Depending on ideas "fairly and objectively presented," a "truly free radio," the commission asserted, "cannot be used to advocate the causes of the licensees" or "to support the candidates of his friends ... [or] principles he happens to regard most favorably." "In brief," the FCC concluded, "the broadcaster cannot be advocate."[24]

23 Toro, "Standing Up for Listeners' Rights," 86.
24 Mayflower Broadcasting Corporation and the Yankee Network, Inc. (WAAB), *FCC Reports*, vol. 8, 1941, 339–41. As discussed earlier, the Supreme Court's decision in *National Broadcasting*

This arrangement presented challenges for the FCC. Policing whether radio programming was balanced or contained editorializing was a daunting task. Moreover, this criterion became important for evaluating broadcasters' performance only during license renewals. As Durr explained to a congressman who had complained about biased news, "the FCC traditionally assumed that balance is the broadcaster's responsibility, considered during license renewal evaluations only if its overall service indicates that the station has been used to promote the point of view of its operators to the exclusion of others."[25] It was "wholly unrealistic," Durr conceded, that all editorializing could be avoided by barring news commentators. "There is editorializing in the selection of the items of news which will be given or omitted in a straight news broadcast."[26] Ultimately, it was political reasons – not inherent difficulties in enforcing these content-related regulations – that led to broadcasters challenging the Mayflower Doctrine.

As early as mid-1946, rumors began circulating that the FCC was relenting in response to broadcasters' demands that the Mayflower Doctrine be reevaluated. This prompted a hastily scrawled note from the former FCC chairman Larry Fly to Durr: "What is this I read about your replacing the Mayflower decision? You scare me!"[27] While the other FCC commissioners' positions were questionable, Durr had actually stated on multiple occasions that he thought preserving the Mayflower Doctrine was of the utmost importance. Nonetheless, the FCC yielded to broadcasters' pressure, and hearings were scheduled for late 1948.

Early on, Durr sought the aid of Edward Heffron, the NAB's former public relations director and now, as the National Conference of Christians and Jews' media relations director, an industry critic. Heffron wrote a strong pro-Mayflower editorial, and Durr hoped Heffron's group, which emphatically favored preserving the rule, would be represented at the Mayflower hearing. Durr wanted progressive voices there to debate issues that were "about as important as any that has ever faced this Commission."[28] Heffron told Durr he was "nonplussed" that *Broadcasting* and two of the more conservative commissioners criticized public participation by calling the FCC's invitations to various constituencies an "unusual step." "Why shouldn't a body entrusted with power to regulate in the public interest, etc., use any lawful and aboveboard means of ascertaining the wishes of the public?" he asked. "Surely this is fairer than what usually happens in public radio hearings," Heffron noted, "when the industry

---

Co. *(NBC) v. United States* further cemented the FCC's regulatory power by determining that denying a broadcaster's license for failing public interest obligations did not infringe upon free speech. *National Broadcasting Co. (NBC) v. United States*, 319 U.S., 1943.

[25] Clifford Durr to Congressman Ellis Patterson, March 31, 1945, Box 30, Folder 3, CJDP.

[26] Ibid.

[27] Larry Fly to Clifford Durr, May 27, 1946, Box 30, Folder 6, CJDP.

[28] Clifford Durr to Edward Heffron, December 9, 1947, Box 31, Folder 6, CJDP.

is represented twenty deep and the poor public goes along oblivious ... that its interests are at stake."[29]

Saying that he was "sick of the self-serving semantics of the radio-as-free-as-the-press crowd,"[30] Heffron sent the FCC a statement roundly criticizing broadcasters' justification for self-regulation. Durr agreed: "'Self-regulation' inevitably ends up with regulation in the interests of the industry rather than the public." Even if the public initially receives industry concessions, Durr argued, "in the long run, the public is more likely to get lip service than protection." Broadcasters' unaccountable power was precisely why the idea of repealing the Mayflower Doctrine was so concerning. The "soundest idea uttered on a street corner, or even in a public auditorium," Durr noted, "can't hold its own against the most frivolous or vicious idea whispered into the microphone of a national network."[31]

Durr remained passionately engaged in these debates for the remainder of his FCC tenure. He described the Mayflower hearing to the former commissioner Ray Wakefield as the current "hot issue," with large numbers of public representatives turning out and offering "intelligent statements" indicating "a lot of hard thinking on the problem."[32] In Durr's view, it was "the most interesting hearing the Commission has held, and the most encouraging. For the first time, groups without personal axes to grind have appeared in numbers to express their views as members of the public."[33] After a week of testimony, the FCC adjourned the hearing until April 19, when, as Durr later described to Everett Parker, "Justin Miller move[d] into action with his big guns." But many public witnesses had yet to testify and Durr was "quite certain that everything won't go Justin's way." Durr marveled at witnessing for the first time radio production people "show[ing] up at a public hearing – writers, producers, musicians, and actors." Observing the high quality and quantity of public statements, Durr enthused, "Perhaps after all the people are beginning to wake up to the fact that the air is theirs."[34]

The Public Awakens

Leading up to and during the public hearings, an increasing number of organized constituencies engaged with the Mayflower debates. A wide range of progressives, including representatives from the American Jewish Committee,

---

[29] Heffron to Durr, December 18, 1947, Box 31, Folder 6, CJDP.
[30] Heffron to Durr, January 28, 1948, Box 31, Folder 7, CJDP. See also, Edward Heffron, "Should Radio Be as Free as the Press," *Commonwealth*, February 26, 1948.
[31] Durr to Heffron, Box 31, Folder 7, CJDP.
[32] Clifford Durr to Ray Wakefield, March 29, 1948, Box 31, Folder 7, CJDP.
[33] Clifford Durr to Rodriguez, March 18, 1948, Box 31, Folder 7, CJDP. Noting how impressed he was by nearly all of the statements' "careful thinking," Durr described his joy in entering Parker's statement into the record.
[34] Clifford Durr to Everett Parker, March 29, 1948, Box 31, Folder 7, CJDP.

the Lawyers Guild, and the CIO, would testify in defense of the Mayflower Doctrine. Hundreds of average listeners' letters came pouring in, as evidenced by the large volume of "Letters of Protest or Endorsement" in the National Archives. The great majority of them – by about a 3 to 1 ratio – were in favor of sustaining the Mayflower Doctrine.[35] While some simply asked that the doctrine be "upheld" or "retained," many others leveled structural critiques against an increasingly commercialized broadcast system and the dangerous power it wielded within a democratic society. These testimonies and letters to the FCC generally fell within three themes.

First, many critics feared that broadcasters' pro-business proclivities would be further amplified if they were given the political power to editorialize. One representative letter phrased it simply: "We cannot allow the air to be controlled by big business."[36] Similarly, others begged that the rule not be repealed because "big business must not control the air as it does the press,"[37] and Wall Street and the National Association of Manufacturers must not "control communications and inflict their poison without a chance to counteract it."[38] The anti-business critique held sway with various constituencies – ranging from social conservatives to remnants of the leftist Popular Front to apolitical citizens – who felt that corporations were rapidly gaining too much power in American society. The fear was exacerbated by the growing lack of any countervailing force as government's regulatory retreat became increasingly apparent.

Unions were especially attuned to this critique. A letter from the CIO Political Action Committee noted that labor groups were particularly sensitized to the "powerful role radio has played and will continue to play in political campaigns and in discussions of political matters which have a direct bearing on the welfare of the American people." The letter stated that for years labor had been "maligned by news commentators and analysts as the breeder of foreign ideology" and had been "met with consistent censorship." If the Mayflower Doctrine were removed, these problems might worsen. "I hesitate to think what would happen when the bars are lifted and a few men in key positions are given the power to beam their views to America's radio audience," the letter declared. By any calculus, "radio is a business, a big business, and as such is bound to represent that viewpoint."[39] Likewise, the Progressive Citizens of America wrote to support upholding the Mayflower Doctrine because given the current "biased distortion of news," presumably any new "editorial policy

[35] Brinson, *The Red Scare, Politics, and the Federal Communications Commission, 1941–1960*, 130.
[36] Mildred Baskin to the FCC, March 29, 1948, Docket no. 8516, Box 3381, FCC Archives.
[37] Tree Ogborn to the FCC, undated letter, Docket no. 8516, Box 3381, FCC Archives.
[38] J. McGowan to the FCC, undated letter, Docket no. 8516, Box 3381, FCC Archives.
[39] Jack Kroll to Wayne Coy, on behalf of the CIO Political Action Committee, March 5, 1948, Docket no. 8516, Box 3381, FCC Archives.

would be slanted in favor of the corporations who sponsor radio programs."[40] A fear of growing corporate power was reflected in scores of letters.

A second recurring theme was concern about ideological imbalance, especially given that most liberal commentators had recently been pushed off the air. One letter exemplified this concern: "The broadcasters are already limiting free speech by discharging liberal commentators. If they are given the freedom to editorialize only one side – their side – will ever be presented. The airwaves belong to all of us, and all of us must have the chance to hear both sides of any dispute."[41] A related argument was that radio programming was already biased and would only become worse without the Mayflower Doctrine. One representative letter noted that anyone listening to radio "must know how much editorializing is now taking place." Citing the preponderance of conservative-leaning commentators, the listener wondered, if even more editorializing were allowed, "how could we possibly bear it?"[42]

The leading figure of the Christian media reform coalition, Everett Parker, challenged the broadcasters' anti–Mayflower Doctrine arguments. Responding to the oft-repeated claim that broadcasters should enjoy the same freedoms as newspapers, he noted, "The situations are not analogous." Whereas newspapers were a "private enterprise," broadcast station licensees were "privileged to use a limited and fixed public facility." Given the medium's limitations, if the Mayflower Doctrine were repealed, listeners might not hear diverse views, especially "in communities which have only one radio station." The situation would become even more acute in communities where the sole station was owned by the local newspaper. In these cases the community would be "effectively limited to the reception of only one editorial viewpoint." In light of this "threat to democratic institutions," Parker concluded by underscoring how "the station operator is already receiving privileges of incalculable value from the public" and "exploiting a valuable public facility for his private gain." This arrangement made sense only if "he operates his station in the public interest" and not simply for the "furtherance of his private views," which would be "wholly unjustified." Finally, Parker doubted that "absentee station licensees or representatives of networks should be considered competent to editorialize on problems affecting the local community."[43]

A third major concern was the fear that radio might come to resemble newspapers in terms of perceived biases and misinformation. One listener wrote, "We get enough half-truths and untruths from newspaper editorials; we don't need them over the air too."[44] Another pleaded that the commissioners not let

[40] Thomas Flynn to the FCC, on behalf of Progressive Citizens of America, March 15, 1948, Docket no. 8516, Box 3381, FCC Archives.
[41] William Schoen to the FCC, March 17, 1948, Docket no. 8516, Box 3381, FCC Archives.
[42] Doris Bryant to the FCC, March 8, 1948, Docket no. 8516, Box 3381, FCC Archives.
[43] Everett Parker to the FCC, January 25, 1948, Docket no. 8516, Box 3381, FCC Archives.
[44] V. Ridmand to the FCC, March 20, 1948, Docket no. 8516, Box 3381, FCC Archives.

the NAB "gang up on the FCC and force a revision" of the doctrine, but rather ensure that radio "be kept free as possible ... for the benefit of the listening audience." "If one political faction [conservatives] is allowed to control the radio as they now do to the newspapers," then American democracy "is on its deathbed."[45] A Chicago AFL-affiliated union that recently had been barred from buying airtime for a short announcement on a CBS station put it bluntly: "Opponents of the policy laid down in the Mayflower Decision simply are seeking a perpetual open season on all progressive forces such as they now enjoy in the daily press."[46]

Many commentators urged the FCC not to cede so much power to broadcasters and lose regulatory authority over such an important medium. The FCC had no direct oversight over newspapers, and many feared the consequences if the agency were to lose such authority over broadcasters. Seeing this debate as part of a larger deregulatory trend that spoke to corporate ascendance throughout society, they offered a critique emphasizing that lofty democratic rhetoric notwithstanding, broadcasters' push was nothing more than a power grab. A *New York Post* editorial captured the growing fatigue with broadcasters' oft-uttered lament that their First Amendment rights were being violated. The column noted that broadcasters, as the "lucky possessors" of radio stations that were prohibitively expensive for most people and reliant on scarce public frequencies, already had tremendous power in deciding "what Americans shall hear when they gather around the family radio." "Since the dangers inherent in the misuse of this power could be great," the editorial continued, the FCC "has the job of watch-dogging [broadcasters'] activities in the interests of the people." The column averred that broadcasters had not lost freedom of speech under the Mayflower Decision, but rather lost "the license to turn our airwaves into propaganda agents." And the American people had gained the "freedom to hear," defined as having access to "all sides of public questions on all radio stations" – a positive freedom that is "integral to democracy."[47]

The Illinois Civil Rights Congress echoed many interest groups' concerns when it noted that the FCC was "being pressured by a number of groups to reconsider the Mayflower policy of impartiality." Its letter stated:

Nothing would be more tragic. Such a step would let loose a flood of libelous and distorted statements leading to violence against individuals and groups fighting to maintain the right of collective bargaining and freedom of assemblage. Already the trend toward such scurrilous attacks is deepening and radio stations are showing a tendency to yield to the pressure of Chambers of Commerce, the American Legion and such forces, and close the air to those who would answer these attacks.... The right of labor

---

[45] R. Tuttle to the FCC, February 26, 1948, Docket no. 8516, Box 3381, FCC Archives.

[46] John Cullerton to the FCC, April 1, 1948, Docket no. 8516, Box 3383, FCC Archives.

[47] "We Rule the Waves!" *New York Post*, April 1, 1948, Docket no. 8516, Box 3381, FCC Archives.

organizations, the Negro people, religious bodies and other minorities, so often sub-jected to oppression to use the air without discrimination, must be protected.

Quoting the Mayflower policy that "freedom of speech on the radio must be broad enough to provide full and equal opportunity for the presentation to the public of all sides of public issues," the letter urged that "the FCC will under no condition retreat" and will "hold inviolate the right of the people to speak freely."[48]

Many letter writers expressed concerns about biased commentary tak-ing over the airwaves if the unchecked power of a predominantly right-wing media were unleashed on the populace. A World War II veteran and University of Pennsylvania graduate student sent a handwritten letter that read, "Surely you must know that the vast majority of stations are owned or controlled by wealthy, ultra-conservative people and that the editorials will overwhelm-ingly reflect conservative opinion," disconnected from "the way the country votes." He insisted that "by no stretch of the imagination can this be regarded as in the public interest and you have therefore disregarded your sworn duty to the people." Citing Goebbels, the veteran argued that "propaganda is the power to kill."[49] Many writers invoked the recent specter of Nazism in their appeals to prevent broadcasters from having too much political power over the nation's discourse.

While letters to the FCC often reflected a fear of rising right-wing extrem-ism, occasionally pro-repeal letters not affiliated with the broadcast industry expressed a fear of left-wing extremism. One such letter writer saw the FCC's efforts to maintain the ban as part of a larger communist plot. He warned, "I have a list of 140 reds and 300 red front organizations, and I have been listening to Fulton Lewis, Jr. expose Communists in our State Department, therefore I can readily understand your attempt." Calling for the FCC to be abolished, he wondered how the commissioners could be so "foolish as to want to destroy our individual form of government which has given the most liberties, opportunities, and the highest living standards in the world."[50] In an unusual twist, a letter signed by several individuals describing themselves as "true Americans" derided the NAB's position as "communistic" and urged the FCC to allow broadcasters the freedom to editorialize only if all perspectives have "equal access."[51]

Indeed, not all who feared too much corporate control of radio thought the Mayflower Doctrine should be preserved; some gave voice to a third-way "fair-ness" position. For example, one letter from the Knights of Columbus, Council 786, based in San Antonio, argued that broadcasters *should* be allowed to

[48] Eleanor Salkind to the FCC, April 6, 1948, Box 31, Folder 8, CJDP.
[49] Howard Goldgraber to the FCC, June 2, 1949, Docket no. 8516, Box 3385, FCC Archives.
[50] J. Kirn to the FCC, undated letter, Docket no. 8516, Box 3381, FCC Archives.
[51] Tallulah Willson, Mathilda Ryckeley, and Doris Whitney to the FCC, February 20, 1948, Docket no. 8516, Box 3382, FCC Archives.

editorialize because otherwise the NAB had the "freedom" of "one-sided editorialization" that gave them the "liberty" to "gag and abuse those people who oppose them." The Knights urged the FCC to "make equal time available for a complete rebuttal."[52] Likewise, a petition taking this position asked that the FCC make "radio as free as the press" by according the NAB the power to editorialize "only on condition that they grant equal time for the presentation of the opposite point of view over their broadcasting facilities."[53] Numerous interest group letters reflected this position, like that submitted by the National Council of Catholic Women president, who thought repealing the ban was fine if fairness and balance could be assured.[54] Even some critics of repealing the Mayflower Decision thought that a content regulation mandating contrasting views was necessary. After stating that "Congress did not intend that the air should be dominated by radio chains, advertisers or large manufacturers," Congressman Emanuel Celler, a Mayflower proponent, agreed that such a fairness condition would be "proper."[55] However, the majority of commentators argued for keeping the Mayflower Doctrine intact without modification, a sentiment also reflected in most statements sent to the FCC and entered into the official record.

Statements

On September 5, 1947, the FCC issued an order that it would hold an early January hearing to debate the Mayflower decision's legitimacy and meaning.[56] The FCC subsequently postponed the hearings until March 1 with a February 1 deadline for written statements. The FCC officially invited some groups, such as the Communication Workers of America, while many others, including the progressive Voice of Freedom, asked to be included.[57] Several members of the Hutchins Commission (discussed in Chapter 6), including Robert Leigh, William Hocking, and George Shuster, sent in statements and some testified.

Most of the statements hewed to the concerns and criticisms described previously. Even some relatively conservative groups came out in favor of either keeping or amending the Mayflower Rule, and a few broadcasters also bucked the overall trend and voiced support. The president of the NAB

[52] Knights of Columbus, Council No. 786, San Antonio to the FCC, undated letter, Docket no. 8516, Box 3381, FCC Archives.

[53] Several petitioners to the FCC, undated petitions, Docket no. 8516, Box 3381, FCC Archives.

[54] Helen Polinski to the FCC, on behalf of the National Council of Catholic Women, March 17, 1948, Docket no. 8516, Box 3381, FCC Archives.

[55] "Radio Fight for Editorial Right Widens," March 3, 1948, Docket no. 8516, Box 3381, FCC Archives.

[56] FCC, "In the Matter of Editorializing by Broadcast Licensees: Order," issued September 5, 1947, Docket no. 8516, Box 3382, FCC Archives.

[57] Paul Walker to J. Beirne, September 25, 1947, Docket no. 8516, Box 3382, FCC Archives; Beirne to Walker, October 10, 1947, Docket no. 8516, Box 3382, FCC Archives; Stella Holt to Slowie, October 4, 1947, Docket no. 8516, Box 3382, FCC Archives.

member station WLYN wrote to Justin Miller (copied to the FCC) that he felt "strongly" that the Mayflower Doctrine should be preserved because broadcasters could not "operate in the public interest" if station owners' personal views drove editorial policy. "The most powerful weapons local radio stations have to justify the belief of their listening audience in their broadcasts of news, political matters or any subject of civic importance, is their directed policy of giving both sides equal time to discuss any controversial subject," he argued. "If the barriers against editorializing are removed ... in all frankness, will the radio station owners give the same opportunity to air his views to another person or group to represent an opposite opinion? I doubt it very much."[58]

Some liberal groups broke ranks and supported repealing the ban, perhaps taking a more absolutist approach to First Amendment protections. However, that argument was generally rare, with even the ACLU (represented by the former FCC chairman Fly) supporting the ban's preservation. Other liberals took a middle road and advocated amending but not completely repealing the ban. Many of these participants supported replacing the ban with an affirmative content regulation, essentially the route ultimately chosen with the Fairness Doctrine. Nonetheless, most articulations were predictable, such as the Motion Picture Association of America (MPAA)'s being pro-repeal and the United Furniture Workers of America's supporting the rule, even going further to ask for an investigation of radio monopolies.[59]

A few participants sent in clips of news articles with their statements, including samples from the liberal magazine the *New Republic* (edited by Henry Wallace at that time), which published dueling pro and con Mayflower positions. While the anti-Mayflower side suggested that radio commentators were already permitted to editorialize and this right should be extended to the station owners themselves, the pro-Mayflower position posited that "large and powerful ... corporate radio interests," allied with newspaper publishers, were threatening the health of a diverse public sphere. "Greater freedom of speech for the broadcast owner means less for the public in the community the station serves," the article stated. "If radio stations are to become instruments for the expression of the views of the private owner, rather than the community, then the idea of public ownership of radio channels has become a fiction."[60] Although less populist than the wide range of statements and unsolicited letters, the hearings similarly offered clear articulations of contrasting policy positions. All of the proceedings were recorded in thick volumes that now collect dust in largely forgotten boxes at the National Archives. But they contained

[58] A. Morgan to Justin Miller, March 2, 1948, Docket no. 8516, Box 3385, FCC Archives.
[59] Morris Pizer, "Statement Submitted in Behalf of the United Furniture Workers of America, CIO," March 4, 1948, 5, Docket no. 8516, Box 3385, FCC Archives.
[60] Saul Carson, "Mayflower: 1948," *New Republic*, October 27, 1947, 33–4, Docket no. 8516, Box 3382, FCC Archives.

kernels of larger – and still vexing – debates about media's normative role in a democratic society.

Public Hearing Testimonies

During the eight days of FCC hearings held during March and April 1948, according to FCC records, "some 49 witnesses representing the broadcasting industry and various organizations and members of the public" appeared before the commission. In addition, written statements were entered into the record by 21 individuals and organizations unable to testify in person.[61] Judging by their correspondence, the FCC went to great lengths to accommodate the NAB, allowing it to go in force toward the end of the hearings, but it resisted when the NAB asked for a delay of the entire hearing. Despite broadcasters' efforts to stack the witnesses against the Mayflower decision, the official roster was well balanced and, if anything, seemed to over represent critics, activists, and media reformers, including Larry Fly, Charles Siepmann, Morris Ernst, Jerome Spingarn, Dallas Smythe, Everett Parker, Morris Novik, and Keith Tyler.[62]

But broadcasters were also well represented by leading advocates, including Louis Caldwell and Niles Trammell. Justin Miller's testimony, which was published as a stand-alone 32-page booklet,[63] articulated several core themes that appeared in many of the pro-repeal arguments: that the Communications Act forbade the FCC to censor broadcasters' speech, that the Mayflower Rule exemplified governmental overreach, that such intervention was unnecessary given radio's already exemplary performance vis-à-vis public interest values, that the Mayflower Rule infringed upon broadcasters' First Amendment rights and amounted to arbitrary treatment, especially in light of the freedoms that the printed press took for granted. Finally, broadcasters challenged the very notion that the FCC had any regulatory legitimacy whatsoever in the matter of radio programming.[64]

Morris Ernst challenged these arguments at the beginning of his testimony: "The purpose of free speech in the First Amendment, and our whole gamble that the truth wins out in a conflict of thought, as distinguished from the Stalin–Hitler theory, lies in the fact that there is diversity of point of view. Only by diversity of point of view can truth come out."[65] From this perspective, Ernst saw no justification to repeal the Mayflower Doctrine, because the

---

[61] In the Matter of Editorializing by Broadcast Licensees, *Federal Communications Commission Reports*, 1246.

[62] Typical of these debates, nearly all of the participants were white men.

[63] Text of Formal Statement Presented at the "Mayflower Doctrine" Hearing before the Federal Communications Commission, National Association of Broadcasters, Washington, DC, on April 19, 1948.

[64] See, for example, the Louis Caldwell booklet "Freedom of Speech and Radio Broadcasting."

[65] *Official Report of Proceedings before the Federal Communications Commission, Washington, DC, in the Matter of Editorializing by Broadcast Licensees*, vol. 3, March 3, 1948, Docket no. 8516, Box 3385, FCC Archives.

definition of editorializing implied that only one perspective was presented and not a diversity of conflicting views.

Perhaps the most poignant testimony was that of Larry Fly, the Mayflower decision's original progenitor. Fly made clear that he was speaking as an individual despite representing the ACLU and delivering its official position. After quoting at length from the original Mayflower decision, Fly noted that the radio industry had objected to it on two major grounds: that it violated the First Amendment, and that it deprived radio of the editorial freedom given to print media. Fly countered that neither objection was well founded, especially since the First Amendment, in Fly's view, safeguards two different interests simultaneously: Individuals should have the freedom to speak their minds without governmental restraint, and all of democratic society collectively should have access to all knowledge and opinion, also without governmental restraint. The ACLU had concluded that the Mayflower decision negatively impacted neither freedom.[66]

Fly clashed with a couple of the commissioners during his appearances. After Commissioner Hyde suggested that Fly was treating radio as a common carrier – to which Fly replied that he instead thought of a broadcaster "as a trustee of a public trust"[67] – Hyde felt compelled to rephrase the question, suggesting it lacked clarity judging from Fly's answer. Fly shot back, "I probably will not give you the answer you want."[68] Fly's tone was combative and confrontational at times, but he had an ally among the questioners in Clifford Durr, who was spending his final days on the commission. It was clear that the two former colleagues still shared many views about media, power, and democracy. While Hyde challenged Fly on the distinction between commentators' freedom to editorialize and station owners' freedom to choose speakers, Durr offered Fly a way out by asking, "In other words, the First Amendment guarantees freedom to human beings or individuals, and not freedom to corporate entities?"[69] Fly agreed, saying that "the primary function or purpose of the freedom" was not "to give the mental or emotional catharsis to the speaker," but rather "to give the benefits of diverse views to the citizenry."[70] Fly asserted that when broadcasters entered the domain of public discourse, they carried special power and therefore warranted special regulation, especially when under "the aegis of an organization, the National Broadcasting Company, CBS, or the locally dominant radio station." Fly thought that individual commentators should have "ample freedom." If not "balanced in their presentation, then they should be counterbalanced by other commentators."[71]

[66] *In the Matter of Editorializing by Broadcast Licensees,* vol. 2, March 2, 1948, 306–8, Docket no. 8516, Box 3385, FCC Archives.
[67] Ibid., 330.
[68] Ibid., 331.
[69] Ibid.
[70] Ibid., 331–2.
[71] Ibid., 330.

While the public's positive versus broadcasters' negative First Amendment protections was a recurring tension throughout the proceedings, many reformers saw in these debates much more at stake. They understood these deliberations as determining not only broadcasters' freedom of speech, but also the social contract among government, the listening public, and commercial radio. In the opening of his testimony Siepmann brought this question into focus:

> It is clear … that more is at stake at these hearings than the right of broadcasters to editorialize. The propriety of the Commission's Mayflower decision is being challenged. But this is not all. The challenge, it appears, extended to the Commission's right to concern itself in any way with program service, whether at the time of granting or renewal of a station's license.[72]

After articulating this "broader and more fundamental issue," Siepmann pointed to two sections in the Communications Act that he believed legitimated the FCC's regulatory authority over programming. The first was in Section 307-C, which stated that Congress was concerned with the provision for "particular types or kinds of non-profit radio programs." Congress deferred to the FCC to determine how nonprofit programming should be managed, thereby justifying the commission's role in overseeing radio content. Refuting one of broadcasters' most frequent arguments – that the FCC should be limited to technical concerns – Siepmann argued, "Thus the contention that the commission has no concern whatever with program content appears to be untenable."

The second section that Siepmann underscored was the "equal time" requirement for political candidates. Siepmann saw in this measure Congress's faith in "the spirit of fair play," and therefore it was reasonable to "read a broad intention into this amusingly specific provision in the act." Together, Siepmann saw these two stipulations as justification for the FCC's affirmative role in ensuring democracy-enriching radio content. Emphasizing positive liberties, he also drew upon the Blue Book and the scarcity rationale (still operative, he believed, despite the advent of FM radio) to argue that while broadcasters, like newspaper publishers, have the right to seek profits, there is a "liberty more precious" than broadcasters' freedom: "the freedom of the people to hear all sides of controversial issues." Siepmann concluded: "Freedom of speech is a cherished privilege in a democracy. But there are other freedoms … which have to be accommodated." "The most urgent of them all," according to Siepmann, is "the freedom of the public to learn … all that may be learned in the free market of thought."[73] But commercial broadcasters had little incentive to pursue this goal, particularly in the area of minority interests, because a "broadcaster's prime interest is in profits."

---

[72] *In the Matter of Editorializing by Broadcast Licensees*, vol. 3, March 3, 1948, 575.
[73] Ibid., 579–80.

Therefore, they should not be entrusted with the power of editorializing. "In a public domain such risks should not be taken."[74]

Ultimately, Siepmann's call for privileging a positive understanding of the First Amendment would not prevail in the FCC's decision, but neither was it entirely refuted. His testimony underscored what many implied but few articulated as clearly and forcefully: The Mayflower debate was actually about defining radio's role in a democratic society and the role of the regulatory state to govern this relationship. In these critical years, during these core policy debates, discursive boundaries were being established – boundaries that still largely endure to the present day.

The Mayflower Gives Way to the Fairness Doctrine

After months of testimony and debate, the decision repealing the ban on editorializing came down on June 2, 1949.[75] When the rule was revoked, however, the FCC installed in its place what later became known as the Fairness Doctrine: Although stations could choose their own programming, they must "devote a reasonable percentage of their broadcasting time to the discussion of public issues of interest in the community served by their stations," and "these programs [must] be designed so that the public has a reasonable opportunity to hear different opposing positions on the public issues of interest and importance in the community."[76] Durr, who clearly agreed with the more reformist views of Ernst, Fly, and Siepmann, did not vote. He left the FCC before the Mayflower decision was final. As one old friend phrased it, Durr had "sail[ed] away on the Mayflower – case."[77] It is unlikely that Durr could have changed the outcome. Indeed, the FCC's lone dissent arose from Durr's replacement – the first female commissioner, Frieda Hennock, who felt that removing the editorializing ban was an open invitation to abuse. She began her dissent by stating, "I agree with the majority that it is imperative that a high standard of impartiality in the presentation of issues of public controversy be maintained by broadcast licensees. I do not believe that the Commission's decision, however, will bring about the desired end." Arguing that it seemed "foolhardy" to allow broadcasters to editorialize, she was not against the idea of allowing

[74] Ibid., 583.
[75] According to the new rule, broadcasters' freedom to editorialize "may not be utilized to achieve a partisan or one-sided presentation of issues." *FCC Reports*, In the Matter of Editorializing by Broadcast Licensees, Docket No. 8516, June 1, 1949. See also Horwitz, *The Irony of Regulatory Reform*, 326, who notes, "The Fairness Doctrine was given statutory recognition when Congress amended section 315 of the Communications Act in 1959. Thereafter, section 315 stipulated the three most direct content-based rules on broadcast licensees: the Fairness Doctrine, the equal opportunities provision for political candidates to purchase airtime, and the personal attack rules."
[76] Editorializing by Broadcast Licensees, 13 FCC 1246 (1949).
[77] Frank Russell to Clifford Durr, May 13, 1948, Box 31, Folder 8, CJDP.

it if "fairness could be guaranteed." However, she concluded, "In the present circumstances, prohibiting [editorializing] is our only instrument for insuring the proper use of radio in the public interest."[78]

Despite public interest concessions, broadcasters crowed with pleasure. The NAB president, Justin Miller, praised the decision as "the greatest single victory on behalf of freedom of expression in this nation since the Zenger case confirming the editorial freedom of newspapers over a century ago."[79] Miller had declared victory nearly two months before the FCC formally announced the decision. In his address to the NAB convention on April 10, 1949, Miller asserted, "Fortunately, the abandonment by the FCC of its Mayflower Doctrine, has resulted in widespread development of news, commentary and editorial analysis in hundreds of broadcasting stations throughout the country."[80] Dallas Smythe, who was now ensconced in an academic position, drafted a letter for the FCC along with a clip of Miller's speech. Decrying the delayed announcement he wondered "whether the public may not get the impression that the Commission has substituted regulation by the closed eyelid for regulation by the lifted eyebrow."[81] For reformers like Smythe, the FCC's so-called compromise was an abdication of responsibility.

Other reactions were mixed. Noting disparate responses of gleeful acceptance and resigned doom, the *New York Times*'s Jack Gould saw the decision's "chief drawback" as being a "confused treatise subject to a host of interpretations." He advised that broadcasters not "dispense with legal counsel just yet." The compromise gave "the broadcaster the green light to include his own voice among those carried by his station" but also "attached conditions to the exercise of that freedom." Given the impracticality of implementing the new policy, he cautioned, the FCC's action cannot yet "be heralded as any notable advance for the cause of radio's freedom, either from the standpoint of the broadcaster, or, more importantly, from the standpoint of the listener." Gould concluded that "it will be interesting to watch the broadcaster play on one team and also umpire the game" because "the report constitutes almost an invitation to any group disagreeing with a station's editorial policy to run to the Government with their complaint and seek redress."[82] Likewise, a *New York Times* editorial wondered "whether the radio industry has not paid a high price for its

---

[78] In the Matter of Editorializing by Broadcast Licensees, *Federal Communications Commission Reports*, 1270. For a book on Hennock's FCC tenure, see Susan Brinson, *Personal and Public Interests: Frieda B. Hennock and the Federal Communications Commission* (Westport, CT: Praeger, 2002). On her dissenting vote, see pages 146–7.

[79] *Newsweek*, June 13, 1949, 51.

[80] Reprinted in various publications, including "Mayflower Doctrine Out, Says Miller in Key Talk," *Billboard*, April 16, 1949.

[81] Smythe to the FCC, April 25, 1949, Container 16-16 F-16-5-1-17, Smythe Papers.

[82] Jack Gould, "Radio Editorials: The FCC Issues a Report on the Right of Broadcasters to Air Their Views," *New York Times*, June 12, 1949, X9.

new-found freedom" because the decision gave the FCC "the power to decide whether a radio station is conducting its editorial policy on an impartial basis and, if it disapproves, to exercise the extreme penalty of putting the station out of business." The editorial cautioned: "Before it cheers the FCC decision too loudly, the broadcasting industry might ponder whether it has not opened a Pandora's box."[83] Other news sources, such as the *Washington Post*, sided with broadcasters against Hennock's argument, seeing the amended Mayflower Doctrine as a positive policy change that gave "the licensee the responsibility of exercising his own judgment on program content and balance ... in the public interest." It concluded that the scarcity rationale no longer justified "a valid barrier to radio editorializing" especially when "there are many more radio stations than daily newspapers in the United States."[84]

Despite the sense that broadcasters decisively won the larger policy battle, the Fairness Doctrine did establish some provisions that many of the fiercest critics demanded, and it salvaged an affirmative function of media policy, a vestige of which would remain in some form for several decades. Meanwhile, the broader trajectory of greater political economic power for commercial broadcasters and less regulatory oversight was abundantly clear. Indeed, broadcasters' triumphalist rhetoric was largely warranted. Although it would become a valuable tool for progressives and conservatives alike to fight prejudicial broadcasts – and serve as a polarizing rallying call to this day – the Fairness Doctrine remained consistent with a libertarian self-regulatory approach that largely ignored structural concerns. Content-related disputes would be handled within the framework of a nominally socially responsible commercial media system. Yet even the relatively weak Fairness Doctrine was antithetical to broadcasters' anti-regulation stance, and they would set to work immediately to undo it – eventually achieving their goal decades later under Ronald Reagan's FCC.

The Political Aftermath

By the late 1940s, industry attacks against the FCC coincided with an increasingly right-wing tilt in Washington politics. Many assumed that President Truman would not appoint Durr to another seven-year term, especially after Durr's vocal stand against Truman's Loyalty Oath executive order. Most likely in response to political pressure from the Democratic base, Truman did try to reappoint Durr in 1948, but he declined. Instead of forcing his staff to sign loyalty oaths, Durr effectively resigned from the FCC. Describing her husband's principled stance against a system that allowed anonymous tipsters to blacklist innocent people and ruin their careers, Virginia Durr recalled: "Cliff just said he refused to carry out such a law, that it was unconstitutional" and "against

---

[83] "Radio Editorials," *New York Times*, June 4, 1949, 12.
[84] "Editorials on the Air," *Washington Post*, June 12, 1949, B4.

everything he believed in."[85] Other progressive commissioners, including the aforementioned Frieda Hennock, occasionally would be appointed over the years, but the critical mass necessary for advancing progressive reforms remained elusive.

Liberals were distraught over Durr's departure. One observer wrote that he was sorry to see Durr leave because "there are very few honest New Dealers left in the government service." Feeling pushed out of the Democratic Party to support Henry Wallace's campaign (as did Durr's wife, the writer noted), he told Durr that he admired him for defying the "loyalty tests," which he believed was "one of the tactics [that Truman used] to kick out all liberals from government service, with the backing of republicans." The letter writer concluded that he was "only worried that President Truman should staff your office with a lot of horse-thieves, Wall Streeters, and militarists."[86] Durr held similar concerns but felt that people were catching on and that "the present tactics will in time be as discredited as the Palmer Raids."[87] Harold Ickes, who, along with Wallace, had been one of the most liberal and powerful New Dealers in FDR's administration, wrote to Durr that, while he understood why he was resigning, "I still regret that you will no longer be able to strike as effectively as you did within the government the sturdy blows that one has come to expect from you in the public interest."[88] Honored to receive such praise from such a progressive stalwart, Durr confessed that he would "stay in the fray" if he thought he "could accomplish anything worthwhile. But the change in the Washington climate has been too great."[89]

Yet Durr hoped others, especially outside government, would carry on the battle. Replying to a farewell letter from the *New York Post*'s Paul Denis, who had joined other columnists from leading magazines to form the "Radio-Television Critics Circle," Durr wrote, "I feel strongly about the role of a radio critic, and am convinced that if we had more of them we would have better broadcasting. May your tribe increase."[90] Many folks, especially educational broadcasters such as H. B. McCarty, begged him to stay on: "Let me try to say again how much your membership on the Commission means to those of us in educational broadcasting ... insisting that people try to think of radio as it might be instead of as it is." Without Commissioner Durr, it would be too easy for reformers to say, "'Oh, hell, what's the use?'"[91] Durr was greatly touched by these entreaties, but he could not be persuaded to reconsider.

[85] Virginia Durr, *Outside the Magic Circle* (University: University of Alabama Press, 1985), 217.
[86] Emanuel Kline to Clifford Durr, April 23, 1948, Box 31, Folder 8, CJDP.
[87] Durr to Kline, June 29, 1948, Box 31, Folder 9, CJDP.
[88] Harold Ickes to Clifford Durr, April 28, 1948, Box 31, Folder 8, CJDP.
[89] Durr to Ickes, May 26, 1948, Box 31, Folder 9, CJDP.
[90] Clifford Durr to Paul Denis, May 20, 1948, Box 31, Folder 9, CJDP.
[91] H. B. McCarty to Clifford Durr, August 15, 1947, Box 31, Folder 4, CJDP. See also Harold Engel letters to Senator Alexander Wiley, and Senator Joseph McCarthy, May 21, 1947, Box 31, Folder 4, CJDP.

Despite a tenure marked by constant battle with numerous foes, Durr was sent off with great fanfare and high rhetoric both in the press and by his fellow policy makers. *Newsweek* described him as the "lone dissenter" on the FCC. In his June 19, 1948, address, the new FCC chairman, Wayne Coy, lauded Durr as "an exultant believer in democracy." "If he is capable of wrath," Coy declared, it "would fall on those reckless sons of America who would sell our soul of liberty for restraints to be imposed by a few."[92] Even some broadcasters expressed regret. One wrote, "As long as I am in the broadcast industry my station policies will reflect the inspiration of your principles and philosophy."[93] Another wrote: "Your influence in the field of radio broadcasting has been greater than your single vote on the Commission. I hope that the trail which you leave behind will not be too stony for others to follow." Durr replied, "It is people like you that have kept me in trouble and made me a nuisance to the industry. But for you I would not have realized what radio is capable of doing when it puts its best foot forward."[94] Nonetheless, Durr's relief upon leaving the FCC was palpable. He observed to a friend that Congress was just then introducing two new investigations against the commission, one in the House and one in the Senate. "It looks like there is fun ahead, and I am going to miss it!"[95]

That Durr's social democratic vision did not prevail does not negate that a well-articulated alternative policy trajectory crystallized in the 1940s, backed by considerable popular support. But with Durr's departure, the possibility of progressive regulatory intervention was greatly diminished.[96] Dallas Smythe would leave around the same time, describing later how he "was about the last New Dealer to leave Washington with his scalp still on. The ones who stayed beyond me got them taken off by the new Un-American Inquisition."[97] A fellow progressive wrote to Smythe that he struggled to find work and his wife was fired from her government job on the basis of an anonymous accusation. DC had become a depressing place, especially for liberals. "People are beginning to leave town," Smythe's friend reported. "This is beginning to take on the appearance of an exodus."[98]

With the last of the progressive reformers fleeing DC, systemic change seemed to be a lost cause. The historian Elizabeth Fones-Wolf described what this exodus felt like for the deflating media reform movement: "By the end of 1948, reformers' expectations that the postwar era would see sweeping changes in American broadcasting had diminished, although labor's FM stations still offered a small ray of hope." Pressure from organized left-wing groups and individuals also receded as radical media reformers "began disappearing into

---

[92] Quoted in Salmond, *The Conscience of a Lawyer*, 97.

[93] Ivon to Clifford Durr, June 21, 1948, Box 31, Folder 9, CJDP.

[94] Clifford Durr to Robert Saudek, June 29, 1948, Box 31, Folder 9, CJDP.

[95] Clifford Durr to H. B. McCarty, June 29, 1948, Box 31, Folder 9, CJDP.

[96] Virginia Durr, *Outside the Magic Circle*, 216–20.

[97] John Lent, *A Different Road Taken: Profiles in Critical Communication* (Boulder, CO: Westview Press, 1995), 30.

[98] Joe Belser to Dallas Smythe, April 1948, Container 16-10 Folder 16-2-1-1, Smythe Papers.

the vortex of anti-communism"[99] As blacklists emerged to demobilize a generation of left-leaning figures and activists, red-baiting became a favorite tool that
media corporations used to crush progressive reform. Fones-Wolf noted that
"It would be twenty years before the FCC, under pressure from the civil rights
movement, again allowed citizen participation in licensing decisions."[100] While
liberals despaired, commercial broadcasters enjoyed a new sense of invincibil-
ity. *Broadcasting* gloated that of the seven FCC commissioners present at the
time of the Blue Book's publication, only one, Paul Walker, remained. "Based on
all outward appearances," the magazine crowed, "the Blue Book is dead."[101]

The scattering of progressives, however, eventually yielded benefits for society. Clifford Durr would become the Lawyers Guild president and defend
blacklisted individuals. Unlike many liberals who took on similar work, Durr
would defend people who were actually communists – not just those who were
unfairly accused of such – according to the principle that no one, including
communists, deserved to have his or her civil liberties violated. Durr himself
would suffer from being blacklisted, and the academic jobs he had been all but
promised suddenly disappeared. He was fired from another job in part because
of his wife's political activism. His social justice work nonetheless continued,
and he and Virginia became key figures in the civil rights movement. The Durrs
helped release Rosa Parks from jail after her historic bus ride and assisted with
her subsequent court battles.[102] Dallas Smythe and Charles Siepmann took
refuge in the nascent academic field of communications. Siepmann became
the long-serving director of the new NYU Communications in Education
Department,[103] and Smythe became one of the first faculty members at the
Institute of Communications Research at the University of Illinois, Urbana-
Champaign, where he taught the first American course on the political economy of communication.[104] Both scholars would teach for decades, leaving their
mark on the new field of communication through their scholarship and by
mentoring a generation of critical scholars. And both would remain engaged
with crucial media policy debates, ranging from spectrum management to the
foundation of public broadcasting.[105]

[99] Fones-Wolf, *Waves of Opposition*, 160.
[100] Ibid.
[101] *Broadcasting*, October 25, 1948, 46.
[102] Salmond, *The Conscience of a Lawyer*, 174–6.
[103] David Berkman, "Charles Arthur Siepmann 1899–1985: A Biographical Tribute and Personal
    Reminiscence," *Television Quarterly* 22, no. 1 (1986): 77–84.
[104] Dallas Smythe and Thomas Guback, *Counterclockwise: Perspectives on Communication*
    (Boulder, CO: Westview Press, 1994).
[105] For example, Siepmann would play a key role in the ongoing debates around educational broad-
    casting and both men were participants at the 1949 Allerton conference, which helped estab-
    lish the vision for educational television. See Glenda R. Balas, Eavesdropping at Allerton: The
    Recovery of Paul Lazarsfeld's Progressive Critique of Educational Broadcasting. *Democratic
    Communique*, 24, (2010): 1–16. See also Victor Pickard, "Charles Siepmann's Legacy for
    Communication Research," in *New Histories of Communication Study*, ed. David W. Park &
    Peter Simonson (New York: Routledge).

However, with New Deal social democrats completely removed from positions of power, the increasingly reactionary political landscape in the late 1940s and early 1950s left a clear imprint on the nation's media system that would last for generations. The broader political context of this era – the HUAC investigations of Hollywood, Truman's implementation of his loyalty program in 1947 – is pertinent to understand the resonance of broadcasters' arguments, a resonance that might not have occurred had the political landscape not shifted so rightward so quickly. The Fairness Doctrine can be understood as an artifact of a receding liberalism and an ascendant corporate libertarianism – an elite consensus that made relatively minor concessions to public service ideals but otherwise solidified corporate control of the American media system.

The Legacy of the Fairness Doctrine

It is somewhat ironic that many contemporary activists hold up the Fairness Doctrine as the pinnacle of progressive media policy – a shining example of, if not a lost golden age, then a whisper of a more progressive time. Few would suggest the Fairness Doctrine did not lead to significant progressive victories, especially in the 1960s, but its romanticized origins should be restored to its postwar political context. The Fairness Doctrine was a concession to widely held concerns that giving commercial broadcasters so much political power would lead to unchecked partisanship and one-sided arguments – a system that many feared would disproportionately benefit conservative voices. Yet even contemporary proponents of the Fairness Doctrine often forget that it had two components. The first, and by far the more progressive, part stipulated that broadcasters must cover controversial issues of public importance; second, they must do so in a way that represents contrasting views. Today the first half of the Fairness Doctrine – a mandate to air "public issues of interest" – is often conveniently overlooked in favor of the mandate to air "opposing positions."[106] This erasure is arguably symptomatic of the ahistorical discourse surrounding media policy in general. Despite its frequent invocation by contemporary progressives, the Fairness Doctrine's history has been largely forgotten. Although both conservative and liberal activists learned how to deploy the Fairness Doctrine with some success until it was repealed in the late 1980s, it evidenced a vague public interest obligation, especially considering the stronger regulation that it replaced. The Mayflower Doctrine repeal would serve as a poignant bookend to a decade of progressive policy activism that began with trust-busting radio chains and ended with weakly enforced public interest obligations.

[106] For a legal history on the Fairness Doctrine, see Steven Simmons, *The Fairness Doctrine and the Media* (Berkeley: University of California Press, 1978). For a discussion of the Mayflower hearings, see Toro, "Standing Up for Listeners' Rights," 91–101. The actual term "Fairness Doctrine" did not become prevalent until the 1960s after further congressional and FCC clarifications. See Fred Friendly, *The Good Guys, The Bad Guys, and the First Amendment* (New York: Vintage Books, 1975), 23–31.

As a closing chapter on radio reform, the Fairness Doctrine was anticlimactic, in some ways presaging the increasingly deregulatory orientation over the ensuing decades.[107] Only after failing to carve out significant space for public media or to establish strong structural constraints on commercial broadcasting did radio reformers begin focusing their efforts on regulating broadcasters' political speech and settling for stipulations on balance and diversity represented within the commercial system. The progression of this early formative stage of broadcasting is clear. An increasingly commercialized medium drew public media criticism, followed by policy interventions and then a corporate backlash that ultimately undermined the potential for long-term structural reform. The next chapter shows how a similar pattern played out for the other major news medium of the time: print media, especially newspapers.

[107] Of course, an aggressive enforcement of the doctrine's two provisions would have amounted to strong regulation, but this never transpired.

5

The 1940s Newspaper Crisis and the Birth of the Hutchins Commission

The 1940s held multiple challenges for American print news media.[1] Newspapers in particular came under withering criticism, and the need for press reform was becoming a matter of public consensus. "It is a fact," stated a 1946 editorial in *Editor & Publisher*, the leading trade magazine, "that newspapers in general have become the national whipping boy."[2] A later piece described how 1947 had subjected newspapers "to the most searching analysis and criticism in all their history."[3] Similar sentiments were shared across a wide range of opinion magazines, trade journals, and journalists' firsthand accounts. Media criticism, according to one historian of the period, had become a kind of popular sport.[4] Critiques that previously had been associated with fringe polemics and leftist elements within the labor movement were becoming mainstreamed. Radicals such as Morris Ernst, who advocated breaking up newspaper and broadcasting chains, had begun to significantly influence media policy discourse. Political elites and broad sectors of the public were increasingly cohering around a structural critique of their press system.

Among the main causes of distrust of the industry were increased concentration of ownership and decreased competition. Charges against newspaper monopolies, absentee ownership, and lack of accountability to local communities became commonplace. As press institutions fought for their very legitimacy, calls for government intervention prompted warnings from people both within and outside the industry that the press must shape up before it was too

---

[1] Parts of this chapter overlap with Victor Pickard, "Laying Low the Shibboleth of a Free Press: Regulatory Threats against the American Newspaper Industry, 1938–1947," *Journalism Studies*, 15, 4, 464–80.

[2] "Heeding Criticism," *Editor & Publisher*, January 19, 1946, 40.

[3] *Editor & Publisher Yearbook*, January 30, 1948, 17.

[4] Margaret Blanchard, *Revolutionary Sparks: Freedom of Expression in Modern America* (New York: Oxford University Press, 1992).

late. Reformist innovations like citizen councils, proposed by the industry to confront the "rising tide of dissatisfaction," gained traction – if only to prevent further public criticism and possible government action.[5] Indeed, the government was already encroaching on multiple fronts, and such interventionist moves put publishers on notice that they were fair game for regulation.

These political troubles coincided with a number of economic challenges facing the industry. On the surface, indicators suggested a postwar newspaper boom: Circulation, advertising revenue, and employment numbers were all increasing. Nonetheless, 1945 marked the beginning of a slow downward spiral for the industry – what the historian David Davies called the "Postwar Decline of Newspapers."[6] The historian James Baughman similarly pegged 1945 as the beginning of the "orderly retreat of the newspaper," which was "wounded but not slain"[7] – a retreat that has greatly accelerated in recent years. Newspapers in the 1940s faced a sudden rise in local monopolies, spiraling production costs, labor disputes, and public distrust.

Despite rising public criticism against commercial journalism, newspaper owners were largely insulated against any falloff in readership by their monopolistic market power. Most newspaper publishers in medium to small towns and cities no longer faced any competition and could safely assume that none would ever arise.[8] The high costs of paper and equipment required to start a newspaper were prohibitive for all but the richest Americans. Further worsening matters was a rapid expansion of newspaper chains – by the end of World War II more than 40 percent of all newspaper circulation was controlled by chains – which accelerated the number of one-newspaper towns. In 1923 there were 502 American communities with two or more dailies. Twenty years later this number had dropped to 137, a marked decline in newspaper competition,[9] dwindling to a mere handful today. Although the problems facing newspapers in the 1940s bear some similarities to the ones our contemporary journalistic institutions are experiencing, their challenges were also inextricably bound up with the politics of the time, especially the fraught relationship between FDR and the press.

FDR and the Press

American newspapers in the 1940s shared some of the same challenges facing their broadcasting counterparts, especially in terms of public criticism. Reform efforts aimed at the press arose concurrently with the radio reform movement. But print and broadcast media's political situations were distinct in several key

---

[5] "Heeding Criticism," *Editor & Publisher*, January 19, 1946, 40.
[6] Davies, *The Postwar Decline of American Newspapers*.
[7] Baughman, "Wounded but Not Slain," 119–34.
[8] Ibid.
[9] Ibid., 122.

respects. One major difference was the relationship they enjoyed with the liberal Democratic President Franklin D. Roosevelt. Unlike today, the trope that the press was at base a deeply liberal institution was not in circulation – in fact, quite the opposite. The press was widely seen as an inherently conservative force, one that protected the class interests of the moneyed and powerful. It was well known that big newspaper publishers were mostly pro-Republican and pro-business, as well as anti-union, anti-regulation, and, especially, anti–New Deal. A book of 1940s media criticism observed a disconnect between newspapers and readers stemming from the "conservative bias of most of the press." This bias was most clearly demonstrated, the book argued, in labor issues, especially publishers' almost uniform opposition to the closed shop, as well as many union protections sanctioned by the Wagner Labor Relations Act.[10] Although FDR cultivated sympathetic journalists among the Washington, DC, press corps, his famous fireside chats were conducted at least partly out of a desire to circumvent newspapers. Live radio broadcasts allowed him to frame his arguments and speak directly to the American public without journalistic mediation.

Despite the press's hostilities toward the New Deal, rank-and-file reporters and other news workers often did not share publishers' anti-labor sentiments. Under the leadership of the charismatic Heywood Broun, a group of journalists formed a national organization, the Newspaper Guild, in 1933. The guild would quickly develop into a powerful and radical leftist CIO union with locals across the country. Its increasingly militant tactics, including a two-year strike against William Randolph Hearst in Chicago, peaked by the end of the decade. Afterward its radicalism subsided to some extent, with many communists being chased out of the union.[11] Nonetheless, judging from its newspaper, the *Guild Reporter,* class antagonisms would remain on full display throughout the 1940s.

FDR may have exaggerated the press's opposition to his agenda – and he even may have sometimes welcomed it, as it generated public sympathy.[12] But he also appeared to hold genuine antipathy toward the commercial press, reflected in his approval of Harold Ickes's *Freedom of the Press Today,* which skewered the news industry as an anti-democratic monopoly.[13] FDR reportedly welcomed the critique, writing that it was a "really worthwhile book." And when the adless newspaper *PM* launched in 1940, FDR sent a congratulatory note expressing the belief that an enterprise that supported itself "simply by merchandising information, with the public [and not advertisers]

---

[10] Leon Svirsky, *Your Newspaper: Blueprint for a Better Press* (New York: Macmillan, 1947), 16.
[11] For a history of the early Newspaper Guild, see Ben Scott, "Labor's New Deal for Journalism: The Newspaper Guild in the 1930s" (Ph.D. Dissertation, University of Illinois, Urbana, 2009).
[12] Graham White, *FDR and the Press* (Chicago: University of Chicago Press, 1979).
[13] Harold Ickes, *Freedom of the Press Today: A Clinical Examination by Twenty-Eight Specialists* (New York: Vanguard, 1941).

as your only customer, appeals to me as a new and promising formula for freedom of the press."[14]

Beyond concerns about the health of American democracy, FDR had legitimate political reasons to harbor ill feelings toward much of the fourth estate. In a private letter in 1936, FDR said he believed that 85 percent of the newspapers were against him.[15] His estimate was not far off, as indicated by newspapers' presidential endorsements. Although he won 57 percent of the popular vote in 1932, he received only 38 percent of daily newspaper endorsements, while Herbert Hoover received 55 percent; in 1936, when FDR won 60 percent of the vote, 34 percent of newspaper endorsements went for him versus 60 percent for Alf Landon. These endorsements dwindled to 23 percent in favor of FDR in 1940, when he won 55 percent of the vote, and to 22 percent in 1944.[16] Not reflected by these numbers is the sheer vitriol hurled at FDR by right-wing publishers including McCormick and Hearst, who went so far as to refer to proponents of regulatory intervention as "Red Fascists."[17] Hyperbolic rhetoric notwithstanding, the already fraught newspaper industry seemingly had good reason to fear the New Dealers.

The troubles facing the newspaper industry – particularly challenges from the labor movement and government regulators – shook the industry's structural foundations. Threats of state intervention were especially alarming, as the industry faced opposition from all three branches of government. As discussed later, FDR encouraged the FCC to scrutinize newspaper chains and prevent them from acquiring radio stations, the Supreme Court issued an important antitrust decision against the Associated Press (AP), and Congress prepared investigations on the disappearance of small newspapers. A severe newsprint shortage, combined with a wave of strikes by printers' unions, negated some of commercial newspapers' other gains. Summarizing these concerns, one historian noted that ownership concentration, especially chain newspapers, reduced the competition by 50 percent in ninety-two cities with 100,000 or more population, leaving overall "fewer total newspapers, more chain ownerships, fewer local features and columnists, and more syndicated columns." This meant that a "few voices reached millions, limiting the number of ideas circulating and giving undue prominence to those that were amplified."[18]

---

[14] Arthur Schlesinger Jr., *The Coming of the New Deal* (New York: Houghton Mifflin, 1958), 566. Frank Luther Mott, *The News in America* (Cambridge, MA: Harvard University Press, 1952), 184. Both quoted in Joon-Mann Kang, "Franklin D. Roosevelt and James L. Fly: The Politics of Broadcast Regulation, 1941–1944," *Journal of American Culture* 10, no. 2 (1987): 25.

[15] Betty Winfield, *FDR and the News Media* (New York: Columbia University Press, 1994), 127–9.

[16] Edwin Emery, *History of the American Newspaper Association* (Minneapolis: University of Minnesota Press, 1950), 689–90.

[17] See, for example, "Outlaw the Red Fascists," October 1948, which reprinted earlier editorials in Hearst papers from June 1, 1940 to June 3, 1948.

[18] Marion Marzolf, *Civilizing Voices: American Press Criticism, 1880–1950* (New York: Longman, 1991), 153.

That press freedoms were reserved only for those wealthy enough to own a newspaper was just one of the industry's legitimacy problems. While economic and labor problems plagued newspapers' production, growing public criticism encouraged regulators' scrutiny. Some scholars have suggested that this press criticism was part of an ongoing radical tradition that was symptomatic of the press system's deeper structural problems, tracing back to the "first great newspaper crisis" of the Progressive Era. This earlier crisis saw arising simultaneously the advent of the modern commercial press, tensions between public service and private profits, and the professionalization of journalism.[19] Placing the 1940s newspaper crisis in this historical trajectory exposes journalism's structural vulnerabilities, suggesting that crisis is built into the very DNA of the commercial press system.

Anatomy of 1940s Press Criticism and Activism

Writing in 1949, the eminent newspaper historian Edwin Emery stated unequivocally that public criticism was "the biggest problem which confronted the daily newspapers of America."[20] Though not as pronounced as the contemporaneous broadcast reform movement, a push for newspaper reform grew out of criticism from academics, political dissidents, former journalists, various social movement activists, and New Dealers. This reform impulse gained further momentum during a crisis of public distrust in the 1940s[21] and was reflected in activist groups' producing their own papers and increasing calls for structural experiments like the previously mentioned adless newspaper, *PM*.[22] Echoing progressive and New Deal era discourses, 1940s press criticism took many of the same forms as radio criticism, mostly falling into the following categories: structural (issues related to the ownership and control of newspapers), informational (the informational deficits in newspaper content arising from these structural factors), racial (misrepresentations of marginalized groups in newspaper content), and commercial (advertising and other commercial values' effects on news selection, omissions, and emphases).[23]

The 1940s structural critique of newspapers is best exemplified by Morris Ernst's arguments for government intervention. Considered a kind of primer for the postwar media reform movement, Ernst's book *The First Freedom* (mentioned in Chapter 1) critiqued media ownership concentration in radio,

---

[19] Robert McChesney, *The Problem of the Media* (New York: Monthly Review Press, 2004).
[20] Emery, *History of the American Newspaper Association*, 244.
[21] Davies, *The Postwar Decline of American Newspapers*, 15–29.
[22] Paul Milkman, *PM: A New Deal in Journalism* (New Brunswick, NJ: Rutgers University Press, 1997).
[23] Like radio criticism, an implicit ideological critique also existed, but despite relatively conservative positions, commercial print institutions had not overtly purged liberal commentators as did commercial broadcasters.

film, and newspapers. Accordingly, Ernst described press-related problems in structural terms:

Ten states have not a single city with competing daily papers. Twenty-two states are without Sunday newspaper competition. Fourteen companies owning eighteen papers control about one quarter of our total daily circulation. Three hundred and seventy chain newspapers own about one fifth of all our circulation. More than a quarter of our daily circulation is absentee-owned. We have a thousand less owners than a few decades ago. Thirty-two hundred weeklies – the backbone of local democracy – have disappeared. One company dominates more than 3,000 weeklies. There are only 117 cities left, in our entire nation, where competing dailies still exist.[24]

To counteract these trends, reformers like Ernst stressed the need for laws preventing joint ownership of media outlets and interlocking directorates, as well as a tax levied against chain newspapers. He proposed such structural interventions as providing tax breaks for smaller newspapers and ending media corporations' vertical integration by forcing newspaper publishers to divest their ownership of wood pulp, paper, and forests.[25] Ernst felt Congress could reverse media concentration if it initiated "a national debate on what to do about our vanishing freedom – the evaporation of diversity of opinion."[26] He recommended a joint Senate-House inquiry aimed at protecting opinion diversity in media content by maintaining ownership diversity, especially among small dailies, weeklies, and magazines. Because "no newspaper has thought it was of interest to the people," Ernst observed, this "anti-democratic story [of concentrated media ownership] has never been told to the American public."[27]

Much of this structural criticism focused on media monopolies. For example, Oswald Villard's *The Disappearing Daily* argued that commercial pressures encouraged propaganda, low-quality reporting, and pro-war inclinations. The book attributed the sudden rise of one-newspaper towns to chain newspapers that acquired smaller papers or drove them out of the market.[28] The rise of media monopolies alarmed both radical and liberal pamphleteers. George Marion, a Newspaper Guild member, penned a radical exemplar, *The "Free Press": Portrait of a Monopoly*. He saw press freedom as being limited to the super-rich, who used newspapers to maintain power and accumulate more wealth: "Newspapers being a Big Business, the views of newspaper owners are the views of Big Business." Thus, those who parroted rhetoric about America's press freedoms served as stooges for a corporate elite.[29] That newspapers

[24] Ernst, *First Freedom*, xii.
[25] Ibid., 249–60.
[26] Ibid., xiv.
[27] Ibid., 135.
[28] Oswald Villard, *The Disappearing Daily: Chapters in American Newspaper Evolution* (New York: Alfred A. Knopf, 1944).
[29] George Marion, *The "Free Press": Portrait of a Monopoly* (New York: New Century, 1946), 11.

presented themselves as victims, Marion insisted, was absurd given generous government-sponsored press subsidies including special mailing privileges estimated to cost taxpayers $10 million to $25 million annually, and indirect subsidies such as expanded capacity for news transmissions via publicly financed telecommunications infrastructure.

Beyond sensationalist news coverage, the worst consequence of the press's becoming a "Big Business" and "brutal monopoly," according to Marion, was its utility to the "fascist fringe" like that represented by the media mogul William Randolph Hearst.[30] To contest these trends, Marion called for a more prominent labor press that would "reduce the wavering" of liberal papers and "combat the commodity-news pattern." He believed this would create "an audience for balanced, trustworthy information" that told the "truth about the American press – that it is the uncontrolled and unlimited voice of monopoly capital." Marion concluded that press reform efforts "must operate within the framework of a larger political program," one that "understands the necessity for curbing the huge monopolies – even within the limits of the capitalist system." This task placed "the heaviest responsibility upon Marxists and class-conscious workers, manual and intellectual, newspapermen not least among them."[31]

While radicals like Marion emphasized the newspaper crisis's systemic nature and pushed for structural reform that required a broad social movement, many liberals were more concerned about protecting First Amendment–guaranteed freedoms. The noted civil libertarian Robert Cushman authored a liberal critique, *Keep Our Press Free*, that viewed the American press system as essentially just and constitutionally protected, and whose greatest threat arose from governmental overreach. Cushman nonetheless concluded his analysis by criticizing newspapers' basic commercial structure. Recounting the Soviet charge that Americans "do not have a free press in the United States because [their] newspapers are controlled by business interests who dictate newspaper policy and determine what the American public shall read," Cushman allowed that this critique "commands serious attention." He also wondered about "private threats to the independence of the press" because "the publishing of newspapers and magazines in this country has become a very big business ... that reflect[s] the political, economic, and social views of the owners and advertisers."[32] Cushman noted that 66 percent of modern newspapers' revenue originated from advertising; thus the public paid for newspapers "by buying the popular brands of cigarettes, toothpaste, or automobiles which advertise in them."[33] Economic concentration, lack of newspaper competition, increased standardization, and homogeneous opinion might necessitate collective legal

---

[30] Ibid., 20.
[31] Ibid., 47.
[32] Robert Cushman, *Keep Our Press Free* (New York: Public Affairs Committee, 1946), 27.
[33] Ibid.

measures, Cushman conceded. Publishers and press associations "have resisted with all their strength every effort by the government to subject them, as business concerns, to the legal controls which are imposed on other forms of business."[34] Cushman concluded that "freedom of the press remains in danger" as long as newspaper owners fail to see "their business as affected with a public interest."[35] However, without legal enforcement – or at least the threat of policy intervention – newspapers were not likely to change their ways.

Besides disaffected intellectuals, disquiet about media monopolies was common among average readers. In November 1946, more than two thousand Akron, Ohio, residents packed into an auditorium for a panel discussion on the question "Is the American Press Really Free?" Broadcasted on the radio program *America's Town Meeting of the Air*, the panel focused entirely on the issue of newspaper monopolies. Panelists included a local newspaper editor, the *New Republic* editor, and Morris Ernst, who suggested subsidizing smaller dailies to help reduce media concentration. When the audience was asked who among them felt that the American press was truly free, only a sprinkling of hands went up.[36] At a similar town meeting in Cleveland, the reported consensus was that the "press is not keeping faith with the public." A guildsman participating in the discussion claimed, "Everybody appears concerned about the papers except the publishers.... They alone seem smugly satisfied with the performance of the properties they own."[37]

A major component of 1940s structural media criticism focused on news workers' labor conditions. Continuing its challenge to commercial newspapers begun in the 1930s, the Newspaper Guild regularly published reports in the *Guild Reporter* on strikes against newspapers. Reflecting a class consciousness largely absent elsewhere in the press, it offered radical structural criticism of the newspaper industry, calling out media monopolies' threat to press freedoms. A leading historian on the subject has noted that it was the guild that directly challenged publishers' definition of freedom of the press with its emphasis on a negative First Amendment.[38] Labor relations abruptly worsened with the printers' strikes led by the International Typographical Union (ITU) against the publishers. The years 1945–8 witnessed a wave of such actions: The ITU struck against 78 papers from 1945 to 1947, and against 50 in 1948. The ITU's strikes, reinforced by walkouts from other craft unions, landed crippling blows against dozens of papers.[39]

---

[34] Ibid., 28.
[35] Ibid., 30.
[36] "Broadcast Audience Doesn't Think Press Really Is Free," *Guild Reporter*, November 8, 1946, quoted in Davies, *The Postwar Decline of American Newspapers*, 25.
[37] "Press Is Not Keeping Faith with Public," *Guild Reporter*, April 8, 1949, quoted in Davies, *The Postwar Decline of American Newspapers*, 26–7.
[38] Scott, "Labor's New Deal."
[39] Davies, *Postwar Decline of American Newspapers*, 8–9.

Publishers were often ruthless in their retaliation. They developed technological workarounds by experimenting with photoengraving, offset printing, and
teletype setting to bypass human labor.[40] They also lobbied policy makers for
advantageous legislation. For example, publishers aggressively advocated the
Taft-Hartley Act for the specific purpose of using it against the printer unions,
which were among the oldest, most powerful, and most effective craft unions.
Taft-Hartley undercut unions' organizing efforts by outlawing the closed shop,
making union foremen part of management, and transforming the National
Labor Relations Board into a kind of strike-breaking agency. "The American
Newspaper Publishers Association and its affiliates believe the Taft-Hartley Act
has provided weapons to smash the [ITU]," the *Guild Reporter* stated. One historian noted that the ITU strikes were seen as guinea pigs for Taft-Hartley, with
Chicago, the site of a massive strike, as the definitive battleground.[41] Labor
conflict underscored a core facet of the structural critique understood by both
news owners and workers: Conflicts over control of newspapers struck at the
nexus of political and economic power in U.S. society.

Other criticism focused on the commercial values permeating news production resulting from advertising's growing influence on news institutions.
Ralph Ingersoll, the founder of *PM*, advocated that newspapers be liberated
from "antagonistic interests" such as advertising and political pressures.[42]
Similarly, the editor of the *Rutherford Courier* observed that the "framers
of the constitution didn't foresee advertising" as "the connective by which
newspapers would come to depend for their existence" and thus become more
dependent on "commercial interests than upon the people."[43] Noting advertisers' increasing influence as newspaper ad sales reached new heights,[44] the
Guild Reporter described advertisers as "corrupt and cynical hucksters, intent
on bamboozling the public out of ready money. And they were paying us [the
journalists] to do it for them ... buying columns, and full pages in our papers
and magazines." While some in the ad-driven press either "gave the matter
little thought" or were "pleased by the tinkling of the cash registers," the article argued, a few "looked ahead and saw that if the free market of thought
became the free market of phony goods, there soon would be no market at

---

[40] "Revolution?" *Time*, December 22, 1947; Davies, *Postwar Decline of American Newspapers*,
10–11.

[41] James Tracy, "'Our Union Is Not for Sale': The Postwar Struggle for Workplace Control in the
American Newspaper Industry," in *A Moment of Danger: Critical Studies in the History of U.S.
Communication since 1945*, ed. Janice Peck and Inger Stole (Milwaukee, WI: New Marquette
University Press, 2011), 57–82.

[42] Ickes, *Freedom of the Press Today*.

[43] Robert Lasseter, "Impossible Role of the Press: Exploring the Low State of Journalism and Its
Causes," *Guild Reporter*, November 28, 1947, 2.

[44] "1948 National Ad Income Hit New Peak in '47 ANPA reveals," *Guild Reporter*, April 23,
1948, 1.

all." If this were to happen, "the public would get tired" and "crack down on the whole mess."[45]

Another category of critique focused on the commercial press's lack of high-quality information. No one better exemplifies the informational critique than George Seldes, who in 1940 launched the weekly *In Fact*. Subtitled "An Antidote to Falsehoods in the Daily Press," the four-page newsletter was devoted to press criticism and investigative reporting. His muckraking work exposed the growing influence of corporate power in American society and inspired future muckrakers and publications such as *I. F. Stone's Weekly*. *In Fact*'s circulation peaked at 176,000 subscribers in 1947, outselling leading left-leaning weeklies at the time. Despite the wide readership, however, Seldes was relentlessly red-baited – falsely accused of being a communist – and in 1950 was forced to close his paper after his subscriptions plummeted.[46]

More mainstream 1940s press criticism arose from the likes of A. J. Liebling and Don Hollenbeck. Credited with establishing "a professional genre of journalism criticism" through the *New Yorker*'s "Wayward Press" column and the 15-minute weekly radio program *CBS Views the Press*, these two commentators posed both stylistic and normative questions about press ethics and responsibility.[47] Liebling criticized what he saw as formulaic news meant to entertain but not inform. He decried the explosion of the one-paper town, which he likened to a "privately owned public utility that is constitutionally exempt from public regulation" and deemed a "violation of freedom of the press."[48] He felt the lack of competition hamstrung journalists and deprived audiences of diverse sources of information. Hollenbeck likewise delivered a consistent critique of mainstream media by singling out particular social issues that were neglected, often because a powerful interest was implicated.[49] He would sometimes supply Seldes with "information about overlooked news stories, pro-business bias, and other press misdeeds."[50]

This emerging genre of self-reflexive press criticism was exemplified by the *Nieman Reports*, a quarterly journal published by the respected Nieman Fellows. This Harvard-based program convened about a dozen working journalists each year to focus on specific media-related issues. In the 1940s they increasingly turned toward media criticism. Announcing itself as "filling a

---

[45] Dillard Stokes, "Supreme Court Rules Misleading Ads Not Protected by U.S. Constitution," *Guild Reporter*, June 25, 1948.

[46] Randolph Holhut, The Forgotten Man of American Journalism: A Brief Biography of George Seldes. http://www.brasscheck.com/seldes/bio.html.

[47] Marzolf, *Civilizing Voices*, 177–83; Davies, *Postwar Decline of American Newspapers*, 26.

[48] Quoted in Marzolf, *Civilizing Voices*, 179. For a book on Liebling's life that draws a lot from his "Wayward Press" background, see A. J. Liebling, *The Wayward Press* (Garden City, NY: Doubleday, 1947).

[49] "Critical but Seldom Criticized; Press Hears Censure of Radio," *Guild Reporter*, 1947.

[50] Davies, *Postwar Decline of American Newspapers*, 26.

void," the 1945–6 class published a significant book of press criticism that portrayed newspapers as failing to serve interests beyond those of their profit-seeking owners.[51] It summarized contemporary criticism that the press was irresponsible, biased in favor of property and privilege, and too narrowly owned and controlled.[52] The authors expressed concern that "it seems unhealthy that so overwhelming a majority [of publishers] should favor and advocate so conservative a philosophy." Although newspaper editors "purport to speak for the people," the authors observed, in reality they "speak for the business community and the advertisers from whom they derive most of their revenue."[53] The *New Republic* heralded the *Nieman Reports* as "a work that deserves to stand with the valuable current investigations of the same subject by A. J. Liebling and Don Hollenbeck."[54] Another report by the 1949–50 fellows criticized newswriting's decreasing quality.[55] These efforts helped professionalize press criticism; what had been the province of the radical Left was now embraced across a broader spectrum.[56]

The racial critique of newspapers addressed both media production and representation. American dailies employed few black journalists, and a vibrant African American press arose to challenge misrepresentations in the national media while advocating civil rights. African American groups endeavored to reform print media by creating their own newspapers and intervening against production processes and issues of representation within mainstream newspapers. As one eminent historian has observed, the number of African American newspapers increased from 150 to 250 in the 1940s. These included the *Chicago Defender*, the *Pittsburgh Courier*, the *Atlanta Daily World*, the *Los Angeles Sentinel*, and the *New York Amsterdam News*. The largest postwar periodicals to emerge were the "picture magazines" *Ebony* in Chicago and *Our World* in New York. A number of smaller press organizations sprang up in the mid-1940s in cities like Nashville and Atlanta.[57]

Despite this vibrant journalistic milieu, few black journalists could get jobs in the mainstream press. As late as 1955, the African American journalist Simeon Booker estimated there were approximately two dozen mainstream black journalists.[58] African Americans typically were either segregated to newspapers' back sections or, especially in the South, restricted to separate "black star" editions distributed only in black communities. Minority groups in general, including Asians, Latinos, and Native Americans, were mistreated in the

[51] Svirsky, *Your Newspaper*, 19.
[52] "Blueprint for a Better Press," *Guild Reporter*, December 12, 1947, 7.
[53] Svirsky, *Your Newspaper*, 16.
[54] "Which Paper D'Ya Read?," *New Republic*, December 15, 1947, 27. Quoted in Davies, *Postwar Decline of American Newspapers*, 27.
[55] "Reading, Writing and Newspapers," *Nieman Reports: Special Issues*, April 1950.
[56] Margaret Blanchard, "Press Criticism and National Reform Movements: The Progressive Era and the New Deal," *Journalism History* 5, no. 2 (1978): 33–7, 54–5.
[57] Frank Mott, *American Journalism* (New York: Macmillan, 1950), 794–5.
[58] Cited in Baughmann, "Wounded but Not Slain," 121.

press. If they were mentioned in the news at all, they were often maligned. As one media critic described it, this pattern was part of the "shameful treatment of those whom [newspapers] seem to regard as second-class citizens – the members of minority groups," and African Americans were "special victims of this discrimination."[59]

African Americans had long sought fairer treatment in the press. Their few mentions in mainstream newsprint were often crime related, and even in the most mundane stories, they usually did not receive the courtesy titles of "Mr." and "Mrs." afforded to whites.[60] In the mid-1940s there was a renewed push to change the stigmatizing practice of identifying African Americans by race in news stories.[61] When the *New York Times* eventually changed its policy after the war, the move attracted the attention of other leading media.[62] A *Times* editorial vowed to cease "extending Jim Crowism to the printed page" to help prevent "the bad moral climate which does encourage violence among the ignorant, the weak and the vicious." Noting that in crime stories, "Negroes are often identified, whereas members of other races are not," the editorial ended righteously: "News that encourages racial discrimination may sometimes be of interest, but responsible journalism has a higher law than a passing interest."[63]

Racial issues also impacted labor organizing – both at African American newspapers, whose workers felt particularly vulnerable, and among organizers of local industries who depended on racial solidarity and fair news treatment.[64] Particularly in the South, papers used racism to combat CIO organizing. The *Guild Reporter* singled out one paper because it "engaged in anti-Semitic activities and ... played on race prejudice" to target specific plants and undermine organizing work.[65] This criticism demonstrated the interlinking relations among media structures, content, political pressure, and their tie-ins with racial issues. Meanwhile, as growing press criticism galvanized the public to confront newspapers in their local communities, the press was being confronted nationally at the policy level by all three branches of government.

The Governmental Assault against the Press

Much of the 1940s regulatory activism had its roots in the 1930s. In 1937, newspapers were declared to be involved in interstate commerce and therefore

---

[59] Svirsky, *Your Newspaper*, 22.

[60] Baughman, "Wounded but Not Slain," 3.

[61] "Dailies Cooperation Asked in Solving Negro Problem," *Editor & Publisher*, August 4, 1945.

[62] "Answer," *Time*, August 19, 1946, 60.

[63] "Race in the News," *New York Times*, August 11, 1946, 8E.

[64] "Recognition Sought on 3 Negro Papers," *Guild Reporter*, April 27, 1945; "Parley Pushes Plans to Organize Negro Press," *Guild Reporter*, July 27, 1945, 1, 4.

[65] "Use 'Freedom of the Press' to Combat CIO in the South," *Guild Reporter*, November 22, 1946.

subject to federal oversight. That same year the Supreme Court decided that the AP had to recognize the American Newspaper Guild's collective bargaining rights.[66] While the guild challenged newspapers over fundamental questions of ownership and control, New Deal liberals hatched plans to rein in – and possibly break up – media monopolies. The FDR administration began to target directly the media industry's definition of freedom of the press, referring to it as a "bogie" and a "shibboleth" that shielded the commercial press from scrutiny and regulation. In 1938, President Roosevelt made the unusual move of issuing a five-page letter to the *St. Louis Dispatch* that questioned whether for-profit newspapers were even capable of serving the public interest or compatible with a free press.[67] Many such signs suggest that FDR was eager to take on the newspaper industry, but he also had to tread cautiously given its tremendous political power.

FDR's Department of Justice (DOJ) quietly began amassing information on the newspaper industry as early as 1938, although its efforts would not come to fruition until the 1940s. A secret report circulating at the highest reaches of the DOJ sheds light on the Roosevelt administration's aggressive criticism and behind-the-scenes tactics toward the commercial press.[68] The first page of this self-described "scouting report on restraints of trade in the newspaper industry" suggested that the newspaper business was ripe for a thorough governmental investigation and possible intervention – a fate that publishers thus far had escaped. The newspaper industry was "notorious" because its "industrial structure was completely overlooked." The DOJ aimed to assess newspapers at a structural level, cautioning that the work must be done "very quietly" and be "limited to government records." "The [monopolistic] restraints that exist are fundamental to the current organization of the industry," the report concluded; "they can easily be dramatized; their mere recitation should forever lay low the shibboleth of 'freedom of the press.'"

This initiative helped create the antitrust case that would be launched against the Associated Press in the early 1940s, discussed later. It also helped direct FDR's approach to cross-ownership concerns, for the greatest threat, the report suggested, was newspapers' increasing acquisitions of radio stations. Although the industry initially feared radio "as an advertising competitor," the report noted, newspapers' worries were "lifted by a determined policy of acquisition of the new medium." Moreover, the memo warned that the FCC had "taken

[66] *Associated Press v. National Labor Relations Board*, 301 US 103, 132 (1937).
[67] This challenge led to a conference at which many of these issues were debated. See Nikki Usher, "Resurrecting the 1938 St. Louis Post-Dispatch Symposium on the Freedom of the Press: Examining Its Contributions and Their Implications for Today," *Journalism Studies* 11, no. 3 (2010): 311–26.
[68] "Confidential Memorandum to Assistant Attorney General Arnold," 1938, "The Newspaper Industry," Hugh Baker Cox Papers, American Heritage Center, University of Wyoming, Laramie. Also titled "Memorandum on Newspapers" (prepared by Irene Till), #3128, Notebook 5, August 3. I thank Dan Schiller for sharing this archival material with me.

a stand-off position; though recognizing the problem, they say their job is to regulate radio stations and not newspapers." The report pinpointed cross-ownership's dangers: "the news policies of the radio stations are, of course, attuned to those of the publishers and their newspapers." For example, "Where newspapers have been closed by strikes, the affiliated radio stations have conveyed the publisher's side of the story; and some libel suits are now pending against newspaper-owned stations by the Newspaper Guild." The report concluded that barring government intervention, "in the next few years the newspapers will own and control most of the radio stations in the country."

As discussed in Chapter 2, FDR responded to cross-ownership concerns by targeting newspapers via the FCC's regulatory authority over radio. Specifically, he sought to reverse newspapers' alarmingly rapid acquisition of radio stations. His efforts yielded only limited success, but FDR did arguably help slow media concentration, while the courts were more successful in constraining media monopoly power.

The Associated Press Decisions

What began as the Justice Department's first serious attempt to bring the provisions of the Sherman Antitrust Act to bear on the newspaper industry led to some of the most progressive First Amendment decisions in American history.[69] The Associated Press, a cooperatively owned newswire service, had long been criticized for anti-competitive behavior.[70] The Justice Department sued the AP in 1942 for hindering trade by refusing to provide wire services to the liberal Marshall Field–owned *Chicago Sun* while maintaining an exclusive market contract with the right-wing Colonel Robert McCormick–owned *Chicago Tribune*. As it went to court, the case generated fierce debate. Those siding with the newspaper industry drew from libertarian interpretations of the First Amendment that, they believed, rendered the press immune to antitrust interventions. The Vermont Republican representative Charles Plumley went even further, condemning the suit as the product of "socialistic, communistic, and paler pinks, intellectuals, radicals, lecturers, and columnists" who opposed the Bill of Rights.[71]

Zechariah Chafee argued opposite points in his "public service theory of the press," articulated during his involvement with the AP antitrust case. Given Chafee's earlier writings, which allowed that healthy democratic discourse may require external nurturing at the structural level, an affirmative governmental role in protecting press freedoms seems consistent. He wrote in 1928 that

[69] For a discussion of the following cases, see Donald Smith, *Zechariah Chafee, Jr.: Defender of the Liberty and Law* (Cambridge, MA: Harvard University Press, 1986).

[70] For an excellent historical overview of this criticism, see Stephen Bates, "Regulating Gatekeepers of Information: The Associated Press as a Common Carrier," *UB Journal of Media Law & Ethics* 3, no. 1/2 (Winter/Spring 2012).

[71] Quoted in Margaret Blanchard, "The Associated Press Antitrust Suit: A Philosophical Clash over Ownership of First Amendment Rights," *Business History Review* 61 (1987): 59.

"freedom of opinion is not safe merely through the absence of legal interference: there must exist affirmative channels of expression."[72] Accordingly, while Chafee would tend more toward First Amendment absolutist positions during his time on the Hutchins Commission (discussed later), he would diverge from strict hands-off laissez-faire approaches to media if he thought artificial barriers such as trade restraints and other monopolistic abuses threatened the health of the country's democratic discourse.

This nuanced view helps explain his opposition to the AP's First Amendment argument, whose most visible proponent was Fred Siebert, the *Tribune*'s associate counsel, who filed a friend-of-the-court brief. Siebert later would coauthor the seminal *Four Theories of the Press*, a foundational text for normative theories of journalism. His and Chafee's debate appeared in the *Chicago Tribune*, gaining much attention. A key quote by Chafee defines his position: "The new conception of public service brings new responsibilities. Within reasonable limits the public can shape the nature of the service which it receives. Prices, quality, wages paid, conditions of employment, etc., are subjected to regulations."[73] For his part, Siebert dismissed the public-service argument, saying that the public interest was better served by allowing market-driven competition among news agencies.

Ultimately the case was decided by a three-judge federal district court that came down 2 to 1 against the AP. Judge Learned Hand drew heavily from Chafee's counsel in authoring the landmark decision – some even accused Hand of virtually repeating verbatim Chafee's instructions. Even if it drew from more long-standing liberal thought regarding the "marketplace of ideas" and related normative theories, the decision was based on a relatively novel argument that democratic imperatives superseded the newspaper industry's interests. The argument also assumed that such antimonopoly measures were consistent with First Amendment protections, as Hand's opinion explained:

Neither exclusively, nor even primarily, are the interests of the newspaper industry conclusive; for that industry serves one of the most vital of all general interests: the dissemination of news from as many different sources, and with as many different facets and colors as is possible. That interest is closely akin to, if indeed it is not the same as, the interest protected by the First Amendment; it presupposes that right conclusions are more likely to be gathered out of a multitude of tongues, than through any kind of authoritative process. To many this is, and always will be, folly; but we have staked upon it our all.[74]

[72] He also wrote, "We cannot afford to neglect methods for obtaining livelier oral discussion and places available for it, and for encouraging fuller presentation of all sides of international and industrial controversies in the press and over the radio." Zechariah Chafee, "Liberty and Law," in *Freedom in the Modern World*, ed. Horace Kallen (Ithaca, NY: Cornell University Press, 1928), quoted in Smith, *Zechariah Chafee, Jr.*, 95–6.
[73] Chafee, statement on AP case, *Chicago Sunday Tribune*, April 18, 1943.
[74] *United States v. Associated Press*, 52 F. Sup 362, 372 (S.D.N.Y.1943).

Predictably, this decision was hailed by progressives as an enlightened position and condemned in many newspapers as an attack on core American freedoms. Noting a "transition from individualism to collectivism," Chafee's biographer observed that the "federal government's assertion of some authority over the media strengthened the hand of press critics who, since the progressive period early in the century, had been saying that if the media did not reform themselves, the government would do it for them."[75]

The decision was appealed to the Supreme Court, where the newspaper industry lost again two years later in a monumental decision. The Supreme Court justice Hugo Black wrote the majority opinion in this case, arguing that freedom of the press protects all of society, not just media owners and producers. In its oft-quoted majority opinion, the court stated that the First Amendment "rests on the assumption that the widest possible dissemination of information from diverse and antagonistic sources is essential to the welfare of the public, that a free press is a condition of free society ... freedom to publish means freedom for all and not for some." The Court further explained, "It would be strange indeed ... if the grave concern for freedom of the press which prompted adoption of the First Amendment should be read as a command that the government was without power to protect that freedom." This notion of state-guaranteed provisions for public interest protections in the press was clear: "Freedom of the press from governmental interference under the First Amendment does not sanction repression of that freedom by private interests."[76]

In his concurring opinion, Justice Felix Frankfurter emphasized the press's unique role in democracies, qualifying it for special protections. He argued that "in addition to being a commercial enterprise," the press required nurturing, for it "has a relation to the public interest unlike that of any other enterprise pursued for profit." More than Justice Black, whose decision mostly focused on whether antitrust litigation was appropriate, Frankfurter adopted Chafee's and Hand's public service rationale in defining the press's role:

A free press is indispensable to the workings of our democratic society. The business of the press, and therefore the business of the Associated Press, is the promotion of truth regarding public matters by furnishing the basis for an understanding of them. Truth and understanding are not wares like peanuts or potatoes. And so, the incidence of restraints upon the promotion of truth through denial of access to the basis for understanding calls into play considerations very different from comparable restraints in a cooperative enterprise having merely a commercial aspect.[77]

Frankfurter's opinion stands out for suggesting that the information produced by press institutions is not a mere commodity but rather an essential public

---

[75] Smith, *Zechariah Chafee, Jr.*, 99–100.
[76] *Associated Press v. United States*, 326 U.S. 1, 20 (1945).
[77] Ibid. See Scott, "Labor's New Deal for Journalism," 269–77.

good, a public service that cannot be reduced to market value. This articulation stands as one of the clearest positive renderings of the First Amendment. And yet it played only a relatively minor role in subsequent legal opinion and media policy making. Although it still stands today, rarely is this decision invoked by anyone beyond media reform activists and intellectuals who call for more affirmative media policies.

Reactions to the decision reflected differing ideological positions. The *Chicago Sun* – whose owner, Marshall Field, initiated the original proceedings against the AP – reflected liberal opinion by hailing it as "a victory for the American people." But overall the commercial press reacted negatively to the verdict.[78] Newspaper publishers' greatest fear, it seemed, was for the press to be categorized as a common carrier (like telecommunications), which would force them to grant greater leeway to the public's positive right to media access. Neither court decision went that far, but they did introduce several new concepts into the discourse around press regulation, including what one press historian described as a "public interest interpretation of the First Amendment" emphasizing the need for positive liberties and diverse sources of information.[79] While many publishers saw these decisions as reflecting partisan desires to cripple the conservative press, some saw even graver long-term threats in having a positive First Amendment guiding media policy.

With so much at stake, some sectors of the press continued fighting the decision. After the Supreme Court refused to grant a rehearing of the case, Colonel McCormick led an effort to negate the court decision by going directly to Congress, where, it was assumed, the newly established Republican majority would sympathize with the publishers' plight. Specifically, McCormick petitioned Congress to amend the Sherman Antitrust Act so that the newspaper industry was exempt from it.[80] Investigations and hearings were held around the proposed legislation, known as the Mason Bill. For the most part, the same arguments were leveled from their respective interlocutors. The ACLU had called upon Thurman Arnold, who was now a sitting judge, to testify. Arnold, who as the former assistant attorney general and head of the DOJ's Antitrust Division filed the original suit against the AP on the government's behalf, argued that the decision's purpose was to protect press freedoms from private tyrannies. Fred Siebert, on the other hand, testified on industry's behalf that government had no legitimacy in taking "a positive position in regard to the freedom of the press" because it was not "the duty of the court or of the Congress ... to see that the American people are furnished ... with information from various channels." Instead, "the constitution was designed to keep the Government from interfering with the private operation of our channels

---

[78] "AP Court Decision Hailed as Victory for Press Freedom," *Guild Reporter*, June 22, 1945.

[79] Blanchard, "Associated Press Antitrust Suit," 63.

[80] William Swindler, "The AP Anti-Trust Case in Historical Perspective," *Journalism Quarterly* 23, no. 4 (March 1946): 40–57.

of news."[81] A clearer articulation of a negative freedom of the press would be difficult to find.

The conservative publishers' campaign to overturn the Court's decision did not pan out as planned. Elite consensus was moving in the opposite direction, albeit briefly, with even conservative congressmen adopting liberal arguments in support of government intervention against the press. In supreme irony, at one point during the hearings a conservative Republican entered into the record various warnings about the dangers of media concentration as recited from Morris Ernst's book *The First Freedom*.[82] Margaret Blanchard cited this episode – a conservative politician torpedoing a conservative bill with a leftist argument – as exemplifying just how far the consensus had moved by the mid-1940s when press criticism "had reached its peak." "Private and government organizations," Blanchard observed, "were studying dwindling newspaper competition around the country, and accusations were flying about the irresponsible exercise of First Amendment rights by the proprietors of the media."[83] Other congressional actions at this time – for a relatively brief moment – similarly supported government intervention against the newspaper industry.

Congressional Investigations

Newspapers' vulnerability was signaled by a number of maneuvers originating within government's legislative branch in the mid-1940s. In particular, congressional critics began probing newspapers' monopolistic practices. One congressional report focused on economic concentration during the war, including concerns about newspaper consolidation: "Free critical inquiry and the open expression of opposing points of view comprise one of the essential ingredients of a political democracy." Thus "citizens in so many communities can buy only one daily paper and that in so many cases these single dailies present the point of view of the same newspaper chain," and "few communities now have more than one version of the news." Noting monopolistic trends in the press and the prohibitive costs of starting a newspaper, the report concluded that "if freedom of the press is to be had only through ownership of a newspaper, it can, under present conditions, be a reality only for the well-to-do."[84]

Around the same time, the U.S. Senate Small Business Committee announced that it was investigating what it referred to as "obstacles to free competition, especially among community newspapers."[85] Near the end of his chairmanship of the Small Business Committee, the Democratic senator James Murray released a 71-page report, *Survival of a Free Competitive Press: The Small*

[81] All quoted in Blanchard, "Associated Press Antitrust Suit," 77.

[82] Ibid., 80.

[83] Ibid., 84.

[84] Reprinted in "Senate Report Shows Trend toward Monopoly in the Newspaper Industry," *Guild Reporter*, July 26, 1946, 3.

[85] "Senate Body Probes Small Paper Newsprint Squeeze," *Guild Reporter*, November 8, 1946, 8.

Newspaper, Democracy's Grass Roots. Drawing a dark portrait of a decimated small-town-newspaper industry, the report called for closer federal scrutiny of chain newspapers and a series of hearings on their effects on small publishers. Instead of limiting itself to economic considerations, the report drew linkages between a monopolistic newspaper industry and the health of American democracy.[86] It also examined the historic role of postal subsidies in sustaining newspaper diversity, describing it as an "ethical issue" based on "the decision by Congress to stimulate the diffusion of knowledge, information, and opinion."[87] Under a section titled "Government Assistance," the report argued for enabling government lending agencies such as the Reconstruction Finance Corporation (RFC) to "lend money to small newspaper publishers and radio-station operators," as they did for other industries, and "allow veterans to acquire loans to start small papers underwritten as provided in the GI bill of rights."[88] Murray's report was dismissive of critics who feared undue governmental influence: "To argue that government loans would make newspapers and stations subservient to the government implies that those who are now able to borrow from private lenders are subservient to them."[89] If the RFC was unable to make nonpartisan loans to papers and stations, then, the report argued, a "new small-loan agency is needed on that basis alone."[90] It also advocated government subsidies in the form of paid advertising in the nation's smaller papers for the War Assets Administration, which was selling off surplus goods.[91]

The report's conclusion, titled "In Defense of Competition," warned the newspaper trade association and the trade press that their "sanguine attitude" would lead to their own ruin. "The whole economic history of America demonstrates that a privately monopolized or highly cartelized press cannot remain free of government regulation for long." Yet the very "private agencies" that stood to lose the most, instead of leading "the fight against the trends towards concentration," seemed "curiously unconcerned" and "strangely cold to even the study of the problem by Congress."[92] By all appearances, the newspaper industry and its allies ignored the report.

Murray also presented his findings to the Senate Small Business Committee, stressing the high mortality rate among daily papers, the continued growth of newspaper monopolies, and the squeezing out of small local papers and weeklies. Murray warned that the competitive press was dying because of the

[86] U.S. Congress, Senate, Special Committee to Study the Problems of American Small Business, *Survival of a Free Competitive Press: The Small Newspaper, Democracy's Grass Roots*, Senate Committee Print 17, Eightieth Congress, First session (Washington, DC: U.S. Government Printing Office, 1947), 1–4.
[87] Ibid., 50.
[88] Ibid., 56–7.
[89] Ibid., 56.
[90] Ibid.
[91] Ibid., 60.
[92] Ibid., 63.

rising costs of operating small newspapers, technological changes, and various revenue losses. He reported that two hundred papers consumed 85 percent of the nation's total newsprint, leaving the rest to be divided among seventeen thousand smaller dailies. This scenario posed a major problem for the 80th Congress and required immediate governmental action, especially because the "future of the small press business is linked with the future of our political democracy" and the "traditionally valued American system of small competing press units is now in such serious jeopardy."[93]

Whether legislation addressing the loss of small local papers could have passed is impossible to know, as the Republicans' 1946 congressional sweep put an end to such talk. Plans for subsequent hearings were aborted as Senate Republicans shifted the meetings' focus to issues such as newsprint shortages, and industry allies in the trade press dismissed Murray's report.[94] Although never amounting to a serious intervention, the congressional investigation, along with regulatory threats from other sectors of government, alerted publishers that their privileged position in society – one that previously insulated them from such interventions – was at risk. Media institutions needed an antidote to such regulatory threats. To inoculate themselves against further criticism, and to preserve their laissez-faire relationship with government, journalists would have to professionalize their craft. They would need to become "socially responsible," while remaining self-regulated.

The Birth of the Hutchins Commission

According to several accounts, the Hutchins Commission's genesis traces back to a casual exchange around 1943 between two former Yale schoolmates: Henry Luce, the founder of *Time* and *Life*, and Robert Hutchins, the educational reformer and University of Chicago president. Both men were at an *Encyclopaedia Britannica* directors meeting, where, according to the official narrative, Luce asked Hutchins about freedom of the press and what responsibilities it entailed. Hutchins said he did not know but would be interested in organizing a committee to study the question if Luce would pay for it, and he did.[95]

---

[93] "Monopoly Strangling Free Press, Senate Report Says," *Guild Reporter*, February 14, 1947, 5. A common concern at the time was that sending facsimile newspapers over FM frequencies to a home receiver and reproducing them on sensitized paper would become a widespread practice. For an in-depth story of facsimile transmissions and their assumed implications for the press, see "Radio Now Will Deliver Your Paper," *Guild Reporter*, April 26, 1946, 3.

[94] *Editor & Publisher*, October 26, 1946, 26; and *Guild Reporter*, November 8, 1946, 8.

[95] Drawn from several accounts, especially Stephen Bates, "Realigning Journalism with Democracy: The Hutchins Commission, Its Times, and Ours" (Washington, DC: Annenberg Washington Program in Communications Policy Studies of Northwestern University, 1995). See also Jerilyn S. McIntyre, "Repositioning a Landmark: The Hutchins Commission and Freedom of the Press," *Critical Studies in Mass Communication* 4 (1987): 154. Other accounts of the commission's origins are found in Elie Abel, "Hutchins Revisited: Thirty-five Years of Social Responsibility

Although it is a charming tale, and probably true to some extent, the likely subtext of the story is that Luce, like other 1940s press barons, saw the writing on the wall: The Roosevelt administration and progressive New Dealers had been gearing up to investigate the newspaper industry since the late 1930s, and these efforts were now coming to fruition. Criticism from fellow journalists, intellectuals, and the broader public was alarming enough, but the industry had also recently endured an FCC investigation of newspaper ownership of radio and television stations and the Justice Department's antitrust crusade against the AP. Facing multiple attacks from the intelligentsia, printers' unions, the Newspaper Guild, the courts, Congress, the Roosevelt administration, the FCC, and the public, newspaper owners awakened to the considerable forces aligning against their laissez-faire privileges. It was common knowledge that newspapers had caused tremendous grief for the Roosevelt administration with their anti–New Deal coverage and their endorsements of FDR's political opponents. Retribution was almost expected. Newspaper trade meetings became rumor mills predicting how the government schemed to break up newspaper chains as it recently had or was attempting to do in the radio, telephone, and film industries. Similar governmental strikes against the press seemed increasingly plausible.[96]

Although surely not entirely precalculated, forming a respected commission to define press responsibility in retrospect seems a shrewd move – almost as if Luce attempted to steal a march instead of waiting for governmental intervention. The recent Court decision shifting First Amendment protections from publishers and toward the public gave the press reason to welcome such an inquiry.[97] With this power shift as a backdrop, Luce asked Hutchins to undertake a high-profile in-depth study investigating the freedom and responsibility of the press, which they defined expansively to include radio, movies, books, and magazines as well as newspapers. Luce would provide $200,000 to fund the endeavor.[98]

Luce had a personal history of being concerned about journalism's democratic and international roles.[99] In 1939 he was quoted as saying that "the

Theory," in *The Responsibilities of Journalism*, ed. Robert Schmuhl (Notre Dame, IN: University of Notre Dame Press, 1984), 39; Frank Hughes, *Prejudice and the Press: A Restatement of the Principle of Freedom of the Press, with Specific Reference to the Hutchins-Luce Commission* (New York: Devin-Adair, 1950), 21; Norman Isaacs, *Untended Gates: The Mismanaged Press* (New York: Columbia University Press, 1986), 100.

[96] "*FCC v. Publishers*," *Time*, Monday, May 5, 1941.
[97] Margaret Blanchard makes this point in "The Hutchins Commission, the Press and the Responsibility Concept," *Journalism Monographs* 49 (1977): 3–6. She also argues that "freedom of the press" had for many newspaper leaders become a slogan with which to ward of government regulation and protect profits.
[98] *Encyclopaedia Britannica* also contributed $15,000.
[99] James Baughman, *Henry R. Luce and the Rise of the American News Media* (Boston: Twayne, 1987). See also Alan Brinkley, *The Publisher: Henry Luce and His American Century* (New York: Alfred A. Knopf, 2010).

present crisis in world affairs may be described as a crisis in journalism."[100] But he also had a reputation for being a shrewd businessman. One historian described Luce as a "self-conscious propagandist for American business, celebrating investment bankers and corporate leaders on the cover of *Time*."[101] While it is safe to assume that he was driven by more than a selfless concern for humanity, Luce's ulterior motives and whether he influenced the commission's agenda are questions of some historical debate.

While many have assumed that Luce took a hands-off approach, evidence also suggests that he remained involved in important ways throughout the process. Drawing on some of the same archival evidence that I have consulted, the historian Jane McConnell has argued convincingly that not only was Luce directly involved in selecting commissioners – for example, he appears to have nixed Hutchins's proposal to invite the famed antitrust crusader Thurman Arnold, and he did not respond favorably to inviting the former FCC chairman Larry Fly[102] – he also played a subtle but significant role throughout the discussions. McConnell has suggested that this role was deliberately obscured, perhaps to protect the commission's reputation.[103]

Regardless, Luce's desires likely influenced the commission even if he later professed to be dissatisfied with its conclusions. Luce was known for expecting his preconceived assumptions to be borne out by the writers he commissioned.[104] It does not appear that Luce had direct editorial control over the commission's published work, but his expectations may have helped shape the parameters of their debates, particularly with regard to government regulation of the press. Nonetheless, Luce provided the resources with which to gather together many of the most respected American intellectuals, and Hutchins immediately endeavored to establish the Commission's autonomy.

Before the first meeting, Hutchins strategized with Harold Lasswell how to guarantee *Time*'s funding regardless of Luce's commitment to their project. "The Commission cannot run the risk that Mr. Luce would lose interest if the conclusions developed were unpalatable to him."[105] By all appearances, Luce remained unobtrusive and mostly accommodating. Judging by the many early letters between them, Luce largely rubber-stamped Hutchins's suggestions,

[100] Quoted in Jane McConnell, "Choosing a Team for Democracy: Henry R. Luce and the Commission on Freedom of the Press," *American Journalism* 14, no. 2 (1997): 153.

[101] Michael Denning, *The Cultural Front: The Laboring of American Culture in the Twentieth Century* (London: Verso, 1996), 84.

[102] McConnell , "Choosing a Team for Democracy," 156–7.

[103] Ibid., 162.

[104] See generally: McConnell, "Choosing a Team for Democracy," 148–63.

[105] Robert Hutchins to Harold Lasswell, November 26, 1943, Box 7, Folder 7, Robert M. Hutchins Papers, Joseph Regenstein Library, University of Chicago (hereafter cited as Hutchins Papers). He also noted that the commission should consult newspaper representatives and the radio and movie industries and should identify media problems in advance via members' memoranda, as became standard procedure.

although Hutchins still felt compelled to run past him major details, such as the selection of commissioners. When asked what his response would be if the commission found that the concentration of information in large media corporations like his own was threatening press freedoms, Luce reportedly said, "If that's what they find, that's what they find."[106] After causing some consternation by showing up at early meetings, Luce mostly kept away throughout the commission's three years of work.[107] Although he was one of the interviewees and occasionally was invited over for drinks and meals, he played no direct role in the commission's deliberations.[108] Nonetheless his presence was undoubtedly felt.

The Commissioners

When the original choice, Judge Learned Hand, declined to chair the commission's proceedings, Hutchins took on the role. He may have seemed a safe choice, but his independent streak was well known. Although not a radical leftist, he had proven himself capable of taking on powerful interests with his reforms at the University of Chicago, where he became the "boy president" at the age of thirty in 1929.[109] He caused a public uproar by disbanding the university's football team as well as its vocation programs. He also reorganized the school curricula around "great ideas" and founded the "Great Books" program.[110] During the war, Hutchins became an ardent advocate of fighting against fascism and helped enlist the university in military efforts, including the Manhattan Project – even offering up the vacant Stagg Field stadium to create the first atomic reaction. After the dropping of the atomic bomb, however, Hutchins became an outspoken activist against nuclear armament and a proponent of world government, creating and serving as the president for the Committee to Frame a World Constitution.[111] Although press issues were not his primary focus, he called for "an endowed press" that could help educate the

---

[106] Kenneth Stewart, "Press RX: Faith healings?" *Saturday Review of Literature*, April 7, 1947, 14, 27.

[107] Robert Hutchins to Harold Lasswell, Box 7, Folder 6, Hutchins Papers. Hutchins hated "to deprive [Luce] of the opportunity" to attend meetings but hoped he still was benefitting from their discussions.

[108] Robert Leigh to Commissioners, June 26, 1946, Box 8, Folder 1, Hutchins Papers.

[109] The following discussion draws from two dissertations that provide excellent intellectual and cultural backgrounds for the commissioners and their worldviews: Frederick Blevens, "Gentility and Quiet Aggression: A Cultural History of the Commission on Freedom of the Press" (Ph.D. Dissertation, University of Missouri, 1995), and Mark Fackler, "The Hutchins Commissioners and the Crisis in Democratic Theory, 1930–1947" (Ph.D. Dissertation, University of Illinois, 1982).

[110] See generally Milton Mayer, *Robert Maynard Hutchins: A Memoir* (Berkeley: University of California Press, 1993).

[111] See Anna McCarthy, *The Citizen Machine* (New York: New Press, 2010).

masses.[112] Hutchins also had regular interactions with the press and maintained a national audience as a public intellectual, publishing widely on issues related to education and appearing regularly on a weekly public-affairs program, the *Chicago Roundtable*.[113] It was up to Hutchins to assemble an all-star cast for the commission.

Hutchins chose for the commission twelve of the most eminent intellectuals in the country, all white upper-class men with unimpeachable pedigrees. Taking counsel from trusted friends and colleagues, Hutchins selected commissioners on the basis of reputation and area of expertise. Although he did not impose a strict ideological litmus test, he did assume that they all shared a commitment to liberal democracy, if not his own center-left political assumptions, and throughout the commission's operations he often pushed for centrist positions.[114]

The aforementioned Zechariah Chafee, a Harvard law professor and vice-chairman of the commission, ironically became a proponent for laissez-faire positions during many of their discussions. Though Chafee served an important role in influencing Judge Hand's decision in the 1943 *AP* case and occasionally allowed for affirmative government intervention, his otherwise libertarian proclivities led him to clash often with William Hocking, a Harvard philosophy professor emeritus. Hocking would represent the opposite perspective, often advocating a collectivist approach to media regulation. He maintained that freedom was not an inalienable right but rather a moral right that must be earned through duties that fell beyond self-interest.[115] At seventy when the meetings began, Hocking was the oldest of the commissioners. He authored the commission's "statement of principles," which would serve as its philosophical foundations. Hocking and Chafee often represented the commission's normative range in terms of recommending regulatory action against the press.

Often challenging these bounds was one of the commission's more colorful characters, Archibald MacLeish. Formerly head of the Library of Congress and an award-winning poet, MacLeish had directed the War Department's Office of Facts and Figures – where he became frustrated that the public lacked access to reliable information – and was the Office of War Information's assistant director. MacLeish was also the first curator for the Nieman Fellowships. In 1944 he became an assistant secretary of state for cultural affairs, and later represented the United States during the United Nations Educational, Scientific and Cultural Organization's (UNESCO's) creation. Though critical of Marxism, MacLeish was the radical of the group, often a lone voice in challenging the commercial

---

[112] "Hutchins Suggests Endowed Press," *Editor & Publisher*, April 26, 1930, 33.

[113] Mayer, *Robert Maynard Hutchins*.

[114] Fackler believes they were influenced by intellectual shifts that were later depicted in Edward Purcell, *The Crisis of Democratic Theory: Scientific Naturalism and the Problem of Value* (Lexington: University Press of Kentucky, 1973).

[115] Nerone, *Last Rights*, 86.

press's legitimacy. He likened the 1940s American press to the model exploited by Hitler, whose aim, he argued, was "to produce the intellectual perplexity, the emotional disorder, the doubt of truth, the distrust of all declarations of principle, all measures of value, all standards of decency, in the midst of which, like thieves in the confusion of a manufactured panic, the gangsters of the age may have their way."[116]

Harold Lasswell was a Yale law professor who authored pioneering work on propaganda and helped with U.S. operations during the war. In 1939 he was appointed as the first director of the Library of Congress's Rockefeller Foundation–supported research division, which conducted analyses, gathered intelligence, and trained workers for other intelligence units. He is well known for defining an "act of communication" as "who says what in which channel to whom with what effect."[117] The youngest member, Lasswell shared many of the commissioners' growing conviction that Mill- and Milton-inspired notions that democratic discourse was inherently self-correcting were being disproven. However, he also believed that the press, if encouraged to provide positive freedoms for the public, could help compensate for deficits in the broader discourse. In 1941, Lasswell wrote an essay titled "The Achievement Standards of a Democratic Press," in which he stated that "the lords of the press cannot suddenly spring to a higher level of social insight than the owners of banks, insurance companies, public utilities, manufacturing corporations" because "all are of the same social structure."[118] Nonetheless, Lasswell believed that social scientists could maintain standards via content analysis to evaluate press performance in covering important policy issues. Lasswell felt that such information was essential to prevent periodic crises from endangering both the "security of the nation and the freedom of the individual."[119]

Many of the other commissioners generally sided with Chafee's laissez-faire approach. John Clark, a Columbia University economics professor, had worked in government during the 1930s and 1940s and was known for developing economic theory positioned between nationalization and laissez-faire frameworks. His notions of "social control of business" were an early

[116] Archibald MacLeish, "The Duty of Freedom," in *Freedom of the Press Today: A Clinical Examination by 28 Specialists*, ed. Harold Ickes (New York: Vanguard Press, 1941), 187–91. Quoted in Blevens, "Gentility and Quiet Aggression," 272. MacLeish resigned from the commission in early 1945 after his appointment as assistant secretary of state for cultural affairs, but remained engaged and attended later meetings. Hutchins considered Larry Fly as a replacement, but the position remained vacant. See Summary and Discussion and Action, Meetings, Document 31, 2, January 22–3, 1945, Box 3, Folder 2–31, Commission on Freedom of the Press Papers, Special Collections, University of Washington, Seattle (hereafter cited as Commission on Freedom of the Press Papers).

[117] Harold Lasswell, "The Structure and Function of Communication in Society," in *The Communication of Ideas*, 37–51. Robert Leigh also had a piece published in this book.

[118] Harold Lasswell, "The Achievement Standards of a Democratic Press," in *Freedom of the Press Today*, 171–8.

[119] Harold Lasswell, "Propaganda and Mass Insecurity," *Psychiatry* 13 (August 1950): 283–93.

version of corporate social responsibility, and he sometimes chided his fellow commissioners' tendency to see governmental intervention as a needed safeguard.[120] John Dickinson, a University of Pennsylvania law professor, shared Clark's reluctance to rely on governmental intervention. Dickinson was one of the commission's more conservative members and was somewhat complacent toward monopoly power. During his time at the Justice Department's Antitrust Division, he was known as a "friend of the trusts," either ignoring infractions or meting out light penalties.[121] When the FDR administration began trust-busting, Dickinson left government to teach in the private sector. George Shuster, president of Hunter College, was generally liberal but tended to see governmental control as the greatest threat to press freedom. Charles Merriam, a University of Chicago professor emeritus of political science, was more amenable to New Deal assumptions regarding governmental management of market excesses but sought a middle way between collectivism and individualism. Reinhold Niebuhr, a professor of ethics and philosophy of religion at Union Theological Seminary, had shifted from his earlier socialism to become more of a "liberal realist." Robert Redfield, a University of Chicago anthropology professor, had advised the War Relocation Authority. Beardsley Ruml, New York City's Federal Reserve Bank chairman, tended to dismiss suspicions about media concentration and thought there should be no governmental checks on media content.[122] Arthur Schlesinger Sr., father of the famous historian Arthur Schlesinger Jr., was a respected Harvard history professor, and one of the commission's least active members.

Robert Leigh, a former Bennington College president, was the commission's director and coordinator. Although not a full-fledged member, he handled much of the commission's administrative work as well as editing and writing some of the published reports. Previously he had worked for the FCC, and he maintained close ties with the agency, especially with Durr. During the war, Leigh, along with a half-dozen of his fellow commissioners, served in an advisory role for the National Resources Planning Board. After leaving the commission in the late 1940s, Leigh would become a major scholar and activist for library- and information-related issues, directing a nationwide Public Library Inquiry study for the Social Science Research Council.[123] While on the Hutchins Commission, Leigh was a proponent of emphasizing positive freedom of the press.

[120] John Clark, *Social Control of Business* (Chicago: The University of Chicago Press, 1926). His later work advocated social ethics based on individual responsibility without necessitating governmental intervention. See John Clark, *Alternative to Serfdom* (New York: Alfred A. Knopf, 1948). Clark later resigned because of health reasons.

[121] Blevens, "Gentility and Quiet Aggression," 214.

[122] See, for example, summary of discussion, July 7–9, 1946, doc. 108B, 93, Commission on Freedom of the Press Papers.

[123] For example, see Robert D. Leigh, *The Public Library in the United States* (New York: Columbia University Press, 1950).

Another key participant who deserves more attention than previous accounts have provided was Ruth Inglis, author of the commission's report on movies. Inglis stands out as the only female staff member on the commission. Although an active contributor, in the commission's meeting notes, she was listed as a "clerk."[124] Previously on Smith College's faculty, Inglis had worked with Leo Rosten on his film industry research and had worked with Paul Lazarsfeld in preparing a review of the early canon for the nascent field of mass communications.[125] After her work on the commission, she became a University of Washington sociology professor. Joining her as a key author and staffer was Llewellyn "Johnny" White, who authored two of the six book-length reports, one on radio and one on international communications. White had been an adviser to the Office of War Information's director on American agencies' international communication and postwar information. After leaving the commission, he directed mass communications on the permanent staff of UNESCO.[126]

None of the commissioners was a working journalist – as would later become one of the press's favorite attack lines – though several had limited journalistic experience. MacLeish, for instance, wrote for *Fortune* for a number of years and was the curator for the journalism-focused Nieman Foundation. Hutchins had considered inviting someone like Walter Lippmann, but he believed that the commission could be more objective without journalists, and Luce seemed to agree. Also noteworthy is that many of these commissioners, including Lasswell and MacLeish, formerly held posts contributing to governmental propaganda activities, and Leigh had directed the FCC's Foreign Broadcast Intelligence Commission and the UN Monitoring Commission during World War II. Leigh and MacLeish also had experience with information policy, particularly regarding libraries. Several other commissioners had held government positions within the FDR administration, a qualification that suggests liberal ideological backgrounds but also that they were generally pro-establishment, vested in the status quo. They simultaneously rationalized anti-democratic functions such as government propaganda and held reformist, social democratic ideals by imagining a progressive role for government in media and social life in general.

The Hutchins Commission's creation marked a watershed moment, the outcomes of which would help establish the modern American press system's

---

[124] See, for example, Summary of Discussion and Action, doc. 26, January 17, 1945, Box 2, Folder 2–26, Commission on Freedom of the Press Papers.

[125] Robert Leigh to Archibald MacLeish, August 24, 1944, Box 7, Folder 7, Hutchins Papers. After her work on the commission, according to an article in *Editor & Publisher*, she would also take a research role with the NAB. Stephen Bates has uncovered the surprising irony that she later became a conservative critic.

[126] Leigh mentioned this to Hutchins regarding a plan for a nonprofit international communications system. Robert Leigh to Robert Hutchins, April 26, 1946, Box 8, Folder 1, Hutchins Papers.

normative foundations. Grappling with a number of core debates about the relationship between media and democracy, the commission's intellectual power gave it tremendous norm-setting influence. The legal scholar C. Edwin Baker noted that the commission's general report "provides the most influential modern account of the goals of journalistic performance" and is virtually treated as the "official Western view."[127] Baker described its work as "the most important, semi-official, policy-oriented study of the mass media in U.S. history,"[128] and the widely respected media scholar James Curran writes that it is "still perhaps the most cogent and elegant report on media policy ever published in the English language."[129] The historian Robert Horwitz noted that the commission's advocacy for a media ethics based on professionalism and responsibility "was taken up in many journalism schools."[130] Indeed, the commission's work inspired the seminal 1956 *Four Theories of the Press*, which in turn became required reading for American journalism students for decades, shaping a generation's thinking about the roles and responsibilities of the press. Media historians have devoted many pages of analysis to the Hutchins Commission's significance in defining media's normative role, yet few have looked at the unpublished transcripts from its meetings and back-channel communications to grasp the true range of the commissioners' discussions as they considered perennial questions about the roles of media, government, and private power in democratic societies.

Together, these thinkers meant to provide a rationale for press freedom. Yet, despite Luce's probable goal of inoculating the industry against governmental regulation, Hutchins, like many 1940s liberal intellectuals, had reformist instincts, and the Hutchins Commission would prove itself to be much more than a reliable whitewash or a simple repair job. Politics aside, the normative question to be settled in the 1940s centered on the still-open definition of American "freedom of the press." It is this question, debated by the Hutchins Commission and contested by an embattled print news industry, that we turn to in the next chapter.

[127] C. Edwin Baker, *Media, Markets, and Democracy* (New York: Cambridge University Press, 2002), 154.

[128] C. Edwin Baker, *Media Concentration and Democracy: Why Ownership Matters* (New York: Cambridge University Press, 2007), 2.

[129] James Curran, *Media and Democracy* (New York: Routledge, 2011), 9.

[130] Robert Horwitz, "Broadcast Reform Revisited: Reverend Everett C. Parker and the 'Standing' Case," *Communication Review* 2, no. 3 (1997): 312.

6

Should the Giants Be Slain or Persuaded to Be Good?

The American Society of Newspaper Editors' (ASNE's) annual conventions were typically grand affairs. Political elites made dramatic appearances and gave what were later hailed as significant speeches. Editors from top newspapers attended, as did prominent commentators and reporters. At the opening of the 1947 ASNE meeting, however, all did not seem well with American newspapers. In his farewell speech, the outgoing ASNE president and *New York Herald Tribune* editor Wilbur Forrest warned the incoming ASNE administration and general membership of a pair of looming threats. Forrest identified the first threat as "the control over the publication of news now exercised by labor union chieftains," whose "manipulation of newsprint supplies and costs" amounted to "a violation of press freedom." These "little dictators" held "power unprecedented in our history," he warned. Labor unions "may shut down one or all of the newspapers in any given community literally overnight.... Vigilance must be constant."[1]

Forrest identified the second threat as government regulation. Decrying "government censorship," Forrest claimed knowledge of a campaign aiming to "tear down the prestige of the American press as an institution in order to obtain government regulation of the press." He asked, "Is not regulation a step in the direction of control?"[2] Recommending a more aggressive defense of laissez-faire principles, Forrest cautioned, "We are ... in an era in which the American press is and will be under attack by those who constantly seek some measure of regulation."[3] Forrest called for ASNE to create a "small but active

---

[1] American Society of Newspaper Editors, annual convention, *Problems of Journalism*, 1947, 18. Several sections and ideas in this chapter are discussed in Victor Pickard, "Whether the Giants Should Be Slain or Persuaded to Be Good': Revisiting the Hutchins Commission and the Role of Media in a Democratic Society," *Critical Studies in Media Communication*, 27, 4, (2010): 391–411.

[2] Ibid., 18–19.

[3] Ibid.

committee" to promote its own definition of "freedom of the press" to combat the "decided misconception" put forth by their critics.[4] Otherwise, invocation of press freedom might give "some commissar a round-about hand on deciding what is proper or improper," thereby justifying a "legislative step" toward regulation.[5] He noted that the "twenty-five or thirty authors who have elected in recent years to needle the press" ignored that the reader is the final judge of press performance by giving "a publisher or an editor the jitters if enough of his kind write in and say they are in complete disagreement with the paper." Forrest dismissed the charge that advertisers control newspaper coverage as "just so much outmoded claptrap."[6]

A primary cause for Forrest's concerns soon became clear. He saw the Commission on Freedom of the Press, popularly known as the Hutchins Commission, as an entering wedge for the government's regulatory agenda against newspapers. He described this shadowy group as "eleven-thirteenths percent pedagogic personnel" and mischaracterized it as a "government commission." Several pages of ASNE's published proceedings are devoted to his detailed rebuttal of the commission's press critique, particularly as it related to ASNE's ethical code. Forrest issued a call to arms for the industry to unite against these threats.

The Hutchins Commission's Intellectual Arsenal

At first glance, it is difficult to perceive how the Hutchins Commission threatened the commercial press. Many of the commissioners held relatively laissez-faire views not unlike those of most publishers. But as we will see, their liberalism sometimes took different turns around two key questions: What is the role of media in a democratic society, and how should that role be regulated? Although a number of policy trajectories were available, ultimately the commissioners concluded that media should practice social responsibility to remain self-regulated. Between their initial questions and final conclusions, however, a number of radical proposals were discussed and ultimately jettisoned. Drawing from archival evidence, including unpublished reports and transcripts, the following analysis outlines the discussions, the tensions, the alternatives, and the compromises that occurred under the Hutchins Commission. To understand the commissioners' approach to these questions, a brief overview of their intellectual foundations is instructive.

In addition to the individual backgrounds described in the previous chapter, the commissioners were steeped in the liberal democratic theory of John Milton, Thomas Jefferson, and John Locke. As discussed earlier, much of this thinking assumes that an open exchange of ideas encourages the best arguments

[4] Ibid., 18.
[5] Ibid., 18–19.
[6] Ibid.

to emerge and truth to prevail. To ensure that all of the commissioners were familiar with this democratic theory, at an early meeting Harold Lasswell distributed a reading list that included Plato's *Apology*, Milton's *Areopagitica*, and John Stuart Mill's On *Liberty*.[7] *Areopagitica* inspired the classical liberal notion of the "marketplace of ideas" as later articulated by Oliver Wendell Holmes, who argued that all voices and viewpoints should be given a fair hearing and that people should have access to diverse information.[8] In *On Liberty*, Mill articulated a utilitarian notion of liberty that the greatest amount of freedom for individuals, barring harm to others, serves the greater good. This formulation arguably privileges private property rights and assumes a relatively equal playing field that naturally encourages egalitarianism. Americans have long believed that impediments to actualizing these democratic ideals lie primarily within state tyranny rather than the private tyranny of concentrated corporate power. Thus, emphasis often is placed on negative liberties that keep people's freedom to speak unhindered. This predisposition has typically given short shrift to positive liberties that consider the collective over individual rights, including a freedom to listen to diverse voices and a freedom of access to different sources of media. Tensions between these concepts were clearly manifest in the Hutchins Commission's deliberations.

Another important foundation for the commissioners was mass society theory, a view of media that recognized its propagandistic potential and therefore saw media ownership concentration as posing a potential threat to democracy. Another influence was qualitative approaches associated with the "Chicago school" of sociology practiced by scholars like Robert Park, a close colleague of several commission members. The Chicago school was grounded in "great community" concepts connected to John Dewey and others emphasizing productive relationships and dialogue between community members and media messengers.[9]

In general, the commissioners believed that media institutions were failing, but they differed on the nature of the problem and potential remedies. Haunted by fears of fascism, they maintained that although "government has an important part to play in communications, we look principally to the press and the

---

[7] Harold Lasswell to the Commissioners, February 15, 1944, Folder 2–6, Box 2, Commission on Freedom of the Press Papers.

[8] It should be noted that Milton and Mill were highly critical of the cultural marketplace. John Durham Peters notes that the "marketplace of ideas" entered common usage at precisely the same moment as the term "mass communication" as a way of acknowledging and compensating for the shrinking media marketplace. See "The Marketplace of Ideas: A History of the Concept," *Toward a Political Economy of Culture: Capitalism and Communication in the Twenty-First Century*, ed. Andrew Calabrese and Colin Sparks (Lanham, Md: Rowman & Littlefield, 2004), 65–82. I thank John Nerone for bringing this argument to my attention.

[9] The Chicago school's dominant position within sociological theory was being challenged by the Columbia School's brand of more quantitative-based empiricism. See Blevens, "Gentility and Quiet Aggression," 55–6 and 138–9.

people to remedy the ills which have chiefly concerned us."[10] The commission sought to define press freedoms in relation to responsibility by codifying a set of public obligations that the press must satisfy to remain self-regulated. A guiding assumption of the Hutchins Commission – one that deserves emphasis – held that an unaccountable press forfeited its privilege of self-regulation and justified legitimate government intervention.

This position would eventually crystallize as the following: "If modern society requires great agencies of mass communication, if these concentrations become so powerful that they are a threat to democracy, if democracy cannot solve the problem simply by breaking them up – then those agencies must control themselves or be controlled by government."[11] The commissioners adamantly wanted to prevent the latter outcome, but neither did they want to reaffirm a laissez-faire position. However, they felt hamstrung by not wanting to overly offend industry, transgress the politically viable and enforceable, or replace private tyranny with state tyranny. Some commissioners saw the latter consideration as a false dichotomy and instead proposed alternative models and regulations, discussed later, that neither relied entirely on state oversight nor conceded everything to laissez-faire market operations, but rather sought to ameliorate the excesses of profit-driven commercial media. Though it was generally cautious, flashes of innovative radicalism punctuated the commission's work.

The Commission's Focus

The University of Chicago announced the Hutchins Commission's formation in February 1944. "The function of the Commission," a press release declared, "is to begin an inclusive inquiry into the nature, function, duties and responsibilities of the press." More than being just a "deliberative body," it would engage in work whose importance was "so apparent that newspaper publishers and editors will be glad to appear before it to give testimony on their experience in operating a free press." The participants planned to hear from "not only ivory tower editors, but also from reporters, desk men, research associates, advertising and circulation directors – and readers." They would examine "areas and circumstances under which the press in the United States is succeeding or failing; to discover where free expression is or is not limited, whether by governmental censorship, pressures of readers or advertisers, the unwisdom of its own proprietors or the timidity of its managers." According to the plan, the study would last two years and culminate with a "definitive report of press freedom." Headquarters and permanent research staff would be based in New

[10] Robert Leigh, ed., *Free and Responsible Press* (Chicago: University of Chicago Press, 1947), 2–3.
[11] Ibid., 5.

York City, but the University of Chicago would administer the funding, mostly provided by Time Inc., publisher of *Time, Life,* and *Fortune.*[12]

The commissioners' budget and prestige enabled them to conduct interviews with fifty-eight leading media critics, policy makers, and journalists, plus testimonies from more than two hundred others. They would generally meet for about three days at six-week intervals (except during summer) from December 1943 (their first meeting predated the official announcement) through December 1946. They gathered seventeen times altogether, with smaller meetings occurring regionally. From these efforts, they would produce six book-length reports, all published with the University of Chicago Press: Robert D. Leigh, ed., *A Free and Responsible Press* (1947); Zechariah Chafee, *Government and Mass Communications* (1947); William Hocking, *Freedom of the Press* (1947); Ruth A. Inglis, *Freedom of the Movies* (1947); Llewellyn White, *The American Radio* (1947); and Llewellyn White and Robert D. Leigh, *Peoples Speaking to Peoples* (1946). One other planned book – by Milton Stewart and Harold Lasswell, on press coverage of the 1945 San Francisco Conference that led to the United Nations – was never published, and no drafts exist in the archives. Although these books are all significant in their own right, most scholarly attention has focused on their main summary report, henceforth referred to as the "Report."

The participants saw themselves as taking on a historic and critical endeavor, noting that these commissions "are important points of influence and reference for periods of a decade or more," usually emerging "in a time of crisis in a specific area such as the present critical juncture as regards information and understanding in matters of public concern." Such forums wield "a sure influence over a longer period of time," they believed, "if their work is done well."[13] Archibald MacLeish laid out his vision of the commission's primary task: "The whole crisis, the whole reason we are here as a Commission ... is that the physical, economic, social circumstances which make that right [of a free press] a useful right ... have so changed that it is no longer possible for a great majority of human beings to exercise the right to that end." For a meaningful freedom of the press that challenged concentrated media power, created new alternative models, or did a combination of both, MacLeish argued, "You have to find some other way."[14]

The commissioners concluded that just as media were becoming more integral to modern democratic society, they were also becoming more commercialized and concentrated – as evidenced by increasingly numerous one-paper

---

12   University of Chicago Press Release, February 26, 1944, Box 7, Folder 7, Robert M. Hutchins Papers, Special Collections, Joseph Regenstein Library, University of Chicago (hereafter cited as Hutchins Papers).
13   Quoted in Jerilyn McIntyre, "Repositioning a Landmark: The Hutchins Commission and Freedom of the Press," *Critical Studies in Mass Communication* 4 (1987): 140.
14   Quoted in Mark Fackler, "The Hutchins Commissioners and the Crisis in Democratic Theory, 1930–1947" (Ph.D. Dissertation, University of Illinois, 1982), 15.

towns, decreasing competition, and the emergence of large national media empires. Magnifying these concerns were fears of propaganda and totalitarianism, suspicion of media monopolies, a changing technological landscape, misrepresentations of minorities, and the press's openly anti–New Deal bias. The commissioners invoked the term "crisis" in assessing the commercial media system's vulnerabilities and resultant threats to democratic governance. For example, Reinhold Niebuhr stated that the "new conditions of technical civilization" and the clash between fascism and democracy had engendered "the greatest crisis in history."[15]

From the beginning, the commissioners endeavored to create a media policy guide.[16] Leigh saw the commission as constructing "a basic chart for American policy in the promotion of free communication in a modern, free, international society."[17] Stephen Bates, one of the few historians to examine the commission's unpublished transcripts, has observed that its "Platonic dialogues show great minds grappling with a fundamental paradox"[18] – the paradox of how to regulate the press. Focusing on how the press could best be molded into a more democratic institution, the commissioners were influenced by contemporaneous progressive media initiatives, including the Supreme Court's articulations in the *Associated Press* case and the public interest arguments outlined in the FCC's Blue Book. They received input from outside institutions and individuals, including Commissioner Durr, who offered advice on educational broadcasting and related issues. During the commission's proceedings, Durr regularly corresponded with Leigh (who had been Durr's colleague at the FCC) and provided extensive feedback on several of the commission's reports.[19]

The Hutchins Commission also received guidance from contemporary thinkers. After its formation was announced in newspapers, a stream of mostly enthusiastic letters arrived from a diverse range of individuals, including fellow

---

[15] Document 16, 22–3, April 26, 1944, Folder 2–16, Box 2, Commission on Freedom of the Press Papers, Special Collections, University of Washington, Seattle (hereafter cited as Commission on Freedom of the Press Papers).

[16] McIntyre, "Repositioning a Landmark," 137–8, notes how the commission's policy orientation is often overlooked.

[17] Robert Leigh, Purposes and Program of the Commission, July 27, 1944, quoted in McIntyre, "Repositioning a Landmark," 142. Leigh thought the name "Freedom of the Press" was "misleading." He preferred "Commission on Freedom of Communication," because "communication" was an "emerging term," more encompassing, and they "could help the term emerge," but Hutchins was not convinced. Leigh to Hutchins, February 20, 1944; Hutchins to Leigh, February 22, 1944, Box 7, Folder 7, Hutchins Papers.

[18] Stephen Bates, "Realigning Journalism with Democracy: The Hutchins Commission, Its Times, and Ours" (Washington, DC: The Annenberg Washington Program in Communications Policy Studies of Northwestern University, 1995), 3.

[19] See, for example, Robert Leigh to Clifford Durr, August 31, 1944, Box 30, Folder 2, CJDP. In one exchange, Leigh tried to coordinate with Durr in convincing a Swiss official who was studying American radio not to establish advertising-supported broadcasting in Switzerland. Leigh to Durr, August 15, 1946, Box 30, Folder 7, CJDP.

intellectuals, politicians, and average news consumers. The sociologist C. Wright Mills sent a copy of his article "The Social Role of the Intellectual,"[20] and the public relations pioneer Edward Bernays sent a copy of his "The Postwar Responsibility of the American Press."[21] Senator Burton Wheeler sent Robert Hutchins a congratulatory note, offering copies of recent radio hearings on freedom of speech issues and government's regulatory role.[22]

A small agricultural newspaper publisher wrote to Hutchins that the commission's study would inspire hope among "many thousands of people" who cared about "the social implications" of press responsibility. He added, "No postwar problem will be of greater importance than the dissemination of unbiased news," but this would require confronting "the power and pressure" from "mammoth advertising agencies," who held "uncontrolled influence in our social order."[23] A Tulane University law professor called for "particular attention to the ownership and control of the American press," suggesting that noncommercial publications such as endowed, university-funded, religious, and labor newspapers be distributed to communities to offset pro-business media biases. He called for a closely regulated press because "a public utility and a business 'affected with a public interest' have always been subjected to American legislative control." He also suggested a newspaper Fairness Doctrine giving "equality of space for controversial issues," and advocated "public ownership of the press, controlled by trustees appointed under an irrevocable trust with the power of self-perpetuation."[24] The professor's ideas would not carry the day, but the commission did consider some similar structural alternatives to the commercial press.

Not all correspondents were in support of the commission. Junius Wood, a veteran foreign correspondent for the *Chicago Daily News*, saw nothing but conspiracy behind the Luce-funded operation. "Mr. Luce paying for an investigation of Freedom of the Press suggests an old game, a gambler paying a policeman to raid a rival joint." He even thought it was possible that Luce had sent agents provocateurs to stage a riot at the opening meeting of the commission. Wood added, "Newspapermen may think that Mr. Luce is paying for this investigation to distract attention from his own publications and that the committee is going along for a pleasant ride."[25]

The Interviews

Throughout its nearly three years of operation, the Hutchins Commission interviewed significant media critics and practitioners, including newspaper

[20] C. Wright Mills to Robert Hutchins, March 20, 1944, Box 8, Folder 4, Hutchins Papers.
[21] Charles Merriam to Robert Hutchins, November 9, 1944, Box 7, Folder 7, Hutchins Papers.
[22] Senator Wheeler to Robert Hutchins, March 1, 1944, Box 8, Folder 3, Hutchins Papers.
[23] Kenneth Quinn to Robert Hutchins, March 7, 1944, Box 8, Folder 4, Hutchins Papers.
[24] Ray Forrester to Robert Hutchins, August 4, 1944, Box 8, Folder 3, Hutchins Papers.
[25] Junius Wood to Robert Hutchins, May 29, 1944, Box 8, Folder 4, Hutchins Papers.

representatives such as Edwin James, managing editor of the *New York Times*; government officials such as Elmer Davis, head of the Office of War Information; Byron Price, director of the Office of Censorship; and Arthur Hays, a civil liberties attorney. Typically meeting with all of the commissioners for a morning or afternoon, interviewees discussed specific topics such as postal policy, libel, and copyright policy, as well as larger issues like the meaning of freedom of the press. As with all commission meetings, the interviews were transcribed and later distributed to each commissioner. These gatherings were usually cordial but sometimes not entirely harmonious. The *New York Times* editor Edwin James left his meeting with the commissioners displeased, writing later that he was "impressed – and not favorably" by their proposal that newspapers should be more critical of advertisements.[26]

The interviews with Morris Ernst and the then–FCC chair Larry Fly are worth examining, both because they influenced subsequent discussions and because their views represented the more progressive parameters within the commission's discourse. Ernst introduced fairly radical ideas to the commission. Through him, the commissioners learned about the history and philosophy of the Newspaper Guild, which, according to his narrative, he represented "when it was not under Communist control." Ernst explained to them the plight of newspaper workers, a largely pro-FDR constituency, who "feel that the publishers for whom they work are out of tune with the times." "Roosevelt had only a few papers behind him in the 1936–40 elections," Ernst recounted, which made the newspaper workers who were often New Deal supporters "feel cheap ... as though they were playing a piano in a whore house."

Ernst talked about his forthcoming book, *The First Freedom,* which presented evidence of a lack of press diversity that tracked closely with media concentration. Ernst informed the commissioners that "five people owned 70% of the total box-office producing theaters" and "when it comes to radio, four men own the air of America." He noted that during the AP antitrust case, there was no newspaper reportage or radio coverage of the FCC's media ownership investigations. "This proves who owns the pipeline of thought in America," Ernst stated. "There can be no pretense of a Bill of Rights if there is no free marketplace for ideas."[27] But Ernst shared the commissioners' fear that "the public will eventually lose faith in the mass media" and then entrust "400 silly Congressmen" with "complete governmental control" of the press. Although he allowed that government-owned British radio had achieved a "competition of ideas," he did not seek government-subsidized American radio. However, he argued, no entity should own more than "one channel of communication," and Congress should also intervene to prevent copyright monopolies. He applauded Learned Hand's "great contribution" toward fostering a free press by insisting

---

[26] Edwin James to Robert Hutchins, May 10, 1944, Box 7, Folder 6, Hutchins Papers.
[27] Meeting with Morris Ernst, Document 21, 28–41, September 18–19, 1944, Folder 2–21, Box 2, Commission on Freedom of the Press Papers.

that "news is a different kind of commodity and that nothing should hinder its widest dissemination."[28]

The commissioners gave a mixed reception to Ernst's ideas. MacLeish seemed intrigued, but he wondered how media ownership diversity mattered if all owners had "approximately the same point of view." Ernst admitted that diversifying ownership was only a first – but a necessary – step toward true diversity of opinion. Without at least the "potentiality" that diverse people could own media, he explained, "it is difficult to defend the concept of free thought." MacLeish and Lasswell suggested that communication channels remain under central control (by either government, private, or nonprofit ownership) but be arranged "for specified degrees of access by accredited groups." As they discussed the merits of changing media ownership structures, Ernst suggested that ideally reformers would "try as many of these devices for achieving greater freedom of expression as possible and then appraise their ... impact."[29]

Ernst disavowed Marxism, arguing against a large state or one that was overly involved in media. When asked to specify, he distinguished his position from the *PM* editor Max Lerner's suggestion of a "TVA of the air."[30] He agreed that the "danger is that the state will start getting into the idea business and the trend will be toward shutting the mouths of its critics." Ernst disapproved of media content regulation, including that by private owners – prevention of which, in his view, necessitated breaking up media concentration. "Look at the Luce empire. He owns four newspapers, a movie company, interest in a radio network, and a seat in Congress. It is going to be very bad taste for this Commission to make certain recommendations." Several of the commissioners assured Ernst of the "toughness and freedom of the Commission itself," but, according to the description in the transcripts, "Ernst looked skeptical."

Whether due to lack of "toughness" or just ideological differences, the commission's behavior may have warranted Ernst's skepticism. Although his media monopoly critique would recur throughout the commission's meetings, at least some commissioners were mortified by his views. In a subsequent discussion about the "implications of [media] monopolistic control," Beardsley Ruml dismissed Ernst's "wild statements."[31] Nonetheless, Ernst's views remained a reference point that helped drive a structural critique into the center of the commission's discussion, even if much of it was ultimately abandoned.

[28] Ibid.
[29] Ibid.
[30] This model referred to Lerner's essay "Freedom in the Opinion Industry," where he proposed a "TVA principle in our radio system" that would place "side by side with, the great broadcasting chains ... two major airways reserved by the government and run for it not by the bureaucrats but by the guild of radio artists." Discussed and quoted in Milton Kaplan, "Radio on the Inoffensive," *Common Ground* VI, no. 4 (Summer 1946), 76.
[31] Summary of Discussion and Action, Document 26, p. 12, November 20–1, 1944, Box 2, Folder 2–26, Commission on Freedom of the Press Papers.

Commissioner Fly, on the other hand, represented a more liberal position among the interviewees. Hutchins abandoned earlier plans to invite Fly to join the commission permanently, but the FCC chair nonetheless made an important contribution to its deliberations by establishing that a holistic approach was necessary to understand the U.S. media system. He advised looking at "the whole range of communication media [including] movies, newspapers, magazines, pamphlets, radio" and even "special channels" like "comic strips." This "tremendously broad" problem involved "various relations of government to communication," including "taxation, labor relations, business regulations," as well as antitrust laws and regulatory commissions like the FCC. Fly rejected a criterion for press freedom as merely the "absence of governmental restraint." He also did not think it was primarily "a problem for legislation." Although he believed that "no paper should own any radio station," Fly stopped short of advocating government control of media, wanting to "avoid, so far as possible, any sort of restraint on communication from the side of government." Drawing from Justice Holmes's "marketplace of ideas" metaphor, he wanted to "promote rather than restrict free speech." He believed anti-monopolistic regulations were applicable to communication but thought antitrust alone was inadequate to maintain a healthy media system. An adversarial FCC was also necessary; impressing upon media institutions their public service responsibilities sometimes "requires preaching instead of law."[32]

Fly summarized the four major challenges facing the nation's media system that required government intervention: the concentration of control of broadcast networks, newspaper ownership of radio stations, public service program policy, and international communications.[33] As they would throughout their deliberations, the commissioners struggled over how to deal with excessive commercialism, especially given their different comfort levels regarding government regulation of media institutions. Leigh observed that they had repeatedly used a "false polarization" between government and individuals while neglecting "intermediate institutions and organizations" – an idea that would recur intermittently throughout the commission's duration. Lasswell suggested "a quasi-public or even private corporation offering shares" to various stakeholders such as "labor and business groups." Fly liked the idea but cautioned that independence had to be assured, citing recent cases in which broadcasters had set up fake independent groups. "Fundamentally, the only hope for improvement is an aroused public opinion – led by the appraisal and subsequent action of some public-minded group," he advised. "It is true that the public may be satisfied with the present situation," Fly further noted, "but this

---

[32] Document 16, pp. 1–15, Meetings, June 19–20, 1944, Box 2, Folder 2–18, Commission on Freedom of the Press Papers.

[33] Ibid. The commission revisited these subjects months later while discussing at great length Fly's report "Freedom of Communications." See Discussion on August 13, 1945, Box 4, Folder 4–3, Commission on Freedom of the Press Papers.

is true of almost every oppression of this kind," when people are not aware of potential alternatives.

While the discussions with Fly and Ernst help focus many of the commission's core tensions and quandaries, three other debates during the proceedings stand out for their direct implications for structural interventions in the U.S. media system. These debates not only were the most contentious but also held the most potential for encouraging – at least at the discursive level – systemic change. They can be thematically categorized as alternative models, laissez-faire versus regulation of the press, and First Amendment protections of the press.

Alternative Models

Early on in the commission's deliberations, fairly radical options figured prominently. Niebuhr set the tone by affirming government's role in media regulation: "There is no evidence that government restrictions have seriously endangered the freedom of the press." While "minor changes" in the relationships between government and the press might be advisable, he claimed, "it is obvious that the peril of governmental interference with press freedom is not great." He continued, "This increase in governmental initiative in the field of communication must not be rejected in the name of archaic laissez faire conceptions." In crafting alternatives, "the essential freedom of communication can be adequately protected by measures designed to prevent the government from having a monopoly in any field of communication." He concluded that "governmental initiative must be introduced merely as a supplementary force in the field."[34]

Arguing that the press's public services were too precious to subject to unbridled market conditions, the commissioners suggested reclassifying the press as a common carrier or a public utility to guarantee reasonable access. Hocking suggested a collectivist approach to the media, declaring, "We cannot leave to private agencies alone the ultimate responsibility for the service of news."[35] He compared the news to the public education system, arguing that neither should be left to the profit-driven whims of the marketplace. Ruml discussed how a federal agency modeled after the FCC should look after the press, making media corporations' submission to its oversight mandatory to retain the legal protections of limited liability incorporation.[36] Merriam spoke in favor of

[34] Reinhold Niebuhr "Document No. 49 General Propositions Deduced from the Investigation of the Freedom of the Press Commission, May 11, 1945, Box 3, Folder 3–18, Commission on Freedom of the Press Papers. Stephen Bates discusses some of the following alternatives in his important study, which informs my own analysis.

[35] William Hocking, Document 66, 51, July 11, 1945, Box 4, Folder 4-1, Commission on Freedom of the Press Papers. Also quoted in Bates, "Realigning Journalism with Democracy," 7.

[36] McIntyre, "Repositioning a Landmark," 155; Bates, "Realigning Journalism with Democracy," 13.

forming citizen councils to oversee local media, based on "mutual, cooperative, consumer types of relations over controls of communication."[37]

MacLeish thought everyone should have freedom of access to the press to "say his say in print if he so desired" – essentially rendering newspapers common carriers. Hutchins disagreed, but the common carrier metaphor would persist throughout the commission's deliberations. Lasswell, who years earlier had argued that a failing press system's self-regulation must be strengthened by legislation, proposed a plan for content regulation of papers that had more than 50 percent of a community's circulation. In lieu of "breaking up the paper concentration," he suggested these newspaper monopolies should be "subject to a special kind of regulation, or a special kind of treatment by the government." He suggested giving such papers "over to public utility regulation," especially in communities dominated by one news organization. "One example of the possible forum would be to make it responsible for carrying a page that would be centrally edited by a government commission," he explained. In response to Lasswell's suggestion, according to the transcripts, Chafee blurted out, "Oh no!" Admitting that "politically speaking," this option "horrifies good Americans," Lasswell continued, "if you are going to think in terms of government means to enforce the common carrier principle, you might imagine a series of steps – one, the liability to present all sides according to the standards determined by the regulatory commission; two, a positive obligation to disseminate certain centrally edited material."[38]

The commission considered increasing competition by aiding start-up newspapers through government-guaranteed loans and other indirect subsidies such as reduced postal rates. Looking for ways to generate revenue for such subsidies, Hutchins asked Chafee in a letter, "Do you think that the Supreme Court would hold a non-discriminatory tax on newspapers unconstitutional?" Hutchins also asked, "Suppose the tax had been clearly for revenue and had applied equally to every publication? Do you think that an equal tax on all radio receiving sets would be held constitutional as a violation of the First Amendment?"[39] Chafee responded carefully that the newspaper tax was conceivably legal and that the radio tax would likely pass constitutional muster as a "rough and ready method of collecting payment for benefits received, something like postage stamps."[40] He even suggested, perhaps out of exasperation,

---

[37] Charles Merriam, Document 11, 1944, Box 2, Folder 11, Commission on Freedom of the Press Papers.

[38] Documents 108c and 108d, 154–6, August 21, 1946, Box 7, Folder 7–11, Commission on Freedom of the Press Papers; see also Hilda Bryant, "A Free and Responsible Press: A Three Year Inquiry: An Intellectual History of the Hutchins Commission Study of the American Press, 1943–1946" (M.A. Thesis, University of Washington, 1969), 76; Bates, "Realigning Journalism with Democracy," 10.

[39] Robert Hutchins to Zechariah Chafee, June 21,1945, Box 8, Folder 1, Hutchins Papers.

[40] Chafee to Hutchins, June 27, 1945, Box 8, Folder 1, Hutchins Papers. He based this on precedents from the Supreme Court's *Grosjean* case.

that "if the plan is to subsidize little papers, let's propose that the government take $25,000 or $50,000 or $100,000 of the taxpayers' money and give it to anybody who wants to start a newspaper."[41]

Of all the alternatives they considered, talk kept returning to the notion, which began congealing in the commission's earliest meetings, of an independent "administrative-judicial board" or "advisory board" to oversee the press. Although Lasswell and Hutchins at first talked of having both a national and many regional councils, the discussion eventually focused on one overarching council. This plan for a national citizen news council would materialize years later, becoming the most substantive reform inspired by the commission's work.[42] Although controversial, it eventually captured many press critics' imagination. Meanwhile, most other recommendations for alternative structures and models gradually faded from discussion.

Laissez-Faire versus Regulation

Partway into the commission's debates, Chafee pinpointed a core tension: "One of the main problems before our commission is whether the giants should be slain or persuaded to be good."[43] As their discussions progressed, the commissioners found themselves repeatedly circling back to the same intractable problems.[44] Many of the recurring themes animating the commission's deliberations are present in most normative debates regarding media's role in a democratic society. Generally, these debates divide into the following categories: the role of government regulation of media, definitions of press freedom, the nature of threats facing press freedom, and the sanctity of private enterprise. All of these areas, however, are arguably subsets of one overarching debate – by far the commission's biggest hurdle: the laissez-faire versus regulation debate.

Also understood as individualism versus collectivism, this debate's furthest-reaching positions were ruled out early in the commission's discussions. At first glance, it even seems that a middle ground was reached between libertarian/laissez-faire negative freedoms and social democratic positive freedoms – represented, respectively, by Chafee and Hocking – when the commissioners

---

[41] Quoted in Bates, "Realigning Journalism with Democracy," 14.

[42] Roger Simpson, "'Our Single Remedy for All Ills': The History of the Idea of a National Press Council," *American Journalism* 12, no. 4 (1995): 477–95.

[43] Zechariah Chafee, Comment to chapter IV, (n.d.), Box 8, Folder 1, Hutchins Papers.

[44] Fackler's quantitative analysis of commissioners' contributions to official meetings shows that Chafee, Hocking, Lasswell, MacLeish, and Niebuhr contributed the most, often leading discussions and contributing much to the written record. Dickinson, Merriam, Ruml, and Shuster made smaller but still significant contributions. Clark, Redfield, and Schlesinger contributed relatively little. Although missing several meetings, Hutchins was the most active and exerted a large if subtle influence both in discussions and in back channel communications. See Mark Fackler, "The Hutchins Commissioners and the Crisis in Democratic Theory, 1930–1947" (Ph.D. Dissertation, University of Illinois, 1982), 364.

began settling on a kind of "social responsibility" idea.[45] But that neglects what is actually a more crucial ideological move. By determining early on that structural intervention was off the table, the commission essentially ensured that the basic precepts of libertarianism would be preserved. This hesitation to recommend structural reforms, combined with an overall bias toward preserving the status quo, negated any call for a systemic overhaul. Challenges to these discursive bounds would periodically arise, especially when the lone holdout, MacLeish, would make a last-ditch effort to establish more radical proposals. But the central debate would pivot on finding an acceptable compromise between aggressive government intervention and absolutist laissez-faire libertarianism.

About midway into its three-year existence, the commission formed a subcommittee to explore the Hocking-Chafee debate further. Hocking challenged the Miltonian "self-righting" principle that assumed truth would organically emerge, for it overlooked preexisting inequities. Hocking believed there was a moral imperative to expand and uphold democratic freedoms that were not accounted for in libertarianism. He believed that positive freedoms needed to be codified further and implemented, thus requiring governmental intervention. In one letter to Hutchins, he asserted: "The first requisite of political liberty is a strong central government."[46] The more libertarian Chafee abhorred the notion of such intervention, particularly when it came to affairs of the press. With some important exceptions, Chafee fell into the absolutist First Amendment camp that lends itself to a libertarian view of press freedoms. At one point, he argued that regulation and legal remedies were unnecessary, using the circular logic that if the commissioners "can show what ought to be done, we need not go into the question of whether it should be done by law or not," because it is "very desirable" and thus will be "done by voluntary action." If not, Chafee maintained, "sooner or later it is going to be done by law."[47] However, some commissioners wondered whether it was realistic to expect a commercial press to sacrifice profits for public service, especially in the absence of any credible regulatory threat.[48]

It is worth reiterating that Chafee had recently and famously argued the opposite position in his "public service theory of the press," articulated during his involvement with the AP antitrust case. Furthermore, in 1928, Chafee wrote, "We cannot afford to neglect methods for obtaining livelier oral discussion and places available for it, and for encouraging fuller presentation of

[45] For a comprehensive discussion of this debate, see Donald L. Smith, *Zechariah Chafee, Jr.: Defender of the Liberty and Law* (Cambridge, MA: Harvard University Press, 1986), 103–15.
[46] William Hocking to Robert Hutchins, January 18, 1944, Box 7, Folder 6, Hutchins Papers.
[47] Summary of Meeting, Commission Document No. 48, April 16–7, 1945, Box 3, Folder 17, Commission on Freedom of the Press Papers.
[48] See, for example, Summary of Discussion, March 31–April 2, 1946, No. 94 A., Commission on Freedom of the Press Papers.

all sides of international and industrial controversies in the press and over the radio."[49] These comments suggested an advocacy of at least some affirmative government intervention in cases when the press failed in its public service to democracy. Nonetheless, Chafee continued to clash with Hocking over defining press freedom and the extent to which government intervention was necessary. They reached some mutual understandings and even sometimes reversed positions, but they never fully agreed. Chafee even visited Hocking on his farm to try to reach consensus, later writing to Leigh, "Frankly, I am getting a little weary of completing his education. He seems to suffer a relapse after every conference."[50] Ultimately, Hocking was somewhat successful in establishing a positive press freedom emphasizing the public's collective First Amendment rights. However, whereas Hocking was willing to give government the final responsibility for protecting this freedom, the commission sided more with Chafee by arguing that government should intervene only as a drastic last resort.

A third-way model that was neither state- nor market-driven was exemplified by the proposal for a citizens' news council. This recommendation invited much debate, with MacLeish passionately for it and Niebuhr unconvinced. When Hutchins worried that the commissioners were not offering anything more substantive, Niebuhr replied that "we don't have startling recommendations but there is a lot of wholesome advice" and "the diagnosis is more important here than a cure."[51] At one point, the commission agreed that "laissez faire does not solve the problem ... that government interference, although on the whole dangerous and to be used charily, has to be used to some degree." This meant that "various devices for regulation have to be set up which neither create the perils of government control nor leave the situation under laissez faire."[52] However, these devices remained cautious and vague in the commission's discussions.

Hutchins revealed some ideological predilections during this debate in his nine-page feedback on Hocking's outline of principles. Specifically, he found the prescribed role for government to be problematic:

> I do not see how a government is the *primary* protector of press freedom, unless primary protection is merely that basic protection which is presupposed for the activities of all citizens, namely, the maintenance of order. Nor do I understand that under American law it is made the duty or function of any government to ferret out the corrupt pressures placed on the expression of opinion. Our courts have protected the press against

---

49 Zechariah Chafee, "Liberty and Law," in *Freedom in the Modern World*, ed. Horace Kallen (Ithaca, NY: Cornell University Press, 1928), quoted in Smith, *Zechariah Chafee, Jr.*, 95–6.
50 Quoted in Smith, *Zechariah Chafee, Jr.*, 110.
51 Quoted in Bates, "Realigning Journalism with Democracy," 16.
52 Summary of Discussion and Action, September 17–19, 1945, Document 75, Box 4, Folder 10, Commission on Freedom of the Press Papers. See also McIntyre, "Repositioning a Landmark," 151.

governments. The attorney-general and the courts have in addition done something about monopoly in the communications industry.[53]

Hutchins feared they were advocating "that the government has specific responsibilities to protect the press against centers of social power," which made him uncomfortable because he did not see "how the government could carry such responsibilities." Hutchins also took issue with characterizing the press as suffering from a lack of diversity; he was not convinced that "the variety of sources of news and opinion reaching the citizen has diminished," especially since "the movies, the radio, television, and the cheap magazines are all products of the last fifty years."[54]

Late in the Report's revision process, Leigh feared his colleagues were moving "too close to aligning the Commission with the sentiments of those who are trying vainly to perpetuate laissez-faire." Regarding the "relation of government to mass communications," Leigh noted that the Report's current wording "does not state the position which the Commission has arrived at – I hope." He cited the commission's earlier articulations that

built up a definition of government vis-à-vis the press which rejects laissez-faire as a principle, which agrees that a free press is not necessarily an unregulated press and develops a careful formula for the proper role of governmental intervention, of activities which promote rather than hinder fulfillment of the modern social requirements for information, ideas and opinions.... What we have arrived at, it seems, is a judgment that the function of the mass communication of information and ideas is one to be carried on *mainly* by commercial enterprise, but *partly* by government and *non-profit* enterprise, with such regulation and appraisal as will promote variety, quality and quantity.[55]

Leigh thought government intervention could be limited to preventing or lessening the media monopolies' negative impacts, but the commissioners did not emphasize a role for nonprofit institutions. Even Hocking, who at times seemed particularly critical of private ownership's economic logic, was a bit lukewarm regarding a section on nonprofit institutions; he felt that urging commercial media institutions to drop their profit motive made less sense than encouraging them to become more public-service-oriented. Leigh attributed the historical lack of governmental intervention not to political elites' complicity or to corporate power but to "the traditional attitude of the American people," who usually seek social goals "without the intervention of government.

---

[53] Robert Hutchins, comments on Document 100, June 18, 1946, 3–4, Box 8, Folder 1, Hutchins Papers.

[54] Ibid., 6.

[55] Robert Leigh to Robert Hutchins, August 1, 1946, Box 8, Folder 2, Hutchins Papers (original emphasis). Leigh was concerned that their recommendations chapter did not define "common carriers." Leigh to Commissioners, 1, Box 8, Folder 2, Hutchins Papers. Leigh noted, "This definition of the government's role is given by Hocking in 100 F, pp 14, first paragraph, and 15 last two paragraphs, in Chafee, document 98, 7, in Peoples speaking to Peoples, vii, viii, 112, and in my sixth revision, 33."

They have suspicions of governmental power, far more so, we believe, than any other democratic nation."[56] Whether this is a fair assessment of the American polity might be debatable, but the report ultimately affirmed the sanctity of a privately controlled, commercial press. It states that "We do not believe that the fundamental problems of the press will be solved by more laws or by governmental action. The commission places its main reliance on the mobilization of the elements of society acting directly on the press and not through governmental channels." However, the commissioners did leave a door partly open for governmental intervention if excesses were to worsen, arguing that no democracy "will indefinitely tolerate concentrations of private power irresponsible and strong enough to thwart the aspirations of the people." If left unchallenged, "eventually governmental power will be used to break up private power, or governmental power will be used to regulate private power – if private power is at once great and irresponsible."[57] The commissioners stated, "The more the press and the public are willing to do, the less will be left for the state."[58] Thus, the notion of "accountability" emerged as a middle ground, later to be replaced with "responsibility." As one historian described it, this resolution reflected "the New Deal's blend of a mixed economy and a managed society" that "offered a way to reconcile individualism and collectivism without rejecting the values or disrupting the basic structures of American economic and political life."[59] At heart, it actually took a relatively conservative position, preserving the broader status quo of political and economic relationships vis-à-vis the commercial press.

The First Amendment Protections of the Press

Throughout their deliberations, MacLeish consistently pushed the commission's radical edge by stressing that media access was critical for any conception of press freedom.[60] Particularly on this issue, MacLeish was a gadfly, constantly needling his fellow commissioners to follow their arguments to their logical conclusions. He wanted them to realize that unless they aimed to redistribute media power structurally, press freedoms effectively served only the rich. Going a step beyond Hocking's position, MacLeish insisted on a radically positive First Amendment that granted everyone direct media access (in other words, the right to be heard through the press). MacLeish felt that Hocking's conception of a community's First Amendment rights was too passive, too ill defined – that it essentially upheld the First Amendment without specifying how it would be actualized.

[56] *General Report*, 1–2.
[57] Ibid., 80.
[58] Ibid., 79.
[59] McIntyre, "Repositioning a Landmark," 139.
[60] For a thorough discussion of MacLeish's embattled status during these debates, see Bryant, "A Free and Responsible Press," 52–81.

MacLeish's First Amendment definition of giving everyone the right to "say his say" through media did not sway the other commissioners. Nonetheless, MacLeish insisted that if in fact not everyone had access to the press, then the Commission on Freedom of the Press should concede that not everyone had freedom of the press. Understanding that First Amendment freedoms were often dictated by power, he felt that any definition needed to address freedom for whom and to what end.[61] To the charge that such a formulation defied the Bill of Rights – or that giving everyone media access was absurdly unfeasible – MacLeish challenged the commission: "How then would these gentlemen answer the question 'freedom for whom?' Are they willing to ask the Commission to define it as freedom for some? For a few? And if so, which few?"[62] When several commissioners became anxious about his implications, MacLeish chided them, "You don't suggest that we obscure certain facts because you don't like the place they are going to take us? All the facts before this commission support the proposition that there is a great concentration of power."[63]

As the Report's primary author, MacLeish repeatedly harped on these issues. Despite his ideological orientation (which became increasingly clear during the commission's deliberations), the famous poet was a natural choice to author the initial draft, referred to as "Document 89." He was, after all, a gifted writer and one of the more engaged participants in the commission's debates. However, the other commissioners aggressively criticized both the style and the substance of his draft. Whereas MacLeish faulted the profit motive for many of the American media system's failings, and he wanted to break up the press's monopolistic concentration of power, other commissioners were uneasy with the prospect of radical structural reform. For example, in a letter to Hutchins, Shuster asserted that, contrary to MacLeish's characterization of media as "bowing to pressure," business norms guaranteed press "neutrality." He feared that removing business pressures would usher in a reinvigorated partisan press, which in turn would force governmental intervention, yielding "the end of freedom as we have understood it." Shuster believed "the real threat to liberty ... does not lie in ownership or in the inevitable concentration of ownership," but in the "subordination of mass media of communication to group propaganda."[64]

Compared to some of the other commissioners, Hutchins was less revolted by MacLeish's unflinching structural criticism. "I am delighted with the style and dash of the draft report," he acknowledged. But he demanded in a long

---

[61] See Commission Document 99, May 28, 1946, 4, Box 6, Folder 6–8, Commission on Freedom of the Press Papers.

[62] Ibid., 7.

[63] Commission Document 108-B, "The Problem," Box 7, Folder 7–10, Commission on Freedom of the Press Papers.

[64] George Shuster to Robert Hutchins, February 6, 1946, Box 8, Folder 1, Hutchins Papers.

critical memo that MacLeish tone it down. "If I have a general criticism," he cautioned, "it is that the draft is too dashing and gives a partisan impression." He continued with a reminder that the commission "should recognize and state the accomplishments of the American press in general."[65] Hutchins thought that the American press was no worse or better than that elsewhere, and that MacLeish seemed to romanticize other countries' and other historical periods' press systems. Moreover, Hutchins particularly took issue with the imputed motivations behind Henry Luce's interests:

I do not think it may be assumed that the principal interest of *Time* in the freedom of the press is its interest in freedom from interference by government.... I think [Luce] had in mind exactly what you have in mind: That the inadequate performance of its function by the press might lead to drastic revision of the status of the press in our society. Such drastic revision might include, in your prospectus as well as in his, governmental interference of the governmental distribution of news on a very large scale.[66]

Hutchins also questioned MacLeish's characterizations that the press had become too concentrated, too commercial, and too inadequate in presenting information about the world. He sympathized with the newspaper owner who was expected to teach people instead of maximize his profits: "He must be an educator even if the people show by the expenditure of their nickels that they do not want education at his hands." "What is he to do," Hutchins asked, "if he sees that he is losing his competitive position in the industry because the newspaper purchasers in his community prefer sensationalism and scandal to the education he offers?" Hutchins also thought MacLeish's draft mistreated the "small and badly financed newspapers whom we have been favoring through this report," because it is the "big ones [who] resist pressure because they can afford to," whereas the "little ones ... can't afford to or because they want to be big."[67]

After receiving a revision of his report, a livid MacLeish wrote to Hutchins: "It is a lovely piece of editing and synthesis, and organization and everything else it ought to be," but it "says nothing which requires contradiction by anybody, including [major newspaper publishers] Frank Gannett, Arthur Sulzberger and Colonel Bertie [McCormick]. Some of our colleagues will consider that a virtue. I, alas, do not." He fervently believed that "the only really useful service our report can perform is to state the problem in clear, uncompromising and realistic terms which will enable public opinion to form around the central issue." "Those members of the commission who believe we can avoid controversy," he argued, "delude themselves." MacLeish framed the debate as one over democracy:

[65] Robert Hutchins to Archibald MacLeish, January 22, 1946, Box 8, Folder 1, Hutchins Papers.
[66] Ibid.
[67] Ibid.

The basic difference between us, I suppose, has to do with the end of the cat to be grabbed. You can talk about a democratic society and the press in terms of the people as consumers of press products and the kind of press service they are entitled to have. Or you can talk about it in terms of the people as citizens and participants in the exchange of ideas and the formulation of opinion in which case you are concerned with the citizens' use of the instrument of communication rather than their consumption of manufactured products.[68]

Soon afterward, Hutchins relieved MacLeish of the Report's primary authorship, editing the final drafts himself with Leigh's help.[69] After eight more revisions, the Report's language was toned down considerably.

Yet MacLeish did not give up trying to produce a more critical document. At the commission's penultimate meeting, on May 6, 1946, he lashed out over the draft's narrow conceptualization of First Amendment rights: "My difficulty with Leigh's latest draft for a general Report goes pretty deep. It goes to the fundamental question of what the Commission wants and what the Commission believes." MacLeish conceded that the commissioners "will not be surprised to hear me say that the three thankless months in which I wrote a draft, absorbed several days of free-for-all criticism and then saw the whole thing shoveled down the drain, left me in some doubt." But MacLeish insisted that his concerns did not stem from bitterness; rather, he felt that the commission's First Amendment definition needed to evolve beyond a negative conception. Although "the Commission proceeded to examine the freedom of the press as a constitutionally sanctioned social belief," MacLeish noted, this freedom developed out of one "economic, social, political and technological [environment]" and "now finds itself in another – with consequences of critical importance not only to this society but to all similar societies and to the future possibility of this kind of society anywhere." MacLeish again challenged the commissioners to consider where their logic took them: By promoting freedom of the press without considering concentration of power, they conveniently ignored the predetermination of who was able to buy a radio station or a newspaper. The commissioners were "shaping the [First Amendment] right to fit the difficulties," he demanded. "Do we really mean that freedom of the press is a right reserved to all people?"[70]

Responding to the final draft, MacLeish wrote to Hutchins with one last plea. Excusing himself for being the perennial dissenter among the commissioners, he nonetheless made clear that he still thought their critique was far too meek: "We can be objective and lawyer-like and scholarly and whatever

[68] Archibald MacLeish to Robert Hutchins, 1946, Box 8, Folder 2, Hutchins Papers.
[69] A frustrated MacLeish told Hutchins that such harsh written feedback was inconsistent with Leigh's in-person disposition, which "makes cooperation so difficult." The two would continue to clash. Leigh prepared discussions based on MacLeish's draft, becoming the new draft's core, Document 93, and later a revised report, Document 97.
[70] Doc. 99, 1–2, Box 6, Folder 6–8, Commission on Freedom of the Press Papers.

else we wish to be without pulling our punches." MacLeish was emphatic that "the issue is not, as John Dickinson suggested, an issue of emotional, dramatic, journalistic writing as opposed to calm, judicial, objective writing." Instead, the problem with the Report was substantive and ideological, and "not one of form." MacLeish asked, "Are we going to state the facts and mark the implications regardless of the probable reactions of the press and its owners?" He saw the Report as unduly cautious, and even resorting at times to a degree of casuistry to evade structural problems in the press. To "drag in prewar Germany to excuse a semi-monopolistic condition in [the U.S.]," for MacLeish was "gratuitous and irrelevant – the kind of thing the Hearst press is forever doing." The commissioners were glossing over "unpleasant facts." He took particular issue with a passage worded "freedom for the press." "Surely," MacLeish argued, this should mean freedom *of* the press." He observed, "Freedom *for* is what [newspaper publishers] think it is," then reiterated, "The freedom belongs, however, to the people, not to the press. And *that* difference is real."[71] The final Report did advocate a positive First Amendment, but nothing that approached MacLeish's ideal.[72]

Compromises and Recommendations

The commission had started out fairly confrontational. Hutchins had made it clear that he wanted to strike out boldly and produce something worthy of discussion in the press and among the general public. The commission's first report, an investigation of the movie industry's self-regulation efforts, was fairly critical. "I do not object to a loud public controversy on the effect of American films abroad," Hutchins wrote. "Let's have all the fights we can."[73] With the General Report, he had called for a "flaming document."

But it was not long before many of the commissioners settled into a more accommodationist mode. Despite general agreement on the Report's recommendations and critiques, concrete proposals for far-reaching alternatives faded from the discussion as the commissioners became uncomfortable with some of their own conclusions. Partly this nervousness stemmed from the analysis that structural reform of the press would require government intervention. Partly it was perhaps due to the dilemma of enforcement, as the commissioners faced the sheer improbability of their recommendations being implemented. And partly it owed to some commissioners growing uneasy about seeming too critical.

---

[71] Archibald MacLeish to Robert Hutchins, July 20, 1946, Box 8, Folder 2, Hutchins Papers.
[72] MacLeish's First Amendment ideal resembles the near-contemporary UN Declaration of Human Rights Article 19, which codified the right to "receive and impart information and ideas through any media."
[73] Robert Hutchins to Robert Leigh, November 15, 1945, Box 7, Folder 8, Hutchins Papers.

As the commissioners finalized the language of the Report, second thoughts proliferated. In a letter to Hutchins, Robert Redfield suggested that a "paragraph or two might well be included making explicit acknowledgement of the many excellent qualities of the American press, its enterprise, its candor and even its variety, taking the little one with the big."[74] In another letter, Redfield expressed disquiet about antitrust measures and admonished his colleagues, "Have we not expressly disavowed government ownership of the media?" However, his letter concluded, "If radio does not reclaim its programs from the advertisers, the public may put its trust, and then perhaps wisely, in government ownership."[75] Others felt that the Report scaled back and hedged more than necessary. Echoing MacLeish's grievances, commissioners like John Clark expressed concern that they were watering down the final report. Clark argued against removing a sentence about reducing profits, saying that "it seems to me probably true that the things we should like to see done by [the press] would involve some reduction of profits." He wondered, "Are we, in these revisions, trying to kid ourselves with the idea that no real financial sacrifices would be involved? I'd be willing to face this possibility and accept the issue."[76]

Though failing to deliver on some of its initial promise, the commission's General Report identified five responsibilities as a basis for evaluating press performance. First, the press should provide "a truthful, comprehensive, and intelligent account of the day's events in a context which gives them meaning" in a factual and objective manner." Second, the press should be "a forum for the exchange of comment and criticism." Third, the press should provide "a representative picture of the constituent groups in society." Fourth, the press should present and clarify "the goals and values of the society." Fifth, the press should provide "full access to the day's intelligence."[77] In addition to criticizing journalistic performance and the concentration of media ownership, the Report included a vague outline for a national citizens' news council to evaluate the press. Although not a radical formulation – and largely voluntary since they lacked government oversight – these recommendations did imply a positive First Amendment conception of the public's right to know. The Report declared that "freedom of the press for the coming period can only continue as an accountable freedom,"[78] implying that a failure to remain accountable to the public might invite government intervention. This emphasis on positive liberties was clearly stated in the following: "The freedom of the press can remain a right of those who publish only if it incorporates into itself the right of the citizen and the public interest. Freedom of the press means freedom from and freedom for."[79]

---

[74] Robert Redfield to Robert Hutchins, November 25, 1946, Box 8, Folder 2, Hutchins Papers.
[75] Redfield to Hutchins, August 20, 1946, Box 8, Folder 2, Hutchins Papers.
[76] John Clark to Robert Hutchins, November 6, 1946, Box 8, Folder 2, Hutchins Papers.
[77] These five points are discussed in the *General Report*, 20–8.
[78] Ibid., 19.
[79] Ibid., 18.

In a final chapter, titled "What Can Be Done," the Report laid out relatively cautious recommendations for government, for the press, and for the public. The commissioners had originally intended to make an explicit statement for antitrust enforcement. But this was gradually tempered, exemplified by Leigh's concerns that such a recommendation seemed like "a bogey-man type of argument 'parading the horribles.'" Leigh felt that "with Congressional and judicial protection and press sensitiveness to government action, such [antitrust] action as is hinted at on the part of the Department of Justice, seems highly improbable."[80] Yet while the commissioners de-emphasized prescriptions for structural reform, they did not completely rule out antitrust action. The Report recommended that while government should "facilitate new ventures in the communication industry," and "foster the introduction of new techniques," it should also "maintain competition among large units through the antitrust laws." However, those laws should only be used "sparingly" to "break up such units;"[81] otherwise the commissioners found anti-trust laws to be "undesirable."[82] "Where concentration is necessary in communications," the Report stated, government should "see to it that the public gets the benefit of such concentration."[83] Stating that "little can be done by government or any other agency to reduce the cost of entering the industry except to adjust governmental charges," the Report rather meekly recommended that "laws and postal rates should be restudied" to see whether they "discriminate against new, small businesses in favor of large, well-established ones."[84]

The Report also stated that "the main function of government in relation to the communication industry is to keep the channels open, and this means, in part, facilitating in every way short of subsidy the creation of new units in the industry."[85] Fearing that it might be used to "limit voices in opposition," the antitrust option was something to be used as a last resort. The Report emphasized again that the "Commission looks principally to the units of the press itself to take joint action to provide the diversity, quantity, and quality of information and discussion which a free society requires." However, "these efforts to raise standards," the Report clarified, "should not be thwarted, even though they result in higher costs [and less profits]." With regard to more socially responsible radio, the commission noted that there were "only two ways of obtaining these results: they can be achieved by the acceptance of responsibility by the industry, or they can be achieved by government ownership. We prefer the former."[86]

---

[80] Robert Leigh to Robert Hutchins, N.D., 1946, Box 8, Folder 2, Hutchins Papers.
[81] *General Report*, 83.
[82] Ibid., 85.
[83] Ibid., 83.
[84] Ibid., 83–4.
[85] Ibid., 84.
[86] Ibid., 86.

The commissioners did not always harmonize their conclusions, and consensus was elusive. Dissenting opinions were sometimes well noted, as reflected in Hocking's and Chafee's individual books. When distributing publications, Leigh sometimes added a note regarding fundamental differences among commissioners in preparing the analysis. Clearly not the "flaming document" Hutchins had originally called for, the Report ultimately concluded that it was better to persuade the giants to be good than to slay them. Yet even in compromised form, the Report generated tremendous controversy.

Public Reactions to the Report

The Hutchins Commission's General Report was published in March 1947, almost a year to the day after the Blue Book. Written responses arrived from average citizens as well as famous figures and intellectual peers. The future senator Russell Long wrote that he seldom had "more thoroughly agreed than the recent account of your report concerning a 'free and responsible press.'"[87] One person self-identifying as "just a newspaper reader" supported the commission's goals and likened newspapers to "educational institutions" as important as public schools, for which the public deserves "effective representation in determining the policies of an instrument which so deeply affects the public welfare."[88] Another example of public engagement was the joint AFL-CIO's institute for union leadership's devoting evening discussions to "what labor might do about the [Commission's] findings and conclusions."[89]

Reactions to the report from fellow intellectuals were mixed, though many were enthusiastic. Mortimer Adler, Hutchins's friend and colleague, wrote, in a reference to Milton's classic text, "This is a masterly document. It out-areos the pagitica." He gushed, "It is forceful without being extreme; it is balanced without loss of power." Adler believed that the Report "should itself become an instrument of public education concerning the problems of a free press ... because your document is so very good, so reasonable, so cogent, so clear." He wanted the commission to continue "as an educational device, as a source of criticism, and the beginning of professionalization, or the setting of professional standards."[90] Walter Lippmann, a respected journalist and intellectual, wrote to Hutchins, "This is an exceptionally able document" that "sets the problems in its true perspective and proportions" and is "brilliantly written." He felt that it justified "the effort that must have gone into producing it" and

---

[87] Russell Long to Robert Hutchins, March 27, 1947, Box 8, Folder 5, Hutchins Papers.
[88] Albert Blassman to Robert Hutchins, N.D., Box 8, Folder 3, Hutchins Papers.
[89] Discussed in a letter from a union representative asking Durr whether he could "talk on the [Report's] findings and lead the discussion." The representative said Durr's participation would be a "valuable contribution to the group ... the first of its kind to meet in Georgia." Frank McAllister to Clifford Durr, June 9, 1947, Box 31, Folder 4, CJDP.
[90] Mortimer Adler to Robert Hutchins, N.D., Box 8, Folder 2, Hutchins Papers.

would "become the starting point of the indispensable inspection of the role of the press."[91]

Others felt the commissioners were letting the press off too easily. Laird Bell, a famous attorney and Hutchins's close friend, thought they had been too "gentle with the newspapers" and later asked, "Where is the line to be drawn between as unfair and destructive a paper as [McCormick's *Chicago Tribune*] and one that is merely Republican in a Democratic administration?" Pinpointing a central tension, he observed

a touch of the Pollyanna when you urge self-regulation of, particularly, newspapers. I have trouble seeing Bertie [McCormick] and [other publishers] working together for their mutual purification. Do you adequately threaten them with sanctions if they don't regulate themselves? The line between proper governmental action and improper is so easy to cross, and the monopolistic and irresponsible activities of the press [are likely enough] to invite governmental attack that I should think the threat very real.[92]

Bell ended by saying, "I'd like to see a punch paragraph – 100% Hutchins – on that score."[93]

Morris Ernst, unsurprisingly, was highly critical of the commission's findings. In 1944, he had drawn up "some observations" in a letter to William Benton and Hutchins in which he offered a list of the press's structural problems that required investigation, including unfair government-enabled advantages such as subsidies and discounts for large publishers, the suppression of unpopular political literature in the mail, market domination by media conglomerates, and a lack of media space devoted to criticizing powerful public figures like Luce. Ernst also expressed reservations about Luce's funding this project:

Obviously I am fearful of any research into the freedom of the press which originated from [Luce] because, whereas I like him, I think he is one the great perils in America in the field of freedom of the press. I have fought him in his attempt to destroy the Newspaper Guild ... and I have discussed with his boys the danger of [Luce] owning radio, movies and press. The separation of banks from security companies raised a problem not unlike the problem of divorce of radio from press, etc.[94]

Three years later, Ernst clearly felt disappointed, especially after having met with the commissioners and urging them to be more critical. Most likely remembering Chafee's performance in the AP antitrust case – and surprised by the libertarian tendencies reflected in the Report – Ernst wrote to him that it "seems so unlike you," and he was "anxious" to get a copy of Chafee's

[91] Walter Lippmann to Robert Hutchins, November 2, 1946, Box 8, Folder 2, Hutchins Papers.
[92] Laird Bell to Robert Hutchins, November 3, 1946, Box 8, Folder 2, Hutchins Papers.
[93] Ibid.
[94] Morris Ernst to William Benton, February 24, 1944, Box 8, Folder 3, Hutchins Papers.

separate book-length report. Ernst wished that "the worthy members had not endeavored to reduce their thinking to the lowest common denominator."[95]

Chafee insisted that Ernst's views had been seriously considered. After all, many of the commissioners had read his book *The First Freedom*, and they all had met with him. Chafee conceded that "You may be disappointed that the members of the Commission, including myself, have disagreed with your reliance on the anti-trust laws and similar legislation, but I can assure you that a very great deal of thought was given to this whole problem." "For my own part," Chafee explained, "I feel that the use of legal methods is somewhat unjustified. We cannot expect the government to employ the anti-trust laws extensively and at the same time be very sparing in legal actions about sedition and obscenity. Once they get going, they will move in many directions." Chafee maintained that overall the commissioners were unanimous in their thinking: "I know that you will not agree with many of our conclusions, but I hope that you will not think of us as giving up any convictions for the sake of log rolling."[96]

The Giants Strike Back

The commissioners generally felt they had published an evenhanded and well-argued report that treaded only gently on the subject of government intervention against the press. So they were entirely unprepared for the uproar that greeted them. At least part of the early reaction to the book can be attributed to the University of Chicago Press's ill-conceived press release issued in advance of the Report's publication date. The promotional material's wording sounded like a frontal attack on the commercial press, declaring that "the media of mass communication, vital to the life of our democracy, have failed" and therefore were "opening the way for the suppression of democratic government, with themselves as the first victims." The press release left out the Report's many nuances and equivocations, making it sound more inflammatory. *Editor & Publisher* further exacerbated the situation by publishing these remarks nearly two months before the Report's release. As a result, a full-fledged preemptive attack on the Report's legitimacy had already launched before its publication, indicating how sensitized the commercial press was toward anything that might be construed as suggesting governmental regulation.

Even before the offensive press release, some publishers had caught wind of the Report and were alarmed – particularly Robert McCormick, who had a long-standing feud with Hutchins over a number of local issues.[97] His proxies

---

[95] Morris Ernst to Zechariah Chafee, February 24, 1947, Box 8, Folder 5, Hutchins Papers.
[96] Chafee to Ernst, February 26, 1947, Box 8, Folder 5, Hutchins Papers.
[97] McCormick had been leading a preemptive strike against government intervention in the press since before the war. See, for example, Robert R. McCormick, "Bureaucracy Is Greatest Threat to Press Freedom – McCormick," *Editor & Publisher*, September 28, 1940, xiv.

at the *Chicago Tribune* had been periodically harassing the commissioners for months. A letter from Leigh to the *Tribune*'s business manager captures a typical exchange over whether the commission was anti-business. Referring to its earlier report on international communications, Leigh noted that the "Commission recommends that private industry should be looked to" for communications "through commercial channels" and that "commercial agencies will provide the main body of international communication." However, where "no commercially profitable [media] market" exists, "non-commercial societies and corporations [should] carry on supplementary communication." Furthermore, the commission "assumes that no private company can perform its services free of charge or without profit or should be asked to do so."[98] This standard reply aptly reflects the commission's attempts to accommodate the commercial press while acknowledging only slight limitations to its market-driven model. But the press attacked nonetheless.

Indeed, in the weeks leading up to and following the Report's publication it was disparaged in various media coverage as the product of a communist cabal endeavoring to subvert press freedoms. Lukewarm positive reception emerged from respected figures like the journalist Marquis Childs, but detractors in the press outnumbered and outmaneuvered supporters. Some observers predicted that any close analysis of press coverage of the Report would show "interesting distortions, omissions, and sensational headlines in the chain and boilerplate press,"[99] and Leigh even suggested to Hutchins that they conduct a study analyzing the content of the press's criticism.[100] *Time* magazine commissioned a clipping service to analyze newspapers' reactions and determined that 99 of 830 newspapers ran editorials (mostly negative) on the Report, a third of which used the same syndicated column.[101] Years later a more comprehensive study observed that "little acclaim and much criticism" greeted the Report.[102] The researcher found that "on the whole, the press treated the commission and the report harshly, and except for learned journals, a few newspapers, and some liberal magazines, quite prejudicially."[103]

The 1947 ASNE meeting discussed earlier contributed to the negative press coverage by whipping up dissent against the commission. Wilbur Forrest's call to arms led the attendees to pass a resolution condemning the commission, arguing that U.S. newspapers' "increasing effectiveness and fairness" kept "the American people the best informed people in the world." The resolution

---

[98] Robert Leigh to Antrim (business manager of the *Tribune*), April 5, 1946, Box 8, Folder 1, Hutchins Papers.

[99] T. W., "A Free and Responsible Press," *New Republic*, March 31, 1947. Quoted in Daniel J. Leab, "Response to the Hutchins Commission," *International Communication Gazette* 16 (1970): 113.

[100] Robert Leigh to Robert Hutchins, April 23, 1947, Box 8, Folder 5, Hutchins Papers.

[101] Robert Brown, "Shop Talk at Thirty," *Editor & Publisher*, July 19, 1947, 60.

[102] Leab, "Response to the Hutchins Commission," 105.

[103] Ibid., 113.

recognized the need for "self-improvement," but it submitted that "public judgment" alone should regulate the press.[104] Around the same time, Forrest was quoted as dismissing the commissioners' work as that of "left-wing individuals and groups [who] have long sought to weaken the American press."[105] Press attacks only increased after the ASNE convention, with critics' hostility hewing to a pattern similar to commercial broadcasters' reactions to the Blue Book, especially in their predilection for red-baiting.

Predictably, McCormick's *Chicago Tribune* was the most reactionary. Under the headline "A Free Press (Hitler Style) Sought for U.S.," the *Tribune* condemned the Report as part of a campaign of "totalitarian thinkers" who were out "to discredit the free press of America or put it under a measure of governmental control sufficient to stop effective criticism of New Deal socialism, the one-world doctrine, and internationalism."[106] The following year, another *Tribune* story, this one on the front page, claimed that "multimillion dollar, tax exempt foundations which have given cash grants to communists or to the publication of communist propaganda also are financing attempts to tamper with the freedom of the press in the United States."[107] The *Tribune* reporter who authored these stories, Frank Hughes, was later given paid leave to write a 642-page book painting the Hutchins Commission as a nefarious communist vanguard "composed entirely of men who have left-wing, Socialist convictions ranging from New Deal 'pink' to Communist 'red'" and further alleging that "so many of them had been affiliated with organizations ... held to be communist fronts."[108] In a *Fortune* article, McCormick struck again, dismissing the Report as "the outpourings of a gang of crackpots." The same article quoted the publisher Frank Gannett as saying that the Report was "wrongly conceived and badly executed" as well as "erroneous, inconsistent, ineffective, and dangerous."[109]

Other outlets dismissed the Report as the academic rants of crazy professors. The *Knickerbocker News* published the headline "Professors Blindly Try to Curb Press by Regulations to End All Our Liberties."[110] The *New York Sun*'s general manager, Edwin Friendly, held that the Report contained "inaccuracies" and "academic double talk," dismissing it as a "grievous reflection upon the discernment and efficiency of the college professors."[111] A columnist for

---

[104] ASNE Proceedings, *Problems of Journalism*, 1947, 232.

[105] "Forrest Says Report Helps Destroy Prestige of the Press," *Editor & Publisher*, March 29, 1947, 11.

[106] Frank Hughes, "A Free Press (Hitler Style) Sought for U.S.," *Chicago Tribune*, March 27, 1947, 36.

[107] Frank Hughes, *Chicago Tribune*, November 14, 1948, 1.

[108] Frank Hughes, *Prejudice and the Press: A Restatement of the Principle of Freedom of the Press, with Specific Reference to the Hutchins-Luce Commission* (New York: Devon Adair, 1950), 62.

[109] "Fortune Letters, Free for All: Freedom of the Press," *Fortune*, June 1947, 24.

[110] Quoted in Mayer, *Robert Maynard Hutchins*, 257.

[111] "Commission Report under Fire Generally," *Editor & Publisher*, April 5, 1947, 13.

the same paper remarked that "a jury of saloonkeepers to determine what is wrong with an irresponsible and amoral educational system would be just as competent as this jury of professors for the American press."[112] The trade press, unsurprisingly, was particularly virulent. Giving a full summary of the Report in its March 29, 1947, issue, *Editor & Publisher* ran four critical articles in addition to a page-long editorial slamming the commission's work.[113] Its following issue carried yet another scathing editorial and an article highlighting other critiques of the report.[114] *Editor & Publisher*'s most colorful diatribe described the commission as the workings of "11 professors, a banker-merchant and a poet-librarian."[115]

Even Henry Luce's reaction was negative. Although not resorting to red-baiting, fear mongering, or ad hominem attacks, he was "disappointed, having perhaps expected too much," and he gave the "general philosophical treatment of the problem" a grade of a "gentlemen's C and no more." Luce believed that "with a comparatively little more effort a much better job can be done." He "earnestly requested" a "special meeting of the Commission" where he could suggest improvements. If not, Luce said, the commissioners should ignore his earlier promise and "expunge from the record [any notion about] publication of the Report in a Time Inc. publication." Although Luce had stated that "Time Inc. had both the right and the duty to publish ... as much of the report verbatim as ... would be of interest to a significant proportion of its readers," he felt that some of the Report's observations "could easily be misunderstood as carrying with them a nasty smell of moral blackmail."[116] A much-discussed *Fortune* editorial that many assumed represented Luce's opinion criticized the Report's "obscurity of academic expression."[117]

A few commentators rose to the Report's defense. A review in the *Public Opinion Quarterly* characterized it as a "challenging study of great current importance" and blamed the *Fortune* piece for triggering subsequent negative and unfair accounts.[118] Some left-of-center publications were congratulatory, including the *New Republic*, which described the Report as "one of the most important books in many years."[119] An *Atlantic Monthly* article by Louis Lyons, then the Nieman Foundation curator, noted that most press commentators

112 George Sokolosky, *New York Sun*, April 8, 1947, 17.
113 "The Critics Meet the Press," *Editor & Publisher*, March 29, 1947, 29; Tom Keene, "Editor Answers Critics in Monopolist Charge" *Editor & Publisher*, March 29, 1947, 10, 57; Jerry Walker, "Press Fails to Meet Needs of Society," *Editor & Publisher*, March 29, 1947, 7, 60; "Journalists, Educators Decry Lack of Facts," *Editor & Publisher*, March 29, 1947, 12, 59; "The Press Is Indicted," *Editor & Publisher*, March 29, 1947, 38.
114 "Commission Report," *Editor & Publisher*, April 5, 1947.
115 Walker, *Editor & Publisher*, 1947.
116 Henry Luce to Robert Hutchins, November 29, 1946, Box 8, Folder 2, Hutchins Papers.
117 "Dangers to Press Freedom," *Fortune*, April 1947, 2–5.
118 Andie Knutson, "The Commission versus the Press," *Public Opinion Quarterly* 12, no. 1 (Spring 1948): 130–5.
119 T. W., "A Free and Responsible Press," *New Republic*, March 31, 1947, 34.

acted as if the very freedom of the press were under attack. While also crit-ical of the report, Lyons observed that "no other institution could have been criticized by as distinguished a group [as the Commissioners] without having the indictment land on the front page."[120] While many major papers entirely ignored the report, a few, including the *Washington Post* and the *New York Times*, provided fair coverage. Furthermore, as James Baughman observes, "some of the new generation of newspaper owners" actually saw in the "rec-ommendations an endorsement of their own management styles." Publishers such as John S. Knight and S. I. Newhouse were assembling successful news-paper chains and "viewed their properties as profit centers, not extensions of their political egos." They "abhorred the prejudiced journalism of Hearst and McCormick," and therefore saw greater press responsibility and similar codes of professionalization as compatible with their business model.[121] But these tended to be minority views.

Criticism also arose from left-leaning media, underscoring inherent tensions in the commission's work. For example, Lyons pointed out that the Report conveniently downplayed the fact that "the press in private hands" is "inevi-tably controlled by large capitalists whose interests are not always in the pub-lic interest." Avoiding this "dilemma is both the weakness of the report and the riddle of the problem."[122] Although generally agreeing with the project, A. J. Liebling assailed the commissioners for being too cautious and missing an opportunity to level a more substantive critique. Left to "wonder unchar-itably ... what they spent the $200,000 on," Liebling dismissed the Report as having "sound, unoriginal reflections, but nothing worth over one grand even at *Ladies Home Journal* rates."[123] Leigh's three-page rejoinder explained how the commission spent the money to gather data that led to original conclusions. He cited the commission's differences with Morris Ernst as evidence of reach-ing an acceptable consensus-based opinion that defied extremes on the right and left.[124]

This attempt at centrism left them appeasing few constituencies. George Seldes, for example, felt the commissioners pulled too many punches. Despite the "25,000 pages of records of evidence" of the press's failures with which

[120] Louis Lyons, "The Press and Its Critics," *Atlantic Monthly*, July 1947, 115–16. See also Louis M. Lyons, "A Free and Responsible Press: A Review of Free Press Report," *Nieman Reports* (April 1947): 1–3; and Louis M. Lyons, "Press Reaction to Free Press Report," *Nieman Reports* (July 1947): 14–20.
[121] Baughman, *Henry R. Luce*, 174. Noting that the "bumbling Wilbur Forrest ... devoted his re-cent presidential address in part to criticizing our general report," and that the previous year then–ASNE president Jack Knight had "devoted a considerable part of his address to criticizing *Peoples Speaking to Peoples*," Leigh asked whether the commission should state its own case at the next year's meeting.
[122] Louis Lyons, "The Reader Also Has Rights," *Atlantic Monthly*, April 1947, 150.
[123] A. J. Liebling, "Some Reflections on the American Press," *Nation*, December 12, 1947.
[124] Robert Leigh to "the Editor of the Nation," N.D., Box 8, Folder 5, Hutchins Papers.

he supplied the commission, they chose to largely ignore the "suppression of news, fakery, corruption of the press" and "dishonest, crooked, distorted, biased news."[125] The historian Frank Luther Mott echoed some liberal critics' disappointment that the "Commission was not able to propose something more constructive or helpful,"[126] and a *Nation* article chastised the Report for its failure to go after the "horizontal combines" that maintained media monopolies.[127] The *American Political Science Review* highlighted the central tension: "throughout the report, one senses the Commission's difficulty in trying to reconcile the communication needs of modern society with private ownership and control of the agencies of mass communication."[128]

This tension pervaded much of the commission's output. The commissioners' hesitation to call for aggressive press regulations is understandable, but in doing so they failed to recognize the structural dilemma at the very center of their inquiry: how to create a democratic press system owned and controlled by monopolists whose primary concern is to accumulate wealth. The degree to which they tiptoed around this quandary is remarkable, and it greatly constrained their potential for recommending meaningful reform. Even mainstream press critiques picked up on this central tension. The *Saturday Review* criticized the report for "mousy platitudes,"[129] and *Time* panned its "timidities and tenuousness," noting how the commission emphasized that "the job of improving the U.S. press ... was largely up to the press itself." This would require "self-examination and vigorous mutual criticism," *Time* observed, but "the U.S. press was plainly demonstrating that it didn't want the advice."[130]

Hutchins Preaches Social Responsibility to the Press

Despite such lively press reactions, the Report began to fade from public discussion within a year of its publication. Although the planned final study of press coverage of the UN's founding never materialized, archival evidence suggests that the commissioners assumed their work would continue in some capacity, perhaps as part of their proposed press council. They were thus surprised by both the hostility they received from the press and the subsequent obscurity into which their work receded. The press's general anti-intellectual tone toward the Report evidenced the degree to which many members of the media felt threatened by its reformist recommendations.

Nonetheless, Hutchins continued to promote the commission's arguments for several more years. Though not as diligent as Clifford Durr was with the

[125] George Seldes, "Truth Not Wanted," *In Fact,* April 29, 1946.
[126] Frank Mott, *Political Science Quarterly* 62 (September 1947): 441–3.
[127] "The Shape of Things," *Nation,* April 5, 1947, 381.
[128] H. L. Childs, *American Political Science Review* 41 (June 1947): 560.
[129] Kenneth Stewart, "Press RX: Faith Healings?" *Saturday Review of Literature,* April 7, 1947, 14.
[130] "The Professionals Reply," *Time,* April 1, 1947, 26.

Blue Book, he gave a number of passionate public speeches that seemingly yielded some results. In a 1947 round table discussion broadcasted over the radio, Hutchins defended the commission's recommendations against the rebuke they received from the press. In particular, he emphasized how the commission sought to help the press save itself by encouraging news media to become more accountable and thus obviate the need to "regulate or control the press." "The Commission's sole logic is to preserve its liberty," Hutchins argued, and therefore the press "must be responsible or ... forces in society, perhaps the government, will deprive it of its liberty."[131] Hutchins continued to call for a national independent council to offer periodic reviews of the press, arguing that the "probabilities of organized professionalization" and "self-regulation" were low without "maximum internal and external criticism."[132] The regulation question, however, would remain the greatest challenge, exemplifying media institutions' reluctance to reform and Hutchins's stubborn belief that the American commercial press system could self-correct if moderated by public criticism.

Hutchins was still publicly defending the commission's recommendations nearly two years later when he presented a lengthy rebuttal to the press's criticism at the National Conference of Editorial Writers. The *Guild Reporter* featured a long transcript of his address,[133] and offered sympathetic treatment as it often had previously, suggesting that the commission's tenets received some genuine grassroots support from rank-and-file reporters.[134] This particular talk, however, was to an elite gathering, one composed of many of the country's leading editorial writers. Systematically debunking the press's main criticisms, Hutchins scolded the editors for resorting to the "straw man and the red herring." Citing one example, he described a *New York Times* editorial that dismissed as a conspiracy theory the commission's argument that newspaper owners and managers "determine which persons, which facts, which versions of facts and which ideas shall reach the public."[135]

Hutchins chided the press for its inference that "you must be doing something right by your readers or you wouldn't have so many." "What a thought that must be," he said mockingly, "for the citizens [who] have to buy the

---

[131] "A Free and Responsible Press," radio address under the auspices of National Broadcasting Company and the University of Chicago, April 6, 1947, 2–5. Cited in Blevens, "Gentility and Quiet Aggression," 151–2.

[132] Ibid., 14.

[133] "A Spotlight Catches the Press," *Guild Reporter*, January 14, 1949, 2–3. Also reprinted in Robert Hutchins, "The Lack of Public Confidence in Newspaper Editorials," *Vital Speeches* 15, January 9, 1949, 175.

[134] See, for example, "Press Threatens Freedom of the Press – Special Commission Urges Changes," *Guild Reporter*, March 28, 1947, 2–3; "Freedom of the Press ... and Government," *Guild Reporter*, November 14, 1947, 6; "If the Patient Is Sick – a Prescription," *Guild Reporter*, October 20, 1947, 19.

[135] Hutchins, "The Lack of Public Confidence in Newspaper Editorials."

papers of one owner or go without!" Hutchins continued, "What a consolation the privilege not to buy must be to the people where, according to Senator
Murray's report ... no locally competing daily newspapers [exist] whatsoever."
Furthermore, he argued, even in regions with competition, when the local
papers "are essentially alike, the reader still has no real choice." That defense
"is like telling the disgusted radio listener that he can turn to three other stations and hear commercials and programs just as bad as the ones he is listening
to."[136] Hutchins continued, "You blame the tone of the press on the people and
say you have to give the public what it wants." But if not "teachers ... what
are you? You are either entertainers or the hired hands and voices of men who
happen to have enough money to own newspapers. In neither case would you
have any serious claim on the public attention."[137]

Clarifying that "the newspaper business was and should remain a private
business," Hutchins broached structural alternatives by suggesting "interesting
experiments" like that practiced by the *Economist* whereby news organizations were controlled by trustees who oversaw stock purchases and the hiring
of editors. Hutchins hoped that such alternative models would not "reflect the
political, economic, and social views of the owner" because, unlike "the sole
test of the success of a steel business or a cracker business" – profitability – the
newspaper business must "meet a further test" by "discharging its responsibility for public enlightenment."[138] Hutchins saw such reforms as part of a "campaign that began a thousand years ago" to instruct educational institutions to
be responsible.

For this campaign to succeed, however, the press must "stop exhibiting neu-
rotic symptoms every time anybody criticizes [it]." To help instill this tradition,
Hutchins emphasized the commission's recommendation for a press council:

> You ought to demand that it be created. You ought to insist that the money be raised
> for it. You ought to build it up as one of the most important and pressing projects in
> American life, so that no man of public spirit could decline to serve on it. You ought to
> point out that through such an agency the principles by which the press can remain a
> private business and perform a public service without governmental regulation may be
> worked out and made effective.[139]

Hutchins believed such an institution could moderate tensions between
newspapers' business and editorial divisions. Until then, he averred, the press
would continue to lack credibility in the eyes of the American public. "No
one will deny that the American press," he argued, "is potentially a tremendous instrument of public enlightenment." The American people should be
"looking to the press for guidance," but "they're not doing so ... they do not

[136] Ibid.
[137] Ibid.
[138] Ibid., 3.
[139] Ibid.

believe what you say ... they do not believe you are responsible." The Hutchins Commission, if nothing else, "showed that freedom requires responsibility."[140]

Hutchins's high-profile speech resonated widely and set in motion immediate, if short-lived, reform efforts. After subsequent conversations between Hutchins and Robert Brown, the editor of *Editor & Publisher*, an informal group called "Panel on the Press" was launched. Composed of publishers, editors, educators, laymen, and several members of the Hutchins Commission, the group was tasked with investigating the commission's recommendation for an "independent critical agency of the press."[141] In his opening address at the group's inaugural gathering Brown stated that since World War II ended

there has been an increasing awareness on the part of newspaper publishers of their responsibilities to the public. This is more and more apparent in the meetings of publisher groups. It is reflected in the pages of our newspapers to the point where their increasing public service to their communities is apparent every day. The presence here today of responsible editors and publishers is an indication of what I mean. Will this awareness of responsibility become more evident? I think so.[142]

The repeated invocation of "responsibility" indicated a new emphasis and, perhaps, a heightened reflexivity regarding the democratic role of the press in society. But despite many self-congratulations, little came out of this specific project; an independent press council was not established until 1973.

Indeed, such public displays in the 1940s were perhaps meant primarily to cement the *appearance* of social responsibility. Beyond establishing a positive image of the press, the pledge to social responsibility also served as a shield against the specter of government regulation. This tactic was in effect during the 1949 American Newspaper Publishers Association (ANPA) annual meeting. While addressing the General Session, the ANPA president warned the audience to beware of "big government" and its attendant threats:

The advocates of big government have been gnawing away at the press. Curtail its freedom, its strength, or its independence and there will be less vigilance, less resistance to corruption and the abuse of power. Likewise, there will be less opposition, less discussion and debate, less parliamentary delay, more free rein for directives and edicts.... The press supplies that check upon government which a free people must have and which no constitution has ever been able to provide. Can we get that back into the schools and in the minds of students and into the hearts of all who love liberty? Fellow newspapermen, it is worth trying.[143]

[140] Ibid.
[141] *Editor & Publisher*, March 26, 1949, 2; ASNE, *Problems of Journalism*, 1949, 18.
[142] *Editor & Publisher*, March 26, 1949, 3.
[143] ANPA, Convention Bulletin No. 6, May 9, 1949 (New York: ANPA, 1949), 119–27. Quoted in John Dille, "Attitude of the ANPA Toward the Responsibilities of the Press" (M.A. Thesis, University of Chicago, 1956), 40.

The press's call for educating the public in the ways of social responsibility would serve as a driving rationale for years to come. This tactic placated both the public and the government and would become a mainstay of media ethics, where it would help professionalize generations of journalists. Although the social responsibility model has its roots in the 1940s, it would not be fully codified until the 1956 publication of *Four Theories of the Press*, authored by three University of Illinois professors at the Institute of Communications Research (discussed in the next chapter).[144]

Meanwhile, Hutchins felt he had failed to effect lasting reform, largely because the commission had been unjustly ignored. He was dispirited about the American media system in general. In 1950 he described commercial radio to *Time* as "a big, unmannerly U.S. industry" and to the *BBC Quarterly*, he concluded that "American radio is a disgrace." Television, which "has adversely affected conversation, reading and the public taste," would complete the ruin, Hutchins argued.[145] The *Time* article reprised Hutchins's "gloomy conclusion" that no improvement is possible "until the day the American people rise up and hurl their radio sets into the streets. But that day will probably never come; we have got so we need the noise."[146] Five years later, Hutchins was still calling for a national press council because the press was incapable of self-monitoring. "Most of you have watched the erosion of freedom without a twinge. When the official line permitted, you have sallied forth, as when you gallantly led the troops from the rear in a belated attack on Senator Joseph McCarthy."[147] Hutchins felt that the press's stenographic reporting during the McCarthy episodes was indicative of how the commercial press could easily become an anti-democratic force in society.

Some twenty years after these remarks, when a group of University of Washington students interviewed several surviving commissioners, Hutchins expressed misgivings about the commission's legacy. The news industry still suffered from many of the same problems, and he continued to argue passionately for a national news council. Interestingly, when he was asked about Luce's support of the commission, he said:

He didn't want you to feel that you knew where he stood. I think he was ambivalent about it. To what extent he was really ambivalent, or only commercially ambivalent, I don't really know. But I got the distinct impression that he was playing it both ways. That if anybody said he had no sense of responsibility in his publications, he could say,

---

[144] Fredrick Siebert, Wilbur Schramm, and Ted Peterson, *Four Theories of the Press: The Authoritarian, Libertarian, Social Responsibility, and Soviet Communist Concepts of What the Press Should Be and Do* (Urbana: University of Illinois Press, 1956).

[145] "Listeners, Arise!" *Time*, April 3, 1950.

[146] Ibid.

[147] Robert Brown, "Hutchins Revives Proposal for Press Appraisal Body," *Editor & Publisher*, April 23, 1955, 21.

"Why, I financed the Commission on Freedom of the Press." On the other hand, if any-body said, "this Commission you financed produced a radical report," he would say, "I had nothing to do with it, and I criticized it afterwards."[148]

Ultimately, Luce did get his wish. "Responsibility" became the dominant norm for modern journalism, and calls for press regulation receded from mainstream discourse.

The Hutchins Commission's Legacy

Although its proposals were largely stamped out by a counterattacking com-mercial press, the Hutchins Commission did encourage greater reflexivity in the news media, which became further internalized within American jour-nalism's professional norms. And while it is true that the commission's rec-ommendations did not lead to significant structural change, it did – at least indirectly – encourage a more responsible commercial press system. On the other hand, the commission's efforts to accommodate the commercial press essentially produced half-measures that were pounced on as if they were radi-cal proposals. The commission's overly cautious recommendations were ripe for co-optation, thereby further inoculating the press against future criticism and structural reform. With growing public disquiet toward newspapers as a backdrop, a new rationale was necessary to justify commercial media's continued independence from government oversight. Social responsibility offered an eminently convenient narrative for the press, but it required legit-imation. Such an endeavor called for a code that was palatable to large audi-ences, one that seemed autonomous from power but did not threaten the fundamental commercial order. With its emphasis on balanced reporting and responsiveness to local communities, social responsibility was a norm whose time had come, and the Hutchins Commission helped articulate it.

Helping codify the social responsibility model of the press was arguably the commission's most important impact, but not the only one. While the commis-sion's recommended reforms were largely symbolic, at the discursive level they further mainstreamed press criticism and influenced international discussions about media policy. As noted earlier, the one recommendation to belatedly manifest for a decade was the national news council, which operated from 1973 to 1983 with foundation support. The commission's influence also can be discerned in the practice of instituting press ombudsmen and other forms of media self-criticism. The commission's tenets also played a role during the New World Information and Communication Order debates at UNESCO in the 1970s and early 1980s and in the public journalism movement of the

---

[148] Box 1, Folder 1, William Ames Papers, Special Collections, University of Washington, Seattle.

late 1980s and 1990s.[149] Another important connection to international press norms was Britain's First Royal Commission on the Press. The British commission, instigated by the National Union of Journalists and ordered by the House of Commons in the late 1940s by a vote of 270 to 157 after much heated debate, was launched to investigate "the finance, control, ownership and management of the British press."[150] To what extent the Royal Commission was influenced by the Hutchins Commission is unclear, but a letter from Leigh stated that Hutchins had "appeared before the Royal Commission on the Press and [had] the reports of the Commission on Freedom of the Press entered as exhibits for their use."[151] Siebert et al. found that the Royal Commission's final report "supports and supplements the writings of the commission on freedom of the press."[152]

Although the Hutchins Commission never had the policy-making authority to mandate systemic change directly, the commissioners' respectability and the Luce publishing empire's political and cultural influence – and financial resources – gave it tremendous norm-setting power. Despite falling short of its original reformist aspirations, the commission codified key democratic benchmarks, inspiring generations of media reformers, especially outside the United States.[153] That the Hutchins Report set the normative dimensions for press requirements within a democratic society – and is now widely considered the blueprint for responsible journalism – is ironic considering how it was mostly greeted with hostility from the newspaper industry or entirely ignored. Nonetheless, elements of the report were gradually incorporated into many journalism schools' curricula as a core set of media ethics.

While the commission was clearly an elite endeavor, it was also an expression of larger social forces, not only from the contemporaneous media reform movement but also stemming from liberalism's contradictions – especially around First Amendment protections – and a broader journalism crisis. Yet despite channeling popular dissent against the press, the commission failed to create a grassroots groundswell connected to 1940s social movements. Operating outside the public's view, the Hutchins Commission did not enlist journalists and lacked a large base of popular support. Ultimately, perhaps out of self-preservation, the commercial press co-opted its already compromised set of normative principles to arrive at its new modus operandi of social

---

[149] Victor Pickard, "Neoliberal Visions and Revisions in Global Communications Policy from NWICO to WSIS," *Journal of Communication Inquiry* 31, no. 2 (2007): 118–39; and Theodore Glasser, *The Idea of Public Journalism* (New York: Guilford Press, 1999).

[150] "Royal Commission to Probe British Press on Growth of Chains, Dangers of Monopoly," *Guild Reporter*, November 8, 1946, 8.

[151] *Royal Commission on the Press, 1947–49* (London: His Majesty's Stationery Office, 1949). Robert Leigh to Robert Hutchins, April 23, 1947, Box 8, Folder 5, Hutchins Papers.

[152] Siebert et al., *Four Theories of the Press*, 75.

[153] Seijiro Tsukamoto, "Social Responsibility Theory and the Study of Journalism Ethics in Japan," *Journal of Mass Media Ethics* 21, no. 1 (2006).

responsibility. Yet despite a fairly critical analysis and recommendations for improvement, the Hutchins Commission's Report's most important finding was that the press should remain self-regulated. The commission's reports and subsequent interpretations essentially removed from conversation any possibility for significant structural regulation. In the next chapter we will consider how the discourse of self-regulation helped define media's normative role in American society.

7

The Postwar Settlement for American Media

Key normative foundations underlying the American media system – and assumptions about government's role in maintaining them – crystallized during a brief yet dynamic period in the 1940s, a critical juncture when technological, social, and political upheavals created crisis and opportunity. A number of potential trajectories opened before policy makers during fundamental debates about the relationships among media institutions, the state, and various publics. What did broadcasters and publishers owe the public? What were media institutions' public service responsibilities? And what was government's regulatory role in enforcing them? Progressive ideas flourished for a time. But as the decade progressed, America witnessed a narrowing of discursive parameters, setting limitations on the potential for government intervention against commercial media. Once this window closed, structural reforms were increasingly off-limits. Commercial broadcasters could feel confident that their licenses would not be revoked regardless of poor public service, and antitrust action against newspaper monopolies ceased to be a serious threat. This era's policy battles resulted in a settlement that media would be self-regulated but "socially responsible" – an industry-friendly arrangement that enshrined a negative conception of press freedom while mandating largely nominal concessions to the public interest.

This outcome is consistent with policy discourses and normative expectations associated with corporate libertarianism, an ideology that conflates corporate privilege with First Amendment freedoms and is girded by a logic that advances individualistic negative liberties at the expense of the collective positive liberties that are central to a social democratic vision of media.[1] Similar

---

[1] For literature on positive First Amendment freedoms see Owen Fiss, *The Irony of Free Speech* (Cambridge, MA: Harvard University Press, 1996); Edward Purcell, *The Crisis of Democratic Theory: Scientific Naturalism and the Problem of Value* (Lexington: University Press of Kentucky, 1973); Matthew Bunker and Charles Davis, "The First Amendment as a Sword:

to the political economic shifts sketched in Michael Denning's *The Cultural Front* – which described a failed social democratic challenge in 1940s America that resulted in a power share among labor unions, government, and big business – this transitional moment marked the Popular Front's dissolution, giving way to a more accommodationist liberalism.[2] For media institutions, the postwar settlement emerging from the resolutions of 1940s policy debates signaled a deregulatory turn – or rather, a "reregulation" under oligopolistic markets. This arrangement systematically obscured structural critiques, foreclosed radical alternatives, and pushed back against social democratic reform movements. In doing so, it kept in place a self-regulating, nominally socially responsible commercial media system.

The Rise and Fall of a Social Democratic Vision of Media

Print and broadcast media policy debates in the 1940s cohered around similar themes, crises, and paradigmatic shifts. While differing in some respects, major policy battles like those connected to the Blue Book and Hutchins Commission

The Positive Liberty Doctrine and Cable Must-Carry Provisions," *Journal of Broadcasting & Electronic Media* 40, no. 1 (1996): 77–95; Thomas Emerson, "The Affirmative Side of the First Amendment," *Georgia Law Review* 15 (1981): 795–849; Lee Bollinger, *Images of a Free Press* (Chicago: University of Chicago Press, 1991), 73; Jerome A. Barron, "Access to the Press – a New First Amendment Right," *Harvard Law Review* 80, no. 8 (1967): 1641–78; William Hocking, *Freedom of the Press* (Chicago: University of Chicago Press, 1947), 172; Ben Scott (2007). "A Broad, Positive View of the First Amendment," in *The Case against Media Consolidation*, ed. Mark Cooper (New York: McGannon Center for Communications Research, 2007): 39–62; Timothy E. Cook, "Public Policy toward the Press: What Government Does for the News Media," in *The Press*, ed. Genevia Overholser and Kathleen Hall Jamieson (Oxford and New York: Oxford University Press, 2005): 248–62; Timothy E. Cook, ed., *Freeing the Presses: The First Amendment in Action* (Baton Rouge: Louisiana State University Press, 2006). Robert Picard, *The Press and Decline of Democracy* (Westport, CT: Greenwood Press, 1985), 38–50; Victor Pickard, "Reopening the Postwar Settlement for U.S. Media: The Origins and Implications of the Social Contract between Media, the State, and the Polity," *Communication, Culture & Critique* 3, 2, (2010): 170–89.

[2] Denning, *The Cultural Front*, 465–6. This outcome is also consistent with a political economic shift concretized in the late Progressive Era that Tom Streeter and revisionist historians have termed "corporate liberalism," in which a façade of administrative neutrality, technocratic expertise, and autonomous policy-making institutions allows for surface-level reforms, but preserves the system's fundamental power relationships by shielding them from deeper structural reform. See Tom Streeter, *Selling the Air*, 120. However, corporate liberalism differs from libertarianism in that it does not account specifically for the particular role of media corporations as political agents protected by First Amendment freedoms. Moreover, corporate liberalism does not capture the core principle at the heart of libertarianism: Government intervention on behalf of public interest and redistributive principles is rendered a priori illegitimate. Whereas corporate liberalism describes the process of glossing over core power relationships, corporate libertarianism – as well as processes commonly identified with the neoliberalism that emerged in the 1970s – underscores the ideological project of elevating individual and corporate property rights over the broader society's collective rights.

displayed a remarkable symmetry. In addition to their synchronicity and similar actors, they shared a common critique: that commercial media were not providing the public services that democracy required. Both initiatives proposed positive and significantly expanded First Amendment freedoms for media audiences, and they faced similar opposition in the form of red-baiting from broadcasters, publishers, and businesses lobbyists, as well as conservative politicians in both major parties.

Allowing for some oversimplification, both the Blue Book and the Hutchins Commission followed a four-stage pattern: originating as a popular critique/ movement, manifesting as a progressive policy initiative based on social democratic normative principles, suffering counterattacks from commercial media industries, and finally, agreeing to industry-friendly settlements. The Blue Book's defeat led to a self-regulated commercial radio (and soon television) system in which broadcasters, under virtually no threat of license revocation, could act with near-impunity. This outcome has had a profound impact on our current media system. For license renewals, broadcasters today simply have to send in a postcardlike form every eight years to be rubber-stamped by FCC engineers – precisely the outcome Clifford Durr fought against. Not only was the Blue Book completely negated by broadcasters and their political allies, its defeat indirectly led to the subsequent repeal of the editorializing ban, which afforded broadcasters still more political and economic power (albeit with concessions to the public in the form of the Fairness Doctrine). Similarly, the Hutchins Commission's resolution helped inoculate the newspaper industry against future regulation, doing little to chasten publishers, even after they had suffered significant comeuppance with the Supreme Court's AP antitrust case. The concession to the public was "social responsibility," but in effect it protected commercial values and helped cement corporate domination of the news industry. The decade's regulatory shift in the relationship between government and the press is striking: Newspaper publishers went from being fearful of imminent government intervention in the early 1940s to being assured by 1949 of near-complete autonomy.

And yet, had progressive reformers such as Durr and Archibald MacLeish prevailed, had policy makers coordinated more effectively with social movement groups, had Cold War anti-communist hysteria not snuffed out much of the 1940s' progressive potential, today's media system would likely be more diverse and less concentrated, more public service-oriented and less commercialized. Instead, policy initiatives like the Blue Book were exiled to the annals of history rather than serving as the foundations for American media policy. The most palpable outcome of the corporate libertarian paradigm's ascendancy was not only keeping the commercial system intact but ultimately strengthening it. The resolutions from these debates consolidated commercial ownership and control of media institutions while solidifying a coerced settlement that in many ways continues to define American media's social obligations. This settlement constrains government's regulatory role, limits the range of public policy, and leaves' de facto governance of media institutions to marketplace relationships, thereby permanently elevating economic motives over social imperatives.[3]

The Blue Book and Hutchins Commission also shared some similar blind spots. Despite the best efforts by such policy makers as Clifford Durr, by not consistently coordinating their activities with grassroots media activists, the commissioners practiced a progressivism that only selectively drew from the broader media reform movement's criticisms. The two commissions did not embrace more radical proposals – for example, calls for public ownership of media, or for news outlets to be considered public utilities or common carriers. Progressive policy elites tended to privilege content regulation over structural reform in their recommendations, especially as the 1940s wore on. Although the Blue Book did pose a credible threat of structural intervention in the form of license revocation, its primary focus was on the regulation of broadcasters' programming choices, not the more fundamental questions about commercial ownership and control.

These initiatives also had important differences. Whereas the Blue Book was largely defeated by broadcasters and their political allies, the Hutchins Commission's recommendations were ignored or co-opted under the guise of "social responsibility." Unlike the Hutchins Commission, the Blue Book attempted to carve out a meaningful role for regulatory oversight and intervention. More than just challenging advertisers' and commercialism's influence, the Blue Book and the social forces buoying it struck at fundamental assumptions about U.S. media's public service responsibilities. Its motivations can be partly attributed to an organized radio reform movement that engaged various constituencies, compared with the more scattershot reform efforts aimed at newspapers. And while the Hutchins Commission report arose organically from public distrust of the press, it was also constrained by mostly elite discourses and communities of experts, disconnected from grassroots constituencies, and, perhaps, somewhat compromised by Luce's and other indirect political pressures.

The Common Sense of Self-Regulation
The Blue Book and Hutchins Commission's similarities were symptomatic of an overarching paradigm clash between two discrete visions of the press's role in a democratic society. Appraising these policy debates together highlights how their resolution solidified commercial media's power and largely immunized news institutions from major structural interventions. The most significant outcome to emerge from both the Blue Book defeat and the Hutchins report was the decision that commercial media – particularly newspapers and

---

[3] For a discussion of social and economic considerations in media policy, see Robert Entman and Stephen Wildman, "Reconciling Economic and Non-Economic Perspectives on Media Policy: Transcending the 'Marketplace of Ideas,'" *Journal of Communication* 41, no. 1 (1992): 5–19.

broadcasting – should remain self-regulated. Although questions about ownership and control and whether mass news media should remain private or public had been largely settled in the 1930s, the nature of the compact between these commercial entities and the public, and the government's role in regulating this relationship, had yet to be determined.

Buttressing this increasingly commonsensical belief in the press's self-regulation were First Amendment arguments that privileged large commercial media producers, technocratic language that skirted important normative debates, and economic paradigms that assumed a benevolent role for market governance. Self-regulation of media industries represented the triumph of an elite consensus, one that was now firmly reasserted as a sacrosanct principle lying beyond the bounds of public scrutiny and facilitated by a simultaneous weakening of reformers' structural critique. Reformers were eloquent in their assessments of news media's shortfalls, but they often offered tepid recommendations that amounted to pleading with, scolding, and shaming commercial media organizations into being good. Such browbeating had relatively little demonstrable effect on media performance. This overall timidity in the face of industry recalcitrance ushered in the social responsibility model of the press.

The Press Finds Social Responsibility

The social responsibility model was founded on the idea that the press should professionalize according to norms of truthfulness and objectivity that benefit the broader community. Situating this professionalization process within a general landscape of public and intellectual criticism establishes the context for newspapers' resolution of the crisis. Despite finding fundamental flaws in the commercial press's structure and content, the Hutchins Commission set codes of professionalization that would, ironically, help shield the industry by elevating an intellectual rationale for self-regulation under social responsibility – a framework that was easily co-opted to serve a libertarian agenda.

Various trends combined to convince policy makers and the general public that changes in the press necessitated a concept of social responsibility[4] – including increased political power and concentration of ownership – but the press also had economic motives to adopt such norms. As an ideological project, the social responsibility model was well suited to preempt regulation of the press – a convenience that has not gone entirely unnoticed.[5] While his University of Illinois colleagues were further articulating the social responsibility model for their *Four Theories of the Press*, Dallas Smythe wrote a

---

[4] See John Nerone et al., *Last Rights: Revisiting Four Theories of the Press* (Urbana: University of Illinois Press, 1995) for an overview of these ideas. A thorough critique of social responsibility theory is found in John Merrill, *The Imperative of Freedom: A Philosophy of Journalistic Autonomy* (New York: Hastings House, 1974).

[5] For example, see Herbert Altschull, *Agents of Power: The Role of the News Media in Human Affairs* (London: Longman, 1984).

scathing critique of their formulation, seeing it as a blatantly political project, "reflecting the public relations program of big business" and "formally equivalent in class and political economic terms to the press doctrine in the Soviet Union."[6]

The social responsibility model purportedly replaced the earlier libertarian model, but a more critical analysis suggests that it essentially enabled a slightly tweaked libertarian model to continue to prevail unabated.[7] Drawing from the Hutchins Commission's relatively cautious recommendations for professionalizing journalism instead of more stringent reforms, it maintained journalistic autonomy from regulation while calling for balanced and informative reporting. Accordingly, such reporting would be protected from business pressures behind a firewall that supposedly enabled reporters to work in the public's interest. However, the Hutchins report's ambiguous language and weak recommendations positioned it for industry co-optation in the form of social responsibility. For example, it stated that the press should offer a balanced account of the day's events without specifying that it should also be adversarial toward those in power. But as long as the press remained socially responsible, the argument went, the public and, more important, the government, could rest assured

The Triumph of the Negative First Amendment

Competing visions of a free press were cast into stark relief in the 1940s. On one side, a positive vision of the First Amendment promoted "freedom *for*" the audience; on the other, a negative, laissez-faire position promoted "freedom *from*" government intrusion into commercial media markets. According to this latter view, which equates freedom with non-regulation, government should defer to market operations to determine who has access to media and on what terms. This approach privileges the interests of media owners and producers over other concerns, with First Amendment freedoms accruing to media corporations.

Despite its many compromises, the Hutchins Commission opposed this corporate libertarian view, advocating instead a positive First Amendment similar to the Supreme Court's decision against the AP. This position of state-guaranteed provisions for positive First Amendment protections was clearly articulated in the court's ruling: "Freedom of the press from governmental interference under the First Amendment does not sanction repression of that freedom by private interests."[8] The Hutchins Commission likewise stated, "Freedom of the press can remain a right of those who publish only if it incorporates into itself the

[6] Dallas Smythe and Thomas Guback, *Counterclockwise: Perspectives on Communication* (Boulder, CO: Westview Press, 1994), 94–8.

[7] For this argument, see Nerone, *Last Rights*.

[8] *Associated Press v. United States* (1945).

right of the citizen and the public interest. Freedom of the press means freedom from *and* freedom for."[9]

Durr and his allies also advanced positive First Amendment freedoms by advocating a "listeners' rights" approach to broadcast policy. In late 1948, after leaving the FCC, a dispirited Durr wrote a series of letters to Dallas Smythe recalling how the primary motivation behind the Blue Book initiative boiled down to concerns about First Amendment protections. He saw radio as an "instrument of free speech" and believed that he and his liberal cohort were championing the Enlightenment traditions reflected in the U.S. Bill of Rights. In an earlier letter to Charles Siepmann, Durr summarized his understanding of the First Amendment vis-à-vis broadcast policy, which clearly contrasted with industry's ideal:

The First Amendment does not require that the government vest in broadcasters the uncontrolled right to control freedom of speech of others. Free speech means effective free speech, and that means that access to the effective instrumentalities should not be denied. There is certainly no denial of free speech when the government, through the FCC, says to a broadcaster, "you must make free speech an effective reality by making the publicly owned radio channels available for the discussion of all points of view."[10]

Durr felt that the main impediments to actualizing positive First Amendment protections were the "emotional blockages" that industry representatives and their conservative allies deliberately employed to obfuscate substantive issues. These red herrings included charges that the FCC's more expansive and progressive view of the First Amendment, codified in the Blue Book, constituted an infringement against "free radio" and "free enterprise" – which therefore meant it was "un-American" and "communistic." Durr's views were consistent with those of the First Amendment scholar Alexander Meiklejohn, who in 1948 lamented the triumph of negative freedoms as he recalled earlier hopes for radio's democratic promise:

It seemed possible that, amid all our differences, we might become a community of mutual understanding and of shared interest. It was that hope which justified making our radio "free," giving it First Amendment protection.... But never was a human hope more bitterly disappointed. The radio as it now operates among us is not free. Nor is it entitled to the protection of the First Amendment. It is not engaged in the task of enlarging and enriching human communication. It is engaged in making money. And the First Amendment does not intend to guarantee men freedom to say what some private interest pays them to say for its own advantage.[11]

[9] Leigh, *Free and Responsible Press*, 18. It must be pointed out, however, that because the commission also advocated for media self-regulation, a more negative freedom gained greater articulation.
[10] Clifford Durr to Charles Siepmann, January 3, 1947, Box 31, Folder 2, CJDP.
[11] Alexander Meiklejohn, *Political Freedom* (1948), reprinted in Meiklejohn, *Political Freedom: The Constitutional Powers of the People* (New York: Harper and Brothers, 1960), 86–7; quoted in Jeff Land, *Active Radio: Pacifica's Brash Experiment* (Minneapolis: University of Minnesota Press, 1999), 5.

Most broadcasters, in contrast, saw those First Amendment principles in more libertarian terms, pertaining primarily to individual liberties rather than the collective good, a viewpoint that – as Meiklejohn bemoaned – resulted in the public's being limited to programming largely dictated by broadcasters' profit concerns. Consequently, as a critic in 1946 put it, "The public does not now hear the voice of its many minorities, of labor, or of consumer groups to any representative extent. Ideas which might arouse vigorous controversy, and antagonize sponsors ... receive no air time."[12] Commercial broadcasters viewed as anathema any redistributive, affirmative logic in giving more representation to marginalized groups and ideas. While political stances played a part, broadcasters' resistance was probably motivated by mostly commercial concerns; they wished to reach large audiences with inexpensive, non-controversial programming. Regardless, the reformers' defeat at the hands of the broadcast industry demonstrated to all that media institutions could effectively use the First Amendment as a shield against unwanted regulation as well as a bludgeon with which to gain more political and economic power. Although it failed to convince the Supreme Court during the AP case, this corporate libertarian understanding of the First Amendment ultimately triumphed and continues to drive much media policy today, even as reformers continue to challenge these assumptions.

The postwar settlement's three components had the collective aim of heading off major structural reform. It contained radical movements, preempted governmental oversight, and bolstered laissez-faire assumptions. Privately-owned, lightly regulated media firms, in many cases monopolies or part of oligopolies in their respective markets, maintained their dominant role within an advertising-supported, commercial media system. While the social responsibility model professed to protect media institutions from political pressures, it also conveniently served to protect revenue, and profit imperatives were not sacrificed in any significant way. Thus, while commercial media had suffered a crisis of legitimacy in the 1940s, that legitimacy was largely restored and even strengthened by the end of the decade.

A pair of implicit questions posed at the beginning of the decade demonstrates the discursive shift during this postwar window that marked the intellectual consolidation of corporate libertarianism: What are the media's public service requirements in a democratic society? And what is the state's proper role in mandating those services? The response in the early 1940s was that media should fulfill a set of criteria or else risk state intervention. But by 1949 the answer had become that media should largely decide for themselves what was socially responsible, and government had only a minor role to play in encouraging this behavior. These assumptions became embedded in subsequent media policies and institutions.

---

[12] Eleanor Timberg, "The Mythology of Broadcasting," *Antioch Review*, 1946, 357.

Other 1940s Media Policies and Subsequent Trajectories

America in the 1940s, this book argues, was closer to following a social democratic trajectory in media policy than is generally acknowledged. While the case studies discussed thus far fall under the rubric of "news media," similar conflicts were playing out in film, telecommunications, and international communications, as well as in the academic field of communication itself, suggesting a broader ideological confrontation. Other media industries were seeing analogous patterns in which a social democratic impulse arose, only to be put down by red-baiting and reactionary politics. These conflicts all deserve closer examination than I am able to discuss here (and in some cases, have already received such attention), but I briefly mention some of them in the following.

Like other mass communications sectors, the film industry was fraught with political struggle during the 1930 and 1940s, and liberal-left films promoting visions of human solidarity and critiques of the capitalist system were not uncommon.[13] Hollywood was riven with labor battles, especially the Conference of Studio Unions strike in 1945 and the subsequent lockout of 1946.[14] Studio moguls used the Red Scare to help undermine the unions and take over the production process. One book on the subject noted that "the crushing of the 1946 studio strike might be taken as the death knell of the Hollywood Left."[15] The trials of the blacklisted Hollywood Ten – a group of prominent directors and screenwriters whose defense in front of HUAC was couched in terms of First Amendment and artistic freedoms – became another crucial battle between corporate control of film and a more social democratic arrangement.[16] Until the eve of the blacklist, people both in and outside Hollywood believed that a standoff over creative control of America's film industry was imminent.[17]

Like other communications industries in the 1940s, the film sector had become a highly concentrated oligopoly, controlled by the "Big Five," Metro-Goldwyn-Mayer, Paramount, RKO, 20th Century Fox, and Warner Bros. Although nearly eighteen thousand theaters operated across the United States in 1945, nearly all their films were produced in large Hollywood-based studios and distributed by those five companies.[18] New Deal antitrust concerns

---

[13] The Hutchins Commission delivered a critical analysis, but ultimately called for more self-regulation. Ruth Inglis, *Freedom of the Movies* (Chicago: University of Chicago Press, 1947).

[14] Gerald Horne, *Class Struggle in Hollywood, 1930–1950: Moguls, Mobsters, Stars, Reds, and Trade Unionists* (Austin: University of Texas Press, 2001).

[15] Paul Buhle and David Wagner, *Radical Hollywood: The Untold Story behind America's Favorite Movies* (New York: New Press, 2002), 376.

[16] For good background on this period, see Larry Ceplair and Steven Englund, *The Inquisition in Hollywood: Politics in the Film Community, 1930–1960* (Berkeley: University of California Press, 1982); Nancy Lynn Schwartz, *The Hollywood Writers' Wars* (New York: Alfred A. Knopf, 1982); Bernard Dick, *Radical Innocence: A Critical Study of the Hollywood Ten* (Lexington: University Press of Kentucky, 1989); and Mike Davis, *City of Quartz: Excavating the Future in Los Angeles* (London: Verso, 1990), 18.

[17] Buhle and Wagner, *Radical Hollywood*, viii.

[18] Baughman, *The Republic of Mass Culture*, 21–2.

led to a major structural intervention in the Supreme Court's 1948 *Paramount* case, concluding a twenty-year court battle. The Supreme Court ruled against vertical integration on the basis of unfair monopolistic practices, and MGM, Warner Bros., and 20th Century Fox were ordered to divest themselves of their theaters, while Paramount signed a consent decree in 1949, agreeing to split its distribution and production arms.

The 1940s also set the mold for television. While national live network programming would not take off until the early 1950s, important parameters for television broadcasting policy were set in place by the late 1940s, including those relating to educational broadcasting, public interest obligations, and the relationship between the FCC and broadcasters. The same big three radio networks – CBS, NBC, ABC – would dominate television with similarly little governmental oversight over programming, even as their influence quickly exceeded that of radio. Much radio criticism easily morphed into familiar indictments against television,[19] and many reformers assumed that Blue Book criteria were applicable and necessary for television.[20]

For telecommunications policy, the notion of "natural monopolies" still reigned, with AT&T dominating telephony and Western Union dominating telegraphy.[21] However, such long-standing verities were receiving increased scrutiny and familiar battle lines were being drawn between corporate telecom entities and progressive regulators. In the late 1930s during an aggressive five-year investigation, the FCC considered aggressive structural interventions against AT&T,[22] and concerns about monopoly control would remain central to FCC telecommunication debates throughout the 1940s.[23] An antitrust investigation against AT&T begun earlier in the decade led to a case formally brought forward in early 1949. However, what began as a progressive intervention against monopoly power devolved somewhat into a more technical debate by the 1950s.[24]

---

[19] Steven Starker, *Evil Influences: Crusades against the Mass Media* (New Brunswick, NJ: Transaction, 1989).

[20] See the Siepmann interview cited in Richard Meyer, "The 'Blue Book,'" *Journal of Broadcasting* 6 (1962): 206.

[21] See William Sharkey, *The Theory of Natural Monopoly* (Cambridge: Cambridge University Press, 1982).

[22] N. R. Danielian, *AT&T: The Story of Industrial Conquest* (New York: Vanguard Press, 1939). See also Victor Pickard, "A Giant Besieged: AT&T, an Activist FCC, and Contestation in Corporate-State Relations, 1935–1939" (paper presented at the Union of Democratic Communications, St. Louis, April 22–5, 2004).

[23] In addition to the organization of the telegraph industry, questions of universal service, rural access, and the plight of independent telecom operators were held in the balance – all issues with considerable relevance for contemporary Internet-related policy debates. In 1943, Clifford Durr would dissent on the Western Union telegraph merger, to great controversy.

[24] Dan Schiller covers these issues extensively in a forthcoming book titled *The Hidden History of US Telecommunications*. See also Dan Schiller, "The Hidden History of US Public Service Telecommunications, 1919–1956," *Info* 9, no. 2/3 (2007): 17–28.

These ideological struggles over media, democracy, and regulation also figured within debates around international communication policy. Archibald
MacLeish took social democratic ideals to the United Nations and authored
the preamble for UNESCO's (United Nations Educational, Scientific and
Cultural Organization) constitution, which promoted international peace,
collaboration, and human rights. Similar issues were addressed by the United
Nations'1948 Universal Declaration of Human Rights,[25] which, among other
things, attempted to articulate an international code of "press freedom." This
doctrine would include Article 19, a code later associated with "The Right to
Communicate," which remains a foundation for progressive global media policy. Inspired by positive freedoms, it states, "Everyone has the right to freedom
of opinion and expression; this right includes freedom to hold opinions without interference and to seek, receive and impart information and ideas through
any media and regardless of frontiers."

At the same time, the U.S. government and its Western allies, business leaders, and well-meaning liberals were advancing a "free flow of information"
doctrine.[26] Often conflating liberal concerns about democratic openness with
the commercial imperatives of Western media companies eager to maintain
preferential positioning within new markets, this debate holds interesting parallels with today's global objective of "Internet freedom." Conflicts around these
norms erupted between social democrats and liberals at the 1948 Freedom
of Information Conference, especially around the issue of press accountability.[27] Other important global communication developments included the 1947
International Telecommunications Union meeting that witnessed the supplant-
ing of the United Kingdom and other imperial powers by the United States.[28]
The 1940s also saw raging debates transpire around questions of propaganda,
state subsidies, and American global hegemony concerning the Voice of America
(VOA), a U.S. government–supported international broadcasting service.[29]

---

[25] See Mary Ann Glendon, *A World Made New: Eleanor Roosevelt and the Universal Declaration
of Human Rights* (New York: Random House, 2001). Page 51 briefly notes MacLeish's involvement in early discussions.

[26] See Victor Pickard, "Communication Rights in a Global Context," in *Battleground: The
Media*, Vol. 1, ed. Robin Anderson and Jonathan Gray (Westport, CT: Greenwood Press, 2008)
91–97.

[27] William Preston, Edward S. Herman, and Herbert I. Schiller, *Hope and Folly: The United States
and UNESCO, 1945–1985* (Minneapolis: University of Minnesota Press, 1989) 54–6.

[28] For an overview and history of the United States relationship with the ITU, see Milfred L. B.
Feldman, *The United States in the International Telecommunication Union and in Pre-ITU
Conferences* (Feldman, 1975). For an overview of the larger power struggles over global telecommunications in the postwar period, see also Jill Hills, *Telecommunications and Empire*
(Urbana: University of Illinois Press, 2007). As it rose in global power, the U.S. government
perceived threats with the rise of an emerging global Left, especially in postwar Europe, where
left-wing partisan groups held the European political mainstream and many center-right institutions were tarnished by their wartime collaboration with fascists.

[29] See, for example, David Krugler, *The Voice of America and the Domestic Propaganda Battles,
1945–1953* (Columbia: University of Missouri Press, 2000). Many conservatives worried that

Some similar ideological tensions were also present within the still-nascent academic field of communication. In addition to differences between propaganda studies (including those who were critical of propaganda and others who were trying to perfect it) and limited effects research, divergences emerged between more critical strands of communication scholarship – like that practiced by the early political economists, the sociologist C. Wright Mills, and the Frankfurt school – and the administrative and positivistic research agendas espoused by Paul Lazarsfeld.[30] While these differences in emphasis all stemmed from particular circumstances and personalities, many also were influenced by larger power shifts such as the retreat of structural criticism, the collapse of a social democratic challenge, and Cold War politics, including instances of red-baiting and state surveillance.[31]

Decline of the 1940s Media Reform Movement

Although 1940s reformers received some sympathetic media treatment and found resonance among the larger populace, they were largely outmaneuvered and were unable to realize the sum of their disparate parts. For print media reform, this was largely due to an absence of a strong base of grassroots support despite tapping into popular sentiments. For radio reform, at least two major strategic errors contributed to the movement's lack of success. First, they failed to maintain a strong inside/outside strategy that keeps reform-oriented regulators connected to outside-the-beltway constituencies. For example, coordination between grassroots activists and policy elites during the Blue Book debates was lacking, leaving reformers ill prepared to withstand the ensuing onslaught. While activist groups could have synchronized efforts more among themselves, little coordination existed between the FCC and grassroots allies leading up to the Blue Book's publication. Some occurred afterward, but by then reformers were already in defensive crouches.

Although grassroots pressures gave rise to the Blue Book, it was composed behind closed doors and released with little advance notice, thus failing to

---

the VOA would have a liberal bias in favor of the Democratic Party (see Krugler, 40), and media industry leaders feared the VOA masked a leftist agenda at work (see Preston et al., 58). For a study of how this ideological struggle played out during America's role in establishing German public broadcasting, see Mandy Troger, "What Makes 'Free' Radio? U.S. Media Policy Discussions in Postwar Germany, 1945–1947," *International Journal of Communication* 7 (2013): 1990–2009.

[30] For a broader discussion of these tensions in the field of communication's early stages of development, see Victor Pickard, "Mending the Gaps: Reconnecting Media Policy and Media Studies," in *Media Studies Futures*, ed. Kelly Gates (London: Blackwell, 2013), 404–21. See also Chris Simpson, *Science of Coercion: Communication Research and Psychological Warfare, 1945–1960* (New York: Oxford University Press, 1994).

[31] Documentation in Smythe's papers at Simon Fraser University suggests that he later came to believe that while he was on the faculty at the ICR the departmental chair Wilbur Schramm had been informing on him for the FBI. "FBI Report – Copy Annotated by Smythe 1/2," 1982, Folder 16-1-4-4, Smythe Papers. See also Smythe and Guback, *Counterclockwise*, 42–3.

give activist allies time to marshal support. Durr's personal contacts and the
activist themes championed in his work demonstrate a clear line from social
movements to the Blue Book. But despite calling for public participation, the
Blue Book's implementation overly relied on its authors' inner circle instead
of drawing support from outside reform groups. To be fair, the secrecy and
lack of coordination preceding the Blue Book may have been necessary to
reduce the risk of leaks. Recalling that Durr formed an "invisible task force,"
Smythe noted that he was not "privy to this triumvirate's [Durr, Siepmann, and
Brecher] work, which was conducted almost secretly" because of "the need to
protect the integrity of the project from industry informers inside the FCC."[32]
This fear of surveillance may have discouraged outside coordination; according to various accounts, by the late 1940s, media reform activism around the
FCC had declined significantly.[33] For their part, activists insufficiently rallied
support when it could have mattered most. An embittered Siepmann wrote in
1948 that media reformers were "conspicuous by their absence" during Blue
Book–related proceedings, and organized assistance was lacking from the very
"non-profit organizations whose interests [were most at stake] ... to let the
FCC know that it had any solid body of opinion behind it."[34]

A second major factor in their decline was the erosion of a systemic critique. Postwar media reformers faced many difficulties beyond their control,
but their decline probably was partly due to losing sight of a structural critique
of the commercial media system. This critique assumes that, short of public
ownership of media, the most effective safeguard against commercialism is a
combination of strong government regulation of media institutions at the federal level and local control and oversight at the community level. Accordingly,
media reform activists in the 1930s and early 1940s prioritized breaking up
monopolies and creating noncommercial radio instead of policing broadcasters' commercial content. But these structural reform efforts faded as the decade
progressed. An attenuated structural critique can be partly attributed to on-
the-ground political realities. Given Washington, DC's resurgent conservatism,
perhaps activists had little choice but to settle for battles over representation
within a commercial media system.

Whatever its underlying causes, despite having the potential to connect with
a critical mass of support, popular media criticism often failed to make the
crucial move from the "symptomatic" (discussing the excesses of commercial
radio) to the "structural" (discussing their underlying root causes). A 1948 article in the academic journal *Public Opinion Quarterly* summed up this erosion
in radical criticism and acceptance of the status quo. Noting that "public criticism ... has continued throughout the decade in cycles of varying intensity,"

[32] Dallas Smythe to Jelena Grcic Polic and Oscar Gandy, June 26, 1991, Box 16–6, Folder 16-1-4-7, Smythe Papers.
[33] Toro, "Standing Up for Listeners' Rights," 133.
[34] Siepmann, "Radio," *The Communication of Ideas*, ed. Bryson, 191.

the article found that "the criticism which continues ... is becoming more temperate, more constructive, more aware of the necessary mass basis for much of radio's programming." Major facets of the status quo were no longer debatable: "Substantial evidence of another notable trend has accumulated during the decade. U.S. radio has become even more securely established as a system of private ownership and operation under government license."[35]

This shift is partly due to the purge of leftist activists most prone to leveling such structural criticism. This political repression created a discursive environment that was hostile to criticizing existing power relationships. Media institutions themselves were culpable in fueling the anti-communist hysteria that hobbled progressive policies and helped demobilize reform movements. Commercial media institutions also helped tamp down media criticism by failing to cover structural issues. Morris Ernst noted, "The greatest single asset of the networks in their drive for continued monopoly of thought lies in the ignorance of the public ... perpetuated by the failure of the networks to allow any debate or discussion [on media ownership and advertising]."[36]

The erosion of a structural critique tracks with the late 1940s decline in media reform activism. As they attempted to persuade media corporations to be good, liberals drifted away from advocating systemic safeguards such as public spectrum set-asides and nonprofit models. This raises a chicken-and-egg question: Were media reformers rendered ineffective by factors beyond their control and thus forced to move away from structural criticism, or did they move away from structural criticism and thus become less effective? Regardless, an unmistakable trajectory emerges, beginning in the 1930s. First, reformers challenged the commercial nature of the broadcasting system itself, with core questions of ownership and control. Then, in the early 1940s, reformers like the FCC chairman Fly pushed for antitrust measures to address media concentration. Next, under Durr's directions, reformers began focusing on programming evaluations and defining commercial media's social responsibilities. Finally, by the end of the 1940s, activists retreated further to focus on content-related matters within what became the Fairness Doctrine, which allowed commercial broadcasters free reign in political editorializing with the caveat that they must provide for balanced discussion of important issues.

Meanwhile, broadcasters steadily pushed forward to create a more perfect corporate libertarian model. While this retreat was not uniform – some groups and individuals held their ground, risking careers and ignoble defeat – the movement away from structural critique and intervention left progressive

---

[35] The article continued, "Virtually No Advocacy of Government Ownership and Operation Was to Be Heard in 1948." Robert Bower, "U.S. Radio Record of a Decade," *Public Opinion Quarterly* (Fall 1948): 441–2. Likewise, the FCC chairman Wayne Coy said in his address to broadcasters that he "knew of no responsible person in the government, including members and staff of the FCC who favors government operation of broadcasting." National Association of Broadcasters Convention, Los Angeles, May 18, 1948.

[36] Ernst, *First Freedom*, 159–60.

media reformers even more exposed to libertarian First Amendment arguments. Without a structural analysis, policy makers and reformers had to fight against the symptoms of a fundamentally flawed media system instead of the root causes – causes often related to commercial media's profit motives and the ensuing market failure to provide adequate communications for a democratic society.

Nonetheless, while political shifts doomed most experiments, reformers were successful in establishing some alternative models in the 1940s. A pro-labor FM network with five licensed stations was founded with access to all major U.S. metropolitan areas.[37] In 1946, the pacifist Lew Hill, inspired by the Blue Book and reformers like Charles Siepmann, initiated the ad-free, nonprofit, listener-supported community radio station Pacifica, which is still broadcasting today.[38] For newspapers, New York City's ad-free newspaper *PM* was a popular and influential exemplar, though it folded in 1948, largely because of poor business practices. Other important advances were the seeds that activists planted for future efforts, including the Fairness Doctrine, which later gave activists some leverage in pressuring commercial media to provide balanced discussion on important issues. Even discursive gains like establishing social responsibility norms arguably helped produce some admirable reporting during journalism's "golden age" in subsequent decades. In some cases, just the threat of regulation may have encouraged media institutions to self-reform.

On the other hand, these modest changes to the U.S. media system afforded business interests a patina of social responsibility, inoculating them from substantive regulation. Even where progressives made some gains, such as the Fairness Doctrine and the creation of educational and labor-oriented radio stations, kept intact were the problematic aspects of what was essentially still a laissez-faire system. After facing significant challenges in the 1940s, this template for self-regulation was solidified, and its general mold has remained in place ever since.

These outcomes raise the question, Were the 1940s media reformers doomed from the beginning? After all, from our current vantage point, it may seem they had little chance of succeeding. Probably the primary reason for the reform movement's demise was the dramatic rightward shift in national politics. Cold War imperatives and a resurgent business community led to a co-optation of more centrist groups, creating a strategic corporatist arrangement among business, labor and other civil society groups, and government. Aggressive reform efforts were largely abandoned amid a purge of progressives and radicals from

---

[37] Fones-Wolf, *Waves of Opposition*, 160–1.
[38] Lew Hill, Pacifica Foundation Radio Prospectus, November 1946. See also Matthew Lasar, *Pacifica Radio: The Rise of an Alternative Network* (Philadelphia: Temple University Press, 2000). I thank Lasar for providing me with Lew Hill's original document. Another alternative model that gained some attention, but apparently never launched, was "subscription radio." See Pickard, "Media Democracy Deferred," 182–87.

postwar social movements, which removed a generation of left-leaning activists from the political arena, from Hollywood entertainers to behind-the-scenes bureaucrats.

This gathering storm of reactionary politics was devastating to the cause of progressive media policy. The impact of the Red Scare and its related blacklists, and the ways media industries exploited them, cannot be overstated in understanding how progressive reform movements were demobilized and radical critics silenced. In this context, all regulatory proposals could be panned as communist plots, and broadcasters and publishers could declare any challenge to their power as un-American and anti-democratic. Indeed, a significant factor driving the anti-communist hysteria can be attributed to business interests reacting to structural threats posed by the New Deal's anti-monopoly/pro-regulation ethos.[39] These politics played a major role in shaping media industries in the 1940s and 1950s.

Though anti-Left repression had existed for years, one of the first systematic blacklists came into existence in 1947 with the firing of the aforementioned Hollywood Ten. Probably the second most notorious of the blacklists was "Red Channels," a pamphlet published by the right-wing journal *Counterattack* in 1950 that listed 151 purported "Red Fascists and their sympathizers" – including Clifford Durr. African Americans and their allies were hit especially hard. One historian noted that "the list was virtually a roll call of the most progressive people in the entertainment industries, especially those most active in the struggles for civil rights and racial equality."[40] Capturing the suddenness and viciousness with which the blacklists struck, the playwright Arthur Miller noted, "In 1946 I do not think we could have believed that such a black list was possible, that the current of one's life and career could simply be switched off and the wires left dead."[41]

Media Policy after the 1940s

With the spectacular defeat of progressive regulation, not only did the FCC become far less ambitious in its efforts to regulate broadcasting, but many media reform groups also backed off from pressuring the FCC and individual radio stations. As attention shifted to television, the hardest-hitting radio criticism dissipated. The Mayflower proceedings remained a high point in public participation until the 1960s. FCC progressivism persisted into the 1950s via Frieda Hennock and, to some extent, Wayne Coy. Hennock was a

[39] Ellen Schrecker, *Many Are the Crimes: McCarthyism in America* (Princeton, NJ: Princeton University Press, 1998); Landon Storrs, *The Second Red Scare and the Unmaking of the New Deal Left* (Princeton, NJ: Princeton University Press, 2013); David Caute, *The Great Fear: The Great Communist Purge under Truman and Eisenhower* (New York: Simon & Schuster, 1978). Brinson, *The Red Scare*, 63.
[40] Barlow, *Voice Over*, 77.
[41] Arthur Miller, *Timebends: A Life* (New York: Grove, 1987), 269.

206 of Americas Battle for Media Democracy

strong advocate for educational television and was instrumental in reserving a significant number of channels devoted to it in the FCC's 1952 "Sixth Report and Order," which ended the 1948 freeze on new television allocations.[42] But overall the new decade marked an increasing conservatism, with even the FCC instituting loyalty oaths for radio operators. Many saw the agency as increasingly captured by communication industries.[43] Although never again reaching the 1940s high-water mark, some progressivism would resume in the 1960s, first when Newton Minow became FCC chairman (famous for giving a speech at the NAB's convention in which he called American commercial television programming a "vast wasteland"), and especially later in the decade when Nicholas Johnson joined the commission to push a number of progressive initiatives, including media ownership restrictions.[44]

In more recent times, the former commissioner Michael Copps embodied this same progressive regulatory tradition at the FCC, seemingly channeling the spirit of Clifford Durr in his defense of public interest principles. Like Durr, Commissioner Copps was often the lone dissenter, exemplified by his vote against the 2011 Comcast-NBC merger. Copps's commitment to progressive media policy was perhaps best exemplified by his "Public Values Test," which, like the Blue Book, defined substantive public interest criteria that broadcasters must satisfy to renew their licenses (every four instead of the now eight years), including a commitment to public affairs, localism, and independent programming. While serving on the FCC together, Commissioner Copps was often joined by Commissioner Jonathan Adelstein to defend media ownership restrictions and Internet safeguards such as net neutrality, but they were still usually outnumbered 3-2.

The trajectory for commercial broadcast media has remained fairly consistent. Even if commercial radio eventually relented on some of its more egregious practices, radio ads did not disappear. While plug-uglies may no longer terrorize the airwaves, even the most casual listener today would note that crass commercialism remains undeterred. And while some anecdotal evidence suggests that broadcasters were chastened by postwar media reform efforts,[45] commercial radio emerged from the period largely inoculated against major structural interventions. To understand the origins of American media's weak public interest standards, knowledge of this 1940s media policy history is

[42] Christopher Sterling, Cary O'Dell, and Michael Keith, *The Biographical Encyclopedia of American Radio* (New York: Routledge, 2010), 169.

[43] Hence its characterization, according to a former FCC chairman, as the commission's "whorehouse era." Quoted in Baughman, *Television's Guardians*, 13.

[44] Stamm, *Sound Business*, 190–1. Also significant was the 1978 Minority Tax certificate program. Statement of Policy on Minority Ownership of Brdcst. Facils., Public Notice, 68 F.C.C.2d 979 (1978). Commissioner Johnson also authored the FCC's Carterfone decision, which allowed consumers to connect their own lawful devices to telephone networks.

[45] Matthew Ehrlich, *Radio Utopia: Postwar Audio Documentary in the Public Interest* (Urbana: University of Illinois Press, 2011).

essential. Indeed, many of the features commonly associated with 1980s media deregulation were already in full force by the late 1940s.

Among policy makers and pundits, it is often noted without much reflection that the public interest standard in American media policy has remained frustratingly ill defined. While it is true that previous attempts to define standards have been fraught with conflict and difficulty, the term "public interest" has not remained ambiguous by a lack of effort or because it is inherently undefinable. Rather, it has remained so because media industries, particularly commercial broadcasters, have fought aggressively to keep standards – and methods to enforce them – vague and ineffectual. Thwarting the Blue Book's muscular definition of public interest responsibilities is a clear case study of this phenomenon. Henceforth, commercial broadcasters and their allies could say that the "public interest" was largely meaningless. This strategy was exemplified by Michael Powell's infamous comment in a 1998 speech where he described waiting up all night after he became an FCC commissioner for the "angel of the public interest" to teach him the meaning of the phrase, but she never visited him.[46]

Exceptions to this broadcast media trajectory sometimes occurred, especially outside the FCC's purview, as in the 1967 Public Broadcasting Act and the Supreme Court's 1969 *Red Lion* case. In the latter decision, which upheld the Fairness Doctrine, the court unabashedly articulated strong support for a positive First Amendment, determining that it is "the right of the viewers and listeners, not the right of the broadcasters, which is paramount."[47] Another historic case occurred in 1966 when WLBT-TV's license was revoked – one of the few times this action has ever been taken – because of racist programming. This case was made possible after the DC Circuit Court forced the FCC to allow citizen groups to challenge a license renewal, thus granting such groups legal standing for the first time.[48] The FCC made other attempts at progressive content regulation during the 1960s and 1970s such as the 1960 Programming Policy Statement, which maintained that government could mandate public interest obligations, and the 1971 Primer on Ascertainment of Community Problems, which mandated broadcasters' commitment to localism. However, many of these public interest obligations, including the Fairness Doctrine, were rescinded during the 1980s under Reagan's FCC.

---

[46] Michael Powell, "The Public Interest Standard: A New Regulator's Search for Enlightenment," before the American Bar Association 17th Annual Legal Forum on Communications Law, Las Vegas, Nevada, April 5, 1998. http://www.fcc.gov/Speeches/Powell/spmkp806.html.

[47] *Red Lion Broadcasting Co., Inc. v. Federal Communications Commission* No. 2 Supreme Court of the United States, 395 U.S. 367, June 9, 1969.

[48] See Erwin Krasnow, *The Politics of Broadcast Regulation*, 3rd ed. (New York: St. Martin's Press, 1982), 55–7; Kay Mills, *Changing Channels: The Civil Rights Case That Transformed Television* (Jackson: University Press of Mississippi, 2004); and Robert Horwitz, "Broadcast Reform Revisited: The Rev. Everett Parker and the Standing Case," *Communication Review* 2, no. 3 (1997): 311–48.

For newspapers, there were occasional glimmers of more positive press freedoms, including arguments for a "right-of-reply" proposed during the 1974
Miami Herald Publishing Co. v. Tornillo case. However, the Supreme Court
decided that a right of media access was contravened by the First Amendment.[49]
Another intervention, the 1970 Newspaper Preservation Act, sought to shore
up the last remaining two-newspaper towns by allowing them to conduct joint
operations at some levels of production.[50] These partial exceptions notwithstanding, many of the trends toward negative freedoms decried in the 1940s
would continue. Critical policy debates would periodically emerge – for example, the 1968 Kerner Commission's report, which indicted the press's deplorable
lack of African American journalists and poor coverage of African American
issues[51] – but discussions about print media's responsibilities vis-à-vis affirmative
public interest regulation were increasingly pushed to the discursive fringes.

The historical record suggests a specific corporate libertarian ideology
ascending from 1940s media policy battles. The logic that emerged led to
a broad accommodation of commercialism, advertising, and concentrated
media ownership, and it would continue to garner intellectual heft throughout the second half of the twentieth century.[52] These trends were evidenced
by an increasingly deregulatory push in media policy – in actuality, a kind of
"reregulation" defined by de facto market governance – that led to repealing
many affirmative policy initiatives. This trend was further exemplified by the
1996 Telecommunications Act,[53] which deregulated telecommunication sectors and jettisoned media ownership caps that had prevented any broadcaster
from owning more than 40 stations nationwide, a policy change that would
allow one corporation, Clear Channel, to own more than twelve hundred stations. This paradigm treats communication issues as primarily technical, bases
media policies on economic efficiency, and strips policy discussions of normative concerns. The former FCC commissioner Robert McDowell, writing in a
Washington Post op-ed, epitomized this position when, in reference to crucial
Internet policies such as net neutrality, he asserted that "engineers, not politicians or bureaucrats, should solve engineering problems."[54]

[49] *Miami Herald Publishing Co. v. Tornillo* (1974). Jerome Barron, who championed the scholarly
argument for a First Amendment–guaranteed access to the press, represented Tornillo in court.
[50] This act has been criticized for doing more to bolster newspaper publishers' profits than encourage local media diversity.
[51] *The Report of the National Advisory Commission on Civil Disorders* (New York: Bantam
Books, 1968), pp. 1–29.
[52] A broader, more encompassing intellectual shift was happening in the postwar years, what the
historian George Nash refers to as the "The Revolt of the Libertarians," which elevated the economic theories of Friedrich A. Hayek into mainstream policy discourse. See George Nash, *The
Conservative Intellectual Movement in America since 1945* (New York: Basic Books, 1976).
[53] To be fair, the entire act cannot be described as deregulatory; it also contained pro-competition
stipulations.
[54] Robert McDowell, "Who Should Solve This Internet Crisis?" *Washington Post*, July 28, 2008.

This focus on technical efficiency and evasion of normative concerns are long-standing traits of corporate libertarian policy discourse. Observing how the United States is unique in treating policy and politics as separate discursive fields, Thomas Streeter noted that this distinction does not exist in other languages, such as German or French, which use a single word (*politik* and *politique*, respectively).[55] This strategic decoupling of the process (politics) and the outcome (policy) is symptomatic of a broader depoliticization of American policy discourse that largely ignores power inequities, both in terms of policy effects and with regard to the political interests that disproportionately lobby for specific policies. Furthermore, this technocratic approach tends to overlook the political economy and history of power relationships underlying specific policy arrangements. Ronald Coase's highly influential 1959 article "The Federal Communications Commission," which argued for privatizing the public airwaves, is a classic example of this technocratic emphasis that privileges concerns related to efficiency rather than concerns about egalitarianism. Launching an intellectual movement in support of spectrum privatization, Coase lamented that earlier laws such as the 1927 Radio Act codified the public interest doctrine and established that the spectrum was public property, albeit under federal oversight of select users with exclusive licenses. According to the "Coase theorem," spectrum management based on public interest grounds was fundamentally flawed. Instead, Coase believed, a clear assignment of exclusive and permanent property rights of the airwaves would allow the free market to allocate resources to their most efficient use. Seeing no difference between an essential communication medium and other commodities, Coase argued, "Since it is generally agreed that the use of private property and the pricing system is in the public interest in other fields, why should it not also be in broadcasting?"[56]

With the increasingly common use of auctions to sell spectrum rights to the highest bidder, the Coase-prescribed private property model has moved from the margins to become increasingly dominant, leaving the "public trustee model" further weakened. However, while some scholars have disagreed with Coase's economic theorizing, others suggest that it is deeply apolitical and ahistorical. Contrary to Coase's narrative that the 1927 Radio Act's focus was primarily technical and economic, more recent revisionist history suggests that officials were less concerned about devising an economically efficient means of allocating scarce spectrum than about preventing the concentration

[55] Streeter, *Selling the Air*, 125.
[56] Ronald Coase, "The Federal Communications Commission," *Journal of Law and Economics* 2 (1959): 1–40. Tellingly, Coase's article devotes much space to contesting Smythe and Siepmann's decade-old ideas. For a broader discussion of Coase and competing models of spectrum management, see Victor Pickard and Sascha Meinrath, "Revitalizing the Public Airwaves: Opportunistic Unlicensed Reuse of Government Spectrum," *International Journal of Communication*, 3, (2009): 1052–84.

of political power and cultivating a diversity of voices on the airwaves.[57] Nonetheless, stripping such normative concerns from media policy debates has become increasingly common and has further reduced meaningful public interest regulation over the past several decades. Cable television, which at first was seen as a potential alternative, has remained even less regulated than broadcast media.[58] And although the Internet arose as a highly regulated telecommunications service, it also was largely deregulated in the 1990s and early 2000s.[59]

A case study of this corporate libertarian policy shift is exemplified by the Fairness Doctrine. Despite its being championed by activists on both the Right and Left and enjoying significant congressional support, the FCC repealed the Fairness Doctrine in 1987. Earlier that same year, a congressional bill that would legislate the Fairness Doctrine passed by a large margin with significant conservative backing – including from luminaries like the then-representative Newt Gingrich – but President Ronald Reagan vetoed it.[60] An attempt at passing a similar bill in 1991 withered in response to President George H. W. Bush's veto threat.[61] In recent years, multiple bills have been proposed in Congress to ban the FCC permanently from ever reinstituting it. After years of right-wing activism, even most liberal Democrats ran away from supporting it, and in 2011 the Democratic-led FCC officially killed it by removing it from the books.[62] These increasingly libertarian positions continue to drive discourse; in recent years right-wing activists have successfully used the specter of a long-since-abandoned Fairness Doctrine to taint nonrelated policies such as net neutrality, accusing the FCC of infringing on basic freedoms and censoring conservatives.[63] Even innocuous FCC reports are branded with the Fairness Doctrine stigma if they remotely sug-

[57] David Moss and Michael Fein, "Radio Regulation Revisited: Coase, the FCC and the Public Interest," *Journal of Policy History* 15, no. 4 (2003): 389–416.

[58] This is partly because cable television does not rely on the public airwaves. For a policy history of cable's early development, including media reform efforts, see Don LeDuc, *Cable Television and the FCC* (Philadelphia: Temple University Press, 1973).

[59] For a fine policy history that sheds light on many of the trends discussed earlier, see Mark Lloyd, *Prologue to a Farce: Communication and Democracy in America* (Urbana: University of Illinois Press, 2007).

[60] It is important to note that the deregulatory project that took hold under the Reagan-appointed FCC chairman Mark Fowler actually began earlier under President Carter and the FCC chair Charles Ferris.

[61] See Victor Pickard, "A Final Farewell to the Fairness Doctrine?" *History News Network*, October 24, 2011. http://hnn.us/article/142541.

[62] Brooks Boliek, "FCC Finally Kills Off Fairness Doctrine," *Politico*, August 22, 2011. http://www.politico.com/news/stories/0811/61851.html.

[63] Matthew Lasar, "Fairness Doctrine: Better Off Dead or Alien Resurrection?" *Ars Technica*, February 17, 2009. http://arstechnica.com/tech-policy/2009/02/eeek-fairness-doctrine/. Allison Perlman provides an excellent historical overview in "Whitewashing Diversity: The Conservative Attack on the 'Stealth Fairness Doctrine,'" *Television New Media* 13, no. 4 (2012): 353–73.

gest the possibility of affirmative media policy or question the infallibility of media markets.[64]

Toward a New Policy Paradigm

The postwar settlement marked the triumph of the corporate libertarian paradigm. But the 1940s also saw the glimmerings of an alternative media system struggling to be born. The policy debates surrounding Larry Fly's anti-monopoly activism, the Hutchins Commission, the Blue Book, and the Fairness Doctrine constituted key discursive moments within a larger reformation of normative assumptions about media. Although a social democratic vision was repressed, its failures can be instructive. Quoting Stuart Hall, Michael Denning reminds us that such losses can still lead to progress: "Social forces which lose out in any particular historical period do not thereby disappear from the terrain of struggle."[65] Media reformers continued their struggle up to and including the present day. Moreover, that our current commercial media system is contingent on past repression calls into question its very legitimacy. And the recognition that this system could have been designed differently is a first step toward undoing the American media's postwar settlement.

Normative assumptions about media are always present; it is incumbent upon scholars to flesh out and expose them to the light of public scrutiny. Rendering these often-implicit principles explicit unmasks core tensions in the U.S. media system – tensions such as media owners' freedom from government intrusion, on one hand, and a public right of access to diverse viewpoints, on the other. Although it clashes with today's corporate libertarianism, the necessity of aggressive state intervention on behalf of liberal ideals was understood then and, though largely forgotten for decades, may be called for again. Given the ongoing failures of journalism, the decline of local broadcast media, and crises across various digital media – including mass surveillance, pervasive advertising, and the rise of new media monopolies and oligopolies – perhaps the time has come for a system-wide correction. However, to actualize democratic ideals based on positive rights of access to media will likely require radical structural reform. The next and final section of the book situates many of these recurring political economic crises in historical and contemporary contexts and proposes a new social contract that rescues media from endemic market failures. For in many ways it was systemic market failure in commercial media that reformers contended with in the 1940s. And it is similar market failure that faces us today.

---

[64] Katy Bachman, "Is the FCC's Latest Study an Attempt to Bring Back the Fairness Doctrine?" *Adweek*, December 10, 2013. http://www.adweek.com/news/press/fccs-latest-study-attempt-bring-back-fairness-doctrine-154422.
[65] Quoted in Denning, *The Cultural Front*, 464.

Conclusion

Confronting Market Failure

In the early decades of the twenty-first century, old problems afflict new media. Once again, America anguishes over the diminished democratic promise of its communication technologies.[1] Like broadcasting in the 1940s, digital media have become dominated by oligopolies driven by a corporate libertarian logic at odds with public interest principles.[2] Recent scholarship has linked these ownership structures to various shortcomings with American broadband, including disparities among communities and socioeconomic groups in terms of speeds and access, costs for service, and impediments to free-flowing information and content.[3] Just as radio's full democratic potential was thwarted by commercial capture in the 1930s and 1940s, a similar fate faces the Internet today. This crisis in digital media coincides with the gradual collapse of journalism's last major institutional bastion: newspapers. Commercial journalism's contradictions were left unresolved in the 1940s, only to erupt in crisis once again in our present times. Now, as then, the newspaper industry faces a structural crisis and intense public scrutiny. However, unlike the 1940s crisis, the one today is likely a mortal blow to the

---

[1] I discuss some of these themes in Victor Pickard, "The Great Evasion: Confronting Market Failure in American Media Policy," *Critical Studies in Media Communication*, 2014, DOI: 10.1080/15295036.2014.919404.

[2] For a similar historical pattern, see Tim Wu, *The Master Switch: The Rise and Fall of Information Empires* (New York: Alfred A. Knopf, 2010). Wu describes a "cycle" in which every major American information industry, beginning with the telephone, has ultimately been taken over by cartels and monopolies.

[3] Sascha Meinrath, James Losey, and Victor Pickard, "Digital Feudalism: Enclosures and Erasures from Digital Rights Management to the Digital Divide," *CommLaw Conspectus: Journal of Communications Law and Policy* 19 (2010): 423–79; Robert McChesney, *Digital Disconnect: How Capitalism Is Turning the Internet against Democracy* (New York: New Press, 2013); Susan Crawford, *Captive Audience: The Telecom Industry and Monopoly Power in the New Gilded Age* (New Haven, CT: Yale University Press, 2013).

industry, and rebranding self-regulatory measures as "social responsibility" will not save it this time.

The 1940s media policy debates are instructive for policy makers as they confront these crises. These earlier debates, to varying degrees, all focused on buffering media's public service mission from undue market pressures. And nearly all of them were resolved in ways that aligned with a corporate libertarian logic that benefited commercial broadcasters and publishers. The 1940s saw a discursive narrowing of possibilities for meaningful public interest requirements and noncommercial alternatives. Similar parameters are at work in today's policy discourse.

This discursive narrowing presents policy problems in two broad, overlapping areas: digital media and journalism. Before I examine potential policy interventions for supporting public service media, I briefly discuss three conceptual areas that were implicit in earlier policy debates but rarely addressed directly: public goods, market failure, and policy failure. Understanding these political economic relationships is the first step toward renegotiating the corporate libertarian paradigm. Integrating these concepts into our political discourses, practices, and institutions might encourage the implementation of sound public policy for the media system our democracy requires.

Public Goods

A growing number of scholars have argued in recent years that the information produced by news media should be treated as a public good.[4] Because public goods are nonrivalrous (one person's consumption does not detract from another's) and nonexcludable (they are difficult to exclude from free riders), they do not operate as other commodities do, such as shoes or cars, within a capitalistic economy.[5] They are, in the words of one economist, "both unique and fascinating because it is virtually impossible to allocate a pure public good through market mechanisms."[6] Journalism is not only a public good in an economic sense (especially in its digital form); it also serves "the public good" in a socially beneficial sense. Put differently, journalism produces *positive*

[4] James Hamilton, *All the News That's Fit to Sell* (Princeton, NJ: Princeton University Press, 2006), 8–9; Victor Pickard, Josh Stearns, and Craig Aaron, "Saving the News: Toward a National Journalism Strategy," in *Changing Media: Public Interest Policies for the Digital Age* (Washington, DC: Free Press, 2009), 1–9; Robert McChesney and John Nichols, *The Death and Life of American Journalism: The Media Revolution That Will Begin the World Again* (New York: Nation Books, 2010), 101–3; Paul Starr, "Goodbye to the Age of Newspapers (Hello to a New Era of Corruption)," in *Will the Last Reporter Please Turn Out the Lights? The Collapse of Journalism and What Can Be Done to Fix It*, ed. Robert McChesney and Victor Pickard (New York: New Press, 2011), 31. See also Baker, *Media, Markets and Democracy*, 8.
[5] Paul Samuelson, "The Pure Theory of Public Expenditure," *Review of Economics and Statistics* 36 (1954): 387–9.
[6] Paul Trogen, "Public Goods," in *Handbook of Public Sector Economics*, ed. Donijo Robbins (New York: Taylor & Francis, 2005), 169–207.

externalities (benefits that accrue to parties outside of the direct economic transaction) – such as increased knowledge and an informed populace – that are vital for a democratic society. Goods that produce such tremendous positive externalities are sometimes referred to as "merit goods," which society requires, but that individuals typically undervalue (are unable or unwilling to pay for), and thus the market under-produces.[7] As an essential public service with social benefits that transcend its revenue stream, journalism is such a good. In its ideal form, it serves as a rich information source for important social issues, an adversarial watchdog over the powerful, and a forum for diverse voices and viewpoints.

Like many public goods exhibiting positive externalities, journalism has never been fully supported by direct market transactions; it always has been subsidized to some degree. Since the late nineteenth century, this subsidy has primarily drawn from advertising revenues.[8] Today, this business model is increasingly unsustainable, as audiences and advertisers migrate to the Internet, where ads sell for a mere fraction of their paper-based counterparts. Despite their growth, digital ad revenues have not offset the enormous losses from traditional advertising. A 2012 Pew study found that declines in print ad revenues, which had fallen more than 50 percent since 2003, exceeded the gain in online digital revenue by a ratio of greater than 10 to 1.[9] The 2013 report found some stabilization, but the growth in digital advertising "does not come close to covering print ad losses."[10] These and other data suggest that as a support system for journalism, ad revenue–dependent models appear to be increasingly unviable, and no other commercial models, including digital paywalls (online subscription models), are filling the vacuum.[11] The inadequacy of commercial support indicates what should be obvious by now: The market's

[7] I thank Chris Ali for bringing the concept of merit goods to my attention. For an excellent discussion of their implications, see Chris Ali, "Where Is Here? An Analysis of Localism in Media Policy in Three Western Democracies" (Ph.D. Dissertation, University of Pennsylvania, 2013). Des Freedman similarly argues that media products, like preventive health care services, are merit goods since individual consumers are likely to underinvest in them. See *The Politics of Media Policy* (Cambridge: Polity Press, 2008), 8–10. See also Richard Musgrave, *The Theory of Public Finance: A Study in Public Economy* (New York: McGraw-Hill, 1959), 13–15.

[8] This characterization of advertising as subsidy might be disputable, but I am using it to drive home the point that advertisers were not paying for news media directly; they instead were paying to have access to eyes and ears. News was produced as a kind of by-product, a positive externality from the main exchange.

[9] Rick Edmonds, Emily Guskin, Tom Rosenstiel, and Amy Mitchell, "Newspapers: By the Numbers," *The Pew Research Center's Project for Excellence in Journalism: The State of the News Media 2012*, accessed February 2, 2013, http://stateofthemedia.org.

[10] Rick Edmonds, Emily Guskin, Amy Mitchell, and Mark Jurkowitz, *The State of the News Media 2013*, http://stateofthemedia.org/2013/newspapers-stabilizing-but-still-threatened/ The 2014 Pew Report found that while other sources of revenue are growing such as capital investment and philanthropy, they account for a meager 1% of the current financial support for news.

[11] Victor Pickard and Alex Williams, "Salvation or Folly? The Promises and Perils of Digital Paywalls" *Digital Journalism*, 2 (2) 2014, 195–213.

systematic under-production of journalistic media qualifies as a clear case of market failure.[12]

Market Failure

Deriving from neoclassical economics, "market failure" is an analytical framework that typically refers to a scenario in which the market is unable to efficiently produce and allocate resources, especially public goods.[13] This often occurs when private enterprise withholds investments in critical social services because it cannot extract the returns that would justify the necessary expenditures, or when consumers fail to pay for such services' full societal benefit. This scenario legitimates state intervention in the provision of public education, a standing military, a national highway system, and other essential services and infrastructures not supported by market transactions. The leading consumer advocate and researcher Mark Cooper has made a convincing argument that various kinds of "pervasive market failure" specifically affect the media industry. In addition to the lack of support for externalities and public goods, other market failures that frequently occur in the American media system are associated with structural flaws like oligopolistic concentration and profit maximization. Uncompetitive markets may lead to perverse incentives and the abuse of market power, which can result in a media system's degradation, including a failure to provide adequate interconnection between communication networks, communication services to all of society, and quality journalism.[14]

In the 1940s, market failure was evidenced by the rise of one-newspaper towns and a loss of local journalism. Signs of market failure in today's American media system are increasingly visible in the ongoing disinvestment in news production, exemplified by the reduction of home deliveries of leading

[12] I generally define journalistic media as based on news gathering that generates new information about socially significant issues.

[13] See, for example, Francis Bator, "The Anatomy of Market Failure," *Quarterly Journal of Economics* 72, no. 3 (1958): 351–79; Joseph Stiglitz, "Markets, Market Failures, and Development," *American Economic Review* 79, no. 2 (1989): 197–203; Steven Medema, "The Hesitant Hand: Mill, Sidgwick, and the Evolution of the Theory of Market Failure," *History of Political Economy* 39, no. 3 (2007): 331–58; John Taylor, *Economics*, 5th ed. (New York: Houghton Mifflin, 2007), 15. See also Allan Brown, "Economics, Public Service Broadcasting, and Social Values," *Journal of Media Economics* 9, no. 1 (1996): 3–15.

[14] Mark Cooper, "The Future of Journalism: Addressing Pervasive Market Failure with Public Policy," in *Will the Last Reporter Please Turn Out the Lights? The Collapse of Journalism and What Can Be Done to Fix It*, ed. Robert McChesney and Victor Pickard (New York: New Press, 2011) 320–39. See also Mark Cooper and Barbara Roper, "Reform of Financial Markets: The Collapse of Market Fundamentalism and the First Steps to Revitalize the Economy" (Washington, DC: Consumer Federation of America, March 2009). To be fair, different market structures may experience some of these failures, but behavior like profit maximization is particularly problematic in noncompetitive markets because it often results in too little production and consumption from society's perspective because the price is set above marginal cost.

metro dailies like the *Cleveland Plain Dealer* and the *New Orleans Times-Picayune* – the latter in a city where approximately a third of its residents lack Internet connectivity.[15] Whether discussing the lack of support for local journalism or deficiencies in providing universal access to affordable and reliable Internet service, a focus on market failure deserves more prominence in American media policy discourse. Indeed, that media policy even requires a "public interest" category is arguably an implicit acknowledgment of endemic market failure in commercial media. Yet an explicit discussion of this subject, especially its role in the journalism crisis, has been noticeably absent among policy makers, a condition that leads us to policy failure.

Confronting Policy Failure

The concept of policy failure is undertheorized in the scholarly literature;[16] here it refers to existing policy mechanisms' insufficiency in dealing with significant social problems including market failure. Beyond policy makers' lack of political will or incentive to act, a number of complications inherent to media policy debates combine to encourage such failure by masking the policy roots of media-related problems.

First, there is the invisibility of media policy. Because so many policy-making processes remain hidden, citizens' relationship to government and the connections between policy and politics in general are obscured. The political scientist Suzanne Mettler highlights aspects of this phenomenon with her very useful formulation of what she calls a "submerged state," in which the state is involved in people's daily lives in profound ways that are rarely recognized.[17] Whereas Mettler is drawing attention specifically to policies impacting households' economic security such as retirement benefits,[18] the influence of the invisible state extends to countless rules and infrastructures including subsidized mortgages, road maintenance, and safety standards. Further, when state intervention is acknowledged, it is often stigmatized for providing "handouts" to disadvantaged (and presumably undeserving) groups. Even expenditures benefiting the general public (public education, public media, public arts) are held suspect, while the more prevalent policy interventions that aid corporations (tax breaks, relaxation of antitrust laws, intellectual property protections) often remain invisible and unscrutinized, or even applauded. Misunderstandings about these largely hidden policy relationships lead to a distorted view of government's regulatory role in society.

[15] The *Picayune* has since resumed daily delivery, but at a much diminished capacity.
[16] Not to be confused with the concept of "government failure," which refers to those goods and services that governments are typically unable to provide.
[17] Suzanne Mettler, *The Submerged State: How Invisible Government Policies Undermine American Democracy* (Chicago: University of Chicago Press, 2011).
[18] Mettler notes that her framework of an invisible state can be applied more broadly. See *The Submerged State*, 15.

In particular, there is much confusion around how government regulates media, which is often elided by celebrations of new technologies and other forms of technological determinism. A widespread assumption is that if society simply allows inventors and entrepreneurs to develop new technologies, the communication system is self-correcting. This ignores market constraints and the state's ever-present role. The Internet's genesis is a classic case. Its early development was largely dependent on state subsidies via military and research institutions, but many see the Internet as a wild, unregulated terrain that emerged naturally from new technologies, market forces, and individual genius. To the contrary, government is inextricably involved at all times, from enforcing copyright laws (often seen by corporations as "good regulation") to applying antitrust laws (or lack thereof). The general confusion about government's regulatory role in everyday communication, combined with policy makers' lack of motivation to raise awareness, discourages public involvement in critical policy debates.

This leads us to the problem of policy inaction – what the political scientists Jacob Hacker and Paul Pierson referred to as "drift."[19] Drift emphasizes policy failure's effect on society over time – how problems often worsen when regulatory agencies do nothing. For example, in the 1940s, as negative externalities such as excessive commercialism in the American media system increased, government could have intervened by applying structural measures like antitrust legislation to break up conglomerates or, with broadcast media, mandated stringent public interest obligations in return for using the public spectrum. But such systemic interventions rarely occur, as a result of both institutional inertia and calculated neglect. Moreover, given what might be called a "submerged state syndrome," the public is unlikely to call for affirmative regulatory intervention. This perceived absence of the state has concrete policy outcomes by limiting the range of possible trajectories in the public imagination. Consequently, vacuums emerge within policy discourses that allow imbalances to continue unabated, particularly given the assumption that a media system has developed according to the natural laws of the market and technological progress. Corporate libertarianism thrives in this discursive environment.

A third major factor that distorts policy discourse and practice is what I referred to earlier as "regulatory capture." This process is often subtle, involving not only media corporations' significant donations to politicians and their campaigns but also the sheer boots-on-the-ground power of having legions of lobbyists crowding the halls of Congress and key regulatory agencies. A media reform advocacy group calculated that in 2009, amid net neutrality and other key telecom policy debates, six leading telecom and cable companies and their lobbying firms employed more than 550 lobbyists – working out to more than

[19] Jacob Hacker and Paul Pierson, *Winner Take All Politics* (New York: Simon and Schuster, 2010).

one lobbyist per member of Congress – and spent more than $70 million on telecom lobbying in Washington, DC, alone.[20]

Perhaps even more significant than direct payoffs to politicians is the much-lamented revolving door phenomenon. Already operative in the 1940s, this shuffling of personnel between the Federal Communications Commission and the communication industries it is meant to regulate remains a common practice. One recent analysis found that of the 26 commissioners and chairs who have served on the FCC since 1980, at least 20 have gone to work for corporations in the industries they previously regulated.[21] Some cases have been quite blatant, as when the former commissioner Meredith Atwell Baker left the FCC to become a Comcast-NBC lobbyist not long after voting to approve those companies' mega-merger. She is now president of the leading trade group for the wireless telecommunications industry, CTIA-The Wireless Association. Similarly, the former FCC chairman Michael Powell now heads the cable industry's top trade association, National Cable and Telecommunications Association (NCTA). The current FCC chairman, Tom Wheeler, formerly headed both NCTA and CTIA, and was a top-level political donor for President Obama. This regulatory capture contributes to a "discursive capture," yielding master narratives that systematically write off alternative policy options such as subsidizing public media and breaking up oligopolies. Much of this ideological framework began to congeal in the 1940s and remains operative today, which leads to a fourth major constraint on media policy discourse.

America's corporate libertarian ideology fails to recognize public goods and downplays the existence of market failure. This, in turn, encourages seemingly commonsensical notions about self-regulation, which, upon reaching the level of ideology, are difficult to dislodge. C. Edwin Baker observed two arguments that have long been used to discredit state intervention in cultivating a vibrant media system: that the government has no legitimate role in markets and that the First Amendment specifically forbids government intervention in media markets.[22] The ideological work that turned these arguments into truisms was still not complete in the 1940s – and such arguments continue to require constant maintenance and repair – but thinking outside their confines today is exceedingly difficult. Des Freedman dubbed these phenomena "media policy silences," which he defined as the "ideological processes of exclusion and marginalization that distort media policy making and undermine the

[20] See "Telecom Lobbying," *Free Press*, http://www.freepress.net/lobbying. Telecom lobbyists arguably have even more influence at the state level where they pressure legislatures to place constraints on municipal broadband services. See Jon Brodkin, "ISP lobby has already won limits on public broadband in 20 states," *Ars Technica*, February 12, 2014.
[21] Personal correspondence with Timothy Karr of Free Press, May 2, 2013.
[22] See generally, Baker, *Media, Markets and Democracy*; *Media Concentration and Democracy*.

emergence of alternative paradigms and policy outcomes."[23] Taken together, these discursive impediments obscure the policy roots of social problems, mask market inefficiencies in providing for society's communication needs, and narrow the possibilities for alternative policy trajectories – all leading to policy inaction and, ultimately, policy failure.

Return of the Nervous Liberals

These corporate libertarian assumptions, first crystallized in the 1940s, continue to permeate American policy discourse, thereby diverting attention from a structural analysis of the media system's problems.[24] This is true even of relatively liberal initiatives like the FCC's 2011 report, "The Information Needs of Communities," which offered a highly critical assessment of American news media's failures but – perhaps fearful of its own logical conclusions – repeated the Hutchins Commission's errors by prescribing only a minor role for public policy in addressing the journalism crisis.[25] A few days after the long-awaited report was issued, its author defended the study's laissez-faire approach to a group of public advocates, arguing that more aggressive policy intervention was inappropriate for two reasons: first, because the government should not be choosing winners, and, second, because the First Amendment forbade it.[26]

This defense sounds remarkably familiar to C. Edwin Baker's description of commercial media firms' standard anti-regulation arguments, and it shows to what extent a corporate libertarian logic is internalized even within the thinking of liberal policy makers. These familiar arguments are also demonstrably false. The government is *always* involved in markets, though often on behalf of corporate interests – a glaring contradiction in corporate libertarianism. Indeed, the American commercial media system could not operate without the state. Particular kinds of state intervention – copyright, relaxation of media ownership restrictions, and generally any measure that privatizes what had been previously in the public domain (such as the public airwaves) – are embraced, whereas any measure that aims to curb profit-seeking behavior is

[23] Des Freedman, "Media Policy Silences: The Hidden Face of Communications Decision Making," *International Journal of Press/Politics* 15, no. 3 (2010): 344–61.

[24] Brett Gary used the phrase "nervous liberals," first coined by Archibald MacLeish, to describe postwar liberals whose selective adherence to First Amendment freedoms allowed them to effortlessly switch from targeting fascists to blacklisting leftists during the ensuing Cold War hysteria. See Gary 's *The Nervous Liberals: Propaganda Anxieties from World War I to the Cold War* (New York: Columbia University Press, 1999). I have adapted the term to describe liberals made nervous by their own conclusions when they stray into a structural critique of commercial media.

[25] Steve Waldman, *The Information Needs of Communities: The Changing Media Landscape in a Broadband Age* (Washington, DC: Federal Communications Commission, 2011), www.fcc.gov/infoneedsreport.

[26] Steve Waldman, *Future of Media Report Public Interest Briefing with Steve Waldman*, New America Foundation, Washington, DC, June 14, 2011.

scorned as regulatory and therefore anti-free market. Furthermore, a proscription on government intervention in media stands on a highly dubious reading of First Amendment freedoms. Given important legal precedents like the Supreme Court's AP decision, government intervention can be justified to ensure a structurally sound and protected press system.

Indeed, a long-standing – if little recognized – tradition exists in which the American government affirmatively mandated that media systems serve public needs. We see this vision briefly take hold in the 1940s and make subsequent appearances in the 1960s, but it traces back to the American republic's earliest days. Richard John's magisterial history of the U.S. Postal Service – a communication network that initially served primarily as a newspaper-delivery infrastructure – demonstrates this precedent.[27] In the first major American media policy debate, the federal government determined that it should privilege the postal system's educational purpose over fiscal considerations, and thus heavily subsidize it. Given the postal system's vital function, the notion that it should be entirely self-supporting was seen as absurd. In recent decades, however, most elite policy discourse has been hermetically sealed off from such ideas, and what was once nonsensical – that media the market no longer supports should be left to wither – is now commonsensical. The first step toward undoing the corporate libertarian paradigm is to realize that government has a legitimate duty to step in where the market has failed. This will require reaffirming what was once better understood: Affirmative media policy based on positive liberties is entirely consistent with American history and democratic ideals. Once the political opportunity arises, reformers will have a rich alternative tradition of positive press freedoms to draw upon, thereby realigning the First Amendment with a more progressive policy orientation.

Policy Reforms for Digital Media

The future of media is a digital one, yet as a society we are still grappling with the implications of this transformation. It would be comforting if concerns about media ownership and public interest obligations no longer mattered in the age of the Internet. For many, caring about the future of news media might seem quaint and anachronistic given the ubiquity of digital communications. But despite dramatic technological changes, similar policy quandaries remain, especially as we witness a new wave of digital media monopolies, oligopolies, and cartels.[28] The commercial Internet faces a norm-defining moment not unlike that of commercial radio in the 1940s. Such moments require normative

---

[27] Richard John, *Spreading the News: The American Postal System from Franklin to Morse* (Cambridge, MA: Harvard University Press, 1995).

[28] For a provocative argument on how we as a society should respond to these Internet cartels and monopolies, see Robert McChesney, "Be Realistic, Demand the Impossible: Three Radically Democratic Internet Policies," *Critical Studies in Media Communication*, 2014, DOI: 10.1080/15295036.2014.913806.

questions: What is the Internet's role in a democratic society? How can the public interest be protected in this digital media system? What is government's role in regulating that relationship? Thus far we have failed to address these questions adequately.

Actualizing this new digital media system's democratic potential requires a paradigm shift. It requires moving away from corporate libertarianism toward a framework that recognizes the public-good qualities of media and embraces government's affirmative role in providing for society's communication needs – especially as systemic media market failure becomes increasingly evident. Nearly a third of all U.S. households still lack broadband Internet, at least partly owing to prohibitive cost.[29] Even for those with access, services are subpar and costly in a global comparison. Among leading democracies, American broadband is the seventh most expensive, and nineteenth in terms of speed. In terms of Internet penetration, the United States ranks fifteenth internationally, having dropped sharply over the past decade.[30] In terms of cost, the U.S. ranked 30th out of 33 countries, with an average price of $90/month for higher speeds of 45 Mbps and over.[31] The average American broadband customer currently pays more than $40/month for 27 Mbps, while an average South Korean pays a fraction of that price for 70 Mbps.[32] A more recent report exposes the degree to which American cities lag in broadband speeds and prices behind other cities around the world. For example, the same broadband speed that fetches $21.75 in Riga, Latvia, costs $112.50 in Washington, DC.[33]

Given that duopolies presently dominate both the wired (Comcast, Time Warner)[34] and wireless (Verizon, AT&T) U.S. markets, it is reasonable to assume that a lack of competition plays an important role in this predicament.[35]

---

[29] Pew Research Center, *Home Broadband 2013* http://pewinternet.org/Reports/2013/Broadband.aspx (accessed October 11, 2013).

[30] Organization for Economic Co-operation and Development, *Fixed and Wireless Broadband Subscriptions per 100 Inhabitants*, Annual Report, 2012 ed., http://www.oecd.org/sti/broadband/1d-OECD-WiredWirelessBB-2012-12_v2.xls (accessed October 11, 2013).

[31] Tom Geoghegan, Why Is Broadband More Expensive in the US? *BBC News Magazine*. October 27, 2013, http://www.bbc.co.uk/news/magazine-24528383.

[32] Organization for Economic Co-operation and Development, *Average Advertised Download Speeds, by Country*, Annual Report, 2011 ed., http://www.oecd.org/sti/broadband/BB-Portal_5a_13July_Final.xls (accessed October 11, 2013).

[33] Hibah Hussain, Danielle Kehl, Patrick Lucey, and Nick Russo, "The Cost of Connectivity 2013 Data Release: A Comparison of High-Speed Internet Prices in 24 Cities around the World" New America Foundation, October 2013. http://oti.newamerica.net/publications/policy/the_cost_of_connectivity_2013. See also Edward Wyatt, "U.S. Struggles to Keep Pace in Delivering Broadband Service," *New York Times*, December 29, 2013.

[34] If the proposed merger between Comcast and Time Warner goes through, this predicament may worsen.

[35] For an international comparison of mobile internet services, see Hibah Hussain and Danielle Kehl, "Americans Pay Six Times More for Mobile Internet Data than the French," *Slate*, http://www.slate.com/blogs/future_tense/2013/10/11/itu_report_shows_americans_pay_high_price_for_mobile_internet_data.html (accessed October 11, 2013).

According to the FCC, 96 percent of American housing units have two or fewer choices for wireline Internet access.[36] In a 2010 report, Yochai Benkler determined that American broadband's relative decline stems from policy differences with other democracies,[37] suggesting that this American exceptionalism is primarily political, with telecom corporations exerting disproportionate control over the policy process.

Because Internet service providers (ISPs) have little incentive to make the necessary investments to address these structural problems, one first step toward increasing capacity is to subsidize the build-out of new networks that can compete with the incumbents.[38] Susan Crawford makes a compelling argument that these digital communications industries wield such influence over the political process that aggressive structural intervention in the form of breaking up monopolies and oligopolies is highly unlikely for the immediate future. However, she sees hope in a smattering of community-owned Internet networks that provide cheap and reliable broadband services to their residents. Therefore, one arrow in the quiver against telecom monopolies should include community broadband initiatives – at least in the 30 states that have not yet passed laws making it extremely difficult or impossible for municipalities to offer these services, essentially ensuring a captive market for companies such as Comcast.[39] These locally owned and controlled wireless or municipal fiber Internet networks could be operated through community media centers supported by local and national tax revenues. These centers could be housed in post offices or public libraries to serve as hubs for community media production.[40]

[36] Federal Communications Commission, *Connecting America: The National Broadband Plan*, 2010 http://download.broadband.gov/plan/national-broadband-plan.pdf (accessed October 11, 2013).

[37] Yochai Benkler, *Next Generation Connectivity: A Review of Broadband Internet Transitions and Policy from Around the World* (Cambridge, MA: Berkman Center for Internet & Society at Harvard University, 2010).

[38] For example, the governments of Japan, South Korea, and Sweden made significant investments in building out broadband infrastructure. See Saul Hansell, "The Broadband Gap: Why Do They Have More Fiber?" *New York Times*, March 12, 2009. President Obama's "broadband stimulus," which viewed the Internet as a crucial infrastructure, was arguably a first tiny step in this direction but insufficient.

[39] Crawford, *Captive Audience*, 256.

[40] A version of the Independent Media Center (IMC or Indymedia) experiment of the early 2000s could serve as a potential model, though it would require reliable funding instead of relying on all-volunteer labor, which challenged many IMCs' sustainability. See Victor Pickard, "Assessing the Radical Democracy of Indymedia: Discursive, Technical and Institutional Constructions," *Critical Studies in Media Communication* 23, no. 1 (2006): 19–38; Victor Pickard, "United yet Autonomous: Indymedia and the Struggle to Sustain a Radical Democratic Network," *Media Culture & Society* 28, no. 3 (2006): 315–36; Victor Pickard, "Cooptation and Cooperation: Institutional Exemplars of Democratic Internet Technology," *New Media and Society* 10 (4) (2008): 625–645. One important model is the Urbana IMC, which purchased the downtown post office building. In addition to providing community wireless services, this space produces a wide range of media, including a monthly print publication, an LPFM station, and a community

Analogous to the 1940s debates over broadcasters' commercial and political power over their programming content, today the gatekeeping capacity of ISPs is in question. Specifically, this debate hinges on whether the Internet should be protected according to "net neutrality" – essentially preventing ISPs from interfering with online content. This controversy traces back to a number of antecedents, including the 2005 Supreme Court's Brand X decision, which permitted the FCC's dubious 2002 reclassification of the Internet (specifically cable modem services) from a carefully regulated telecommunications service to a lightly regulated "information service." Without explicit net neutrality protections, ISPs can potentially interfere with users' online activities by slowing or blocking specific kinds of content, creating "fast lanes" for prioritized services, and thereby fundamentally altering the Internet's basic design principles.[41] The net neutrality debate's long, ongoing saga is beyond this book's scope; its most recent permutation has left the issue in limbo after the DC Circuit Court of Appeals struck down the weak protections that the FCC had enacted in 2010.[42] Verizon, who successfully sued the FCC to have the rules thrown out, used an all-too-familiar negative liberty argument that communication firms typically use to protect capital and shield themselves from regulatory intervention. It stated that "contrary to the FCC's assertion, broadband providers are speakers protected by the First Amendment."[43] Also problematic, open Internet protections have not thus far fully pertained to mobile services, which increasing numbers of Americans use to access the Internet. To maintain a free-flowing and democratic digital media system, net neutrality should be mandatory across platforms.[44] However, while

news website. See Sascha Meinrath and Victor Pickard, "The Rise of the Intranet Era: Media, Research and Community in an Age of Communications Revolution," in *Globalization and Communicative Democracy: Community Media in the 21st Century*, ed. Kevin Howley (London: Sage, 2009), 327–40. Another institutional exemplar is Philadelphia's Media Mobilizing Project, which uses new communication technologies to produce media in coordination with poor and working class communities. See Todd Wolfson, *Digital Rebellion: The Birth of the Cyber Left* (Urbana: University of Illinois Press, 2014).

[41] Arguing that net neutrality is actually a type of ancient nondiscriminatory law – essentially common carriage – adapted to twenty-first-century infrastructure, Tim Wu reminds us that a "vibrant information economy cannot countenance discrimination at a level so basic as transmission on a public network." Wu, *The Master Switch*, 311.

[42] *Verizon Communications Inc. v. Federal Communications Commission*, DC Cir., No. 11–1355, 1/14/14.

[43] Joint Reply Brief for Verizon and Metropcs, *Verizon v. Federal Communications Commission*, No. 11–1355 (DDC filed Dec. 21, 2012), p. 2. Elsewhere Verizon argues that these rules "infringe broadband providers' speech by, among other things, stripping providers of control over which speech they transmit and how they transmit it," p. 26. See also Paul Barbagallo, "Verizon First Amendment Challenge of Net Neutrality Tests Century of Regulation," Bloomberg, January 24, 2013 http://www.bna.com/verizon-first-amendment-n17179872014/. In its decision, the court ultimately did not address Verizon's First Amendment argument.

[44] This requires reclassifying broadband as a telecommunications service protected by Title II of the Communications Act, thereby reaffirming the FCC's regulatory authority over Internet communications. See Sascha Meinrath and Victor Pickard, "The New Network Neutrality: Criteria for Internet Freedom," *International Journal of Communications Law and Policy* 12 (2008): 225–43. Of course, other kinds of online discrimination and preferential treatment not involving

having an open digital infrastructure is necessary, it does not specifically address the American journalism crisis, which I turn to next.

Taking the Profit out of News

American journalism lives a double life as a public service and a commodity. It is the latter identity – news as a profitable commercial entity – that has collapsed in recent years. With nearly all signs suggesting a slow but sure demise for advertising-supported journalism – seen most spectacularly in the newspaper industry – traditional news organizations continue to flounder for a last-minute rescue, whether through digital paywall models or some other technological fix. The Internet, paradoxically, is seen as both journalism's destroyer and its potential savior. The latter view assumes that new digital media will somehow combine with market forces and organically produce new models for citizen journalism. Thus far, little evidence suggests that this will manifest at sufficient levels. Saving commercial journalism from itself – or rather, extricating its good parts – must happen quickly before its slide toward ruin leaves behind hundreds of hollowed-out newsrooms. For while its business model has collapsed, journalism's public service mission is as vital today as any point in history. Salvaging it, however, will require public policy interventions.

Even modest policy changes could bolster public service journalism. Lessening market failure within the digital realm as described previously would greatly benefit news media, but policy reforms aimed specifically at journalistic institutions are also necessary. A three-pronged approach to reinventing journalism would involve new tax laws, subsidies for a new public media system, and research and development efforts for new digital models. Together, these initiatives would remove or lessen profit pressures and help restore journalism's public service mission. An immediate stopgap measure like tweaking tax laws would help struggling news outlets transition to new low- and nonprofit business models while also eliminating barriers to new ventures.[45] A number of promising initiatives have been waiting for months and years to be granted nonprofit status, and the IRS's inexplicable delays have caused unnecessary hardship for these news organizations.[46] Other worthwhile tax reform

ISPs occur with other large Internet firms, including those that often side with public interest groups during net neutrality disputes such as Google.

[45] For a discussion of these tax models, as well as historical models such as municipal-owned newspapers, see Victor Pickard, "Can Government Support the Press? Historicizing and Internationalizing a Policy Approach to the Journalism Crisis," *Communication Review* 14, no. 2 (2011): 73–95.

[46] Josh Stearns, "No News Is Bad News for Nonprofit Journalism," *Yes Magazine*, May 3, 2012. http://www.yesmagazine.org/people-power/no-news-is-bad-news-for-nonprofit-journalism. See also: "The IRS and Nonprofit Media: Toward Creating a More Informed Public," Council on

proposals have been floated in recent years but have yet to receive a full public hearing.[47] The finer details of tax law might not be the most compelling activist issue, but reforming them could induce both old and new media institutions to provide public service journalism.

Strengthening the already existing public media system would be a strong first step toward funding an alternative media infrastructure insulated from the commercial pressures that accelerated our journalism crisis. Right now, the United States is a global outlier among democracies in how little it funds public broadcasting.[48] The current crisis presents a rare opportunity to revitalize and repurpose this public media infrastructure by dedicating it to local news gathering as well as international and state-level news. Existing community and public radio stations could transition into multimedia centers (as many already are) that create digital media across multiple platforms and support investigative reporters in local communities, replacing the news media production often vacated by commercial newspapers. Funding for public media should be guaranteed over the long term and carefully shielded from political pressures, a process that would require removing it from the congressional appropriation process. A permanent trust could be supported by spectrum fees paid by commercial operators, a small consumer tax on electronics, or something equivalent to the universal service fund added to monthly phone bills. In the meantime, the United States could allocate targeted subsidies toward increasing public media's capacity, reach, diversity, and relevance. These subsidies could help broaden public media to include not just the Public Broadcasting Service and National Public Radio but also low-power FM stations, public access cable channels, and independent community Web sites, as well as the aforementioned community media centers.

All of these efforts would benefit from R&D investments in new digital start-ups.[49] Similar to private initiatives like the Knight News Challenge,[50] this federal R&D program could nurture promising journalistic experiments to help them become self-sustaining. Recent years have witnessed numerous creative proposals to jump-start innovative forms of multi-platform public media, including federal support for a journalism jobs program based on the Americorps model,[51] instituting $200 tax vouchers to put toward taxpayers' choice of

Foundations, March 4, 2013, http://www.cof.org/nonprofitmedia?ItemNumber=18708#sthash.NHD3Y8Ui.dpuf.

[47] See, for example, Senator Ben Cardin's proposed bill, the "Newspaper Revitalization Act of 2009," to help struggling newspapers become nonprofits. See also his op-ed "A Plan to Save Our Free Press," *Washington Post*, April 3, 2009.

[48] Rodney Benson and Matthew Powers, *Public Media and Political Independence: Lessons for the Future of Journalism from around the World* (Washington, DC: Free Press, 2011).

[49] Discussed in Pickard et al., "Saving the News," 44–5.

[50] The Knight News Challenge is an annual contest offering rewards of between $1,000 and $1,000,000 to promote innovative ideas in "news and information."

[51] Pickard et al., "Saving the News," 43–4.

media,[52] repurposing funds currently used for international broadcasting,[53] charging commercial broadcasters for their use of the public spectrum,[54] and having journalism schools take over news operations abandoned by professional organizations.[55]

Given corporate libertarianism's control over American political discourse, such a policy reorientation may seem like a nonstarter, especially when conservative politicians routinely target public broadcasting for proposed budget cuts – at a time, no less, when the need for public media should be most self-evident. But polling data consistently show high levels of support for public broadcasting,[56] suggesting one clear example where the corporate libertarian paradigm is not based on popular consent. Regardless, establishing new reforms and expanding public media are possible only if we create a counter-narrative to corporate libertarianism.

Beyond Corporate Libertarianism

How we think about journalism is largely determined by how much we buy into a corporate libertarian paradigm that sees news and information primarily as commodities whose existence is dictated by their profitability. If we see journalism first and foremost as a public service or public good, then it must be sustained regardless of market support. Thus, an argument for subsidizing public media can be condensed to the following points.

- Despite its continued commercial devaluation, journalism produces a public good that is essential to democracy.
- The advertising model that has subsidized this public good for the past 125 years is no longer sustainable.
- No new commercial models are emerging that offset the loss of journalism within legacy media.
- Once society acknowledges this market failure, the need for policy interventions to promote public service journalism and to encourage new journalistic experiments becomes paramount.

---

[52] McChesney and Nichols, *The Death and Life of American Journalism*, 201–206.

[53] Shawn Powers, "U.S. International Broadcasting: An Untapped Resource for Ethnic and Domestic News Organizations," in *Will the Last Reporter Please Turn Out the Lights? The Collapse of Journalism and What Can Be Done to Fix It*, ed. Robert McChesney and Victor Pickard (New York: New Press, 2011), 138–150.

[54] Benjamin Lennett, Tom Glaisyer, and Sascha Meinrath, *Public Media, Spectrum Policy, and Rethinking Public Interest Obligations for the 21st Century* (Washington, DC: New America Foundation, June 2012).

[55] Leonard Downie and Michael Schudson, "The Reconstruction of American Journalism," in *Will the Last Reporter Please Turn Out the Lights? The Collapse of Journalism and What Can Be Done to Fix It*, ed. Robert McChesney and Victor Pickard (New York: New Press, 2011), 55–90.

[56] Public Broadcasting System, Today's PBS: Trusted, Valued, Essential, 2013 http://www-tc.pbs. org/about/media/about/cms_page_media/625/2013_Trust%20Brochure.pdf (accessed October 11, 2013).

This reframing of the journalism crisis allows for commercial and noncommercial models to coexist by restoring balance between profit-making and democratic imperatives and creating a mixed, structurally diverse media system that is not overly dependent on market relationships. The historical record as well as recent events would suggest that a wholly commercial news system focused on advertising revenue optimization and profit maximization cannot easily withstand market fluctuations and is inadequate in supporting democratic society's communication requirements.

Of course, advocating public subsidies does not mean that the state should exert direct control over media; rather, it should help foster the structural conditions necessary for public service media to thrive. Despite Americans' discomfort with press subsidies, a growing body of academic research demonstrates that publicly owned media and government-subsidized privately owned media are no less critical of government than non-subsidized privately owned media.[57] Critical journalism and continued media independence – despite state subsidies – are exemplified by the often-confrontational BBC. Arguably, in liberal democracies with predominantly commercial media systems that overly rely on access to official sources (such as politicians), the state can play a larger role in shaping the news than it does in publicly subsidized media systems. Subsidies might liberate journalists to become more autonomous and thus more adversarial toward those in power. Drawing from a number of respected studies showing a strong correlation between public media systems and vibrant democracies, recent research has convincingly debunked the arguments that public press subsidies automatically create a slippery slope toward totalitarianism.[58] Likewise, research suggests that subsidies do not encourage subservient, uneducated publics; often the opposite appears to be true.[59]

Over the past decade, American scholars have begun to examine the subsidy approach more closely,[60] and proposals for press subsidies long considered off-limits are gradually being reconsidered, as evidenced by a number of reports

---

[57] Rodney Benson, "Public Funding and Journalistic Independence: What Does Research Tell Us?" in *Will the Last Reporter Please Turn Out the Lights? The Collapse of Journalism and What Can Be Done to Fix It*, ed. Robert McChesney and Victor Pickard (New York: New Press, 2011), 314–19. For a fine example of this research, see also Rodney Benson, *Shaping Immigration News: A French-American Comparison* (New York: Cambridge University Press, 2013).

[58] Robert McChesney and Victor Pickard, "News Media as Political Institutions," in *Handbook of Political Communication Theories*, ed. Kate Kenski and Kathleen Hall Jamieson (Oxford: Oxford University Press, 2014).

[59] James Curran, Shanto Iyengar, Anker Brink Lund, and Inka Salovaara-Moring, "Media System, Public Knowledge and Democracy," *European Journal of Communication* 24 (2009): 5–26. See also Rasmus Kleis Nielsen and Geert Linnebank, "Public Support for the Media: A Six-Country Overview of Direct and Indirect Subsidies" (Reuters Institute for the Study of Journalism, Oxford University, 2011), http://reutersinstitute.politics.ox.ac.uk/publications/risj-reports.html.

[60] I synthesize much of this scholarship in "The USA: Unfounded Fears of Press Subsidies," in *State Aid for Newspapers – Theories, Cases, Actions*, ed. Paul Murschetz (Berlin and Heidelberg: Springer-Verlag, 2014), 357–72.

and op-eds.[61] Even as these proposals incur wrath from those who still view press subsidies as dangerous, the beginnings of a new "popular front" consensus among liberal and radical intellectuals might be crystallizing around what James Curran refers to as "public reformism."[62] This position calls for strengthening public media to sustain the journalism that the private sector no longer supports. Since public media's future is bound up in the political appeal of state activism, proposals for supporting journalism must convince broad constituencies that subsidies would not influence the press's editorial viewpoints or news coverage. All public media subsidies should be based on complete transparency, systems of accountability, and multiple firewalls to prevent them from becoming instruments of the state. For example, one potential safeguard is to mandate a new kind of "ascertainment" by which subsidized media institutions must consult local communities to find out what stories residents would like to see covered. Reform proposals also should emphasize that they are not focused on simply propping up corporate incumbents and paper-based print media.

To be clear, the objective should always be stated as protecting journalism, not necessarily legacy newspapers. Few proponents of subsidies are advocating a direct bailout of the commercial media system or the preservation of traditional news organizations as they currently exist. Furthermore, sentimentality about ink-stained fingers notwithstanding, we should think proactively about digital journalism and aim beyond saving "dead tree" broadsheets. A restructured newspaper industry combined with a fully funded public media infrastructure could bring into existence, with time, not just reform, but a *transformed* media system, one less beholden to commercial interests and more accountable to diverse communities.

Presently, the politics to drive these policies are absent, and as long as the corporate libertarian paradigm that ascended in the 1940s remains predominant, they likely will remain so. Recent developments in media law and policy have only strengthened this paradigm as corporations are increasingly empowered and emboldened to act as political agents, seeking to undermine even weak redistributive mechanisms in U.S. society.[63] Moreover, the case for government

---

[61] See, for example, Federal Trade Commission, "Potential Policy Recommendations to Support the Reinvention of Journalism" (discussion draft, Washington, DC, 2010); Lee Bollinger, "Journalism Needs Government's Help," *Wall Street Journal*, July 14, 2010. Lee Bollinger expands on these arguments in *Uninhibited, Robust, and Wide-Open: A Free Press for a New Century* (New York: Oxford University Press, 2010).

[62] James Curran, "The Future of Journalism," *Journalism Studies* 11, no. 4 (2010): 472.

[63] This is especially true after the 2010 Supreme Court decision in *Citizens United v. FEC*, which stands to reorder the political landscape along corporate libertarian lines by unleashing nearly unlimited and unaccountable corporate influence in political campaigns. For a penetrating analysis of this and related phenomena, see John Nichols and Robert McChesney, *Dollarocracy: How the Money and Media Election Complex Is Destroying America* (New York: Nation Books, 2013).

intervention has been further weakened in the public imagination with increasing disclosures of run-amok state surveillance via digital media. While dismantling this surveillance state must become a key policy battle in the years ahead, a progressive role for state intervention is still possible and necessary. After decades of American media policy largely favoring incumbent media corporations, a rare chance has emerged to create a truly public media system.

Media Reform Deferred

Ideas themselves do not lead directly to social change; reform requires the energy of grassroots movements, as well as long-term organizing and institution-building. In considering lessons from the postwar settlement's ascendancy and prospects for moving beyond it, a long view is useful. The history of media reform is one of missed opportunities and deferred alternatives, but the purpose of this research is not to mourn a lost golden age or to lament what could have been. Rather it is meant to link previous struggles to alternative futures, to learn lessons from past failures, and to see contemporary media reform movements as part of a long historical tradition, one that continually engages with the vexing intersections of media, democracy, and policy. Radical policy formations and ideas for new models typically exist at the margins of political discourse. It is incumbent upon scholars to bring those alternatives to light and to challenge dominant ideologies and relationships. The history discussed in this book is more than a declension narrative. In answering the "How did we get here?" question, this history reminds us about forgotten options – lost possibilities that we recover not only to correct the historical record by reclaiming agency and resistance but also to inspire future reform efforts. As we look back to the paths not taken, we may consider changing course.[64]

Just as the New Deal era has been described as a period of chaotic experimentation, our current critical juncture calls for testing alternative models. But without a structural analysis we are left to fight against the symptoms of a fundamentally flawed media system instead of root causes. This evasion of structural reform in the 1940s poised newspapers for their current dissolution. However, a possible silver lining to the crisis is that new journalistic models are becoming more viable. Unlike in the 1940s, when prominent figures in the media industry viewed any suggestion of structural reform via state intervention with knee-jerk suspicion and hostility, now some industry leaders, perhaps out of desperation, indicate a greater willingness to experiment, as do many working journalists whose jobs are at stake. This trend may combine with a

---

[64] I discuss some of these themes in "Revisiting the Road Not Taken: A Social Democratic Vision of the Press," in *Will the Last Reporter Please Turn Out the Lights? The Collapse of Journalism and What Can Be Done to Fix It*, ed. Robert McChesney and Victor Pickard (New York: New Press, 2011), 174–84.

resurgent media reform movement to build the crucial public support that was lacking or disconnected from policy makers in the 1940s.

Concerns about unaccountable media monopolies and government complicity articulated in the 1940s continue to galvanize media reformers and public outrage. In 2003, nearly 3 million people wrote letters to the FCC contesting proposed plans for loosening ownership restrictions.[65] In 2006, more than 1 million people petitioned Congress to protect a then-obscure policy called net neutrality to maintain a nondiscriminatory Internet.[66] In 2012, 4.5 million people signed a petition to roll back two proposed Internet piracy bills that would have given government and corporations tremendous power over Web content.[67] With increasing numbers of Americans attempting to renegotiate the power dynamics between communities and media companies, uncovering the origins, contingencies, and contradictions of this relationship is timely. This study strives to recuperate lost alternatives by presenting a usable history and showing that "the public interest" is still a meaningful category in the digital era.

This analysis reaches the uncomfortable conclusion that the current commercial model for media is not adequately serving democracy. In particular, commercial journalism is failing; the normative framework of socially responsible media has too often failed; and the market-driven build-out of communication infrastructures has been insufficient. It is unreasonable to think that we can awaken tomorrow and jettison the entire apparatus. However, it is reasonable – in fact, it is absolutely necessary – for policy makers, media reform activists, and other stake-holding constituencies to begin pushing for structural alternatives. For this goal to be realized, we will have to renegotiate the postwar settlement, and to do this, we must know its history. The postwar settlement for American media marked a failure of reformers' vision of media democracy, one privileging access over corporate profits and diversity over commercial values. It is this vision that has been deferred, still awaiting its moment.

History shows that democratization can occur when government, pushed by social movements, enters the fray on the public's behalf. More than seventy years ago, an opportunity was lost. Instead of confronting the problem for what it was – the result of deeply systemic flaws endemic to commercial media – policy makers either avoided this task or were squelched by pro-industry counterattacks, especially red-baiting. Ultimately they fell back on palatable halfway measures, helping ensure that future generations of Americans would be forced to face similar crises. The American public has inherited the legacy of policy

---

[65] For a history of the early 2000s media reform movement, see Eric Klinenberg, *Fighting for Air: The Battle to Control America's Media* (New York: Metropolitan Books, 2007).

[66] Stephanie Kirchgaessner, Patti Waldmeir and Richard Waters, "Google Action Tests Power of Cash vs Votes in Washington," *Financial Times*, July 18, 2006.

[67] SOPA Petition Gets Millions of Signatures as Internet Piracy Legislation Protests Continue, *Washington Post*, January 19, 2012.

decisions from the 1940s that left intact a nominally socially responsible, self-regulated commercial media system. This corporate libertarian paradigm would prefigure much of the American media system for decades. The time has arrived for a renegotiated social contract. Instead of being constrained by past policy failures, we must learn from them and move forward with bold new models.

Bibliography of Primary Sources

Manuscript Collections

Clifford J. Durr Papers, Alabama Department of Archives and History, Montgomery, Alabama.

Commission on Freedom of the Press Records, Accession No. 0078-011, Special Collections Division, University of Washington Libraries, Seattle, Washington.

Dallas Smythe Collection, Simon Fraser University, British Columbia, Canada.

Federal Communications Commission Archives, National Archives and Records Administration, College Park, Maryland.

James Lawrence Fly Papers, Rare Book & Manuscript Library, Columbia University, New York.

James Lawrence Fly Project, Oral History Research Office, Sally Fly Connell Papers, Special Collections, Columbia University, New York.

James Rowe Jr. Papers, FDR Presidential Library, Hyde Park, New York.

National Association of Broadcasters Papers, State Historical Society of Wisconsin, Madison, Wisconsin.

National Broadcasting Company Records, State Historical Society of Wisconsin, Madison, Wisconsin.

Robert M. Hutchins Papers, Joseph Regenstein Library, University of Chicago, Chicago, Illinois.

William Ames Papers, Special Collections, University of Washington, Seattle, Washington.

Newspapers, Periodicals, and Trade Publications

Advertiser
Advertising Age
American Mercury
American Political Science Review
Annals of the American Academy of Political and Social Science
Antioch Review

Arizona Quarterly
Atlantic Monthly
Billboard
Boston Daily Record
Business Week
Broadcasting
Chicago Tribune
Common Ground
Commonwealth
Cooperative Consumer
Editor & Publisher
Evening Bulletin
Federal Communications Bar Journal
Federal Register
Fortune
Forum
Guild Reporter
Harpers
In Fact
Journal of the National Education Association
NAB Reports
Nation
New Republic
New York Sun
New York Times
Newsweek
Nieman Reports
Progressive
Psychiatry
Public Opinion Quarterly
Reader's Digest
Saturday Review of Literature
St. Louis Post-Dispatch
This Week
Tide
Time
Variety
Washington Post
Western Political Quarterly
Yale Law Journal

Index

Other Books in the Series *(continued from page iii)*

Daniel C. Hallin and Paolo Mancini, *Comparing Media Systems: Three Models of Media and Politics*

Daniel C. Hallin and Paolo Mancini, eds., *Comparing Media Systems beyond the Western World*

Robert B. Horwitz, *Communication and Democratic Reform in South Africa*

Philip N. Howard, *New Media Campaigns and the Managed Citizen*

Ruud Koopmans and Paul Statham, eds., *The Making of a European Public Sphere: Media Discourse and Political Contention*

L. Sandy Maisel, Darrell M. West, and Brett M. Clifton, *Evaluating Campaign Quality: Can the Electoral Process Be Improved?*

Pippa Norris, *A Virtuous Circle: Political Communications in Postindustrial Society*

Pippa Norris, *Digital Divide: Civic Engagement, Information Poverty, and the Internet Worldwide*

Victor Pickard, *How America Lost the Battle for Media Democracy: Corporate Libertarianism and the Future of Media Reform*

Margaret Scammell, *Consumer Democracy: The Marketing of Politics*

Adam F. Simon, *The Winning Message: Candidate Behavior, Campaign Discourse*

Daniela Stockmann, *Media Commercialization and Authoritarian Rule in China*

Bruce A. Williams and Michael X. Delli Carpini, *After Broadcast News: Media Regimes, Democracy, and the New Information Environment*

Gadi Wolfsfeld, *Media and the Path to Peace*